JOB RIGHTS IN THE SOVIET UNION:
THEIR CONSEQUENCES

SOVIET AND EAST EUROPEAN STUDIES

Rudolf Bićanić *Economic Policy in Socialist Yugoslavia*

Galia Golan *Yom Kippur and After: The Soviet Union and the Middle East Crisis*

Maureen Perrie *The Agrarian Policy of the Russian Socialist-Revolutionary Party from its Origins through the Revolutions of 1905–1907*

Paul Vyšný *Neo-Slavism and the Czechs 1898–1914*

Gabriel Gorodetsky *The Precarious Truce: Anglo-Soviet Relations 1924–1927*

James Riordan *Sport in Soviet Society: Development of Sport and Physical Education in Russia and the USSR*

Gregory Walker *Soviet Book Publishing Policy*

Felicity Ann O'Dell *Socialisation through Children's Literature: The Soviet Example*

T. H. Rigby *Lenin's Government: Sovnarkom 1917–1922*

Stella Alexander *Church and State in Yugoslavia since 1945*

M. Cave *Computers and Economic Planning: The Soviet Experience*

Jozef M. Van Brabant *Socialist Economic Integration: Aspects of Contemporary Economic Problems in Eastern Europe*

R. F. Leslie ed. *The History of Poland since 1863*

M. R. Myant *Socialism and Democracy in Czechoslovakia 1945–1948*

Blair A. Ruble *Soviet Trade Unions: Their Development in the 1970s*

Angela Stent *From Embargo to Ostpolitik: The Political Economy of West German–Soviet Relations 1955–1980*

William J. Conyngham *The Modernisation of Soviet Industrial Management*

Jean Woodall *The Socialist Corporation and Technocratic Power*

Israel Getzler *Kronstadt 1917–1921: The Fate of a Soviet Democracy*

David A. Dyker *The Process of Investment in the Soviet Union*

S. A. Smith *Red Petrograd: Revolution in the Factories 1917–1918*

Saul Estrin *Self-Management: Economic Theories and Yugoslav Practice*

Ray Taras *Ideology in a Socialist State*

Silvana Malle *The Economic Organization of War Communism 1918–1921*

S. G. Wheatcroft and R. W. Davies *Materials for a Balance of the Soviet National Economy 1928–1930*

Mark Harrison *Soviet Planning in Peace and War 1938–1945*

James McAdams *East Germany and Detente: Building Authority after the Wall*

J. Arch Getty *Origins of the Great Purges: The Soviet Communist Party Reconsidered 1933–1938*

Tadeusz Swietochowski *Russian Azerbaijan 1905–1920: The Shaping of National Identity*

David S. Mason *Public Opinion and Political Change in Poland 1980–1982*

Nigel Swain *Collective Farms Which Work?*

Stephen White *The Origins of Detente: The Genoa Conference and Soviet–Western Relations 1921–1922*

Ellen Jones and Fred W. Grupp *Modernization, Value Change and Fertility in the Soviet Union*

Catherine Andreyev *Vlasov and the Russian Liberation Movement: Soviet Reality and Émigré Theories*

Anita J. Prazmowska *Britain, Poland and the Eastern Front, 1939*

Allen Lynch *The Soviet Study of International Relations*

JOB RIGHTS IN THE SOVIET UNION: THEIR CONSEQUENCES

DAVID GRANICK

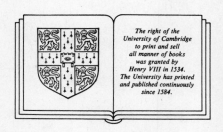

The right of the
University of Cambridge
to print and sell
all manner of books
was granted by
Henry VIII in 1534.
The University has printed
and published continuously
since 1584.

CAMBRIDGE UNIVERSITY PRESS

CAMBRIDGE

LONDON   NEW YORK   NEW ROCHELLE
MELBOURNE   SYDNEY

Published by the Press Syndicate of the University of Cambridge
The Pitt Building, Trumpington Street, Cambridge CB2 1RP
32 East 57th Street, New York, NY 10022, U.S.A.
10 Stamford Road, Oakleigh, Melbourne 3166, Australia

First published 1987

Printed in Great Britain at the University Press, Cambridge

British Library cataloguing in publication data
Granick, David
Job rights in the Soviet Union: their consequences. –
(Soviet and East European studies)
1. Labor supply – Soviet Union
1. Title. 11. Studies
331.12'0947   HD5796

Library of Congress cataloguing in publication data
Granick, David.
Job rights in the Soviet Union.
(Soviet and East European studies)
Bibliography.
Includes index.
1. Manpower policy – Soviet Union. 2. Labor supply –
Soviet Union. 3. Central planning – Soviet Union.
4. Labor turnover – Soviet Union. 1. Title. 11. Series.
HD5796.G72   1987   331.11'0947   87-26392

ISBN 0 521 33295 8

Contents

List of tables and figure		*page*	vii
Acknowledgements			viii
List of abbreviations			ix

1   Introduction   1

PART 1

2   The Soviet labor market: its characteristics   11
    The labor market   12
    The setting of prices in the labor market   40
    The trade-off available to enterprise management   65

3   Overfull employment and job rights   70
    Overfull employment   70
    Job rights   84
    The rival hypothesis   105

PART 2

4   Maximization model for testing the JROE hypothesis-set   117
    Extensions of the neoclassical approach   118
    The objective function and constraints in Model A   121
    Model B   135

5   Fixed prices and JROE   136
    The problem   136
    A proposed solution for producer goods   148
    The proposed solution for consumer goods   157

The proposed solutions and the Models 159
Alternative explanations of the existence of Soviet fixed
prices 167

6 Fixed investment and JROE 171
Data explained by either set of constraints 171
Data explained only by Model B 183

7 Education and JROE 202
Soviet education as investment in human capital 202
Supply and demand conditions for different levels of
education 205
Explanations of the excess supply of human capital 219

8 The labor market and JROE 235
Phenomena to be explained 235
A JROE model explaining continuous overfull employment
in the presence of shocks 240
Alternative explanations of overfull employment in the
face of shocks 256
The Shchekino movement: explanations 259
Conclusion as to the testing of the JROE Model B 262

PART 3

9 Some applications 267
The supply side of the second economy 267
Inventories as an employment buffer 272
Primary and secondary labor markets 282

10 Conclusion 300
Labor market equilibrium 300
The costs of the JROE policy 303
The JROE policy: its reasons and future 306

Appendix: Easy-reference verbal treatment of algebraic formulae 310
Bibliography 316
Index 326

Tables and figure

2.1 Soviet annual quit rates and total-separations rates in international perspective   15

2.2 Channels used for hiring personnel in all sectors of the economy of the Russian Republic   22

2.3 Female labor-force participation   25

2.4 Structure of earnings of industrial manual workers, Soviet Union   41

2.5 Relative earnings of piece-work manual workers in the electrical equipment industry   46

3.1 Labor-force participation in the socialist sector   80

3.2 Annual disciplinary dismissals as a proportion of the average labor force   89

3.3 Relocation of redundant manual workers within the enterprise   95

6.1 Annual rates of increase in the Soviet capital/labor ratio   172

6.2 Labor-force reductions during the 1960s in the Soviet Union and the U.S.   176

6.3 Proportions of all Soviet manual labor-force reductions in declining occupations, by category of occupation (1959–1970)   177

6.4 Unskilled materials handlers, warehousemen and packers in Soviet industry   184

6.5 Retirement rates for fixed assets in the economy as a whole   194

7.1 Annual graduations   204

7.2 Full-time students as percentage of all graduates   205

7.3 Probability of a pupil continuing education beyond secondary level, depending upon parental occupational position   231

9.1 Age and sex of labour force engaged in primarily physical work   287

9.2 Quits by manual workers according to branch   289

FIGURE

5.1 Non-taut planning with all actors being price takers   153

Acknowledgements

The research for this book has been supported by the Kennan Institute for Advanced Russian Studies of the Woodrow Wilson International Center for Scholars, the National Science Foundation under Grant No. SES-8319905, the National Council for Soviet and East European Research, and by the Graduate School of the University of Wisconsin-Madison. Any opinions, findings, and conclusions or recommendations expressed in this publication are those of the author and do not necessarily reflect the views of the National Science Foundation or any of the other supporting organizations. I am also grateful to the Osteuropa-Institut of Munich, and to its director Professor G. Hedtkamp and its assistant director H. Clement, for the warm hospitality extended to me over fifteen months during the actual writing. The Hoover Institution on War, Revolution and Peace assisted with the typing and provided support for final correction of the manuscript.

Edward Albertini, Richard Kistler, Andrew Krikelas, and Gary Krueger have been my assistants at various stages of the research, and I am indebted to them. The index was prepared by Fiona Barr. Of the many people who have commented on my writing at various of its stages, I am particularly grateful to Peter A. Hauslohner, D. M. Nuti, Wolfram Schrettl, and Volkart Vincentz. None of them, of course, bears any responsibility for the final product.

Some of the results of this research have been previously published, and are again presented – although usually in a considerably altered form – in the current book. I am grateful to the publishers for having given their permission. The relevant articles are "Soviet use of fixed prices: hypothesis of a job-right constraint," in Steven Rosefielde (ed.), *Economic Welfare and the Economics of Soviet Socialism* (Cambridge University Press, 1981); "Institutional innovation and economic management: the Soviet incentive system, 1921 to the present," in Gregory Guroff and Fred V. Carstensen (eds), *Entrepreneurship in Russia and the Soviet Union* (Princeton University Press, 1983); "Central physical planning, incentives and job rights," in Andrew Zimbalist (ed.), *Comparative Economic Systems: An Assessment of Knowledge, Theory and Method* (Kluwer-Nijhoff, 1984).

Abbreviations

B.B.O.I.S.	*Berichte des Bundesinstituts für ostwissenschaftliche und internationale Studien*
C.D.S.P.	*Current Digest of the Soviet Press*
Employment and Earnings, 1909–75	U.S. Department of Labor, Bureau of Labor Statistics. *Employment and Earnings 1909–75* (Bulletin 1312–8. Washington, D.C.:G.P.O., 1976)
E.G.	*Ekonomicheskaia gazeta*
E.K.O.	*Ekonomika i organizatsiia promyshlennogo proizvodstva*
E.N.	*Ekonomicheskie nauki*
Izv. AN SSSR	*Izvestie Akademii Nauk SSSR, Seriia ekonomicheskaia*
Izv. sib. otd.	*Izvestiia sibirskogo otdeleniia AN SSSR, Seriia obshchestvennykh nauk* (*Seriia ekonomiki i prikladnoi sotsiologii,* from 1984 on)
J.C.E.	*Journal of Comparative Economics*
J.E.C.	*Joint Economic Committee of the United States Congress*
J.E.L.	*Journal of Economic Literature*
Narkhoz SSSR	TsSU pri Sovete Ministrov SSSR. *Naraodnoe khoziaistvo SSSR v . . .*
P.Kh.	*Planovoe khoziaistvo*
Ref.	*Referativnyi sbornik; Ekonomika promyshlennosti*
R.E.S.	*Review of Economic Studies*
S.I.	*Sotsiologicheskie issledovaniia*
SP SSSR	*Sobranie postanovlenii pravitel' stva SSSR*
S.T.	*Sotsialisticheskii trud*
V.E.	*Voprosy ekonomiki*
V.M.U.	*Vestnik Moskovskogo universiteta, ekonomika*
V.S.	*Vestnik statistiki*

I

Introduction

This book is organized around the twin hypotheses that an employee's right to his existing job, unless he deliberately misbehaves or voluntarily quits the job to search for another, together with overfull employment in all regional labor markets, are interlinked conditions whose preservation takes precedence over most other objectives of central planners in the Soviet Union.[1] The term "overfull" is commonly used in recognition of the economically harmful effects that occur when jobs chase men; but note that it is defined in terms of the proportion of the labor force that, at a given moment, is unemployed – often meaning no more than between jobs. The higher the degree of overfull employment, the easier and quicker it is for an individual worker to find another job when he either quits or is dismissed from his old one. The achieved level of overfull employment in the Soviet Union may have been no higher than that observed in most of Northern Europe during the post-war years prior to the first oil crisis.

These hypotheses of Job Rights-Overfull Employment (JROE) may be viewed in either of two ways which are indistinguishable from one another with regard to their effects upon economic behavior. The first possible treatment is to say that JROE is an argument in the welfare function of central planners that must be satisfied fully before other objectives are pursued. (This does not mean, of course, that it is the only such argument that is thus lexicographically preferred. One might, for example, hold that there is also a lexicographic preference for some minimum level of income equality. It is only important that the list of lexicographic preferences not be so long as to eliminate the possibility of pursuit of other objectives: i.e. of decision making other than the reversal of some previous lexicographic

---

[1] These objectives/constraints are intended to apply only within confidence intervals, and their realization is subject to a further stochastic element. Only in a sense to be defined in Chapter 3 can they be linked to directly observable phenomena; the "facts" from which they spring are stylized.

choices. The parallel with the more customary maximization under constraints – where more than one constraint is possible – is exact.) In this treatment, central planners are viewed as first meeting conditions that are described as constraints, then as pursuing the lexicographically preferred degree of fulfillment of the JROE objective, and only thereafter as maximizing the welfare function by engaging in a trade-off among other objectives. The alternative possible treatment is to treat JROE as one among a number of constraints imposed upon central planners, with central planners maximizing a welfare function that does not contain JROE.

Mathematically described, the planners' welfare function is:

If $g(y_{\text{lagged}}) \geqq \bar{y}$

welfare function $= f(\text{JROE}, y)$

$= y$ if $\text{JROE} \leqq \text{JROE}^{\circ}$

$= 0$ if $\text{JROE} > \text{JROE}^{\circ}$

If $g(y_{\text{lagged}}) < \bar{y}$

welfare function $= h(y)$ (1.1)

where y is a vector of all arguments (e.g. rate of growth of gross national product) other than JROE that are contained in the welfare function, there is lexicographic preference for holding $\text{JROE} \leqslant \text{JROE}^{\circ}$ provided that $g(y_{\text{lagged}}) \geqslant \bar{y}$, and this lexicographic preference in the welfare function disappears if $g(y_{\text{lagged}}) < \bar{y}$.

One might choose to interpret this approach as implying that in the central planners' own ranking of the welfare contribution of JROE, compared to any objective that is not similarly lexicographically preferred, the relative contribution to planners' welfare of a marginal change of JROE compared to a marginal increase of any other objective is infinite.[2] (This, of course, applies only until the lexicographically preferred amount of JROE is obtained; thereafter, the ratio falls abruptly to zero.) In contrast, one might interpret the second approach of constraints as implying that JROE represents a constraint imposed upon central plan-

---

[2] The following two authors seem to consider JROE as entering directly as an argument into the planner's welfare function, although neither of them provides a lexicographic interpretation. L. Tyson in *International Organization*, 40, 2 (Spring 1986), p. 244 calls a commitment to job security an important outgrowth of socialist ideology. T. H. Hilker (1983, p. 5 and in private discussion) considers the central leaders as historically having had as a major goal the maintenance of the employment security characteristic of an agricultural feudal system, while at the same time adapting the new urban recruits from the countryside to industrial life. Hilker holds that economic efficiency was considered to be a much less important goal.

ners against their will – a constraint arising out of an "implicit contract" with labor.[3]

However, both approaches yield identical results with regard to the behavior of central planners whose decisions reflect a maximization of their own welfare function. Thus, for purpose of this study, there is no need to choose between the above two explanations as to why JROE should be given its great importance. While the lexicographic approach will be used, such use should not be taken as representing such a choice. Rather, this usage simply respects the convention that constraints are imposed inequalities and that the decision maker has no alternative but to respect them. Since central planners would have the option of breaking an "implicit contract" with labor, provided that they were willing to pay the price in reduced work effort or in social disorder, it seems preferable not to treat JROE as a constraint. But although it must be admitted that this choice as between treatments is fundamentally arbitrary, the significant point is that it makes no difference which treatment is used.[4]

An apparent difficulty with the treatment of JROE either lexicographically or as a constraint is that it seems hard to understand why the relevant function – the partial derivative of planners' welfare with respect to an increase of JROE – should take the same value at all points except one, and there that it should shift discontinuously from plus-infinity to zero. Such a shift is best seen as an abstraction from a function which varies continuously, but takes values other than "extremely high" or "extremely low" only within a narrow range of JROE. Given any refinement of measurement that we might conceivably hope to attain, this abstraction does no harm.

Like any function, the partial derivative of planners' welfare with respect to JROE holds only within a given domain. The relevant domain is presumably bounded from below by certain minimum values that are attainable for other arguments in the planners' welfare function while respecting the lexicographic preference for JROE. Thus, if the environment in which Soviet planners operate should change sufficiently so that

---

[3] See Alex Pravda in Bornstein *et al.* (1981), p. 163 and R. W. Campbell in Byrnes (1983), p. 114 for such an interpretation of JROE in application to Eastern Europe, but not explicitly to the Soviet Union.

[4] In this regard, it is interesting to note the evolution of the treatment in Hauslohner (1984). This able American political scientist begins his dissertation by treating overfull employment and job rights as part of a social contract. However, by the time he reached his final chapter, he believed that these policies represented rather an appeal for political support from particular groups in Soviet society. (See especially pp. 663–65.)

Given the difficulties in the concept of an implicit social contract, and the differences in possible interpretation of the motivation of Soviet leaders, I am grateful for the fact that it is unnecessary for my purposes to take a stand on the matter.

the expected secular value of annual increase of gross national product per capita – under conditions of continued lexicographic preference for JROE – should become zero, one might predict that we would have passed outside the domain in which the hypothesized function holds. What is maintained in this book is that during the period that this study covers, roughly the 1960s through the early 1980s, the Soviet economy and Soviet society in general fell within the domain relevant for this function (i.e. $g(y_{\text{lagged}}) \geqslant \bar{y}$). It is through considerations of the domain of the function that trade-offs can be introduced as between arguments in the central planners' welfare function.

My interest in the twin hypotheses of JROE is in inquiring into their implications for Soviet economic policy. Applying a neoclassical economic approach, extended to include the shaping both of economic institutions[5] and of fundamental policy decisions by central planners who are perceived as maximizing under constraints, this book inquires into the significance of lexicographic preference for JROE in the choice of institutions and policies. I ask here which stylized facts of the Soviet economy of the 1960–80 period can be explained only in an *ad hoc* fashion by a neoclassical model of the above type which ignores JROE, while being satisfactorily explained by an otherwise identical model that incorporates lexicographic preference for JROE. The significance of this treatment is the suggestion that, of the significant malfunctions of the Soviet economy which have been commonly attributed to the existence of a central planning system organized primarily along non-market lines, many of these malfunctions can be attributed to the addition of JROE to this central planning system.

If this suggestion is correct, then these particular malfunctions cannot properly be treated as "inefficiencies" of the Soviet economic system in terms of the realization of the welfare function relevant to the functioning of the Soviet economy, even when we exclude the preservation of central planning from this welfare function. Moreover, given that, holding other things equal, social welfare in non-socialist countries is also increased by changes in the level of JROE, we cannot even treat these particular Soviet malfunctions as inefficient in terms of the maximization of a social welfare function which contains only the same arguments as might be found in those of a non-socialist economy. In short, the issue of "inefficiency"

---

[5] This has a similarity to the treatment by North and Thomas (1973) of the development in Western Europe, during the tenth through the seventeenth centuries, of institutions affecting property rights and the internalization of what had previously been externalities. In my case explicitly, and in theirs implicitly, the underlying assumption is made that the actors who alter economic institutions are rational economic men whose motivations can be treated in economic terms.

should disappear from our discussion of the Soviet economic system with regard to these particular malfunctions.

The mirror image to the concern expressed above as to the policy implications of the JROE hypotheses is the inquiry into how far the JROE hypotheses help in understanding other aspects of the Soviet economy, particularly aspects of the Soviet labor market. To the extent that they do "cast light" on a variety of problems, and that such "light" emanates from a core concept (JROE), we have here the type of integration of diverse data by a single theory which is what we should look for in science.

The stylized facts underlying JROE have come to be widely accepted as applicable both to the Soviet Union and to the other centrally planned economies of eastern Europe. This holds both for the existence of overfull employment, as indicated by the brevity of the period required for a typical job seeker to find a new post, and for the failure of state enterprise to dismiss workers except in very narrowly specified situations. What is in question, however, is the explanation of these stylized facts.

An explanation competitive to JROE is that these phenomena are neither desired by central planners nor imposed upon them as constraints by pressure from workers, but are rather predictable outcomes of national and local labor markets that are in permanent disequilibrium (through over-heating). In the simplest form of this explanation, state enterprises are described as subject only to "soft constraints" on their effective demand for the employment of labor, while subject to "hard constraints" (through allocation) with regard to complementary factors of production. Output is viewed either as a variable to be maximized, or at least as a variable whose value should be made equal to or greater than the plan value, with planned value being sufficiently ambitious so that there is a premium upon obtaining greater quantities of labor than are in fact available to the enterprise. Labor is supplied through a market relationship, in which workers can freely choose the jobs for which they apply and can quit them on fairly short notice; such labor mobility is a function of money wages which, in turn, are determined by central planners. It is this concatenation that results in the permanent disequilibrium. (While this very simple explanation of labor market disequilibrium does not strike me as being particularly realistic for the Soviet case, the same result can be generated by other causal sequences.)

Given such permanent disequilibrium, the consequence of overfull employment follows by definition. Rarity of dismissals is a natural consequence for enterprise managements who are unconstrained in constantly trying to hire more workers than are available to them on the labor market-place. No JROE postulate is required in order to explain the stylized labor market facts.

Since we cannot distinguish very well as between the JROE and the market-disequilibrium hypotheses, with regard to their explanation of the above labor market facts, the obvious testing procedure is to generate subsidiary hypotheses arising from these primary ones, and to examine their fit with regard to additional stylized facts. This approach will be followed in the case of the JROE postulate, which will be combined with "maintained hypotheses" concerning maximizing behavior by all actors, central planning, and incentive systems in Soviet production sectors of the state economy. It will be suggested that the labor-disequilibrium hypothesis provides no unified system for explaining these additional stylized facts, and that instead recourse must be had to a variety of specific and unrelated hypotheses in explaining Soviet behavior in these diverse areas of the economy. It is due to its greater breadth of explanatory power in diverse areas of the Soviet economy that I find the JROE hypotheses more satisfactory than their competitor.

Logically, the reader might reasonably inquire as to how the two basic hypotheses fare when compared against other stylized facts that may be unified by the market-disequilibrium hypothesis. A symmetrical treatment of the competing basic hypotheses would require the addition of this latter approach, but the compass of this study seems to be already large enough. Such complementary treatment is left to the future attention of some advocate of the market-disequilibrium hypothesis.

So far as the JROE hypotheses are concerned, the hypotheses-testing procedure outlined above is identical to the hypothesis-implications procedure described earlier. The treatment adopted will be the hypotheses-testing procedure, so that comparison may be made with the market-disequilibrium hypothesis. But the reader should keep in mind throughout that the results of testing the joint JROE hypotheses can be interpreted with equal validity as exhibiting the implications for Soviet economic policy of the JROE postulate. My interest is in both interpretations equally, although my treatment will be only in terms of one of them.

The materials and analysis of this book are specific to the Soviet Union during recent decades. However, it must be recognized that the domain of the theorizing is much wider. Suppose that the same malfunctions which are here explained by the JROE hypotheses should be found in other centrally planned periods of Soviet history, or in other centrally planned economies, in which the specified brevity of required job search and/or the extreme reluctance of enterprises to dismiss workers are absent. In that case, the nature of the argument developed in this book in defense of the JROE hypotheses would be vitiated.

Like the earlier issue of a symmetrical treatment of the competing basic hypothesis, this matter will have to be left for possible future research. My own hunch, based on considerable empirical research on the Soviet Union of the 1930s and on three of the East European planned economies in the early 1970s, is that the above empirical underpinnings of the JROE hypotheses would be found generally in those centrally planned economies in which these particular malfunctions have been observed. In fact, the job-rights hypothesis was first formulated as an explanation of Hungarian economic behavior in the early post-1968 reform years.[6] Other authors[7] have continued to apply it to later years in the history of the development of this most reformed of the East European centrally planned economies.

This introduction may well give the reader the impression that this book will be almost wholly theoretical. My own view is that it is a study in applied economics; it is intended to be a study of empirical data as informed by theory. Soviet labor market literature of the late 1960s through 1984, conceived as broadly as possible, has been followed fairly exhaustively both in book and in journal form. In particular, all of the relevant Soviet journals have been read through 1984. Hauslohner (1984) has been particularly useful in providing reassurance from the literature of the earlier post-Stalin period that similar labor market conditions extend back earlier. Writings by Soviet sociologists, demographers, and lawyers, as well as the works of Soviet economists and administrators which form the core of my materials, have been examined. Where I have failed properly to understand the current Soviet labor market behavior, it is not due to slighting the available Soviet literature (with the exception of newspapers, that have been ignored aside from specific references). On the other hand, I have given no serious attention to the historical dimension of Soviet labor market conditions; my reading on the period prior to 1960 has been done essentially in secondary sources consisting of English-language monographs.

A word of explanation may be appropriate here as to technical features that are found in the footnotes and bibliography.

(1)   Sources referred to in the footnotes are the original sources, even

---

[6] D. Granick in *World Politics*, XXV, 3 (April, 1973).
[7] E.g. Michael Marrese in Adam (1982), pp. 107–19.

when I have been led to them by secondary sources, provided that I have checked the original. Where I have not checked the original, it is the secondary source that is cited.

(2)   The publishers of Soviet books are listed. For the knowledgeable reader, the name of the publisher provides some limited information as to the trustworthiness of the work – just as is the case for western publishers.

(3)   The transliteration system used is that of the Library of Congress.

(4)   In the footnotes, the Russian abbreviation SSSR is used to stand for the Soviet Union. This system is intended for the specialist so as to avoid confusion with the Ukrainian Soviet Socialist Republic.

I have followed the old fashioned custom of using only the male pronoun when referring to men and women, unless this leads to confusion. I beg the reader's indulgence.

Part 1

2

The Soviet labor market:
its characteristics

The first question to be considered in this chapter is the degree to which a labor market exists and the restrictions under which such a market operates. It would, for example, be wrong to consider the purchase of most intermediate products and capital goods by state enterprises and collective farms as passing through a market, since such goods are allocated by planners. To what degree does similar planning replace a market relationship in the case of labor? (The first section deals with the question. Because of the nature of the issue, this section is institutional and non-theoretic to a degree unique in this book.)

The second question concerns the working of such a market. If the market is to function effectively, its prices cannot be allowed to depart too far from equilibrium. Yet base wages are fixed for long periods of time and on a universal basis; if relative earnings of different categories of workers were kept proportional to their base wages, one could hardly expect to see a satisfactory approximation to shortrun equilibrium. In what fashion are relative earnings permitted to deviate, while the aggregate demand for labor on the part of employing enterprises is still constrained? For state employees, investigation of this question involves the study of the workings of the enterprise wage fund.

The third question is that of the trade-off that exists for the management of the individual enterprise in the use of its wage fund. In particular, there is investigation of the trade-off between employing a larger number of workers – thus combating labor "shortage" – and reducing the quit rate of those already employed in the enterprise, who have developed enterprise-specific skills. This is a particular form of choice between quantity and quality of labor inputs.

THE LABOR MARKET

The existence of a labor market

The fact that the very existence of a genuine labor market in the Soviet Union is not universally acknowledged is shown by the writing of Peter Wiles, who distinguishes Soviet labor policy from capitalist policies by the following features *inter alia*: (1) an unwillingness to come to terms with supply and demand, indeed, to admit that a labor market exists at all; (2) a tendency to neglect, at least in theory, the role of differentials in earnings in enticing workers to jobs in which their marginal productivity is highest; (3) a further tendency, again at least in theory, to direct or nearly direct people to a job.[1] It is true that the above statements may be interpreted more as an interpretation of Soviet theory than of practice with regard to labor markets, but they would at a minimum seem to imply that Soviet theory in this regard has at least some carry over.

This questioning of the existence of a genuine labor market is entirely separate from the effects of both compulsory military service and of forced labor camps. By convention, the armed forces are usually excluded from treatment of the national labor market, although of course they need not be and indeed were not in American debates about elimination of the military draft. The forced labor camp population in the Soviet Union had declined presumably to minor proportions by the mid-1960s, which is close to the beginning of the period being examined.[2] In any case, Wiles and I both exclude these two groups from the laborforce universe under discussion.

In contrast to Wiles' apparent position, support of the appropriateness of the labor market notion in application to the Soviet Union's practice stems primarily from two well-documented phenomena: (1) the high rate at which individual workers leave state enterprises through quitting; (2) the low production of job vacancies that are filled through any form of planned hirings.

The quit rate. The most reliable Soviet labor turnover data refer to "quits plus dismissals."[3] The dismissals portion refers only to dismissals for reason

---

[1] Wiles in Schapiro and Godson (1981), p. 17.

[2] The United States Department of State, Intelligence and Research Bureau, in a declassified report of 1960, estimated the number in labor camps in the Soviet Union as being one to one-and-a-half million in 1959. S. Rosefielde presents an estimate for that year of four million. (S. G. Wheatcroft in *Soviet Studies*, 25, 2 [April 1983], pp. 232 and 236–37.) These figures range between 1 and 4 per cent of the total Soviet labor force (including military) working for the State or on collective farms.

[3] *Tekuchest'*.

of violation of labor discipline;[4] as we shall see in Chapter 3, such dismissals are in the range of 6 to 10 per cent of the total. Quits do not include departures for military service or for fulltime studies; these are instead treated as transfers. They exclude retirements. Nor do they include refusals to sign up again for employment at the end of a fixed-term contract.[5]

Historical series for state employees in various sectors running from 1950 through 1975 have been assembled in Western sources.[6] The most reliable data are for manual workers in industry (Soviet definition, which includes extractive industries, logging and fishing – and thus might be expected to yield somewhat higher figures than for manufacturing alone). The best of these appear to be for 1967, and it is implied by a 1981 Soviet source that no truly good data have appeared since.[7] For the Soviet Union as a whole, the 1967 figure was 22.1 per cent;[8] in following years, the figure fell in the range between "insignificantly lower"[9] than the 1967 figure and something in the order of 18.2 per cent by 1978.[10] If the latter figure is correct, the 18 per cent decline between 1967 and 1978 is all the more impressive because of the growth of the sixteen-to-thirty year age group as a proportion of the pre-pension age population;[11] it is this age group which has by far the highest quit rate both in the Soviet Union and in developed capitalist countries.

[4] L. M. Danilov *et al.* in *Problemy ispol'zovaniia* (1973), p. 204. Cases of arrests were included in such dismissals, at least up to the mid-1960s (Bliakhman, Zdravomylsov, Shkaratan [1965], p. 11).

[5] *Otnoshenie* (1970), pp. 9–10.

[6] McAuley and Helgeson (1978), p. 38a, and Feshbach (1978), p. 31.

[7] Sukhov (1981), p. 98.

[8] Rusanov (1971), p. 111. Logging and woodworking was 27.6 per cent, but coal was only about 17.1 per cent.

[9] Sukhov (1981), p. 98.

[10] *SP SSSR*, 1980, Nr. 3, Article 17, p. 43. (However, the 1978 figure may well apply to all personnel rather than only to manual workers; if so, it could well be biased downward as an estimate of quits plus dismissals of the latter.) An 18.6 figure for 1978 would be obtained independently by assuming the same proportional decline in the Soviet Union as a whole as in the Russian Republic. In 1967, the figure for the Russian Republic was 21.4 per cent – 97 per cent of the figure for the entire country. (Compare Rusanov [1971], p. 111 and A. G. Sozykin in *C.D.S.P.*, XXXII, 32 [September 10, 1980], p. 7.)

If one assumes that the figure in Markov (1980), p. 145 for decline in "quits plus dismissals" refers only to manual workers, then the 1976 figure was about 18.3 per cent.

A further decline to 16.1 per cent in 1980 for all personnel in industry is indicated by authoritative authors but, since this explicitly amounts to a decline in some 12 per cent in one year, I tend to regard the 16.1 per cent figure as being either incorrect or an aberration unlikely to be repeated in future years. (See Kotliar and Trubin in *Zaniatost' naseleniia* [1983], p. 50 and L. A. Kostin [1981], p. 52.)

[11] S. Rapawy and G. Baldwin in *J.E.C.* (1983), Part 2, pp. 288–92.

A 1973 estimate by a reliable Soviet sociologist spoke of a 15 to 20 per cent annual "quit plus dismissal" figure for agriculture (presumably only state-owned) and of 40 per cent and more for construction and services.[12] Data are unavailable for collective farms, but it is my impression that resignation from a given collective farm is most frequently accompanied by migration to an urban area and least often by movement to another collective farm;[13] in agriculture generally, we do not appear to have anything resembling the movement from one economic unit to another within the same branch that is so common in urban occupations.

The total proportion of the industrial manual labor force that leaves its existing enterprise in a given year for all reasons combined is unknown; but commonly referred to is a guess by the Research Institute of Labor that it is in the neighborhood of 30 per cent.[14] This is consistent with national data for industrial manual workers for 1965 (31 per cent)[15] and with Ukrainian data for the same group in 1975 (28 per cent).[16] What seems in 1976 to have been the only study of the subject showed that some 78 per cent of the "quits plus dismissals" in Moscow enterprises in 1963 were followed fairly quickly by employment in another enterprise rather than constituting departures from the labor force.[17]

For purposes of placing these Soviet figures into an international perspective, it is the crude 30 per cent separation rate for all employees in industry which seems to lend itself best to comparisons. This is both because there is no breakdown of separations for most of the countries for which data exist, and because quit-rate comparisons are bound to be heavily influenced by the sharp international differences in the relative importance of dismissals. But quit rates will also be compared where possible. Comparisons are intended only as orders of magnitude.

The data of Table 2.1 suggest that Soviet separation rates are of the same

---

[12] T. I. Zaslavskaia in *Problemy ratsional'nogo* (1973), p. 88. See also V. Churakov in *S.T.*, 1970, 2, p. 124.

    The 1967 figure for manual workers in construction was 38.2 per cent (Rusanov [1971], p. 115), and the 1976 figure was probably about 26.3 per cent (Markov [1980], p. 145).

[13] See the wide variance among collective farms in Belorussia in the proportion of "labor needs" to workforce age personnel shown by F. Romma and F. Gilitskii in *S.T.*, 1972, 12, p. 120.

[14] See Danilov *et al.* in *Problemy ispol'zovaniia* (1973), p. 156; Maslova (1976), p. 19; Sukhov (1981), p. 98. This 30 per cent is alternatively described as one and one-half times "quits plus dismissals."

[15] A. M. Korneeva in *Problemy ekonomicheskoi* (1968), p. 114.

[16] Dolishnii (1978), pp. 213 and 216.

[17] Pavlenkov (1976), pp. 76–79. The data presumably were taken from a study of 129 enterprises. Of the remaining 22 per cent, 17 per cent represented movement into the private household economy.

Table 2.1 *Soviet annual quit rates and total-separations rates in international perspective*

Country	Total separations (percentage of labor force)	Quits
Soviet Union		
manual workers in industry		
1967		20.8[a]
1978		16.4[a]
1970s	30	
United States		
all employees in manufacturing		
1958–74 range across years	47–59[b]	13–32[b]
1958–74 range adjusted to approach Soviet definition	39–50[c]	
United Kingdom		
all employees in the economy		
1971–72		
males	32–34[d]	
females	52[d]	
German Federal Republic		
all employees in the economy		
1959–62 range	34–38[e]	
German Democratic Republic		
all employees in the economy		
1965		15[f]
1978 and 1980		7–8.1[f]
Australia		
all employees		
in the economy, 1974	66[g]	52[g]
in manufacturing, 1974	85[g]	67[g]

[a] The figures are calculated on the assumption that dismissals for violation of labor discipline constituted 6 per cent of all quits plus dismissals in 1967, and 9.6 per cent in 1978. (See *Otnoshenie k trudu* [1970], p. 9 and L. Kartashova in *P.Kh.*, 1984, 9, p. 84.)

[b] U.S., B.L.S., *Employment and Earnings, 1909–75*. In contrast to the Soviet data, but in accord with the data for the U.K., the B.R.D. and Australia, the termination of temporary jobs is included.

[c] The adjustment is made by eliminating temporary jobs: 18 and 13 per cent of all separations in 1955 and 1961 respectively (*Wages and Labour Mobility* [1965], p. 6).

[d] United Kingdom, *Department of Labour Gazette*, January 1975, p. 24.

[e] *Amtliche Nachrichten der Bundensanstalt für Arbeitsvermittlung und Arbeitslosenversicherung* (ANBA), 1963, 3, p. 152.

[f] All data include disciplinary dismissals. The 1965 and 1980 data are from J. Stolzel in *Wissenschaftliche Zeitschrift der Hochschule für Ökonomie Bruno Leuschner Berlin*, 1982, 3, p. 21 and are taken from a doctorate dissertation by G. Pietrzynski (cited by Belwe [1982]). The 1978 figure is from K. Lubcke in *Arbeit und Arbeitsrecht*, 1980, 4, p. 152. The definition is from Belwe (1982), pp. 1 and 21–25. Schaefer *et al.* (1982), p. 26 refers to a large number of studies of individual units, and thinks of the average as currently lying between 7 and 8 per cent.

Table 2.1 (*cont.*)

Other data are also given by Lubcke, but they should probably be ignored. Although the data appear to refer to the entire economy, O. Aninova in *S.T.*, 1983, 3, p. 126 interprets what is almost certainly the Lubcke 1978 figure as referring only to industry. Both the Russian Aninova and the West German Belwe seem to take the 1978 figure of 8.1 per cent seriously. I am indebted to Dr Belwe for having supplied me with the sources from the German Democratic Republic.

  g Australian Bureau of Statistics, "Labour turnover, March 1974" (Canberra; looseleaf), pp. 5–19. The original data are surveys for March only; the March data are multiplied by twelve by me to give an annual rate, and seasonality may cause this approach to be grossly misleading.

  Note: Other United Kingdom data with regard to separations are given on the basis of quarterly data, and show very low separations data. However, these are based on quarterly surveys which disregard all separations of employees hired in the same quarter. Data used suffer from the same exclusion, but it consists of exclusion only on a monthly basis.

For France, separations data for 1958–60 are given as being in the range of the American figures (*Wages and Labour Mobility* [1965] pp. 50 and 257–58). However, in view of other comments as to the quality of French separations data, they are not cited here.

order of magnitude as those of the United Kingdom and the German Federal Republic. (The Soviet figure is understated relative to the others because it excludes the ending of temporary jobs; on the other hand, one might guess that manual workers have a higher separation rate than white-collar employees.) The Soviet figure appears, on the other hand, to be low compared with the American and, particularly, with the Australian data. With regard to the quit rate, the Soviet figures stand in or near the lower third of the American annual range and are low by Australian standards. American-Soviet comparisons are influenced by the fact that part-time employees (and thus fulltime students during the school year who might be expected to have a high quit rate) are included in the figures for both countries, but that there are very few part-time jobs in Soviet industry. As to summer employment, Soviet students are much more likely to take jobs for specified periods – and thus to be excluded from both the quit and separation figures.[18]

[18] The most significant difference in the definition of "quit" between the two sets of statistics is that separations due to leaving for fulltime education are treated as quits in the American data but not in the Soviet. (Even this difference is modified by the fact that a fair proportion of the Soviet leavers will quit in order to study for the entrance examinations.) Those workers having unauthorized absences for more than seven days at the end of the month, or never having reported to work after being hired, are treated as quits in the American data but as dismissals in the Soviet. However, due to the existence in the Soviet Union of work books in which dismissals are supposed to be entered, these types of dismissals are probably rare except in those cases where the Soviet worker has no legal right to quit.

  Definitional differences clearly lead to some over statement of the American compared to the Soviet quit rate. The direction of this effect on a comparison of quit rates of fulltime, year-round workers is the same as that of the considerations cited in the text.

I would sum up these data by suggesting that Soviet separation data look quite normal in comparison with those of developed capitalist countries in non-depression times, and that the quit rates are normal compared to the American. Only with regard to the Australian and German Democratic Republic data does the Soviet Union appear to be distinctive, and too little is known by me about the figures for either of these countries for such comparison to be taken too seriously. Thus, with respect to both quit rates and total separation rates, Soviet industry – and, probably, the Soviet economy as a whole – seems to have a labor market with a quite normal degree of activity as judged by the standards of developed countries.

Planned hiring in the filling of job vacancies. The only civilians who are directed to work in the Soviet Union are graduates of fulltime schools (other than the standard general secondary education). Members of the Communist Party are also subject to such direction by Party bodies, but there is no indication that such direction is carried out to any substantial degree.

For 1981, we may calculate that graduates of vocational schools (PTU) who were in either of their two years of job assignment constituted about 14 per cent of all job hires of manual workers in industry.[19] This may be taken as a good estimate of the degree of planned obligatory direction of manpower in the manual-worker sphere, although even here the assignment of graduates to cities other than where they have trained sometimes meets substantial resistance and resulting labor turnover.[20]

---

[19] Only graduates of fulltime vocational schools are subject to job direction. These constituted 1,915,000 in 1981 (*V.S.*, 1982, 12, p. 71). In 1983, the percentage of fulltime daytime graduates directed to work in industry constituted 33.2 per cent of the total (*V.S.*, 1984, 11, p. 49). This proportion of the 1981 graduates is taken, and then multiplied by two since the period of direction is for two years (I. S. Poltorak and Iu. E. Shul'ga in *S.I.*, 1984, 2, p. 79). The resulting number was divided by the estimated hirings in 1981 of manual workers in industry; 30 per cent of the 1980 figure plus the net increase between 1980 and 1981 (*Narkhoz SSSR 1922–1982*, p. 402).

    The figure of 14 per cent is quite consistent with percentages of first-year job directions to industry as a proportion of all industrial worker hirings: 6 per cent in the Russian Republic in 1972 (*Trudovye resursy: formirovanie* [1975] p. 118) and 7.7 per cent in the Ukrainian Republic in 1975 (Dolishnii [1978], p. 202).

    Back in 1966, the period of job assignment was said to be normally four years (Prudinskii [1966], pp. 63–64), although Hauslohner believes that such assignment, if it existed at all, had no serious implications. At a minimum, it seems clear that it had no legal force.

[20] See Poltorak and Shul'ga in *S.I.*, 1984, 2, p. 79. In a major steel plant studied in 1982, the vast majority of assigned graduates of vocational schools in other plants had either never appeared, had quit (illegally), or had been dismissed for violations of labor discipline.

    It should be noted that, at least in the middle 1960s, the job allocation of vocational school graduates was done through administrative acts which had no legal force. There were no legal consequences for the graduate who refused to take the assigned job. In a discussion of penalties for those refusing to take assigned jobs, reference is made to the fact

Graduates of daytime junior colleges (*tekhnikumy*) and higher education are also subject to job direction, usually for three years. These constituted 71 per cent of total daytime vocational school graduates in 1981.[21] While we have no total job-change data for white-collar personnel in the economy, we might make a calculation that assumes that all the above graduates go to white-collar jobs (which is a substantial exaggeration) and that the separations rate for all white-collar personnel in the economy is equal to that of manual workers in industry (which is probably a major offsetting assumption). On the basis of these two assumptions, these graduates on assignment in 1981 constituted over one-third of the new hirings of white-collar personnel. As in the case of vocational school graduates, anecdotal Soviet data suggest that a significant portion may avoid serving out their assignments. Furthermore, their period of obligatory service includes an on-the-job training period (*stazhirovka*) of up to one year, all time spent in the armed forces, and leave taken in order to care for a child of up to one year (or one and one-half) of age.[22]

Transfers of industrial manual workers between enterprises ranged between 3.2 and 3.9 per cent of all hirings per annum during the years 1967–74.[23] Such transfers include temporary transfers – e.g. to and from seasonal branches – and the individual worker can always reject a permanent transfer without losing his rights to his old job.

Organized recruitment (*orgnabor*) and social recruitment (*obshchestvennyi prizyv*) are equally unimportant, together constituting 2.6 to 4.7 per cent of all hirings of manual workers in industrial enterprises during 1970–74, and 11 per cent in construction in 1971.[24] Organized recruitment is essentially of unmarried males over twenty-five years of age; since the mid-1950s, some three-quarters of the recruits have come from urban areas. One-third of these recruits are seasonal, and the remainder sign contracts for one to three years (the overwhelming majority in the Russian Republic signing for

that other enterprises are forbidden to employ such graduates of daytime technical schools and higher education, but no such statment is made as to graduates of vocational schools. It is conceivable that such graduates could be made to repay the costs of their education; but discussion of this in the case of apprentices who do not stay on in the plant (where legal precedent is split) did not mention it for vocational school graduates (Pashkov [1966], pp. 72–74 and 156–73).

It was only beginning in 1981 that job allocations of fulltime vocational school graduates were given a legal basis, and then for assignments of two years (Hauslohner [1984], p. 412) in comparison with the apparent norm of four in the mid-1960s.

[21] *Narkhoz SSSR 1922–1982*, pp. 411 and 513.
[22] E. Khlystova in *S.T.*, 1982, 1, pp. 111–12.
[23] Maslova (1976), pp. 95–96.
[24] *Ibid.*, pp. 204–05. The construction figure may refer only to the Russian Republic. Social recruitment of students for summer work is not included here.

two years). An analysis of those serving out two-year contracts in the Russian Republic showed that two-thirds left the job at the end of their contract period. As one might expect, organized recruitment is more important for the eastern than for the western part of the Soviet Union. People sign up voluntarily for adventure, to get away from home, and to gain high earnings for relatively short periods.[25] Such fixed-term contracts are legal only where the employee is given some economic advantages as compensation.[26]

Even in seasonal branches of industry, and in the underdeveloped portions of the country, they have constituted only a very minor source of hirings. In 1970, they constituted 12 per cent of manual-worker hirings in the fishing and lumbering industries where (in addition to peat) such seasonal recruitment is concentrated.[27] In 1974, some 16 per cent of the total number of labor-force age personnel migrating to Eastern Siberia and to the Far East from other parts of the Russian Republic came through organized recruitment.[28] Furthermore, according to data of the labor recruitment administration in the Russian Republic, two-thirds of the personnel so recruited to Siberia and the Far East in fact leave before the expiration of their contracts.[29]

Social recruitment (with the Comsomol organization playing a particularly important role) has been used to recruit working youth for tasks of major importance in northern and eastern regions. Primarily, it has been employed for filling construction jobs. The hope was to recruit people to move permanently, rather than on contract. This is a movement that is said to have declined sharply after 1966.[30]

Organized recruitment and social recruitment represent, from the employee's point of view, no more than an alternative voluntary means of finding a job. In the case of contractual period organized recruitment, the recruit obtains material advantages in return for binding himself (theoretically) for a stated period. In the case of social recruitment, there is strong emotional recruitment fever mounted by the Comsomol organization in its recruitment drives. But once the individual has arrived at his place of work, he has no obligation to remain in the enterprise or even in

---

[25] *Ibid.*, pp. 155–62. These data cover the first half of the 1970s.
[26] *Trudovoe pravo* (1972), pp. 32–36.
[27] A. V. Shteiner in *Dvizhenie rabochikh kadrov* (1973), p. 42. Studies of the Research Institute of Labor of the Soviet Union.
[28] Maslova (1976), p. 209.
[29] *Osnovnye problemy* (1971), p. 27 footnote. No date is given, but the data are presumably for the late 1960s.
[30] Maslova (1976), pp. 105–08.

the region. Similarly, the enterprise has no obligation actually to hire him.[31]

From the point of view of the Center, however, both of the above forms of labor recruitment represent a planned allocation similar to the job assignments of school graduates. Enterprises are not allowed freely to compete with one another for the recruits from these sources; it is not the enterprises who are doing the recruiting. The Center does not have control over the numbers recruited in this fashion in any year, but it does directly determine their disposal. This seems to be the justification as to why Soviet statistics generally treat this joint form, together with job assignments of graduates and with transfers, as the only types of labor recruitment in industry that are considered as other than "recruitment by the enterprises themselves."

Within agriculture, there has also been a system of organized recruitment; this is called organized resettlement of families to Siberia and to the Far East. Only 20 per cent of these have been collective farmers. But what matters is the numerical insignificance: within the Russian Republic as a whole, only some 11,000 farm families were resettled annually this way during the 1966–74 period.[32] Furthermore, in various regions studied, only one-third of those settled in 1975 were still in their new location five years later.[33]

This leaves a residual that has varied between 85 and 88 per cent of all manual workers hired in industry during six indicated years of 1963–74. It is this that is described as "hiring by the enterprises themselves."[34] But since only part of this residual constitutes genuine hiring at the factory gate, it is important to investigate the other categories.

Municipal employment offices were created in 1968–69. In 1971, 8.7 per cent of all manual workers hired in industry came through them; the figure rose to 12.5 per cent in 1973 and to 14.1 per cent in 1974 – at which point it constituted 16 per cent of all hirings "by the enterprises themselves."[35] It is said to have risen to over 20 per cent of all hirings by 1980–81.[36] In a few cities, hiring by enterprises was permitted only through such employment bureaus; but this experiment (initiated in the cities of Ufa and Kaluga) was

---

[31] Topilin (1975), pp. 128–29.
[32] A. Z. Maikov in *Migratsiia naseleniia RSFSR* (1973), p. 81; Maslova (1976), pp. 119–30.
[33] T. Galkova in *Naselenie i trudovye resursy RSFSR* (1982), p. 90.
[34] Maslova (1976), pp. 139 and 146.
[35] *Ibid.*, p. 146.
[36] By this time, the coverage of such employment bureaus was almost complete in cities of over 100,000 population, and one-third in cities of 50–100,000 (I. Maslova in *S.T.*, 1981, 7, p. 67).

restricted in scope.[37] Furthermore, in some cities (which, however, included both Moscow and Leningrad in 1978) employees who have quit their jobs twice within a given year or who have been dismissed for violation of labor discipline are permitted to seek a new post only through the municipal employment office.[38]

Despite these restrictive aspects in the operation of some employment offices, these offices should be viewed primarily as a mechanism intended to speed up and reduce the costs of labor placement through improving the availability of information to job seekers. That job applicants and prospective employers retained rights of refusal are shown by national data:[39] of all job applicants to the employment bureaus, the percentages placed by these bureaus were 58 per cent in 1971, 65 per cent in 1973, and 72 per cent in 1981.[40]

Aside from the absence of compulsion in job placement through employment bureaus, the other aspect of their work that is important for our purposes here is the degree to which they have attempted to channel job applicants to particular employers in line with planned objectives. The principal author dealing with labor morbidity recognizes the potential in this regard (as a result of the bureau's monopoly of *centralized* information as to job vacancies in the city), and implicitly seems to favor the use of this potential.[41]

However, it seems unlikely that such powers have in fact been used. This is shown first by the fact that, about 1980, nationally only some 29 per cent of new hirings in cities serviced by employment bureaus were of persons

---

[37] E. Voronin in *S.T.*, 1977, 1, p. 29. The experiment was initiated in 1970–71 in the cities of Ufa and Kaluga; from the first, enterprises in these cities retained the right to reject job candidates sent to them (L. M. Danilov in *Problemy ratsional'nogo* [1973], p. 133). In 1974, 15 per cent of those cities that had employment bureaus used this compulsory feature (but, it would seem, these users were mostly or entirely smaller cities) (Maslova [1976], pp. 170 and 190–91). Although the experiment may well have been interrupted during the 1970s in the city of Kaluga, it was functioning there in 1984 (*C.D.S.P.*, XXXVI, 31 [August 29, 1984], pp. 13–14).

[38] *S.T.*, 1978, 4, p. 130.

[39] About one-third of all job applicants sent by the employment bureaus are rejected by the employers (Maslova [1976], p. 191). Kotliar and Trubin (1978), p. 102, cite a 1974 study which appears to conflict sharply with Maslova's figure. Moreover, accepting Maslova's one-third figure does not mean that only a negligible number of job applicants reject jobs; in the figure cited here, the unit is the job referral, while the percentages in the text take the job applicant as the unit.

[40] Maslova (1976), p. 175 and I. S. Maslova in *Problemy povysheniia effektivnosti* (1983), p. 235. Similar and better data are also available for the Russian Republic (1969–74 in A. Kotliar in *S.T.*, 1975, 3, p. 111) and for the Ukraine (1975 and 1980 in N. Panteleev in *S.T.*, 1982, 4, p. 22).

[41] Maslova (1976), p. 183.

Table 2.2 *Channels used for hiring personnel in all sectors of the economy of the Russian Republic (percentage of all personnel hired)*

Channel	1970	1980
Assignment to work of graduates completing fulltime studies in		
vocational school	5.9	9.3
junior colleges	2.0	3.0
higher education	1.1	1.9
Transfers	4.3	3.8
Organized recruitment of manual workers	0.6	0.7
Social recruitment	...	0.5
Organized agricultural resettlement	0.2	0.2
Placement of youth by local commissions	4.7	2.8
Hiring by enterprises through labor offices	3.5	9.7
Hiring by enterprises directly	77.6	68.1

Note: 1970 percentages are all slightly overstated, because they are calculated on the assumption that social recruitment was zero in 1970. These percentages are also subject to rounding error, in contrast with the 1980 data.
Source: A. Kotliar in *E.N.*, 1984, 3, pp. 53 and 56. The 1980 column is given directly; the 1970 column was calculated. Data, at least for 1980, are from a sample study carried out by the Central Laboratory of Labor Resources of the State Committee of Labor of the Russian Republic (*Zaniatost' naseleniia* [1983], pp. 3 and 45–46).

referred by these bureaus.[42] Bureaus seem to have been judged by their record of job placement, and one might have expected that their concentration would have been on raising their success rate rather than complicating their task. Secondly, there is the 1982 evidence of the chairman of the Committee on Labor of the Ukraine – a republic with a higher-than-average proportion of recruitment through labor bureaus. Until recently, wrote the author, the criterion of the bureaus for sending out candidates for jobs was simply the knowledge of the existence of a vacancy and the willingness of the job applicant to apply for it; there was no screening whatsoever. Recently, however, the first priority has become the interests of the *specific* would-be employer.[43] Nowhere is there suggestion of a plan-implementation function for the bureaus.[44]

Of the remaining 74 per cent of all hirings of manual workers in industry in 1974 which represented hirings at the factory gate, local commissions exist to aid in the placement of youth going to work directly from general education, of people with physical disabilities, and of others. In the case of

[42] Maslova in *S.T.*, 1981, 7, p. 67.   [43] N. Panteleev in *S.T.*, 1982, 4, p. 19.
[44] As has been pointed out to me, my conclusions regarding the bureaus are essentially the same as those reached in the more extensive examination of the data in Hauslohner (1984), Chapter 7.

youth, enterprises are given minimum quotas of such people whom they must employ;[45] presumably these quotas exist both because of labor legislation regulating the use of teenagers[46] and because of the high quit rate associated with youth, both of which factors may make the employment of such youth unattractive to the enterprise. But none of these commissions seem to have any substantial role in guiding labor to jobs in sectors determined by planning priorities.

Table 2.2 depicts the relative importance of these various channels of hiring personnel in the entire economy of the Russian Republic. Presumably, but not explicitly, collective farms are excluded.

General limitations on the working of the labor market

If one can assert that Soviet labor distribution is determined essentially by market forces (on which, of course, central planning impinges at least through determination of the wage funds available to the different organizations), the next step is to examine the limitations on the operation of this market.

The obligation to work in the socialist sector. Soviet authors have constantly asserted the general obligation of Soviet citizens (with specified exceptions) of labor-force age to work fulltime in the socialist sector. In the case of collective farmers, this obligation has been enforced partly through the linking of the occupancy of a house and private plot by labor-force age people to the observance by at least one member of the family of the conditions of membership in the collective farm – notably, working at least the minimum number of days required annually by that farm.[47] More significantly, since the above establishes only a lower limit to family participation, the trade-off for the collective-farm family in working on the collective farm versus working on the private plot has been sharply

---

[45] Postanovlenie TsK KPSS and Soveta Ministrov SSSR of February 2, 1966, Nr. 83 (*SP SSSR* 1966, Nr. 3, p. 26), reprinted in *Normativnye akty* (1972), p. 523. See also P. Grossman in Kahan and Ruble (1979), pp. 48–50. A study of hirings in the city of Orel' – taken as representative of cities of 250–500,000 population in the Russian Republic – in industrial enterprises in 1976 showed that ten per cent of all hirings of all personnel were done through these commissions, and that this constituted one-quarter of all youth hired that had recently completed studies of any sort (*Dvizhenie rabochei sily* [1982], pp. 30 and 194).

[46] Youth under eighteen years of age are forbidden to work night shifts and must also be paid on a fulltime basis for a shortened work-day (*E.K.O.*, 1977, 4, pp. 220–22).

[47] Wädekin (1967), pp. 30, 31, 35. In the past, minima were determined by public authorities. But this appears not to have been the case for some decades (Chandler [1978], pp. 34–35).

constrained by the fact that animal fodder and machine services for the private plot are provided almost entirely by the collective.[48] As a result, in 1970 when daily earnings from work on the collective farm were substantially lower than in the 1980s, the number of days worked by non-disabled males of labor-force age on collective farms were nevertheless said to be 99 per cent of those worked by industrial manual workers in the Soviet Union as a whole; for females, the figure was 76–79 per cent. By 1975, the figures were 106 and 89 per cent respectively.[49]

In urban areas, there was not only social pressure to work but also legislation, applied in the Russian Republic first in 1961, allowed for the administrative sentencing of unemployed people to compulsory work.[50] A Western source reported that the first deputy prosecutor general of the Soviet Union stated that in 1983 some 90,000 parasites had been successfully prosecuted.[51] A Soviet description applicable to Uzbekistan in 1980 was that these habitual parasites and vagrants rarely remain in work centers more than a year or two.[52]

Nevertheless, this obligation to work is far from absolute. With regard to the anti-parasite laws, for example, procedure in at least some regions has required that local police organizations cannot take action against an individual unless he has been without a job for at least four months. He then receives an order to take a job; if he does so, even though he quits immediately afterwards, the procedure must begin again.[53] More significantly, the proportion of female participation in the labor force rose dramatically between the 1959 and 1970 censuses: the proportion of non-disabled workforce age (sixteen to fifty-four years) women working in the socialist economy rose from 68.4 to 82.1 per cent (in fulltime equivalents), while the additional proportion who were fulltime students rose from 4.2 to 7.6 per cent.[54] It is particularly interesting to see Census data as to female workforce participation by age, comparing them with American data.

---

[48] Wädekin (1967), p. 35. See also V. Sheiko *et al.* in *S.T.*, 1982, 7, p. 78.

[49] Sidorova (1972), pp. 150–52; Tatarinova (1979), p. 89; *Narkhoz SSSR 1922–1982*, p. 148.

[50] Experiments in some smaller republics began in 1957. See Butler (1983), pp. 275–77.

[51] *Le Monde*, October 20, 1984, p. 6.

[52] *C.D.S.P.*, XXXII, 38 (October 22, 1980), p. 13.

[53] For similar reports from different cities, at periods seven years apart, see *C.D.S.P.*, XXV, 14 (May 2, 1973), pp. 27–28 and XXXII, 50 (January 14, 1981), p. 19.

   Beginning in January 1983, however, the previous legal requirement that parasitism had to be practiced over a protracted period of time was dropped (R. Sharlet in Nogee [1985], fn. 51 on p. 105).

[54] G. P. Sergeeva in *Trudovye resursy: Sotsial'no* (1976), p. 103. These data show 1.5 per cent greater increase than do sources using the Census materials directly, because the latter ignore the issue of whether work is fulltime.

Table 2.3 *Female labor-force participation*

Age (years)	Soviet Union			United States	
	1959 (percentage of age group)	1970 (1959=100) (index)	1970 (1959=100) (index)	1961	1967 (working full year and full-time) (percentage of age group)
16–20	65.0	...	...	29.5 (15–19 years)	
20–29	76.0	85	112	46.9 (20–24)	
30–39	71.4	91	127	36.2 (25–34)	
40–49	65.7	89	135	43.6 (35–44)	
50–54	53.1	74	139	49.7 (45–54)	30 (45–54)
55–59	29.0	...	...	37.5 (55–64)	30 (55–59)
60 and over	10.0	...	...	10.4 (65 and over)	9.5 (60 and over)
16–54	70	82	117		

Sources: Soviet Union

Labor force participation is limited to that in the socialist sector. The entire age group is encompassed, including the disabled. While no data for the age group 55–59 for 1970 are available, 1979 census data show the same 29 per cent participation rate as in 1959.

Sources are the original unpublished Census figures. Slightly different variants are also given for two of these age groups, but their use would not affect the case made in the text.

TsSU, *Naselenie SSSR 1973* (1975), p. 143. Tatarinova (1979), p. 10. (This latter source defines the figures used in the former.) M. Sonin in *Problemy ratsional'nogo* (1973), p. 356. L. Chizhova in *S.T.* 1984, 8, p. 90.

United States

1961. Sonin in *Problemy ratsional'nogo* (1973), p. 356. The late Soviet author was a careful scholar, who was citing the American figures as a base of comparison with the 1959 Soviet figures. Since his knowledge of the Soviet sources would allow him better to choose comparable American data than I could do, I have not gone into American sources for the American data.

1967. *Demographic* (1975), p. 89. Full-year is defined as being 50 to 52 weeks. Data are those of the Bureau of Labor Statistics.

Table 2.3 demonstrates two things of interest. The first is that the most rapid growth in the labor-force participation rate of the female population was in the age groups forty to fifty-four – i.e. right up to pension age and well beyond the age of mothers caring for pre-school children. (Indeed, while the increase in the total female participation rate is somewhat exaggerated,[55] such exaggeration does not apply to these age groups.) Second, the Soviet 1959 participation rate for pre-pension age, fifty to

---

[55] Census data refer to those having a job on the day of the census. In 1959, a woman could take leave from work and retain her job for five months after giving birth; by 1970, the period had been extended to twelve months (McAuley [1981], pp. 32 and 169–70).

fifty-four year old women, was not much above the United States 1961 figures for the same age group; after the Soviet pension age for women, the Soviet participation rates were below the American. These results prove that, at least in 1959, the obligation to work in the socialist sector for women without young children has been far from absolute.

It should also be pointed out that the 1959 phenomenon of women who were neither working in the socialist economy nor studying full-time is not peculiarly rural. In urban areas in 1959, non-working females constituted 15 per cent of the total (male and female) non-disabled workforce age population; of such women, 43 per cent did not have children under fourteen years of age.[56] This implies that the rural and urban proportions of women not working in the socialist sector was much the same, although rural women had a much greater likelihood of enjoying the opportunity to work on a private agricultural plot instead.

What occurred between 1959 and 1970 to raise the female participation rate so dramatically? The only Soviet explanation that I have seen points exclusively to factors of labor demand.[57] That labor demand should have become more acute is understandable when one considers that the percentage growth in the country's workforce age population was only 57 per cent as high in the 1960s as it had been in the 1950s; it was essentially by raising the female participation rate that the employed labor force outside of agriculture increased by some 94 per cent of the rate of the 1950s.[58] What is less understandable is why supply should have changed in this fashion; I know of nothing to indicate that demand had been the constraining factor and that urban female unemployment existed in the 1950s or, indeed, in earlier decades after the 1920s.[59]

The obvious question that comes to mind is whether participation rates

---

[56] *Puti razvitiia* (1967), p. 65.

[57] G. P. Sergeeva in *Trudovye resursy: sotsial'no* (1976), pp. 108–19.

[58] Feshbach (1978), Tables 2, 7 and 9.

[59] Gail W. Lapidus, in private discussion during 1979, also laid all of her stress upon supply factors.

See the discussion in the section of Chapter 3 entitled "regional aspects of unemployment" for a treatment of the issue of whether demand constraints on female unemployment existed at the regional and local level. While it must be admitted that such constraints may have existed in the 1950s in some rural areas and small and middle-sized towns, data from one Soviet source make it appear unlikely that the easing of such constraints was important in explaining the increase in the female labor participation.

The source claims that in towns of less than 20 to 50,000, and in particular in towns under 10,000 population, the labor force participation rate actually declined during 1954–64 (F. B. Anikeeva and I. F. Chubuk in *Naselenie, trudovye resursy SSSR* [1971], pp. 121–22). This period includes the first half of the 1960s – i.e. the heart of the participation increase that we are concerned with explaining.

rose in this dramatic fashion because of new and sudden pressure from the authorities, who were redefining the "obligation to work." If so, this would have had to have been during a very compressed period; some 71 to 84 per cent of the number of women moving into the socialist labor force because of the higher participation rate came during the first half of the 1960s.[60] If this had occurred as a result of official pressure, one might expect that such pressure would have had to be sufficiently sharp so that Westerners would have become conscious of it whether through Soviet publications or otherwise. So far as I am aware, such special pressure during the first half of the 1960s has not been noted either by Soviet or non-Soviet sources.

A Soviet emigre, Mr Leonid Khotin, has suggested to me a supply-side explanation that is completely independent of official pressure. He pointed to the pension law of 1956 which revolutionized old-age pensions for workers and employees both with regard to coverage and to payments. He stated that he personally knew at least eight women who took jobs in the 1960s so as to raise their length of covered service to the minimum requirement under the new law.

This explanation does have the problem of positing a lengthy lag in this effect of the law (over three years), since it assumes that the major part of the effect was not registered in the 1959 population census. But such a lag is possible. Another explanation, suggested by Peter Hauslohner, is that the reduction in the length of the normal work week from 48 to 41 hours made participation in the labor force both more feasible and attractive to many women. This explanation has the advantage of fitting the timing of increased participation without the need for positing a lag.

The only other explanation that I can offer is that the dramatic 1959–70 development is explained by the same "change in taste" among women that occurred both then and in the 1970s in Western countries. Here is a topic in the history of women in the Soviet Union that cries for research.

The absence of anything approaching a self-clearing market for intermediate goods in production was noted earlier in this section as constituting a strong incentive for collective farmers to work sufficient days a year to remain in good standing on their farms. The same holds for urbanites who engage in private work for individuals as the urban counterpart of the private plot. Both the small tools and the materials needed for this work seem to be mainly unavailable on the market; normally, they would appear to be obtainable (even though illegally) only from the socialist employer of

---

[60] For this range of Soviet estimates, see V. Kostakov in *V.E.*, 1974, 4, p. 39 combined with A. Dadashev in *V.E.*, 1974, 4, p. 119; L. A. Kostin in *Trudovye resursy SSSR* (1979), p. 11; Afanas'evskii (1976), p. 19; Sbytova (1982), p. 80.

the urbanite engaged in petty second-economy activity.[61] Thus the average second-economy urbanite could not, regardless of whether he were permitted to avoid working in the socialist economy, consider socialist-economy and private-economy work as substitutes.[62] Particularly for males, whether they be rural or urban, incentives match obligations to work in the socialist sector.

Geographic restrictions on job changes. The first set of such restrictions to be investigated are those that have been placed on collective farmers. Until 1976–82 under the law of 1974[63] (and I know nothing of how this law has worked in practice), most rural inhabitants and collective farmers in particular did not have internal passports like other Soviet citizens; farmers were instead allowed to leave the collective farm only with the permission of the farm itself.[64] Thus their ability to change jobs was, at least in theory, sharply restricted by their absence of the right to leave their locality.

However, the author of the first sociological study of rural life in the Soviet Union found that this restriction seemed to be ineffective. In a special study, he compared villages in the Moscow area only a few miles apart, with practically identical economic conditions, in some of which the restriction applied while in others all residents had been given internal passports. He found that the rate of out-migration was in fact higher in those villages whose residents did not have internal passports.[65]

Similarly, Peter Wiles writes (although without references) that the

---

61 With regard to auto repair, the director of the Russian Republic Automotive Service Association estimated in 1981 that 50 per cent of private cars were repaired by "mechanics working 'on the side' either on state time and at state service stations or after work but using state materials." (*C.D.S.P.*, XXXIII, 52 [January 27, 1982], pp. 14–15.)

62 The Soviet procuracy is reported to have given the official count of the total number of "parasites and vagabonds" in the Soviet Union as being 500,000. The statistic is said to refer to those who have been without work and without an official dwelling for more than four months (*Le Monde*, October 20, 1984, p. 6). This figure can presumably be taken as a rough estimate of the number of second-economy urbanites who are not working in the socialist sector. (I am indebted to Philip Hanson for this source.)

63 Decree of August 28, 1974 of the Council of Ministers of the Soviet Union in *SP SSSR*, 1974, 19, st. 109. For controversy as to the meaning of this decree, see *Osteuropa*, 1977, 5, p.A 251; 1977, 6, pp. 532–33; 1977, 9, p. 801; 1978, 3, pp. 250–51; and Ioffe and Maggs (1983), p. 251.

64 Decrees of 1932 and 1940 specified that rural workers on state farms should have internal passports, and a 1973 article states that all those working for state enterprises in rural areas should have passports. On the other hand, a 1953 decree makes no special mention of rural workers on state farms, in construction or in transport as receiving passports. (Ann Helgeson, "The Soviet internal passport system," University of Essex Department of Economics Discussion Paper No. 126 [March 1979].)

65 Arutiunian (1971), p. 285 fn.

restriction was never well enforced. Wiles also declares that it has been lifted region by region since January 1, 1975.[66]

That there has been extensive out-migration from collective farms is not in question. Unfortunately, we cannot separate this from other rural out-migration, but total rural–urban migration accounted for 63 per cent of the urban growth between the 1939 and 1959 censuses, 46 per cent between the 1959 and 1970 censuses, and presumably close to that figure between the 1970 and 1979 censuses.[67] During 1968–69, the gross migration from one locality to another in the Soviet Union totalled 14 million. Of these migrants, 49 per cent moved from rural localities[68] – although in 1970, only 44 per cent of the country's population was rural. These migration data include youth going to other areas to study and presumably also include some moves within the confines of a single collective farm; although these limitations of the data certainly introduce bias into comparisons of rural compared to urban moves for purposes of changing civilian jobs, there is no suggestion here of a rural population forced to keep its residence. Since the number of personnel working in collective farms in 1970 still constituted two-thirds of those working in collective and state farms combined,[69] a large share of the rural migration must have come from the collective-farm population.

Nevertheless, these data tell us nothing as to what rural migration would have been if it had not been restricted. Limitations on migration have taken the form both of restrictions specifically on collective farmers, but also apparently on most (but not all) rural residents who require a specific permit to leave the areas even if they have a passport.[70] But the limitations specifically on collective farmers appear not to have applied to children under the age of sixteen years, to demobilized soldiers,[71] or to those going to study in urban areas in daytime vocational schools or other educational institutions from which they would be subject to temporary job allocation. There is even a suggestion that it has not applied to those with resident family members working outside of the collective-farm system.[72]

One Soviet sociologist, as part of a study of rural migration in an oblast of the Northwest Region of the Soviet Union where the rural population in the 1960s was declining by almost two per cent annually and where the

[66] In Schapiro and Godson (1981), p. 28.
[67] *C.D.S.P.*, XXXIII, 9 (April 1, 1981), p. 20.
[68] TsSU, *Itogi perepisi 1970*, Vol. VII, pp. 3 and 8.
[69] *Narkhoz SSSR 1922–1982*, pp. 285 and 303.
[70] Staroverov (1975), pp. 85 and 121.
[71] *Ibid.*, p. 205 and A. Zalevskii in *Ekonomika sel'skogo khoziaistva*, 1972, 4, p. 68.
[72] Staroverov (1975), p. 97.

labor supply was sufficiently restricted so that ten per cent of those working (compared with three per cent in the Russian Republic as a whole for rural and urban combined) were outside of the workforce age, asked in the second part of the 1960s about the effect on migration of the "special passport regime for rural areas." Despite the fact that the demography of the area might lead one to have expected particularly sharp efforts to restrain out-migration, the sociologist reports that not one of the agricultural leaders questioned could name a single rural inhabitant whose settlement had been able to retain him on the basis of this special rural legislation. On the other hand, he also reports on steps taken by individuals in the area to avoid becoming subject to this legislation.[73]

I have seen only one study comparing collective-farm and state-farm separation rates. The data are for Novosibirsk oblast' in West Siberia and cover the 1959–67 period. It is noteworthy that the collective-farm rate is only one quarter of that of the state farms.[74] This would argue for the likelihood of effective restriction on collective-farm out-migration in this area.

On the other hand, national data for tractorist-machinists[75] are striking. During 1965–69, 3.6 million of these were trained in the Soviet Union. But if one looks at the increase in the number of tractorist-machinists working in Soviet agriculture as a whole, and considers replacement needs for those retiring or leaving for health reasons, on a net basis 79 per cent of these trainees moved completely out of agricultural employment. This is explained (almost certainly as an exaggeration) by the author as the result of the trainees being young and transferring to other branches after their later demobilization from military service.[76] (Only some four to seven per cent of all machinist-tractorists under twenty-eight years of age in a large-scale study of 1969 were female.)[77] A similar pattern seems to have continued during 1971–74.[78] Yet this is the group which the collective farms would be most anxious to retain.

Clear conclusions cannot be drawn from this material. But it seems safe to say that restrictions on collective-farm (or indeed all rural?) labor

[73] *Ibid.*, pp. 77–78, 97, 205.

[74] R. K. Ivanova in *Migratsiia sel'skogo naseleniia* (1970), p. 170.

[75] This term is identical to "mechanizers." It refers to all manual workers doing agricultural work with tractors, combines, excavators, or other agricultural equipment. They are registered on their farm as having this trade; normally, at least, they have appropriate certificates and have had special training in school (S. Sazonov and V. Chupeev in *S.T.*, 1979, 6, p. 104 and N. Rogovskii in *Kommunist*, 1976, 16, p. 58).

[76] Zalevskii in *Ekonomika sel'skogo khoziaistva*, 1972, 4, p. 68.

[77] A. V. Bezrukov in *S.I.*, 1976, 1, p. 89.

[78] D. Palterovich in *P.Kh.*, 1980, 9, p. 102.

mobility did significantly constrain the labor market opportunities for this important category of worker at least through the 1970s, but that the restrictions operated very imperfectly. The imperfections of operation seem to have applied particularly to young males, although it is precisely those under thirty years of age that we would expect to be most mobile.

A second sphere of geographic restrictions concerns a number of the largest cities in the Soviet Union (as well as some smaller but attractive ones such as Tallin) where it is intended to restrict population growth, and thus where special permission is required for anyone to become a permanent resident. Certainly this has not had the effect of stopping net in-migration into these cities, particularly the more attractive ones.[79] Nevertheless, between the 1959 and 1970 censuses, the ten cities which had passed one million population by 1970 had had only two-thirds of the growth rate of the Soviet Union's total urban population. Of the seven that passed one million during the 1960s, only one had a higher growth rate than the total urban population.[80] Between the 1970 and 1979 censuses, the above ten cities had 87 per cent of the growth rate of the urban population.[81] One may surmise that these restrictions have had at least some effect.

At the same time, there are complaints that the planned employment in industry in these same cities is determined by national ministries, rather than by the cities. This is given as the explanation for why Leningrad's planned population for 1980 was exceeded by 1971, and why Moscow's plan for 1990 was almost reached in 1978.[82]

In-migration into such cities seem to occur particularly to fill manual labor jobs for which it is difficult to recruit locally. Thus in a 1970 study of the workforce of seven machinebuilding enterprises of Leningrad by a very careful Soviet scholar, 48 per cent of the non-commuting personnel under the age of thirty were found to have been born outside of Leningrad and 29 per cent had lived in Leningrad for less than sixteen years. Of the twenty to twenty-nine year olds who had lived in Leningrad for less than one year, 75 per cent worked as machine operators (a trade generally disliked); the proportion declined with the stay in Leningrad, being 43–49 per cent for those in the city for one to ten years, 35 per cent for those ten to fifteen

[79] V. Bialkovskaia and V. Novikov in *V.E.*, 1982, 11, p. 92.

[80] TsSU, *Itogi perepisi 1970*, Vol. 1. Of the total of ten cities, Kiev and Tashkent were the only two that grew more rapidly than the urban average.

[81] TsSU, *Chislennost'* (1984), Tables 2 and 4. The same two cities that had grown faster than the urban average during 1959–70 repeated their performance, and were joined very narrowly by Baku.

[82] V. Cherevan' in *V.E.*, 1982, 2, pp. 52–53.

years, and 17–19 per cent for those living there longer or having been born in Leningrad.[83] In Moscow during 1976–80, 41 per cent of the total hirings of manual workers were of out-of-towners; this high proportion is described as a result of the steady net shift of Moscow personnel out of industry and into the service sector.[84]

In Moscow, much of the in-migration is said to take the form of organized recruitment (*orgnabor*) for heavy physical labor; presumably[85] these workers signed contracts for several years and thus could not use the job as a means of searching for housing and a better job.[86] Such workers would be given only temporary residence permits in Moscow.

What happens to these in-migrants who have arrived as manual workers in undesired trades and with temporary residence permits? In Moscow, about 30 per cent of the stock of such manual workers leave the city every year. But these are mainly low-skilled workers. The same authors who report this figure also say that out-of-towners working in machinebuilding usually quit once they receive their permanent residence permit;[87] the implication is that such receipt is fairly normal for those who are not totally unskilled. This implication receives a crude confirmation from the implied statement of one migration authority that the flow of net in-migration into Moscow through temporary permits is of the order of 70,000 annually,[88] while the same author elsewhere tells us that, as of 1971, there was a stock of only 55,000 manual workers with temporary residence permits.[89]

Writing of Leningrad, another author says that permanent settlement there by rural youth from the surrounding region (but outside of commuting range) is intense. Usually such in-migrants stay with relatives and friends, with whose help they get around the difficulties connected with registering for permanent residence.[90]

To some unknown but presumably substantial degree, then, youths are able to enter restricted cities as permanent residents – and then exercise as

[83] Vasil'eva (1973), pp. 7, 8, 121–124, 194.

[84] A. Kosaev and S. Il'in in *V.E.*, 1981, 10, p. 74.

[85] "Presumably" because different Soviet authors use the term for organized recruitment with different meanings. The labor category of *limitchiki* is included here.

[86] Another source writes of Moscow temporary residence permits for work in engineering enterprises being linked to their continued work in that sector (Ia. A. Davidovich *et al.* in *S.I.*, 1981, 4, p. 126).

[87] Davidovich *et al.* in *S.I.*, 1981, 4, p. 126.

[88] B. Khorev in *E.N.*, 1984, 3, p. 63. Khorev describes this number as pertaining only to the requests by organizations for additional temporary jobs, but gives the impression that these requests are honored. During 1985, there were 60,000 requests for such permits by employers in Moscow (*Pravda*, January 25, 1986, pp. 1–2, as indicated by Hauslohner).

[89] B. S. Khorev and N. M. Timchuk in *Migratsionnaia* (1974), pp. 149–53.

[90] Staroverov (1975), p. 162.

free a choice as any other Soviet citizens in the job market – but only by working for a period of time in manual-labor occupations for which it is difficult to recruit locally. Thus, in such cities, it is possible for enterprises to recruit for unpopular jobs at what would not be a market-clearing wage without such special entry rights.

A second type of interference with the labor market concerns the reluctance of specialists of various types who already have permanent residence permits to leave for better opportunities elsewhere. In a discussion relating to Moscow, this reluctance is laid to the fact that such out-migration would be a once-and-for-all decision.[91] This type of imperfection, like the first, leads to people working at jobs that would be inferior to their other options if it were not for the existence of the system of residence permits.

Still undiscussed up to this point has been the role of daily commuting from outside of the restricted city as a means of improving the efficiency of its labor market. Daily net commuters (defined as those travelling across administrative boundaries) for both work and study purposes into cities of over one million population in 1971 were estimated to have totalled eight per cent of the total number of the inhabitants of these cities who studied or worked there. Round-trip commuting time was normally distributed, with 42 per cent of the commuters spending 60–90 minutes daily, and only 15 per cent spending less than 40 or more than 120 minutes.[92] In 1960, the gross percentage of inward commuters to work alone was ten per cent of the total population in Moscow, five per cent in Leningrad, and 13 per cent in Khar'kov.[93] Thus, as is not surprising, commuting from outside the city's limits is a significant means of entering the labor market of restricted cities.

To a significant degree, such commuting simply eases the geographic labor market barriers for those already living in suburban areas. Thus we are told that, of suburbanites working in engineering plants in Leningrad in 1970, there was very little effort to move into the city.[94] It would seem that this was probably due to the difficulties of migration into Leningrad. Data of 1979, that seem to relate to L'vov, show that the bulk of inward commuters of all ages would have liked to have moved into the city;[95] for them at least, commuting was not primarily voluntary.

Most interesting is the view taken in one of the key migration studies where it is claimed that population growth in the suburbs of large cities is

[91] V. Perevedentsev in *C.D.S.P.*, XVIII, 11 (April 6, 1966), p. 11.
[92] B. S. Khorev *et al.* in *Migratsionnaia* (1974), pp. 107, 114, 117. The data base was a one-time study by TsSU SSSR of June 1, 1971.
[93] Iu. L. Pivobarov in *Materialy* (1968), p. 239.   [94] Vasil'eva (1973), p. 123.
[95] F. D. Zastavnyi in *S.I.*, 1981, 3, p. 119.

determined primarily by the growth in jobs in the city itself rather than in the suburbs.[96] This suggests that those who do not live within commuting distance of a restricted city have open to them another possible option besides that of entering the city with a temporary residence permit; they may, instead, move to a suburban area and then commute. Of course, housing shortages in the suburbs make this difficult; but it is certainly not impossible for a single individual who is willing to rent part of a room in someone else's domicile.

Restrictions on change of the specific job. We have already looked at legal restrictions on the employee which arise out of his status as a recent graduate of particular educational institutions, of his having signed a labor contract for one or more years, or of his being a collective farmer. Other restrictions emanate from the need to give notice before quitting one's job: what used to be a two-week notice requirement has become a one to two-month period depending on the grounds for leaving.[97] Another recent change of significance has been the shift from one month to three weeks in the normally (and minimally) permitted period between quitting one job and starting another without losing the privileges of continuous work service.[98] The length of continuous work service is relevant for pensions, vacations and for sickness benefits, but the vacation significance is very minor and the other elements (especially concerning pensions) are least important for workers under thirty among whom – as in other countries – the quit rate is by far the highest.[99]

The restriction that one might have thought could be very important, but which from all accounts is not binding, is that of housing. Some three quarters of all urban housing space is rented,[100] and a great deal of this

---

96 *Migratsionnaia* (1974), p. 155.
97 It was changed to one month in January 1980, and then to two months in August 1983 (see "Konsul'tatsii," in *S.T.*, 1984, 8, p. 108). However, the enterprise has the right to waive the notice period ("Konsul'tatsii," in *S.T.*, 1984, 1, pp. 110–11) and one might expect that this clause would be used frequently since an unwilling worker is not much use to his employer.
98 The one-month period was established in 1960 (*Opyt*, p. 10). In 1980, the qualification was added that the interruption of employment could not be more than once a year (*Pravda*, January 12, 1980, p. 1). The three-week period dates from late 1983.
99 Boderskova (1975), pp. 1–23 is a good source for distinguishing between the rights accompanying "total work service," "continuous work service" and "continuous special work status." For seasonal workers, see *Dvizhenie rabochikh kadrov* (1973), p. 105. Also see the discussion by R. Livshits in *S.T.*, 1982, 11, pp. 78–79 which is similarly disparaging as to the effect of various recent financial encouragements for remaining within a given enterprise.
100 *V.S.*, 1984, 9, p. 62.

belongs to individual enterprises that have built for their own employees.[101] The remainder of the rented housing belongs to the municipalities, but much of this space has been granted to individuals on the basis of an allocation by the city to their employing enterprise.[102] Since the housing is built or assigned to the enterprise for purposes of housing its labor force, one might expect that employees who quit would be evicted. Given the housing shortage in the Soviet Union, such practice could be decisive in constraining most quits.

A well-regarded Russian émigré economist, Katsenelinboigen, reports that the practice of evicting quitting workers from apartments received from their employer was discontinued in 1956 – i.e. in the same year when such quits once again became legal. In the late 1960s, when an individual enterprise attempted to return to such evictions, the national procuracy halted the evictions.[103]

In searching for relevant information from the Soviet press, I have found one reference from 1964 and four from the period between 1974 and 1984; all of them supported the position of Katsenelinboigen.[104] In addition, a 1975 decision of the Supreme Court of the Russian Republic, that confirmed the right of collective farms to evict hired employees who left the employment of the farm, did so on the ground of the special legal status of collective farms.[105] Three of the four press references referred to above discuss the problem that receiving housing from one's employer often serves as a sufficient incentive to quit working for him; the employee stays only so long as he is building seniority to get housing, and then feels free to go to another enterprise where the employment terms other than housing are superior. One enterprise in Kiev is reported to have had 176 employees waiting for housing in 1959; as of 1966, although the enterprise had received 800 more apartments to allocate and, by implication, had not grown much in employment, the waiting list had nevertheless increased to 300 employees.[106]

---

[101] In the mid-1970s, employers' contributions accounted for 70 per cent of all appropriations for the building of houses (*C.D.S.P.*, XXXIV, 10 [April 7, 1982], p. 7).

[102] For a 1979 statement of this with regard to Moscow, see *C.D.S.P.*, XXXI, 1 (January 31, 1979), p. 11.

[103] Katsenelinboigen (1978), p. 223.

[104] V. Acharkan in *S.T.*, 1964, 8, pp. 129–30, cited in Hauslohner (1984), Chapter 2, fn. 100; E. G. Antosenkov in *Dvizhenie rabochikh kadrov na promyshlennykh predpriiatiiakh* (1974), p. 215; Pavlenkov (1976), pp. 108–09; *C.D.S.P.*, XXXIV, 10 (April 7, 1982), p. 7; *E.K.O.*, 1984, 5, p. 59. The 1964 reference is the least clear in this regard.

[105] Hazard (1983), p. 90.

[106] Hauslohner has informed me that the post-war history of legal prohibition of eviction of workers who had quit their jobs goes back to 1953. Exceptions always existed, but these were further restricted in 1981 national housing legislation.

Of course, none of this should be taken as suggesting that housing shortages do not limit the labor turnover. That would be absurd. The point is that such shortages have less of an effect upon such turnover, within a given city, than one might have expected, given the assignment of much of urban housing to specific enterprises.

The discussion so far has concerned restrictions upon the employee. But equally interesting are restrictions placed upon the employer in changing the tasks set for the individual employee. This discussion will be limited to Soviet law; the topic will be taken up again in Chapter 3.

Both the particular trade, and the locality within a multi-plant enterprise at which an individual employee can be used, are limited by the employment arrangement established when the individual was first hired unless the employee agrees to a change.[107] With regard to trades, it is "spetsial'nost'" that is determinant,[108] and this is so narrowly defined that in 1973 alone there were 6,300 such trades listed for industry alone.[109] Locality is defined by a "population point"; there may be several such within a single administrative district (*raion*).[110]

The above restrictions apply to permanent job transfers either within the enterprise or to other enterprises. Transfer within an enterprise refers to any change in "trade, skill, duty, scale of earnings, privileges, advantages, or any other existing conditions of work."[111] Such transfers cannot occur against the employee's will, nor can he be dismissed on the ground of refusing such transfer.[112] Indeed, even refusal of permanent transfer to another trade for disciplinary reasons has been rejected as a ground for dismissal by the Russian Republic's supreme court.[113]

However, dismissals can occur when an individual is unable to carry out his work properly because of either lack of skill or health, or when the

---

[107] Smirnov (1969), pp. 21–23 and L. Okun'kov in *S.T.*, 1975, 5, pp. 131–34. For example, a worker might have been originally hired as a driver of all kinds of vehicles, or alternatively only for those of specified tonnage. Which of these is the case will determine whether his being shifted to a vehicle of different tonnage constitutes a "transfer" and so requires his agreement. If a change is agreed upon by the worker, the new "job" constitutes the elements of the labor contract which are binding in the future. The restrictions on obligatory transfer within an enterprise may have been eased somewhat by a 1979 decision of the Supreme Court of the Russian Republic (see Hazard [1983], pp. 86–87).

[108] V. Pirogov and M. Pankin in *S.T.*, 1972, 2, p. 134; Okun'kov in *S.T.*, 1975, 5, p. 131.

[109] Gur'ianov and Kostin (1973), pp. 15–16. This represents a reduction from 23,170 in an unstated year.

[110] Gershanov and Nikitinskii (1975), pp. 28–29. Travel time from the worker's housing seems to be the issue here (Okun'kov in *S.T.*, 1975, 5, p. 133).

[111] Article 25 of the Russian Republic's Code of Labor Laws, reprinted in *Normativnye akty* (1972), p. 218.

[112] See articles 29 and 35 in *ibid.*, pp. 219–21 for grounds for dismissal.

[113] Prudinskii (1966), p. 48.

enterprise has a surplus of workers in a given trade.[114] Thus in these major cases, the individual who does not accept transfer is liable to some probability of dismissal. Nevertheless, it should be noted that surplus of workers in a given trade can be narrowly defined; in at least one court case, such redundancy was denied by the court on the ground that it existed only because some personnel in the enterprise were working in such a fashion as to combine trades other than their own.[115]

In case of redundancy of personnel, the law lists individual labor productivity and skills as the two prime criteria for determining which workers would be dismissed. Only if there is equality among individual workers in these regards, are other criteria such as seniority in the enterprise or the family situation to play a role.[116] From a purely legal point of view, enterprise managements in this respect have greater freedom than would most American managements operating under trade union contracts.

Obligation to change the specific job. In contrast to permanent job transfers, temporary transfers – both within an enterprise and between organizations – are permitted without the consent of the worker. Such transfers are limited to one month per calendar year, and must be due either to idleness of the factory or shop or to production conditions which could not have been foreseen;[117] the main exception refers to transfers for disciplinary reasons, where duration can now be three months.

Social recruitment of students for construction work during the summer vacation might be regarded as a form of temporary transfer as well. This began to develop sharply after 1966 as a substitute for permanent social recruitment of youth. By 1977, such recruitment from daytime higher-

[114] See Nikitinskii and Paniugin (1973), pp. 42–46 for this interpretation of the legal provision that dismissals can occur when staff is reduced. It is explicitly denied in this legal source, written for a broad audience, that such staff reduction must be overall in the enterprise. Presumably, it was the latter interpretation given to the wording in the Soviet Union's 1970 Fundamentals of Labor Law that caused Blair Ruble to write that technological obsolescence could not be cited as justification for the abolition of a worker's job and thus for the dismissal of the worker if he were unwilling to shift to another (in *Comparative Labor Law*, 2, 3 [1977], p. 181).

[115] A. Vladimirov in *Sovetskie profsoiuzy*, 1967, 7, pp. 24–25.

[116] *Normativnye akty* (1972), article 34, p. 221. It is not surprising, however, that the "subsidiary" criteria seem to get more attention in practice than do the "primary" ones. See the treatment by a lower court in the case of Berezina as reported in *Sovetskie profsoiuzy*, 1965, 4, pp. 30–31.

[117] *Ibid.*, articles 26–27, p. 219 and *Trudovoe pravo* (1972), p. 8. For the interpretation, see Pirogov and Pankin in *S.T.*, 1971, 2, p. 140. In forestry, however, such temporary transfers can be for up to three months and also may be for clearly foreseeable reasons: e.g. seasonality and the logging of new forestry tracts (Sevost'ianov [1975], p. 23).

educational and junior college institutions reached 741,000. Both in 1973 and 1977, some 16–17 per cent of all daytime higher educational students participated in this summer construction work. In 1973, at least, one-third of them also studied construction trades during a preparatory period.[118]

By far the most important of the temporary transfers, however, occur entirely outside the law. Urban workers are sent on a very large-scale to work in farming, not only at the height of the season but throughout the year.[119] Others are mobilized in urban areas for unloading and storage work connected with agriculture,[120] or are sent for street and building maintenance work by their own towns.[121] Still others are seconded by their own enterprises to suppliers as the only means for the sending enterprise to obtain certain goods or services; construction work and construction materials are particularly singled out as fields for which such seconding is essential.[122] These missions are not covered under the law treating temporary transfers, since it is neither production necessities in the sending enterprise nor absenteeism of a specific worker in the receiving one that constitutes the cause. Expert commentators say that, although tractorist-machinists and truck drivers are obliged to accept agricultural missions under pain of violating labor discipline, no legal sanctions can be taken against other workers who refuse and that only "social pressure" can be exerted on them.[123] Yet the amount of such agricultural work increased by 150 per cent between 1950 and 1960, by 20 per cent between 1960 and 1970, and by a further 117 per cent in the following decade.[124]

If we limit ourselves to personnel detached by their State organizations for temporary agricultural work, we can estimate their number as 11.3 million urbanites and 16.8 million urban and rural employees in 1982.[125]

118 Maslova (1976), pp. 107–08. V. Barinov and A. Semenchenko in *Demograficheskie* (1975), pp. 96–100. This construction activity is the main form of student work (Zaitsev and Uvarov in *E.I.*, 1984, 4, p. 94).
119 *Trudovye resursy SSSR* (1979), pp. 267–68.
120 *C.D.S.P.*, XXXIII, 48 (December 23, 1981), p. 7.
121 *C.D.S.P.*, XXX, 22 (June 28, 1978), pp. 20–21. *Trudovye resursy SSSR* (1979) pp. 267–68.
122 A. Brovin in *S.T.*, 1984, 9, pp. 80–82.
123 A. Gudilin in *C.D.S.P.*, XXX, 39 (October 25, 1978), p. 6 and *E.K.O.*, 1982, 4, pp. 179–80.
124 TsSU, *Sel'skoe khoziaistvo SSSR* (1971), p. 446 and *Narkhoz SSSR 1922–1982*, p. 315. Data for 1979 onward describe the category as consisting of "all personnel sent by other enterprises and organizations to work on collective- and state-farms; hired personnel on collective farms." One might assume that the data are thus the sum of both categories; but data given here for earlier years are identical with other data given earlier by the Central Statistical Office with a definition that ignored hired personnel on collective farms.
125 The total figure of 16.8 million workers and employees is taken from *Narkhoz SSSR v 1982 g.*, p. 287, after adjustment by the common Soviet assumption that these personnel work for an average of one month (*Osnovnye problemy* [1971], p. 128; E. Manevich in *V.E.*, 1981,

These constituted 11 and 16 per cent respectively of all state-employed workers and employees in the Soviet Union whose principal employment was outside of agriculture. When we remember that we are not including temporarily mobilized labor for non-agricultural purposes, and particularly when we note the fact that older people and mothers with young children must have been largely exempt, one can see that the probability of such mobilization, sometime during the year for urban males under age thirty-five, must have approached something like 25 per cent. Of course, the quantitative dimension of this restriction is much less when measured in efficiency units of farm work as opposed to number of persons; a reliable Soviet demographer reports that farm managers are agreed that the proportion in efficiency units must be reduced by at least two-thirds.[126]

Not only the sending of urban personnel to work temporarily in agriculture, but also its use within urban areas, has grown greatly within recent years. Such seconding has clearly become much more than a response to seasonal labor needs. Instead, it is a widely used non-market method of getting work done that is low-skilled, physically hard, and unattractive at prevailing earning levels. An author who is deeply concerned with certain negative effects of its extension nevertheless rejects the market solution of raising the earnings for these jobs; such a solution, he insists, would violate the principle that earnings should be directly proportional to the quantity and quality of work.[127]

Soviet writers and officials are evidently very uneasy about this development. It is attacked as anarchic; seconding by order of local government is unplanned and unregulated.[128] Work is inefficiently done. The system is said to falsify the financial accounting both of the sending and of the receiving organization, since the former bears much or all of the wage costs. It serves *de facto* as a device for violating pricing regulations governing

9, p. 60; V. I. Perevedentsev in *C.D.S.P.*, XXXV, 8 [March 23, 1983], p. 5). The one-month figure is elsewhere stated to be a maximum figure (*Trudovye resursy SSSR* [1979], p. 32), so the bias of our 16 per cent estimate is probably downward.

Urban data are obtained by taking the estimate made by the Research Institute of Labor of the Soviet Union for man-days worked during 1976 by urban workers and employees (L. Kostin in *S.T.*, 1978, 9, p. 20). This is converted into full-year equivalents by using the Central Statistical Office conversion rate for temporarily employed personnel in agriculture (Mashenkov [1974], p. 76). Dividing the resultant figure by the TsSU statistic for 1976 for all (urban plus rural) employees, we end up with a ratio of 67.3 per cent urban. This ratio is then applied to the TsSU statistic for 1982 for all employees.
126 V. I. Perevedentsev in *C.D.S.P.*, XXXV, 8 (March 23, 1983), p. 5.
127 Brovin in *S.T.*, 1984, pp. 81 and 84–85.
128 A. I. Shokin, Minister of the Electronic Industry of the Soviet Union, in *Pravda*, May 17, 1984, as quoted by Brovin, p. 84.

transactions between enterprises.[129] Yet there are no signs of its decline. When the problem was addressed by central authorities in 1979, it was only *unjustified* secondment of personnel that was ordered to be curtailed.[130]

Currently, this obligatory secondment seems to be one of the most important limitations on the working of the Soviet labor market. Soviet attacks upon it are not made on the basis of its interference with the Soviet citizen's right to choose his occupation provided that he can find an employer; rather they stress the inefficiency of the system in terms of cost effectiveness to the State. The nature of these attacks probably reflects the basis for Soviet leaders choosing by and large to maintain a market for labor: the market as the means for distributing this factor of production is considered more efficient from the viewpoint of the ultimate buyer (the state) than would be centralized methods. The welfare of the labor supplier is not the issue.

THE SETTING OF PRICES IN THE LABOR MARKET

Wage rates versus the wage fund

If, as already argued, the distribution of labor in the Soviet Union is carried out primarily through the market-place, there are very significant efficiency advantages to be gained if relative prices are such as to clear the closely inter-connected markets for each type of labor. It is true that one might conceive of a central authority, provided that it possesses considerable knowledge of the supply of each type of labor skill within each small region, as setting a quantity of each sort of labor for each enterprise as the maximum that it can employ. Given that a single individual can usually perform various kinds of work, one might conceive of relative prices that are above the market-clearing set existing for the more skilled jobs with individuals sorting themselves out into specific jobs through queuing. But the information demands of such a system, both with regard to the supply of labor and to the trade-off among different kinds of labor in the individual enterprises' production functions, would make reliance on such a queuing system of labor distribution peculiarly unsatisfactory. In any case, Soviet authorities have never attempted to establish a large set of

---

[129] *Ibid.*, pp. 80–87.
[130] Decree of December 13, 1979 of the Central Committee of the Communist Party of the Soviet Union, of the Council of Ministers and of the trade union central organization, quoted in *ibid.*, p. 83.

Table 2.4 *Structure of earnings of industrial manual workers, Soviet Union*

Source of earning	Machinebuilding & metalworking (probably end of 1970s)	All industry					
		1957	1961	1965	1968	1970	1972
Determined by the Center	68%	65%	84%	79%	79%	73%	68%
Of this:							
Minimum wage	43	33	43	39	51	46	43
Payment above the minimum according to wage rate[a]	16	23	30	28	17	17	16
Supplementary payments	10	9	12	11	11	10	10
Incentive payments	32	35	16	21	21	27	32

Note: Incentives paid from the material-stimulation fund are included. Sickness pay is excluded from the total.

[a] This includes reclassification of workers to higher skill categories, and so can embody an element of what is really incentive. But McAuley (p. 249) has shown this component to be insignificant.

Sources: Machinebuilding and metalworking: V. Markov in *S.T.*, 1980, 1, p. 101.
All industry: Estimated in McAuley (1979), pp. 247–49. Very similar proportions for 1961 and 1971 are given by R. Batkaev in *S.T.*, 1973, 4, p. 89.

labor inequalities for each enterprise. (The furthest that they have ever gone is to establish such inequalities for three aggregates of labor.)

On the other hand, the State Committee of Labor has twice in the post-war years worked out very detailed compilations of wage rates. Since these wage rates, following the model of producer prices of products, are expected to remain unchanged for fifteen years or so, one could hardly expect them to be market clearing during most of their lifetime regardless of how accurately they were originally set. The difference, however, between stable relative wages and stable relative producer prices is that the latter set does not operate within a market-place but rather is accompanied by physical allocation to receiving organizations. Relative wages are much more important. We are thus left with the puzzle: How can Soviet authorities afford to rely upon centrally determined – and thus, inevitably, extremely sticky – prices for labor under conditions of the distribution of labor through the market-place?

The answer, it seems to me, is that they neither can nor seriously try to do so. It is labor earnings, not wage rates, that should be considered as the price of labor. Incentive pay, that is not regulated from the Center with regard to particular types of labor, constitutes a large proportion of total earnings. This is illustrated in Table 2.4.

From Alistair McAuley's original table that serves as the base for the "all industry" part of Table 2.4, we can calculate the ratio of the increase in average incentive pay to the increase in total average earnings of manual workers in industry. The ratios show considerable scatter between periods: 1957–61: −126% (absolute decline of incentive payments); 1961–65: +81 per cent; 1965–68: +16 per cent; 1968–70: +91 per cent; 1970–72: +98 per cent. Of all five periods, only in 1957–61 and 1965–68 was the rate of growth of average earnings dominated by growth of wage rate set by the Center.

From these data I conclude that it is not the sticky wage rates that are of primary importance in determining relative earnings, but rather the allocation as between employees of the funds available for incentive payments. This conclusion points us toward concentrating on the wage fund and the material-stimulation fund, from both of which such payments are made, that are available to each enterprise.

Moreover, virtually all manual workers in Soviet industry have a substantial component of incentive pay built into their wage system. Between 1965 and 1982, it is true that piece-workers constituted only some 54–58 per cent of all manual workers, but time-workers not on a bonus scheme – and this is the truly relevant portion of the manual labor force – declined from 5 to 1 per cent.[131]

McAuley interprets his data in terms of wage drift which is "most likely to be undesired (by the Center) and unplanned."[132] This strikes me as a curious view, since it is the Center that determines the wage fund, and to some degree the material-stimulation fund, available to each enterprise. It seems to me more appropriate to hold that the Center determines the total change in incentive payments each year – but not the distribution of such payments within the individual enterprise. It is not sheer accident that, when we consolidate McAuley's periods above into four of roughly equal length, the two in which the incentive portion declines or grows negligibly in absolute terms are the same two in which the centrally determined portion grows most rapidly as expressed in rubles.

In the Pechorskii coal basin of the far north, producing 4.5 per cent of

---

[131] *V.S.*, 1976, 10, pp. 91–95, and 1983, 6, pp. 60–68.   [132] McAuley (1979), p. 246.

Soviet underground coal at this period,[133] average earnings of coal-mining workers increased by 5.8 per cent annually between 1959 and 1963. However, the total amount of this increase was due to the sharp expansion in the average period of employment in the basin for which a wage supplement was paid. Despite the fact that labor productivity grew by 18 per cent over this period, there was no increase either in the wage rate for a given skill grade or in per capita incentive payments.[134]

How can we account for this complete absence of "wage drift" during these years *after* wage rate and piece-work norm revision had been completed here? Presumably, by the fact that piece-work norms were further revised downward.[135] Yet why should such revision have occurred, quite contrary to usual Soviet practice, immediately after the general revision was over? It can probably only be explained by the pressure upon the management of the basin to remain within its assigned wage fund – which had to cover all of the increases arising out of the expansion of seniority of the labor force in the basin. Such expansion of seniority may have been desired, but it could scarcely have been planned in the sense of being directed as opposed to being predicted.

Assuming that my explanation is correct so far, the interesting question is that of why the basin's wage fund did not expand so as to permit incentive-payment increases to accompany productivity growth. McAuley's logic would suggest that in setting the wage fund, the Center was unaware of, or at least took no account of, the dramatic increase in seniority that was occurring. My logic is rather that the Center believed that 5.8 per cent annual increase in average pay was sufficient – whatever the cause of such increase. Clearly either explanation might be correct for a particular instance such as this; but as a generalization covering many specific cases, I find it difficult to credit either the ignorance or "benign neglect" explanations.

The pattern of changes in the structure of total earnings stands out most clearly in the analysis of piece-work payments. In the periods of wage-rate revision in industry of 1956–60 and 1973–75, basic wage rates, paid for one hundred per cent fulfillment of work norms, were raised significantly, but

[133] Kharchenko, Minevich and Chaika (1970), pp. 7–11.
[134] Kaminskii (1967), pp. 96, 99, 102. Between the end of 1958 and the middle of 1963, the proportion of manual workers with less than one year's service in the basin fell from 40 to 12 per cent, while the proportion with more than five years rose from 11 to 48 per cent. The significance of this fact for average earnings was that the northern supplement (accounting for 59 per cent of the total increase), above normal vacations (32 per cent of the increase) and direct seniority payments were all attached to the number of years of service.
[135] Bonuses for manual workers in Soviet industry in general were fairly small in this period.

these raises were each accompanied by a sharp increase in the amount of production required for fulfillment of the piece-worker's basic quota. During the 1973–75 reform, the average percentage of norm fulfillment was reduced to 118 per cent from the 135 per cent (155 per cent in the large sub-sector of machinebuilding) to which it had crept since circa 1960. This was accomplished by raising the norms of piece-work by 23 per cent at the same time that the basic wage rates were being increased by 28 to 30 per cent.[136] The result of these offsetting revisions, but also of the increase in the minimum wage, was that the rate of growth of average earnings of manual workers in industry rose by 11 per cent compared with the previous four years – certainly nothing spectacular. Thereafter, the percentage of norm overfulfillment once more began to mount.[137]

Similarly, in three out of four industrial branches listed, the average skill grade of manual workers fell during the period of the 1973–75 wage reform. The authors of the article presenting these data of the Central Statistical Office comment that reductions of grade of individual workers are frequent in such a period,[138] playing the same role as the increase of piece-work normatives.

This is not to argue that the periodic wage-rate changes are irrelevant to relative earnings, although one labor economist comes close to arguing this.[139] Particularly in sectors of the economy like education and health, where earnings are primarily of a straight-salary nature, there seem to be large percentage increases across the board that are granted only every few years.[140] Furthermore, it would be surprising if relative changes in wage rates both within and between enterprises had no effect at all on relative earnings. It is clear that relative earnings will be affected directly by the fact that the floor of earnings for any individual worker is determined by the base wage for his category, and that some workers (although probably few aside from those at the minimum wage) will be affected by a change in this base. But we would also expect an indirect effect, both through the influence on higher authorities in terms of the total wage fund granted to a

---

[136] S. Novozhilov in *S.T.*, 1979, 1, pp. 9–11.

[137] D. Dymentman in *P.Kh.*, 1980, 8, p. 111, and M. E. Belkin in *E.K.O.*, 1982, 10, p. 111.

[138] V. Moskovich and V. Anan'ev in *V.E.*, 1979, 6, p. 58.

[139] S. Shkurko in *P.Kh.*, 1983, 8, pp. 74–80.

[140] In 1964, there was an increase of an average of 21 per cent of earnings in various "non-productive" branches. In 1972, earnings of physicians and teachers were again raised by 20 per cent (I. Zaslavskii in *Pered vykhodom* [1982], p. 24). It is interesting, however, to note that McAuley is unable to find the degree of irregularity in the average earnings of such sectors as education and health as we might expect (McAuley [1979], pp. 243 and 251). Perhaps reclassifications of personnel serve as a major smoothing device here.

given enterprise or other organization, and in terms of the psychological effect on enterprise managers (and trade union leaders) in their determination of relative earnings among the personnel within their unit.[141]

Officially recognized wage supplements, linked at an early stage to the Shchekino movement (see Chapter 8), were generalized in the 1970s, and have been further extended in experiments during 1984. But commentators describe their significance as being that of giving both manual and white-collar personnel the belief that their individual work discipline, their initiative and creativity will be recognized and rewarded regardless of their production results which can depend on other factors as well – e.g. on supply of materials.[142] In short, wage supplements do not directly affect total earnings within the enterprise; rather, they perform the same function for the individuals as do base wage rates in protecting them against reductions in these items if the enterprise's actual wage fund falls below expectations. They are removed from the large residual category constituted by bonuses of various types paid from the wage fund.

Despite the likely effects of the sum of base wage rates and supplements on the planned wages of enterprises, it is not uncommon for Soviet writers to argue that actual relative earnings of individuals are determined on the labor market rather than through centrally determined wage rates. It is true that the language used tends not to be that of the market-place. Thus Shkurko says that the wage rates take into account only a limited number of indicators of work, and totally neglect others (such as the monotony of the job) which today are of major importance in determining actual earnings. It is through considering these other (and quantitatively unweighted) elements of work that he comes to the conclusion that relative earnings must and in fact do deviate from relative wage rates so as to secure a correspondence of earnings with work done. Yet Shkurko goes on to make his market logic reasonably explicit: "Any other relationship in the enterprise," he writes, "would simply lead to many categories of personnel simply disappearing from the enterprise; production would stop."[143]

That does not mean that Soviet writers are comfortable with this market logic.[144] The same Shkurko, who here would seem to accept the market

---

[141] The position taken here is not too dissimilar from that of Doeringer and Piore (1971) in commenting upon the formal instrument of job evaluation as an influence upon relative earnings in large American firms. "Though limited by economic forces, the formal procedures of wage determination can and do exert an independent influence upon wages," (pp. 84–85).

[142] L. Bliakhman and T. Zlotnitskaia in *S.T.*, 1984, 1, p. 86.   [143] *P.Kh.*, 1983, p. 75.

[144] Some, however, are comfortable. See L. Bliakhman and T. Zlotnitskaia in *S.T.*, 1984, 1, p. 88. In reporting on a 1978 study by the SSSR Central Statistical Office in which earning levels of manual workers were found to depend not only on approved wage rate

Table 2.5 *Relative earnings of piece-work manual workers in the electrical equipment industry*

Trade (in order of skill)	Skill grade					
	Lowest	2nd	3rd	4th	5th	Highest
	(metal turner of lowest grade = 100)					
Machine tool setup man	148	130	126	129	138	203
Metal turner (machinist)	100	105	127	146	167	159
Workers knocking off the spurs of castings	117	125	154	128	—	—
Workers engaged in manual loading and unloading	141	126	119	—	—	—

Note: The skill grades listed cover virtually the full range used in setting wage rates in this industry, only some 2.2 per cent of the aggregated trades being excluded as "without grade" because completely unskilled (L. Ignat'ev in *S.T.*, 1980, 10, p. 103). In the engineering industry generally, it is believed by at least one group of Soviet authors that "skill category" represents skill reasonably well (*Problemy ispol'zovaniia*, p. 69).
Source: S. Shkurko in *P.Kh.*, 1983, 6, p. 76.

logic as inevitable within an enterprise, had earlier called for annual revisions of wage rates and salaries so that the Center could exercise control over relative earnings and so that there would not be differences in these relationships between different enterprises.[145] The varying positions of the same author may be explained by the time of writing (1983 vs. 1977), but it seems at least as probable that the explanation lies in a fundamental Soviet ambivalence. Nevertheless, while there may be confusion in Soviet normative evaluations, there seems little disagreement among Soviet labor experts as to what forces are actually dominant in the enterprise.

Here we find a fundamental difference between the position of the individual enterprise, deciding how to distribute its wage fund among individual suppliers of different kinds of labor, and the state in distributing the national wage fund among organizations. In the former case, there is no way to avoid market pressures. In the second, it is possible (although at a serious efficiency loss) to find non-market resolutions of the problem of the absence of market-clearing relative wages because of the insufficiency of the wage funds for organizations making particularly heavy use of certain

factors but also on sex, trade, and region, the authors consider such dependence as a reaction to labor market conditions. As such, they are not critical; instead, they view it as reflecting a realistic adjustment on the part of enterprise managers.

[145] Shkurko (1977), pp. 198–99.

kinds of labor. As we saw in the previous section, the temporary assignment of workers from one organization to another is the current prominent non-market solution. But temporary assignment to particular jobs within the organization is not a solution usually available to the individual enterprise, because of the worker's ability to respond by resigning and going to work elsewhere in the same locality.

Data for piece-rate earnings of different categories of workers in the electrical equipment industry as a whole are presented for an unstated year that is presumably in the 1980s. These earnings have been converted by me into relative terms for different aggregated trades and skill levels in Table 2.5. Within a given trade, they indicate very little correlation between skill grade and earnings. Within a skill grade, the differences in earnings between trades are striking; but such differences are not, as we might have expected, systematically and inversely related to the possibilities for skill improvement within the trade. Thus they do not represent investment by the worker in improving his own human capital. Although these differences may be partially explained by variation as between grades in average work conditions, or in average age and thus willingness to work overtime, it seems difficult to believe that such factors can explain much of the results taken at the level of an entire industrial branch. It would thus seem reasonable for us to follow Shkurko in attributing these differences to market forces.

Data for a 30 per cent sample of all manual workers in two large heavy industry enterprises in the Urals some time in the late 1960s, showed that the range of monthly earnings within a given skill grade was greater than the average earnings of that grade in that enterprise in eleven of the thirteen cases of different skill grades (six in one plant and seven in the other). Only 0.3 per cent of all manual workers in one plant, and 7.1 per cent in the other, had a skill grade for which the enterprise range of earnings was less than the average earnings.[146]

A 1976 study of hourly paid time-workers in engineering enterprises, shortly after they had completed wage-rate revisions, showed that the average earnings of top-skill grade workers as a proportion of those of the lowest grade was some 11 to 17 per cent greater than the proportion of wage rates.[147] A 1978 study by the Central Statistical Bureau showed that, for eight branches of industry, the earnings spread was 15 to 30 per cent greater than the spread of wage rates. The author of the article reporting

---

[146] V. V. Skvortsov and V. V. Chichilimov in *Sotsial'nye problemy truda i obrazovaniia* (1969), pp. 102–07.
[147] Iu. Anan'eva in *S.T.*, 1979, 10, pp. 88–89.

these data believed that such a relationship was the rule rather than the exception, reflecting labor market conditions, and said that the data have led many specialists in wage administration to believe that future changes in wage rates should follow (rather than attempt to direct) the skill variations in earnings. Indeed, he reports that 1982 changes in relative wage rates in underground coal mining were in the direction of following the observed earnings differentials between skill categories.[148]

In between the periodic revisions of wage rates these market forces, as we would expect, exert their influence through a wide variety of payments. Regional percentage supplements to wages for special construction and production projects have grown over time with a growing general labor shortage; the proportion of senior specialists to rank-and-file specialists, as well as the number of staff managers among specialists, have increased as a joint recruitment and labor-retention device; annual payments from the material-stimulation fund of the enterprise are differentiated according to the relative shortage of different trades in the enterprise.[149] Supplements to pay are allowed to workers who learn new trades and practice them in combination with their old. The theory is that this will better fill up the work day. But a statistical analysis in the chemical industry showed that manual workers in low-skill categories constituted the absolute majority of those receiving such supplements, and were over-represented in numbers of such recipients by 240 per cent in relationship to their number in the workforce of the industry. The explanation given was that such supplements were used as a device for reacting to market pressures.[150] The earnings of bus drivers in Moscow and Leningrad have been pushed up to some 150 to 180 per cent of the average earnings of manual workers in Soviet industry by the introduction of a whole series of supplements and bonuses (since piece-rates are not paid to these drivers).[151] It is true that Shkurko complains that it is easier for market forces to work through piece-rates than through these other mechanisms,[152] and that for this reason equilibrium earning rates are not attained. The justification of this complaint is quite believable,[153] and such imbalance would constitute a significant imperfection in the Soviet labor market. Still, it is doubtful that this imperfection is any greater than that observed through trade union monopolies in capitalist countries.

If earnings are really determined on the labor market, one would expect

[148] L. Kheifets in *V.E.*, 1982, 6, pp. 37–38.   [149] Shkurko in *P.Kh.*, 1983, 8, pp. 76–78.
[150] S. Efremov in *S.T.*, 1977, 1, p. 75.   [151] Shkurko in *P.Kh.*, 1983, 6, p. 76.
[152] *Ibid.*, p. 78.
[153] L. Kheifets in *V.E.*, 1982, 6, p. 37 does not seem to accept it for manual workers paid by the hour, although he does accept it for managers and professionals.

those for a given trade to differ among enterprises at any moment of time because of the play of supply and demand for workers of this trade under the impact of disequilibrating shocks. I have data in this regard for only two cities. In one city of 400,000 in the late 1960s, data for manual workers of a single trade in four engineering enterprises – all of which enterprises appear to have had much the same priority level – showed that average monthly earnings in two enterprises were represented by an index number of 100–104, while for the two others the index number was 150–154. The author claimed that the same variations existed for a variety of other trades, some of which were defined so narrowly as to place milling-machine operators and lathe operators into distinct groupings.[154] In a second similar sized city in 1978 in a distant part of the country, the range of average earnings for a particular skill-grade within a single trade among four engineering enterprises varied for three trades between 115 and 120 per cent.[155] Since each enterprise was constrained in its total wage payments to all personnel by its wage fund, presumably the individual enterprises that provided high earnings for a particular trade did so by paying workers of other trades – less needed in those enterprises – low earnings relative to what they would earn elsewhere.[156] One would expect that the mobility of workers of a given trade moving between enterprises within the same city, motivated by differences in earnings of the magnitude indicated, would be sufficient to improve rapidly upon the original disequilibrium of different types of workers as between enterprises.

Quantitative restrictions on personnel

One might reasonably ask whether my emphasis upon the wage fund in the individual enterprise does not unduly neglect the role of planned constraints upon the number of personnel who may be hired in an enterprise.

[154] B. P. Gailgalas in *Sotsial'nye problemy truda i obrazovaniia* (1969), p. 56. Much more detail is given in the original source, written by the head of the State Committee of Labor of the Lithuanian Republic, and this lends authenticity to the data.

[155] N. V. Chernina in *Izvestiia sib. otd.*, 1981, 11 (vypusk 3), pp. 130–31.

[156] One would expect such a relationship to be particularly sharp for Soviet enterprises, whose wage-paying constraint is a relatively fixed over-all wage fund. But the only two relevant studies for the United States that seem to have been written by 1981 (see R. B. Althauser and A. L. Kalleberg in Berg [1981], p. 143) claim to have found either that not many enterprises consistently pay high or low wages across the whole spectrum of occupations (Rees and Shultz [1970], p. 46) or that the hypothesis must be rejected of equal wage effects on each of four aggregative categories of the labor force as a result of working in a particular industry (R. M. Stolzenberg in *American Sociological Review*, 40 [1975], pp. 655–57). Here, I would speculate, we have a similarity across socio-economic systems among individual production units operating within a labor market.

It is my belief that physical planning of effective demand in the field of labor, in sharp contrast to the physical planning of such demand in the area of intermediate products, has generally not acted as a constraint upon the hiring practices of enterprises. At least this has been true during the recent decades which are the period covered by this book.

It is true that, either prior to 1958 or prior to 1965 for all enterprises, and continuing therafter till the early 1970s for the "unreformed" ones, enterprises received a quota as to their maximum average employment during the year.[157] Moreover, this quota was subdivided into three categories: manual workers, clerical personnel (*sluzhashchie*), and professional and managerial personnel. There was then an extended intermediate period when all such quantitative restrictions were abandoned; but the quota (this time, however, a unitary one) was reinstated in 1980.[158] Particularly since the interim period was declared to have been a disappointing failure in its effort to restrain labor demand by enterprises solely through financial means,[159] one might legitimately question my disregard of these labor quotas during the years when they have been legally in force.

During the period from at least 1972 through 1979, enterprises received approved plans from their ministries; but these plans were non-binding on the enterprises, and were used only to calculate labor productivity which was, however, a significant indicator in affecting the size of the material-stimulation fund. Between 1971 and 1977, the sum of the approved plans for the total number of employees exceeded the actual number available (and the previous calculation of the State Planning Commission of the Soviet Union) by some 1.3 to 2 million. If we assume that these numbers refer to industry alone, the plan excess was some six per cent. This is consistent with the Soviet calculation for the late 1970s that in the Russian Republic the number of approved "working places" in industry exceeded the number of employees by ten per cent.[160] A Soviet researcher's

---

[157] N. Rogovskii (of Gosplan SSSR) in *S.T.*, 1981, 1, p. 17, says that this period ended in 1957, and that thereafter through 1979 there were no quantitative restrictions on the number of personnel in enterprises. This may have continued right until 1980 for those enterprises that were still "unreformed." In the Azerbaidzhan Republic as of January 1983, 21 per cent of all enterprises and organizations under republic administration had still not been subject to the 1965 reform, but few if any of these enterprises seem to have been in the industrial sector (S. Divilov in *S.T.*, 1984, 2, p. 78).

[158] But it was not reinstated for all sectors; at a minimum, not for trade or the state farms in 1980 (*ibid.*, p. 18).

[159] *Ibid.*, p. 17.

[160] A. Dadashev in *V.E.*, 1979, 8, pp. 41–42. The figure of two million is also reported as current by A. Solov'ev in *S.T.*, 1980, 7, pp. 104–05. These data are presumably restricted

calculation, based on data from industrial enterprises in a city of 450,000 during 1975–77, is that so long as an enterprise's actual employment is no less than 95 to 99 per cent of its planned employment, the enterprise is not threatened through labor shortage with the inability to produce its planned output.[161]

I know of no similar data for the 1980s when binding manpower plans were once again given to enterprises. But enterprise manpower plans are influenced particularly by local planning bodies, who are concerned with the local availability of labor. Their function seems to be to match demand and supply of labor within individual localities, and not particularly to raise labor productivity. Although approved plans in the Russian Republic in 1982 and 1983 did cut back industrial enterprise requests for growth by one-third, and in Lithuania by one quarter, it is significant that the resulting plans bore the imprint of the relatively weak regional authorities rather than that of the national ministries to which the enterprises are responsible.[162] Sanctions for the violation of manpower limits by enterprises subordinate to any authorities higher than the local level are described as having been virtually inoperable in the Russian Republic during at least the first two years after the reintroduction of these limits.[163] In a recent period (presumably 1983), industrial ministries whose total employment was less than provided by plan were able to hire only 94 per cent of the total separations they incurred, while those ministries whose employment was greater than plan hired 107 per cent of their losses.[164]

It is also significant that I have seen no Soviet claims of an improvement in the ratio of planned to actual numbers of employees, despite the reading of materials where such a claim would have been appropriate. Furthermore, both in 1982 and during at least part of 1983, one-fifth of all industrial enterprises in the Russian Republic had average employment exceeding their allowed limits. For industrial enterprises in the Soviet Union as a whole in 1982, the figure was also one-fifth. Although sanctions

to industry, although this is not specified in the sources. (See the percentage figure for the Russian Republic's industry in Solov'ev.)

[161] Chernina in *Izvestiia sib. otd.*, 1981, 11 (vypusk 3), p. 127. The author indicates the basis for her calculations. Since the data base is heterogeneous within a region rather than being confined to a single industrial branch, it must reflect the labor plans approved by many different ministries.

[162] N. Zenchenko in *P.Kh.*, 1983, 6, p. 24, and L. A. Kostin in *E.K.O.*, 1984, 1, p. 35. In contrast, Veretennikov *et al.* in *Voprosy* (1983) claim that the plans are to be agreed upon between the regional authorities and the ministries.

[163] Veretennikov *et al.* in *Voprosy* (1983), pp. 73 and 80.

[164] The first group of ministries numbered nineteen, and the second group six. (A. Kotliar in *Pravda*, May 13, 1984, p. 2; this was called to my attention in Hauslohner [1984], p. 576.)

for such excess are legislated, I infer from the Soviet discussion that they are enforced only unusually and then with very mild effect.[165]

The wage fund

Each state enterprise in the Soviet Union is given a single planned wage fund for each year. The actual wage fund available to it may differ from the planned fund as a result of the enterprise overfulfilling or underfulfilling its production targets during the planned year, but such deviations are also governed by centrally predetermined norms. Although the material-stimulation fund is an important source for professional and managerial personnel in industry, this is not so for manual workers or for the labor force as a whole. In 1975 and 1977 for all personnel in industry as a whole, 91–92 per cent of earnings came from the wage fund.[166] For manual workers alone, the figure was roughly 96 per cent in 1975–77.[167] These magnitudes constitute my justification for concentrating here upon the wage fund as the source of earnings for an enterprise's labor force as a whole.

Three problems concerning the use of the wage fund by the enterprise are of particular interest in the current context. The first is that of the fungibility of the wage fund within a given year. The second is the degree to which a given year's wage fund is a "hard" rather than "soft" constraint, to use the language of Kornai. The third is that of the "ratchet effect": what is the effect upon the planned wage fund for year $(t+1)$ both of the use made of the wage fund of (t) and of the ratio during (t) of actual to planned labor productivity?

Fungibility of the wage fund. Concentration will be on fungibility at the level of the enterprise. Ministries appear from all indications to be fairly free from control by higher authorities as to how they allocate their own wage fund to

---

165 Tkachenko *et al.* in *P.Kh.*, 1983, 11, pp. 91–94; N. Zenchenko in *P.Kh.*, 1983, 6, p. 26; and *Zaniatost' naseleniia* (1983), pp. 32–33. During 1981 and the first half of 1982, 8–14 per cent of the number of violating enterprises were sanctioned by the State Bank, and these lost only 1 per cent of the earnings which would have otherwise gone to the above-plan number of personnel. Bonus losses by management are also treated as insignificant.

166 Iu. Artemov in *V.E.*, 1980, 11, pp. 65–66 and Markov (1980), p. 32. A range among industrial branches in 1975 was some 86–95 per cent. This had not changed by 1982 (Zh. Sidorova in *V.E.*, 1984, 10, p. 32).

167 Calculated from Artemov in *V.E.*, 1980, 11, pp. 65–67 and V. Rakoti in *P.Kh.*, 1982, 12, p. 72. All of these 1975–77 figures are slightly overstated, as they take no account of supplementary bonus funds when these are not channeled through either the wage fund or the material-stimulation fund. But supplementary bonus funds in industry constituted only 1.4 per cent of the total wage fund in 1969 (Vasil'ev and Chistiakova [1972], p. 99),

their member enterprises. To the degree that this is not so, the difficulties of fungibility for ministries do not seem to extend beyond those existing for enterprises.[168]

As a generalization, it seems that the wage fund of an enterprise is completely fungible provided that all employees receive at least the salary or wage rate provided for their category. Thus a 1982 Soviet writer declares that savings out of wage funds simply do not occur; when the management sees that it may have such savings in a given trimester, it takes all measures needed to avoid them, "all the more so since such liquidation of savings is not difficult."[169] Rules as to allowable bonuses, supplements to salaries, and piece-rate norms do not serve as effective constraints on the freedom of the enterprise to allocate its total wage fund as it sees fit.

Some support for this view is found in statistical studies. A 1967–68 study of 15,000 manual workers in eighteen engineering enterprises showed that 35 per cent of them were performing work graded at a higher level than the grade at which the worker himself was classified and paid.[170] If the wage fund of these enterprises had been larger, it would have been easy for the managements to have justified raising the skill classification of these workers. While supplemental payments to employees for combining trades are allowed, they are most widely found – and in the highest proportions to their wage rates – in those branches of industry where labor shortage is the greatest; moreover, in at least one of these major industries the maximum permissible supplemental rate is frequently grossly violated through reclassification.[171] A study of forty-nine enterprises with an employment total of over one hundred thousand showed that 40 per cent of the enterprises gave special privileges, with regard to the standard norm on which piece-rates were based, to women over forty-five years of age – so as to attempt to keep them working after the legal retirement age of forty-five or fifty for such workers.[172] The point here is the even split among the number of enterprises adopting this practice, although all were within the same industry, and the fact that it took a special study – rather than simple questioning of the branch ministry concerned – to reveal this diversity of

---

and 1 to 2 per cent of earnings in the 1980s, however they were channeled (L. Kunel'skii in *S.T.*, 1984, 2, p. 12).

[168] See A. Katsenelinboigen in *Revue d'études comparatives est-ouest*, 9, 4 (1978), p. 17 for a 1950s example; this is the only discussion I have seen of problems of fungibility at the ministerial level.

[169] A. P. Zaitsev in *E.K.O.*, 1982, 9, p. 120.   [170] Aitov (1972), pp. 3–4 and 70–71.

[171] Dubovoi and Zhil'tsov (1971), pp. 33–40. Neither the nature of the sample nor the period are described.

[172] L. Shokhina in *Pered vykhodom* (1982), pp. 69–70. The period of the study was probably sometime after 1975.

practice. Finally, it is pointed out by the head of the labor section of the State Planning Commission of the Soviet Union that no regulations exist which restrict the proportion of the wage fund that can be paid in bonuses, that this situation exists both at the level of the ministry and of the enterprise, and that as a result there are sharp differences in this proportion as between industrial branches.[173]

Counter evidence falls into two categories. The first category relates to the enterprise's freedom in distributing its wage fund without altering the average (mean) earnings.

First, there is the implication that the earnings of managerial and professional personnel, relative to that of manual workers in industry, have declined over time because of the inability of enterprises to compensate those in the first category who have low base salaries. If this were the case, then we would see an increase in the ratio during the period of changes in wage rates and salaries. In fact, the ratio fell steadily during both post-war periods of centralized change in industry: 1956–60 and 1973–75.[174] The absolute number of managers and professionals in industry who received supplements to their base salary for economizing labor was halved during the period of the 1970s wage reform – a phenomenon which is the counterpart of increases in work norms for piece-workers during the same period.[175] The decline in the ratio seems to be a result of market forces and/or of central policy, and to have little or no relationship to the issue of the fungibility of the wage fund.

A second phenomenon which at first appears to be counter evidence is the replacement in various textile mills of the electric motors of shuttleless looms so as to reduce the volume of cloth produced per loom. The reason for this was an imbalance between spinning and weaving capacity in individual enterprises after these shuttleless looms were introduced, resulting in idleness of the looms, reduction in the earnings of the operators, and worker quits as an end product. Replacement of the motors slowed down the looms and thus eliminated equipment idleness and raised operator earnings back to their old level.[176] Since the cloth output for the factory as a whole was unaffected by the motor change, one might think that the replacement was due to the need to pay operators according to

[173] N. Rogovskii in *S.T.*, 1981, 1, pp. 20–21 and *S.T.*, 1982, 1, p. 37.

[174] *Narkhoz SSSR*, various issues and TsSU, *Trud* (1968). The force of these data for my argument is, however, considerably weakened by the fact that the minimum wage in industry was raised during both periods of centralized change, and that this would hardly if at all have directly affected the earnings of managerial and professional personnel.

[175] L. S. Kheifets in *Izv. AN SSSR*, 1978, 1, pp. 53–54.

[176] Iu. D. Kosykh in *E.K.O.*, 1984, 4, pp. 61–63.

work-norms that were specific to shuttleless looms having the original motors.

But this explanation does not stand up, when one considers that the quitting of operators which was occurring would have solved the problem. Some looms could have been left permanently idle, while the rest were operated at the designated speeds and with no injury to the operators' income. The explanation must lie elsewhere than indicated by the Soviet author: either in the effect on the enterprise manager's reputation with higher authorities of having permanent idleness of equipment (since it showed that he had ordered too many looms), or in wear and tear on the motors due to their original high speed.

The evidence for this first category of counter evidence to fungibility can be seen to be so weak that it should be ignored. The second category, however, must be taken more seriously. It relates to the increase in the average wage fund per employee in an enterprise as a result of the number of employees being fewer than had been assumed by higher authorities when the planned wage fund was assigned. Can such increases be paid out freely as supplements and bonuses?

In retail trade, it is implied that the answer is categorically affirmative. Indeed, most state retail stores were said in the mid-1970s to have fewer store personnel than indicated in setting the planned wage fund, and the store personnel received the extra income.[177] However, the source is not explicit as to whether 100 per cent of the planned wages of the missing personnel are divided up among the personnel working. Presumably, the legal justification for the higher average income is the right to wage supplements, that can be up to 100 per cent of the wage funds that would otherwise have been economized, as a result of replacing absent workers.

For the 1950s, one reputable source tells us that the answer was negative at the ministerial level: a ministry could not sub-divide its own wage fund among its enterprises in such a way as to increase the average planned earnings of personnel in an enterprise which had reduced the number of its employees.[178] In 1984, a legal opinion in a journal refers to a 1965 decree as still being in force; this decree referred to the setting of salaries of white-collar personnel of enterprises as being constrained by the average planned earnings of all personnel in the enterprise.[179] But once the Shchekino experiment had begun in the late 1960s, and particularly as its reward features were generalized during the 1970s, the ministerial restric-

[177] Lokshin (1975), pp. 20–21.
[178] A. Katsenelinboigen in *Revue d'études comparatives est-ouest*, 9, 4 (1978), p. 17.
[179] *S.T.*, 1984, 8, p. 109.

tion became increasingly formal rather than substantive. Given the room for salary supplements and bonuses for white-collar personnel, the restriction upon their basic salaries also seems to have little substance.

More significant as counter evidence is the experience with the Shchekino experiment. Enterprises which reduced the number of their personnel in comparison with specified standards have been permitted to keep 50 to 90 per cent of the resulting wage-fund economies – the exact percentage depending upon the standard employed in the comparison.[180]

In fact, however, such enterprises have regularly used less than the permitted moneys for wage fund expenditures during the course of the same year. A study conducted during 1975 in 326 industrial enterprises that were operating on the Shchekino principle showed that, of the funds generated during January–October of that year, 45 per cent remained unused at the end of 1975 and thus were lost to the wage fund. This lost portion constituted 0.5 per cent of the total wage fund and, during the year that this study was conducted, the implication of this failure to spend the available moneys was that they were permanently lost to the enterprise and reverted to the State budget.[181]

Nor was this a phenomenon of a single year. The pattern of permanent loss to the enterprise of unused funds was introduced in 1971, four years after the beginning of the Shchekino experiment, and lasted through 1976. Then for two years, only half of the unused funds were lost to the enterprise. Since 1979, the enterprise has been legally allowed to keep all of the unused portion (transferring it into its material-stimulation fund); nevertheless, a 1983 article writes of the legal provision of transfer not being carried out in the Belorussian Republic.[182] It is clear that throughout the years a substantial portion of the earned sums has remained unspent during the current year. Although the non-use of the funds did lead to an increase in profits, and thus positively affected the material-stimulation fund, this effect was far from fully compensating. The question of interest is: Why were these funds not used by the enterprises?

If one takes Soviet authors literally, this was a free decision by the enterprise managements themselves. One explanation offered for this decision is that if supplements are added to salaries or wage rates, these supplements are viewed by the personnel affected as relatively permanent

---

[180] Shkurko (1971), p. 57. The figure was raised to 100 per cent in 1977 (L. S. Kheifets in *Izv. AN SSSR*, 1978, 1, pp. 47–48).

[181] S. Ivanov in *S.T.*, 1977, 4, pp. 13–17.

[182] Kheifets (1974), p. 72; Kheifets in *Izv. AN SSSR*, 1978, 1, pp. 47–48; G. E. Schroeder in Adam (1982), p. 14; F. Gershtein in *S.T.*, 1983, 6, p. 41.

– while the funds may be unavailable in future years.[183] This explanation is hard to credit, since paying the money in the form of bonuses would avoid this problem. Other explanations provided are that part of the labor savings were achieved through investments assigned without cost to the enterprises, and – most significant of all – that there was no "production necessity" compelling the enterprise to pay out all the funds allowed.[184] It seems to me reasonable to believe that these latter explanations are more to the point, and that they were more likely persuasive to higher authorities than to the enterprise managements themselves.

If one adopts the view, as I do, that the reason the enterprises did not spend all the funds legally available to them was that there was pressure upon them from higher authorities not to do so, then this counter evidence to the thesis of fungibility of the wage fund disappears. One instead reinterprets the evidence as indicating that the "effective" increase in the wage fund from the reduction in the labor force compared to standard has been in fact only half to two-thirds of the amount legally granted. But within this "effective" increase, there is no indication of constraints on fungibility.

The wage fund as a "hard" constraint. János Kornai is the father of the terminology discriminating between "hard" and "soft" constraints on socialist enterprises, the latter referring to restrictions on behavior that can be transgressed without serious consequences. Basing himself primarily upon the Hungarian experience, he considers the wage fund and its counterparts elsewhere to be "hard" constraints.[185] In contrast, one Soviet author in 1984, writing specifically of the Soviet economy, considers the wage fund as a "soft" constraint. He bases this statement on the frequent revision of the wage fund by higher authorities when it would otherwise be overspent.[186] What credit should we give to these contrasting views?

Let us for the moment put aside revision by the ministries of the planned wage funds of the enterprises, and consider only overexpenditures of the annual wage funds as these were finally approved.[187] Such overexpendi-

---

[183] Shkurko (1971), pp. 56 and 63. See also G. Kulakin and Z. Khabarin in *S.T.*, 1982, 6, p. 92.

[184] Shkurko (1977), p. 130.

[185] Kornai (1980), Chapter 16, and especially pp. 377–78, 405–06, 408.

[186] D. Ukrainskii (head of a section of Gosplan SSSR) in *P.Kh.*, 1984, 4, p. 51.

[187] Among other things, this means ignoring the fact that employment growth, as projected in five year plans, has in fact been consistently surpassed both in industry and in the state sector as a whole. (For statistics covering 1951–1975, see Anna-Jutta Pietsch in Lane [1986], p. 181.) Such exceeding of planned employment growth presumably implies similar overexpenditure of projected wage fund. But these five year plan projections have

tures do not seem to be effectively controlled by the State Bank's refusal to release funds for wage payments beyond the allotted amounts; the State Bank is not really in a position to refuse enterprises the cash needed to pay wages due.[188] Nevertheless, we are told that overexpenditures that remained unrepaid constituted during 1975–80 about 0.7 per cent of the wage fund; these data presumably refer to the entire state-owned economy, although they may refer only to industry.[189] In contrast, industry wage funds as set forth in five year plans have typically been drastically overfulfilled and clearly constitute "soft constraints." But since five year plans are in general non-operational, "softness" at this level is of no special significance.

Which organizational level of Soviet industrial administration has made whatever repayments of annual wage funds to the state bank that do occur? According to one Soviet writer, it cannot be the ministry since its wage fund is simply the sum of that of all of its subordinate organizations and none of these will fail to spend fully its allocated wage fund.[190] Even taking this statement with the due degree of salt, it would seem that repayments must be made primarily by the individual enterprise. The incentive for such repayment does not exist for manual workers – their wage rate supplement and bonuses are unaffected by unrepaid overexpenditures of the wage fund[191] – but managers do have such an incentive. All managers (apparently roughly above the foreman level) can be deprived of up to 50 per cent of the bonuses they have earned if the wage fund for their unit has been overexpended, but half of their loss is returned to them if the bonus fund overexpenditure is made up within six months.[192] Given the high proportion of managerial earnings that consists of bonuses,[193] this provision should provide managers with a strong personal incentive to avoid overexpenditures of the wage fund, and particularly unrepaid ones. It would thus seem that the 0.7 per cent unrepaid overexpenditures at the

not been hard and binding plans; only the annual plans are so binding. In general, and not just with regard to employment, five year plans have been poor predictors of the future.

188 This obligation to provide the funds to meet enterprise wage requirements is similar to, but doubtless much stronger than, the obligation to provide enterprises with temporary credits to meet bills due to suppliers (see the Resolution of July 12, 1979 of the Central Committee of the Communist Party and Council of Ministers of the SSSR, article 57, in *Resheniia* [1981], p. 116, and V. Alkhimov in *E.G.*, 1985, 21, p. 13).

189 V. Rakoti in *P.Kh.*, 1982, 12, p. 73.

190 A. P. Zaitsev in *E.K.O.*, 1982, 9, pp. 119–20.

191 *S.T.*, 1980, 12, p. 116; L. Kheifets in *V.E.*, 1982, 6, p. 35.

192 *S.T.*, 1980, 1, p. 113 and 1980, 12, p. 116. Prior to the 1965 reform in industry, managerial bonuses could not in theory be paid at all if there had been overexpenditures of the wage fund which had not yet been repaid (Steklova [1976], pp. 18–20).

193 Iu. Artemov in *V.E.*, 1975, 8, p. 42.

national level are unlikely to represent more than, perhaps, one per cent at the level of aggregation of the individual enterprise. This degree of slippage does not seem excessive, and is consistent with treating the wage fund as a "hard" constraint.

The real issue here is the extent to which planned wage funds of enterprises are revised. As indicated above, it seems unlikely that the individual ministry can find on its own the funds needed to permit it to do this. A paper based on a project interviewing Soviet émigrés to the United States during the second half of the 1970s suggests that enterprises were very reluctant even to ask for such revisions from their ministries.[194] What we have no information about, however, is the degree to which the ministries themselves are granted supplements to their planned wage funds.[195]

Since this key question cannot be answered, what we must ultimately appeal to is the excellent post-1955 Soviet record with regard to national inflation (both open and hidden), at least until the late 1970s.[196] We have seen that the managements of enterprises compete with one another for workers in a reasonably free labor market, and that no substantive restrictions exist with regard to their wage offers other than their allotted wage funds. If the wage funds allotted to them at the beginning of the year were treated by them only as "soft" constraints, it seems impossible to explain why Soviet inflation rates have not been at the very high levels of the 1930s. It is for this reason that I conclude that the constraints are "hard."

[194] The paper is based on intensive interviews with managerial and staff employees, mainly at the enterprise level (Linz [1986], p. 27). The paper's author wrote me privately that only one respondent dealt with the issue of covering overruns of the originally allocated wage fund by asking the ministry for wage fund revision versus getting a loan from the State Bank; this respondent thought that going to the bank was the lesser of the two evils. The author's impression from interviews with six respondents was that overspending of the originally allocated wage fund was generally regarded by them with considerable disfavor, no matter how such overspending was covered.

[195] In 1939, ministries overspent their allotted wage funds and did not appear overly concerned about the matter (Granick [1954], p. 180). But pre-war control over wage funds is generally believed to have been far more lax than control later.

[196] According to Richard Portes, Western estimates show an annual rate of 0.8 to 1.2 per cent for 1955–70. He thinks it would be difficult to make a case for more than 1.5 to 2 per cent for the 1970s (Cambridge [1982], p. 363). See A. Bachurin in *P.Kh.*, 1982, 9, p. 5 for a statement that wage fund over-expenditures in various branches have increased in recent years. For the situation in 1981, see G. Kiperman in *C.D.S.P.*, XXXIV, 37 (October 13, 1982), p. 10. Such over-expenditures would be consistent with the increase in the rate of open plus disguised inflation.

A recent summary of the data and treatment of the topic is given by D. M. Nuti, "Hidden and repressed inflation in Soviet-type economies" (paper at the Third World Congress for Soviet and East European Studies, 1985).

The "ratchet" effect on the wage fund. The wage fund of a given year may be fungible, as I have argued above, without this fungibility property holding across years. Yet clearly both enterprise managers and employees are concerned with the inter-temporal dimension.

A glance at the Shchekinskii chemical combinat in its earliest, most publicized, and most successful years is informative. This enterprise was centrally chosen to start the movement to reduce staff and use a substantial part of the wage savings to reward the remaining personnel. Yet, although labor productivity rose by 131 per cent between 1966 and 1970, average earnings increased by only 33 per cent. If we can assume that without the movement, average earnings would have increased in this enterprise at the same rate as they did in industry as a whole,[197] the average employee of the enterprise gained net over the four years a total of fifteen rubles a month as of the last year – or 6 per cent of his 1970 income.[198] This seems like very little inter-temporal retention of gains for the showcase enterprise of a major national movement at the time of its greatest publicity.

The way that the planned wage fund for an enterprise is determined is critical for the inter-temporal issue. In principle, it is set on the basis of the planned number and skill-occupation mix of the employees, multiplied by the vector of basic wage-rate scales and of supplements for such factors as the region of the enterprise and whether particular work performed is heavy or dangerous. The resulting single ruble figure is then multiplied by one hundred per cent plus the percentage of above-scale payments expected to be common to the industrial branch in the planning year. The result is modified somewhat to take account of the existing above-scale payments being made in the given enterprise during the current year.

What is important to note is that both the current labor productivity and the planned productivity improvement of the enterprise are largely irrelevant in determining the per capita wage fund of the enterprise.[199] (This, of course, is very different from saying that they are irrelevant to the

197 In evaluating the likelihood of this, one should observe that at the time the movement began, the average earnings in this enterprise were slightly below the average in all industry and were the lowest of all enterprises in the branch (Kheifets [1974], pp. 15–16). Thus this assumption is probably a conservative one.

198 Basic data for the enterprise was provided by V. I. Slepykh, chief engineer of the combinat, at a symposium reported on in *Vestnik Akademiia Nauk SSSR*, 1972, 5, pp. 110–12.

199 This is implicitly denied by the head of a section of Gosplan SSSR who says that bonuses planned to be paid from the wage fund in $(t+1)$ depend heavily on the actual bonuses paid out in (t). He points to coal and metallurgy as branches suffering from this treatment (N. Rogovskii in *S.T.*, 1982, 1, pp. 36–37). But a year earlier, the same author had explained the low bonuses paid out in the iron and steel industry by the fact that many enterprises of that industry do not meet their plans (in *S.T.*, 1981, 1, p. 20).

determination of the total wage fund; they are fundamental to the determination of the planned number of enterprise personnel.) They can enter only into the enterprise-specific adjustment to the calculation of the ratio of above-scale payments; this adjustment seems to be made largely to prevent declines in total planned earnings for individual enterprises that have had exceptionally high ratios in the current year. It is my impression that such adjustments are fairly minor, and the data presented above for the Shchekinskii chemical combinat is consistent with this impression. Thus there is very little carry-over between planning periods in the realized per capita wage fund.

The size of the realized wage fund available to the enterprise during a given year (t) is determined by the planned wage fund for (t) plus a percentage (that is specific to that enterprise) of the above-plan or below-plan value of output in (t). Thus within a given year, changes in labor productivity affect the realized per capita wage fund; but this effect is intended to be restricted to that single year and to have no carry over. The wage fund plan for year $(t+1)$ is intended to take account of, and to factor out in the setting of its improvement effect on the per capita planned wage fund, all increases of labor productivity achieved in (t). It is this that constitutes the "ratchet."

Since 1970, there have been efforts to allow enterprises to enjoy Schumpeterian quasi-rents for the length of a five year plan. The notion is that a non-rolling five year period should constitute the basic planning period for the enterprise, and that it is to be broken down into annual figures. Annual wage fund plans are still developed later, but the enterprise gains or loses in its per capita planned wage fund for the year depending upon whether that year's planned wage fund per unit of output is higher or lower than the figure in the enterprise's five year plan. The actual wage fund available during a given year is determined in relation to the annual plan in the earlier fashion. Since the five year plan is always adopted at least one year late, these quasi-rents can in principle be enjoyed by the enterprise for one to four years depending upon the year of the above-planned productivity improvement.

In fact, even these briefly enjoyed quasi-rents appear to be more fictitious than real. As one Soviet labor economist wrote in 1977, the stability of the five year plan of the enterprise's wage fund rests upon the assumption that the actual production conditions, including product mix, will each year be what had been predicted. Such realization of assumptions he regards as virtually impossible.[200] This sensible position seems in fact to

[200] Shkurko (1977), pp. 248–49.

be implemented, with resulting instability of the enterprise five year plans to the degree that they actually exist at all.[201]

The fact that Plan $(t+1)$ is a function of Realization (t), and that a basic building block of the wage fund plan is the skill-occupation mix of the unit, creates an inter-temporal limitation upon the fungibility of the wage fund in (t) that we have not yet considered. So far, we have envisaged the enterprise management as optimizing under the combined constraints existing for it during year (t) of the total planned wage fund, the elasticity of substitution among different labor occupations and skills under the production conditions of the specific enterprise, and the labor market. But once we allow the optimizing process to extend over time, we must reckon with the fact that if relative earnings paid out in (t) to employees of different skill levels are such as to lead to a reduced average wage rate (as opposed to earnings) in the enterprise, this reduction will in and of itself have a negative effect on the planned per capita wage fund in $(t+1)$. Such reduction can be a result of the single-year optimization process through the combined effect of quits and recruitment failures in the higher wage-rate categories of employees. It is unclear how important in practice is this restriction on the fungibility of the wage fund during (t), but the existence of the restriction is unquestionable.

The ratchet effect on the per capita wage fund also has its implications for the amount of effort put forth by the individual employee. We may think of the employee as attempting to equalize his marginal earnings per unit of effort (the purest case of this is the piece-worker) with his personal opportunity cost of effort. The issue is: What is the individual's marginal earning rate?

If we think of the individual as an isolated being, his earnings per unit of marginal effort during (t) consist of what he actually receives during period (t). He need not worry about any effects of his actions on the earning rate in $(t+1)$, since Soviet enterprises are typically large and no ordinary individual's effort will have a significant effect upon the total labor productivity of the enterprise. We have here the counterpart of perfect competition in a capitalist product market, where each firm produces so as to equate marginal cost with the price of the product and ignores the effect of output on the price.

On the other hand, the individual is also a member of a group. The combined membership of a shop or enterprise group can place informal pressure upon each individual to restrict his effort in such a way as to take

---

201 See R. Iakovlev in *S.T.*, 1979, 1, p. 53, and the discussion circle in *E.K.O.*, 1980, 1, pp. 77–78.

account of its effect on the planned wage fund per unit of effort in $(t+1)$. Thus it is important to ask what the individual's earning rate is when he is considered as a member of a group.

Defining his monthly earnings in (t) as an isolated being as $w_{1,t}$, his earnings as a member of a group constitute the lower figure $w_{2,t}$ where

> $w_{2,t}$ = discounted monthly pay earned by (i) in (t) but received during t, $t+1, \ldots, \infty$. This is the amount earned and received today for today's effort, minus the negative effect on tomorrow's earnings of today's effort being greater than $\bar{E}$ for the group of all (i) in the enterprise

$$(2.1)$$

where (i) refers to the individual employee, E_t is effort per man in period (t), and $\bar{E}$ is normal effort per man

Thus the group always has an economic interest in keeping labor productivity in (t) below what the individual, if he were to act as an isolated being, would wish. We shall explore in Chapter 8 the conditions under which $w_{1,t}$ or $w_{2,t}$ may be expected to determine $E_{i,t}$.

What is of interest here is the fact that, to some degree, enterprise and shopfloor management can be viewed as the upholder of group values. The working group, through social pressure, is the enforcer of attention to $w_{2,t}$ rather than to $w_{1,t}$; but management, through direct administrative pressure upon the individual (e.g. in the way that it allocates "good" versus "bad" jobs for piece-work, or that it distributes bonuses), is in this respect the ally of the group. Moreover, to the degree that wage funds should be viewed as being given only to enterprises rather than to smaller work groups, while on the other hand it is only the smaller work groups that can place effective pressure for work restriction upon the individual worker, management is in this respect an essential ally of the combined workers of the entire enterprise.

The reason for this managerial role is that bonuses of managers – far more than is the case for any other group in the enterprise – depend upon the fulfillment of the various elements of the production plan while remaining within the planned wage fund. If planned per capita marginal earnings during $(t+1)$ (defining these as $\partial w_{1,t+1}/\partial E_t$) become sufficiently low so as to cause reduction in the enterprise's labor force and/or reduction of per capita effort, it is the earnings of managerial personnel at all levels of management that will suffer the most both in absolute and in percentage terms. One might even hypothesize that $\partial w_{3,t}/\partial E_t$ – defined as marginal return to effort which managers would like individual employees to equate to their opportunity cost – is even lower than the group $\partial w_{2,t}/\partial E_t$.[202]

The material-stimulation fund

The material-stimulation fund of the enterprise, created since 1965, is the source of virtually all earnings not paid from the wage fund. Despite the fact that less than ten per cent of total earnings of all personnel come from this fund, it is nevertheless worth pointing out that its properties are the same as those of the wage fund with regard to fungibility and the "ratchet" effect, although only to a lesser degree with regard to its constituting a "hard" constraint.

The material-stimulation fund, just like the wage fund, is planned, and the planned form of each of these two funds is intended to be independent of the degree of planned improvement in the unit's various success indicators. Although the size of the realized fund appears to be more sensitive to production success relative to plan than is the realized wage fund, nevertheless 40 per cent of the material-stimulation fund is guaranteed to the enterprise almost regardless of its degree of success. The annual plan, formally built upon the five year plan as is the case for the wage fund, is similarly said to be more important in practice than is the five year plan.[203]

Fungibility within a year is comparable to that of the wage fund; similarly, part of the material-stimulation fund can be frozen.[204] Intertemporally, its fungibility is even greater than that of the wage fund; the composition of the labor force appears to be important primarily in terms of the proportion of manual workers to total employees.[205]

Since 1980, some 10 to 15 per cent of the total material-stimulation fund is intended to be centralized at the association and ministry level for reapportionment among individual enterprises. Such reapportionment appears to have become of greater importance as an increasing number of associations were created during the 1970s, and this trend has been criticized as weakening the link between the magnitude of an enterprise's fund and the fulfillment of the various success indicators on which its size is supposed to depend.[206] Because of this redistribution phenomenon, the

---

[202] See G. Plotnitskii in *S.T.*, 1983, 11, p. 86 who claims that the foreman in an enterprise is disadvantaged when labor productivity exceeds plan. Plotnitskii's argument, however, is restricted to period (t).

[203] Shkurko (1977), pp. 232, 252–254; G. Egiazarian in *V.E.*, 1974, 8, pp. 18–19; Zh. Sidorova in *V.E.*, 1984, 10, p. 33; Rzheshevskii (1975), pp. 83–84; R. Iakovlev in *S.T.*, 1979, 1, p. 53.

[204] Iu. Shatyrenko in *S.T.*, 1983, 2, p. 109.   [205] G. Egiazarian in *V.E.*, 1974, 8, p. 18.

[206] V. Rzheshevskii in *S.T.*, 1980, 5, pp. 15–16, and Zh. Sidorova in *V.E.*, 1984, 10, p. 32.

material-stimulation fund planned and realized for an individual enterprise seems by the 1980s to be a "softer" constraint than is the wage fund. At the organizational level of the ministry, however, there is no indication that the constraint is any less "hard" than it had been earlier.

THE TRADE-OFF AVAILABLE TO ENTERPRISE MANAGEMENT

So far in this chapter I have shown the existence and general freedom of the Soviet labor market, the fact that the enterprise's wage and material-stimulation funds represent a "hard" constraint upon the amount of wages that it can pay out, and the fungibility of these funds. This section builds upon these three empirical results.

We shall treat the enterprise decision problem of how to divide the available wage fund among the available personnel as being a management problem. In fact, it is not strictly this. The trade union of the enterprise plays a formal role of some significance in this decision, and we could well imagine that its decision criteria might be very different from those of the enterprise management. Although the general Western impression seems to be that the actual union role in such matters is negligible, this impression does not rest upon research and may well turn out to be incorrect. Nevertheless, for lack of information which would force us into a complex model of decisions made jointly by two players with different decision criteria, we shall follow the simpler approach.

The maximization problem of the enterprise management can be stated in the following terms:

Maximize the Objective Function *(o) subject to:*

$$o \leq \gamma\,[f(k,m,l),P]$$
$$k_i \leq K_i$$
$$m_j \leq M_j$$
$$\sum_{e=1}^{E} e_s = g_s(w_s\, w_t)$$
$$\sum_{e=1}^{E} \sum_{s=1}^{S} e_s w_s = W$$
$$W = \hat{W} + h(o)$$

with P, W_p and the functional forms γ, f, g, and h being exogenous

where o is a positive vector expressing all of the rewards and punishments imposed upon enterprise management in relation to the enterprise results; γ is the reward function; f is the production function of capital, materials, and labor; P is the performance plan; k_i represents utilization of a particular piece of capital equipment while K_i represents its availability; m_j represents the utilization of a particular type of material, semi-fabricate or energy source and M_j represents its allocation; e_s is an employee of a given type (skill), and $\overset{\Sigma}{e} \, e_s$ represents the availability of a given number of employees of a particular type (s), and is a function of $(w_s \, w_t)$ – the average earnings of (s) and of $(t{\neq}s)$; $\hat{W}$ is the planned wage fund plus material-stimulation fund of the enterprise, while W is the realized sum of these two funds.

Although the above constraints make no mention of fringe benefits paid to workers (housing, passes to rest homes, the opportunity to shop in enterprise stores, etc.), non-monetary earnings should be viewed as implicitly included in w_s, w_t, $\hat{W}$, and W. The sum of these available within a given enterprise is, in any year, limited in the same fashion as is the wage fund. Also, similarly, these non-monetary earnings are distributed unequally among the labor force of the enterprise.

The maximization problem can be viewed inter-temporarily, in which case the dependence of P, $\hat{W}$, γ, and h in $(t{+}\text{I})$ upon decisions made by enterprise management in (t) must be considered. But it is simpler to treat the problem as limited to one period, and this simplification will create no difficulties in the analysis of this section.

The distinctive part of the problem as posed in this chapter is that inputs other than labor are treated as non-fungible, while labor inputs can be meaningfully expressed in fungible, monetary terms. Given this statement of the problem, we can concentrate upon a major joint-decision problem of the enterprise management: how should W be apportioned among the individuals employed, and what is the optimal size of $\overset{\Sigma}{e} \, e_s$?

We have already treated this problem partially in terms of apportionment of per capita earnings among occupations and skill grades. The determination of w_s, and consequently the size of $\overset{\Sigma}{e} \, e_s$, depends upon the marginal rates of substitution between e_s and $e_{t{\neq}s}$ given both the objective function and the constraints of vectors γ, f, h and of K_i and M_j.[207] In this treatment, s represents the occupation-skill category of labor which is to be paid w_s. What is new here is that we depart from the conventional wisdom of Western writers about the Soviet labor market who treat enterprise managers as though their demand for number of employees was unbounded upward. Given the relevant constraints (which do not include the

---

[207] If we wish to state the problem inter-temporally, the expected response of planners to changes in the number of employees in category (s) becomes an additional constraint.

central determination of the maximum number of employees for a given enterprise), management desired $\sum_e e_s$ is a well-determined number.

Let us now turn to a treatment of the labor categories e_s and $e_{t \neq s}$ along another dimension. This will be the dimension of whether a given employee has also been working in that same enterprise during the previous period. Here we are using the conventional wisdom in human-capital theory that many skills are enterprise specific, and thus that a new recruit to an enterprise must go through a learning stage.[208] Thus, within a given occupation-skill category, a current worker is viewed as more valuable than would be his replacement if he quits.

Seen in this dimension, enterprise management is faced with a trade-off between the total size of the labor force $\sum_e \sum_s e_s$ and the proportion of old to new workers for a given matrix of relative numbers in given occupation-skill grades. If the enterprise chooses to be a low-paying employer, it can expect its quit rate and thus its turnover rate to rise. The quality of an average employee will be lower, but the number of employees that it can afford will be higher, than if it were to adopt a different strategy. By using its power to manipulate bonuses, wage-rate supplements, and piece-rate norms, enterprise management in the Soviet Union can enjoy the same freedom of choice of strategy as does the non-unionized capitalist firm. As suggested by the Western literature on dual labor markets, it might be hypothesized that a Soviet management which decides to be a high-paying employer for certain jobs may optimally determine to fill other jobs on the basis of paying low wages.[209]

All of this can be summarized by saying that the enterprise management, given its other constraints, will optimize by distributing its wage fund in such a fashion as to maximize its objective function. This implies that the number of employees engaged will not be maximized. Soviet constraints on the enterprise are not those supposed by writers who conceive of management as having an unbounded hunger for more employees, and who for this reason suppose that the Soviet Union is inevitably faced with a permanent "labor shortage." As in any market

[208] Soviet conventional wisdom on this subject is symmetrical, concentrating both on the decline of productivity during the months before a worker quits, and on the required adaptation period of the new recruit. Manual workers who have decided to leave a given job are viewed as suffering a drop in labor productivity of 5 to 15 per cent until they actually leave; after they are hired in a new enterprise, their productivity is again perceived as being 10 to 20 per cent below normal for two to three months (*Trudovoe pravo* [1972], p. 63 and *Dolishnii* [1978], p. 211).

[209] This choice of strategy by the employer plays an important role in the distinction made between the primary and secondary labor market in the Western literature on dual labor markets.

system, demand must be "effective" to be relevant to the market-place; enterprise demand for labor is "effective" only within the constraint of its realized wage fund.

Of course, none of the above has any direct bearing on the demand of enterprise management for inclusion of additional personnel in its labor-force plan. This demand is indeed upwardly unbounded – not particularly because of its implications for the number of personnel, but rather because the formation by higher authorities of the enterprise's planned wage and material-stimulation funds (and thus also its cost and profit plans) takes this figure into account. The expression of such demand is a free good for management (except as exaggeration awakens the suspicion of higher authorities), and the concept of "effective" demand has no place here.

It is true that, if such demand is accepted by higher authorities, the increase in the planned wage fund for the enterprise will normally (under the optimization process described earlier) also lead to an expansion in the enterprise's actual labor force. But this is because of the change in the enterprise's former wage fund constraint, not *per se* because of the increase in the planned number of personnel.

Here we must make a sharp distinction between enterprise demand for labor as expressed in requests to higher authorities, and enterprise "effective" demand through offers made on the labor market. The first is indeed unbounded upward, but higher authorities have the choice of whether to accept or reject such requests. The second is bounded upward by the constraint of the wage plus material-stimulation funds, and such bounding is essential from a macroeconomic standpoint since the higher authorities are powerless in this area once they have set these planned funds.

The writing of János Kornai easily lends itself to misinterpretation in this regard. He writes that the enterprises are subject to an expansion drive which is not at all restrained by labor becoming more expensive, and that the firm is not particularly responsive to relative wages in its choice of employment mix. He also regards managers at all levels from the shop floor to the individual ministry, but not higher, as acting as the representatives of their own workers in wage claims on higher authorities. These phenomena are ascribed particularly to the "soft" total budget constraint under which managers operate; i.e. to the relative unimportance of total costs, profits, and balance-sheet position *per se* as opposed to non-financial objectives.[210]

But the above must be reconciled with Kornai's other views, expressed

[210] Kornai (1980), pp. 391, 396, 400–06.

in the same chapter, that the wage fund constraint is a "hard" one and that in socialist economies the Center is almost completely successful in resisting wage-drift pressures to increase average earnings.[211] The reconciliation, it seems to me, is that Kornai's discussion supporting the thesis of the "soft budget" constraint on labor relates exclusively to requests to higher authorities for future planned wage funds, rather than to the shortrun situation where the enterprise must live within the wage fund that it has been granted. My concern, instead, is with the shortrun. If we accept Kornai's view as to the wage fund, we should reject any shortrun application of his view as to the irresponsiveness of managers to relative wages.

Furthermore, however, Kornai writes that the socialist economy inevitably evolves over time into one of labor shortage, and then remains in this state.[212] Unlike his treatment in earlier work, Kornai's writing in 1978 de-emphasizes the role of central economic policy and concentrates upon what he calls the almost insatiable demand for investment by managers at all levels below that of the very Center.[213] But since in Kornai's model little or nothing is invested without the approval of the Center, it is difficult to understand how in centralized socialism the adaptation of its plans by the Center to such hunger by lower bodies can help but be a necessary condition for the investment strains that lead to labor shortage. Indeed, Kornai's treatment of investment cycles[214] is consistent with this objection to his shift in approach. Thus we perforce return to seeing the enterprises' insatiable demand for labor as relating only to their requests to higher authorities, and as having significance only to the degree that the Center ratifies an undue proportion of these requests. This, in my opinion, is far from constituting a longrun "soft" budget constraint imposed on any particular enterprise. In the longrun, just as in the shortrun, the effective demand for labor by an enterprise must be subject to a "hard" constraint.

[211] See note 185 for sources.   [212] Kornai (1980), Chapter 11.
[213] *Ibid.*, pp. 63, 209–10, 556, and 569.
[214] *Ibid.*, pp. 211–15.

3

Overfull employment and job rights

This chapter discusses the empirical phenomena in the Soviet labor market which must be explained by any set of hypotheses claiming to deal with full employment in the Soviet Union. It presents the set of hypotheses of overfull employment and of job rights (JROE) by decision of the Center; these hypotheses provide the core around which this book is constructed. A rival hypothesis resting upon labor scarcity is also presented. Finally, the two competing theories are compared with regard to how well they fit the facts of the labor market, but all broader comparisons of the theories are postponed.

The JROE set of hypotheses

The two full-employment hypotheses to be presented here represent lexicographic preference by the Center for a specified degree of full employment over any attainment of other objectives such as growth in final product. (Of course, as pointed out in Chapter 1, the Center may have more than one such lexicographic preference.) While such lexicographic preference can exist only within a certain domain of obtainable values of all arguments in the Center's welfare function, it is maintained that the Soviet economy fell within the relevant domain during the period of this study. (See Chapter 1 for a fuller discussion of this lexicographic preference, and for the relationship between this and a "constraint.")

Although the hypotheses are statements as to observable phenomena, these observables do not arise from reduced form equations representing the interaction of the demand and supply of labor. The first full-employment hypothesis (3.1) in particular relates only to the demand for labor which is of the form:

Overfull employment and job rights

$$L_S = f(X)$$
$$L_D = g(L_s, Y)$$

where L_S = labor supply, L_D = labor demand, and X, Y are matrices of independent variables.

This hypothesis describes the maximum degree of involuntary unemployment that is observed, but with an unusual definition of "involuntary." All search activity by an unemployed person is defined as constituting "voluntary unemployment" to the degree that it extends beyond what is required to find some job within his own locality for which he is qualified (i.e. capable of performing) both physically and with regard to skill.

The logic of this approach is twofold. Most important, these postulated lexicographic preferences of the Center represent restrictions on the Center's ability to pursue other goals. Full employment, as treated here, is not a means to such objectives as growth of national income and of minimum family income. Instead it stands as a goal in its own right and, to the degree that overfull employment is pursued, the attainment of these other objectives suffers. The right of each individual to a job is valued for its own sake rather than for its income-creation or income-distribution attributes.

Given this trade-off feature of the preferences, it would seem unreasonable to posit that the Center would allow its preferences to be directly affected by actions of suppliers of labor. Planners' preferences that referred to the observed degree of frictional unemployment would compel counteracting Central action if suppliers of labor decided – say, because of a larger stock of family monetary savings – to raise their aspiration level concerning acceptable jobs and thus to increase their period of "search" during the interval between leaving the job and taking another. Central lexicographic preferences which were to refer to the observed period of job change might force the Center to ensure that a higher proportion of "good" jobs were being offered – a choice which would further restrict the ability of the economy to attain other objectives. Such obligatory validation of the increase of popular aspiration levels in the single domain of employment, pushing the costs of such validation completely into other domains, would presumably appear to the Center as an unreasonable restriction upon its own choice-making process.

None of this discussion is intended to suggest that the Center is uninterested in the final outcome of the demand and supply of labor, nor that it is unwilling to take actions affecting the structural supply equation. The reduction in 1983 from one month to three weeks in the period allowed between jobs without jeopardizing the job searcher's right to certain financial benefits was an effort to influence the supply function. But this and similar actions are directed toward the goal of increasing the level of national income rather than of reducing frictional employment *per se*. The second is only a means to the first.

The second branch of the logic of stating hypotheses as relating only to the demand for labor is that this approach allows us to avoid much of the thorny problem of defining "unemployment" that arises in Western treatments. Should the unemployed include those who could indeed find jobs, but not those full-time jobs that they wish to have? Should it include those who find full-time jobs, but not the part-time jobs that they wish, and who thus remain temporarily out of the labor market? (Full-time students are probably the largest category of this last group of "unemployed" in the Soviet Union.)[1] How about mothers of young children who would like to work if nursery facilities were locally available, but who find that they must go onto a waiting list for such childcare; are they unemployed? In summing up the number of unemployed, should we apply unequal weights to different categories or are all types of unemployment of equal consequence?

These are the sorts of problems observed in the United States, particularly in the 1970s and 1980s, in defining "unemployment." Once our interest in "unemployment" is informed by questions relating either to income creation or to income distribution, a differential interest in different categories of "unemployed" becomes inevitable. Furthermore, we are pushed to wrestling with such issues as "under-employment" – particularly the case of individuals working at jobs below their skill level.

If in this study our interest in unemployment were to include both the absence of jobs for would-be part-time workers, and the absence of jobs at the prevailing earning rate for a given skill for job applicants having such skills, it is unclear whether we would find the average rate of unemployment lower in the Soviet Union than in the United States. If we were to include as unemployment the proportion of unused to total time on the job of all "working" employees, the results would be tipped still more sharply against the USSR. But such results would be highly misleading. For they would suggest that the Soviet economy has been no more successful than the American in eliminating the types of unemployment which are

---

[1] Soviet studies have shown that 35 to 45 per cent of full-time students in higher education (and, perhaps, in junior colleges; the source is unclear) would like to work part-time during the school year. Yet of the very few full-time students who do work during the school year, over 60 per cent work for more than thirty-one hours weekly (G. Zaitsev and V. Uvarov in *E.I.*, 1984, 4, p. 94).

considered *per se* to be major problems by both the central authorities and the public in the respective countries. This would be manifestly untrue.

Concern with unemployment per se. A good statement of the position taken in the Soviet Union is the following proposition of János Kornai:

The unemployed are not only deprived of wages (this might be partly or fully compensated by unemployment dole), but they also suffer from the humiliation of idleness. Full employment not only increases wages, but also strengthens security, and human dignity. It establishes the material foundations for equal rights for women. That is why we are justified in recording it as a separate item among the benefits (of expanded employment).[2]

A similar position is taken by various writers in capitalist countries. Here the finding of Angus Campbell in reference to the United States is of interest: the unemployed as a group, regardless of income, score low in self-perceived well-being.[3]

This position is in reasonable accord with a criterion of being "unemployed" which I have developed as being consistent with the generally held view – both in the Soviet Union and in the West – that full or overfull employment prevails. The criterion is stated in terms of categories that are excluded from the definition.

(1) Those who would like only part-time work are excluded. This is shown by the fact that, as late as 1981, less than 0.5 per cent of all employees in the state sector were working part-time. Moreover, an earlier study suggests that a high proportion of these were moonlighters.[4] In contrast, 11.2 per cent of the American labor force plus discouraged workers in 1982 consisted of those who were voluntarily working part-time.[5] The Soviet press concerned with the labor market is filled with complaints as to the extent of the popular demand for part-time jobs by pensioners, women with young children, and students. But the complaints are directed to the negative effect on national income of the fact that many

[2] Kornai (1980), pp. 273–74.
[3] Campbell (1981) as reported in Social Science Research Council, Center for Coordination of Research on Social Indicators, *Social Indicators Newsletter*, 16 (August 1981), pp. 4–5. The conclusion is based upon national surveys conducted between 1957 and 1978.
[4] N. Rogovskii in *V.E.*, 1982, 1, p. 6 and V. Acharkan in *S.T.*, 1972, 7, p. 140. The 1981 data are consistent with the results of a study in September 1974 by the Central Statistical Office of the SSSR, which showed that 0.32 per cent of all those working on that day were working part time (T. Skal'berg *et al.* in *S.T.*, 1977, 2, p. 105).
[5] United States Bureau of Labor Statistics data as reported in the *New York Times*, August 14, 1983, p. 14.

of these people constitute "discouraged workers," rather than being aimed at the disappointment of the employment desires of the individual.[6]

(2) Those who cannot obtain jobs at their own skill level are excluded, so long as they can find work at some job within the socialist sector.[7]

(3) Excluded are those women with young children who would like to work but cannot do so because of the absence of pre-school facilities.[8]

(4) People of pensionable age may also be excluded, although this is less clear.[9]

---

[6] See Tsepin (1973), pp. 28–29.

[7] This is best shown by the data regarding graduates of junior colleges working in industry (see Chapter 7).

[8] In 1975, about half of all pre-school age children (under seven years) in urban areas were attending nurseries and kindergartens. For the country as a whole in 1979, the figure was 43.3 per cent (G. Sarkisiants in *S.T.*, 1976, 6, p. 13 and E. Manevich in *V.E.*, 1981, 9, p. 63). No separation can be made within this age group because the vast bulk of pre-school attenders go to institutions that are mixed nurseries and kindergartens.

Swedish national pre-school coverage in 1978 of all children up to school-entrance age (which is seven as in the Soviet Union) was 46 per cent – i.e. roughly the same as the Soviet coverage. Swedish coverage of three to five year olds is low in comparison with France, the German Federal Republic and the United States, but coverage is high (some 30 per cent) for the under-three cohort (Kamerman and Kahn [1981], Chapter 3 and especially pp. 101–02).

Another one-third of Soviet families with pre-school age children had, about 1970, "helping" members in the family other than children (G. Sergeeva in *Demograficheskie* [1975], p. 29); these were primarily grandparents. Still other couples had parents living separately but in the same neighbourhood who could take care of the children. Of course, the need for providing such aid in raising children is one reason for pensioners to stop working. In three urban samples where women aged 55–58 (60) and men aged 60–63 (65) who were not working were questioned during the 1970s, 11 to 16 per cent of the sample explained the fact of not working by their "desire to take part in raising their grandchildren" (Shapiro [1983], pp. 47–51 and 61).

It is true that, between the early 1960s and the end of the 1970s, the proportion of pre-school children attending nurseries and kindergartens increased fourfold (see G. Sergeeva in *Demograficheskie* [1975], p. 27). But Soviet discussions of this increase have been more in terms of its effects on national income than on female employment *per se*.

[9] From time to time, questions have been posed by readers of Soviet journals as to whether people of pensionable age may be dismissed from their jobs for that reason alone, and it has been necessary to insist that age is not a proper legal ground for dismissal (e.g. A. Solov'ev in *S.T.*, 1970, 5, pp. 139–40, and "We answer readers" in *S.T.* 1974, 6, p. 156). For new hirings, the 1970 pension law recommended to managers that they employ pensioners who are both fit and who are needed for the organization's production – qualifications that could well have been interpreted as applicable to all hirings, but that clearly were in fact interpreted by at least some managers as being considerably more restrictive (*S.T.*, 1970, 5, pp. 139–40).

Writing in 1969, one labor economist said that prior to the 1956 law on pensions – which both expanded the coverage and made pensions more generous – enterprises had to keep in employment a significant number of personnel who could not work at full capacity for reasons of health or age. This was the case then for humanitarian reasons, he declared, and this justification ceased with the new pension law (E. G. Antosenkov in *Opyt* [1969], p. 15).

(5) Collective farmers who, either because of the seasonal nature of their work or because of an excessive population density of farm families, are unable to work an appropriate number of days in the socialist sector and thus have lower annual incomes than they would otherwise. There seems to be no perceived obligation on the part of central authorities to provide sufficient state employment in the localities of these farmers to take up the slack.[10]

The above five categories that are excluded from the Soviet concern for unemployment *per se* share the common feature that their members are all engaged in socially approved activities and are not subjected to the ego-threatening "humiliation of (socially defined) idleness." It is for this reason, I suggest, that they are of concern to Soviet planners only because of their instrumental effect on other desiderata such as higher levels of national income. This suggests that "unemployment" is not a fundamental concern of Soviet central authorities because of its connection to poverty; although poverty is deplored, it is nevertheless accepted.[11] It is, instead, only the social aspects of unemployment that are truly unacceptable.

The description of the following hypotheses as being those of overfull employment rather than of full employment alone will not, I trust, cause difficulties for the reader. As mentioned in Chapter 1, what is meant is only

The clear inference in the book was that no right to work existed for such people. See also Chapter 9.

[10] Differences in the number of days worked per annum on the collective farms by members of "working age" (16 to 55/60 depending upon sex) seem to vary much more by type of work done than by region. In a year that must have been 1975 or thereabout, field workers in the Soviet Union who were not direct users of self-propelled mechanical equipment constituted 47 per cent of all collective farmers; but they worked an average of only 71 per cent of the number of days worked by all the other collective farmers (calculated from Soskiev [1978], pp. 133–34). If we were to make the extreme assumption that all the work done by all collective farmers in 1975 on work that fell out of their normal duties was done by this underemployed group, their days worked would still not rise above 80 per cent (*ibid.*, p. 143). The slack period in collective farm work is also, of course, precisely the period of greatest slack in labor demand on the farmers' own private plots.

In general, one can say that there has been little effort to develop state-owned enterprise in rural areas that would take up the seasonal slack among collective farmers. (Even where auxiliary industrial enterprises exist on collective farms or state farms, they are not normally operated in such fashion. See L. Kostin in *P.Kh.*, 1978, 12, p. 25). Nor in Central Asia, where rural youth claim that they would prefer to engage in non-agricultural pursuits provided that these are located in their native rural areas, is there any indication as yet of the State attempting to expand the employed work-year for collective farmers through the location of full-time industry in rural regions. The Central Asian textile industry, for example, is peculiarly concentrated in very large mills which must inevitably be located out of commuting range of rural inhabitants. (D. I. Ziuzin in *S.I.*., 1983, 1, pp. 109–17; E. Afanas'evskii in *P.Kh.*, 1982, 4, p. 86; Afanas'evskii [1976], pp. 55–61.)

[11] McAuley (1979) estimates that in 1967–68, one-third of the Soviet population had per capita incomes below the "official" poverty line (pp. 18–19, 70, 74–78 and Chapter 3).

that the period of necessary search by a job seeker between two positions is kept very brief, regardless of whether he left the previous job as a result of dismissal or of a quit, and that new entrants on to the labor market should similarly find no difficulty in being placed. The degree of brevity of this period that is desired by Soviet leaders is posited to be such as to be typically associated in capitalist countries with the various macroeconomic ills that one thinks of as accompanying "overfull" employment. Whether the combination of social gains and losses from this condition represents a net worsening or improvement over the situation described commonly as "full" employment is a matter of judgment and social preference.

The reason for such high Soviet concern with the provision of jobs is uncertain, and shall not be pursued. It is evident that such concern is regarded as a fundamental characteristic of a socialist economy, favorably differentiating it from capitalist society. But whether the willingness to sacrifice other goals to this one stems from the value system of the Soviet political leadership, or whether it is imposed upon this leadership by the demands of the Soviet public, is less clear – perhaps even to the Soviet leadership itself. In any case, as was discussed in Chapter 1, this is not an issue with which we are forced to concern ourselves in this book.

The two hypotheses. The first hypotheses is as follows:

Within each small locality of the country – defined in terms of the practicality of commuting to work from an individual's current residence – the probability is minimal that an unemployed individual will remain unemployed for longer than a month,[12] provided that he is willing to take

---

[12] The month of acceptable frictional unemployment is a figure intended only as an order of magnitude. Between 1960 and 1983, this was the length of time allowed between jobs without a worker suffering financial penalties other than loss of wages; thereafter, it was reduced to three weeks.

Data as to average time between jobs come from sample studies, and a fairly wide range is shown; a statement in *Pravda* of 23 to 35 calendar days seems about the best that can be said here (A. Laskavy in *C.D.S.P.*, XXXII, 43 [November 25, 1981], p. 20). Figures for manual workers hired on in two temporally differentiated samples of industrial enterprises in Novosibirsk, with the later sample having a 60 per cent overlap with the former, showed a 30 per cent increase in the average period between 1970 and 1981 (Z. P. Kupriianova in *Izv. sib. otd.*, 1984, 7 [vypusk 2], pp. 33 and 38). Of this period, it would seem that two weeks or more are required for the formalities of signing off and signing on (see *ibid.*, and V. Parfenov in *C.D.S.P.*, XXIX, 47 [December 21, 1977], p. 4).

On the other hand, some of this average period represents other than involuntary unemployment. Paid vacation time is included here, although it is common for employees to use at this time part or all of their accumulated vacation from their last job (E. G. Antosenkov in *Opyt* [1969], p. 33 fn. and V. Pirogov and M. Pankin in *S.T.*, 1971, 2, p. 144). Judging by some studies of manual workers carried out during 1966–70 by the Labor Research Institute of the Soviet Union, the average period between jobs was then 33

any job which he is capable of performing. This job may well require a skill level below that of the job seeker. (3.1)

It is the proviso in this hypothesis which makes it an equation governing only demand for labor. "Unemployed" is defined to exclude the fourth and fifth categories treated in the previous section (the other three are excluded by the qualifications stated in the hypothesis itself). Thus involuntary unemployment is restricted to the frictional variety, and is sufficiently limited so as to fall within the usual definition of "overfull" employment.

In this hypothesis, it is not assumed that the available job is necessarily with an organization other than the one for which the employee worked before he became unemployed. Specifically with regard to collective farmers, this restriction implies that an individual cannot give up his membership in the collective farm and be assured of state employment in the same rural locality.

The above hypothesis (3.1) is stated formally as an inequality expressed in a two-way categorization of skills and of the physical difficulty inherent in particular jobs. This could readily be generalized to an n-way categorization.

$V_{z_j}^*$ is chosen so that

$$\Pr \left\{ f(Z_j) \,\middle|\, V_{z_j}/s_{z_j} \right\} \langle\ \varepsilon_1 \qquad (3.1)$$

where

$f(Z_j)$ = duration of unemployment of individual (i) for $> y_1$ calendar days when this individual has the characteristics Z_j and is willing to take any job offered within his own locality which he is able to perform, given his skills and physical condition

Variables

V_{Z_j} = number of job vacancies with the characteristics Z_j

S_{Z_j} = number of job seekers with the characteristics Z_j

calendar days. But this average was heavily affected by the figure for women aged twenty-one to twenty-nine, for whom the average period was 56 days, and by both sexes under twenty-one, for whom the average was 41 days. According to the Soviet author, the former figure reflects family formation and child bearing, while the latter reflects youths quitting jobs so as to prepare for entrance examinations for specialized secondary and for higher educational institutions (I. I. Matrozova in *Dvizhenie rabochikh kadrov* [1973], pp. 5–6, 203–05). Those working youths who wanted to take entrance exams for higher education were said in the mid-1960s *generally* to quit in order to have more time to study (E. G. Antosenkov in *Opyt* [1969], pp. 14 and 80). Another source talks of youths who are rejected for admission into full-time higher educational studies spending six months before taking a job (E. Manevich in *V.E.*, 1981, 9, p. 63).

Constants

y_1 = roughly, thirty

ε_1 = a very small number

Characteristics

Z_j = $Z_I, \ldots, Z_{IV}$

Z_I = z_1

Z_{II} = $z_1 \cup z_2$

Z_{III} = $z_1 \cup z_3$

Z_{IV} = $z_1 \cup z_2 \cup z_3 \cup z_4$

z_1 = $a\ u\ e$ ⎫ where the righthand side is a

z_2 = $a\ u\ h$ ⎪ vector of characteristics whose

z_3 = $a\ s\ e$ ⎬ elements include all non-zero

z_4 = $a\ s\ h$ ⎭ values

a = a locality of the country, and takes values $a_1, a_2, \ldots, a_N$

u = unskilled jobs (or workers), and takes values 0 or 1

s = skilled jobs (or workers), and takes values 0 or 1

e = physically undemanding jobs (or workers who are desirous of filling them), and takes values of 0 or 1

h = physically demanding jobs (or workers who are both physically capable and desirous of filling them), and takes values 0 or 1

The second hypothesis is based on the supposition that (3.1) is not intended simply to provide a minimum-income guarantee to all who wish and are able to work – it is needlessly restrictive if that were its only concern – but also to allow individual (i) to earn such income rather than to receive it as a transfer payment. This is motivated by the avoidance of the "humiliation of idleness."

On this basis, (3.2) below prevents "slack" in any enterprise's use of labor time from being concentrated on any particular group of employees. While underemployment within the enterprise can exist, it must be spread around. (Thus labor hoarding by an enterprise would not necessarily violate this constraint.) This hypothesis is expressed formally in our second inequality.

$$Pr\ \{\ A_i > y_2\ \} < \varepsilon_2 \qquad\qquad (3.2)$$

where

Ai = days per annum of unwanted idleness within his current enterprise of individual (i)

y_2 = a moderately substantial number (e.g. thirty) of working days per year

ε_2 = a very small number

"Idleness" is defined to include the effect of working less than a pace that is normal in that enterprise.

Inequality (3.2) guarantees (*i*) that he will be given the opportunity of actually earning his paid income, rather than receiving it as a transfer payment made on condition of his physical attendance at the job. In this sense, it represents more than a policy of income maintenance. But it is also the latter, since idle employees need not be paid as much as those working at a normal pace; piece-rate workers constitute the clearest example of this fact. The income-maintenance effect of (3.2) should not be confused with the guarantee of a minimum income; instead, it represents an attempt to preserve whatever income level the individual worker had previously attained.

Furthermore, inequality (3.2) constrains any potential employing enterprise (*k*) – where $k = \epsilon \{k_1, k_2, \ldots, k_K\}$ – against maintaining a labor force whose structural imbalance transcends certain limits; this constraint on (*k*) is a necessary condition of the guaranty to (*i*).

Observed degree of labor participation and frictional unemployment

When we turn to data regarding observable unemployment as this is usually defined, it is not necessary that low unemployment and a high labor-force participation rate should be accompaniments of an overfull employment policy as this has been defined in the JROE hypotheses. The "search" effect of the supply side of the labor market is ignored in these hypotheses, but clearly it will be highly relevant to the observations made. Nevertheless, whatever the structural supply equations look like, we would hardly expect to observe a combination of low unemployment and high participation if the demand for labor were unfavorable. Thus we might think of a combination of low unemployment and high participation as a sufficient, but not a necessary, condition for belief in high demand for labor.

Labor-force participation data are available from the Population Censuses by age and sex. The data come from a 25 per cent population sample, with the question referring to the main source of income of the individual. Draftees, people only seasonally employed, women on leave from their jobs because of having children under one year of age, and those who had left their previous job less than one month ago and who planned to return to work were all included in the category of "working in the socialist sector."

Table 3.1 *Labor-force participation in the socialist sector*
(percentage of age group)

Census year	People in the normal working age			People in the first five years of pension age	
	Total group	Men (16–59)	Women (16–54)	Men (60–64)	Women (55–59)
1959	77.4	89	69	...	29.0[b]
1970	84.8	87	82	27.8	23.7
1979	85.7[a]	87	84	29	29

Notes:
[a] Calculated on the assumption that the total working population of this age had the same sex composition in 1979 as it had had in 1970.
[b] It is not explicitly stated that this figure comes from the Census.
Sources: M. I. Sonin in *Problemy ratsional'nogo* (1973), p. 356. *Naselenie SSSR* (1974), p. 143. Lantsev (1976), p. 119. L. Chizhova in *S.T.*, 1984, 8, p. 90.

Pensioners and students receiving scholarships were included only if working on permanent and full-time jobs at the time of the census.[13]

Table 3.1 provides data as to the percentage of different age groups that were at work in the socialist sector at the time of the last three censuses. If we were to add to these the number of full-time students receiving scholarships (75–77 per cent of all full-time students in 1983/84),[14] the totals for people in the normal working age would be 92.4 per cent in 1970 and 94 per cent in 1979.[15] A study of families in Leningrad in 1974–75 showed that, normally, families in which only the husband worked were of this type either because children were still of nursery-school age or because the wife had already gone on pension.[16] Soviet writers treat participation rates as being currently as high as possible; in fact, they are frequently considered as being too high for women and are viewed as a cause of undesirably low birth rates.[17]

It is quite true that the labor-force participation rates for men sixty to sixty-four years of age, and for women fifty-five to fifty-nine, seem surprisingly low. However, since these are pension-age people, there is no

[13] Knabe (1979), pp. 27–31 and Rapawy (1976), p. 13.
[14] *Narkhoz SSSR v 1983 g.*, p. 410.
[15] E. P. Chernova in *Regional'nye* (1978), p. 210 quoting *Pravda*, April 17, 1971. *Ref.*, 1983, 2, 2E51.
[16] Vasil'eva (1981), pp. 57–58.
[17] A. Tkachenko in *Demograficheskie* (1975), pp. 33–42. *Zaniatost'* (1978), p. 59. Z. V. Kupriianova in *E.K.O.*, 1982, 3, p. 122.

inconsistency here with the notion of overfull employment as Soviet leaders are hypothesized to view it.

Given these high participation rates, we turn to the percentage of unemployed. For this, we must lean primarily on data as to the period between jobs; we shall consider all such periods as constituting unemployment, although periods of over one month lead to the individual being excluded from the labor force as defined in Table 3.1. In fact, as was discussed in footnote 12, some of this frictional unemployment is clearly voluntary.

Let us take the figure of 18.2 per cent of Chapter 2 as the annual "quit plus dismissal" rate for Soviet industry in the late 1970s, and assume that it holds for the economy as a whole. (It is clearly higher in construction and lower in the collective farms; comparisons for other sectors are uncertain.) Since we wish a point estimate of the period between jobs, let us take thirty-six calendar days, a statistic coming from a single Soviet study and one of the very highest figures I have seen.[18] Together, these provide a frictional-unemployment rate of 1.8 per cent at the end of the 1970s. If we further posit that youth completing full-time education wait for a 50 per cent longer period before taking their first job than do people between jobs,[19] and count them as being in the labor force during this period,[20] we obtain a total unemployment rate of some 2.3 per cent. This is probably close to the upper bound of what is likely but, because of the very crude basis of the calculations, let us take 1.5 to 3 per cent as our range of estimate for the end of the 1970s, recognizing that such "unemployment" must include a fair proportion of informal vacation time taken before starting a new job. (Such informal vacation should have become particuarly large by the end of the 1970s when repressed inflation increased and it thus became increasingly difficult for Soviet families to spend usefully all of their money income. The Novosibirsk data of footnote 12, showing a thirty per cent increase during 1970–81 in the period between jobs, is reflective of the results of other Soviet studies.)

Observed frictional unemployment rates of 1.5 to 3 per cent are strikingly low by American standards or by West European standards of the late 1970s and the first half of the 1980s. But they were fairly normal for

[18] R. Rogovskii, head of a sector in the State Planning Commission of the SSSR in *P.Kh.*, 1979, 10, p. 41, and Z. P. Kupriianova in *Formirovanie* (1982), p. 60. See also footnote 12.

[19] Youth who fail to win acceptance into full-time higher educational courses are described as being typically unemployed for six months (E. Manevich in *V.E.*, 1981, 9, p. 63).

[20] This treatment is consistent with the labor participation figures of Table 3.1, since the figures are from population censuses that were taken outside of the first few months following the end of the school year.

many developed countries from the 1950s through the mid 1970s. Thus the Soviet overfull employment policy, as posited in JROE, has not led to observed results that are strikingly different from those seen in a number of capitalist countries over a quarter of a century. This should not particularly surprise us in view of the importance of "search" in determining observed unemployment. What matters, however, is that the rate of Soviet unemployment is fully consistent with a belief in the existence of a high demand for labor.

Regional aspects of unemployment

The JROE hypothesis (3.1) is very strong in that it calls for sufficient offers of jobs within each locality so that the probability of involuntary unemployment will be minimal. Empirical objections to this hypothesis are most likely to concentrate upon its provision that would-be workers should not be forced to change residence. Examples of phenomena subject to the interpretation of reflecting local unemployment are the following:

Migration of males occurs from cities like Ivanovo, where employment opportunities are dominated by a textile industry which is primarily "feminine."[21] The proportion of "housewives" is particularly high in coal mining and steel towns, that combine shortage of employment opportunities for women with very high wages (by Soviet standards) for men.[22] Discussion of the reasons for high rural migration to particular neighboring cities rather than to others concentrates upon demand factors.[23] In a study of a small rural region, it was found that both in-migrants and out-migrants in the middle 1960s showed an increase in the proportion who were neither students, pensioners nor working in the social economy.[24] Given this increase in comparison with the situation prior to the move, lasting at least throughout the first year after their move, the Soviet finding may be taken as demonstrating long-term frictional unemployment among migrants.

However, all of these instances seem better interpreted in terms either of efforts by individuals to move to areas where they have greater opportunities to obtain "good" as opposed to "poor" jobs, or as resulting from the preference for leisure as opposed to "poor" jobs in an area where one is living because of the work of one's spouse or parents.

The desire for self-betterment has been used by the prominent sociolo-

---

[21] Afanes'evskii (1976), p. 13.   [22] Kurman (1971), p. 8.
[23] Staroverov (1975), p. 162.
[24] *Ibid.*, pp. 172–73.

gist Zaslavskaia as a partial explanation of migration: the individual of given skills often has to accept both a lower skill rating and lower earnings in an old and thickly populated region than he might receive in a newly settled, developing region.[25] This phenomenon emerges inevitably in a national labor market.

The preference for leisure as opposed to "poor" jobs seems a likely explanation of the phenomenon of comparatively low female labor participation rates in the coal and steel towns of the Donbass region. In the study carried out in 1968 which reported these low participation figures, we are also given quit rates by sex in four large steel plants. Among manual workers, the female quit rate was 96 per cent of that of the male. Moreover, female quits were not concentrated in production shops where the work must have been particularly hard. Instead, women also accounted for 67 per cent of all quits from jobs in non-production departments (kitchens, dining rooms, nurseries, infirmaries, etc.) – a figure which was probably not too far from their proportion of the total number of such employees.[26] If women in these towns were truly eager to work at any job offered, and if an unemployed woman were likely to remain without an offer for a long time, we would have expected to see a very low female quit rate in these towns.

Two different Soviet writers have commented negatively upon the experience with creating enterprises of light industry in the coal towns of the Donbass, the Urals and Siberia in order to reduce the proportion of housewives in these towns. Such enterprises do not attract housewives to work, it is explained; the families already have too high a standard of living to make such work attractive. It is only young girls finishing secondary school who take such jobs instead of leaving town to work as they had done previously.[27] These statements do not suggest long-term involuntary unemployment of women in these small towns that are arch examples of localities where jobs are primarily male. As to the girls finishing school, it is not suggested by the Soviet writers that there was no work at all available for them in their native towns; rather, the material presented is consistent with the interpretation that jobs did exist there prior to the building of the facilities of light industry, but that these were not such as to entice youth of a mobile age and without marital commitments not to migrate.

Of all the reports I have seen as to the existence of labor-demand constraints, the only serious one that cannot readily be interpreted in one of

[25] T. I. Zaslavskaia in *Migratsiia sel'skogo naseleniia* (1970), p. 45.
[26] Kurman (1971), pp. 82–83.
[27] V. A. Kremliakov in *Problemy razmeshcheniia* (1973), pp. 54–55 and E. A. Iankovskaia in *Regional'naya* (1978), p. 67. It is jobs in garment and knitting factories that were most accepted by school leavers.

the two ways suggested above refers to a study conducted at the end of 1967 in the Urals. Here, over two-thirds of the 14 per cent of the labor age population that was neither working in the socialist sector nor studying on scholarship expressed a desire for employment. The principal single reason that was given for not working was the "absence of work." The second main reason was the need to look after children, and the authors commented that this reason was closely connected with the first. Given the absence of work, there was little pressure on the state to build nurseries and kindergartens since their existence could not lead to an increase in the employment of housewives.[28]

One reason for the apparent absence of regional unemployment has been pressure placed "from outside" upon enterprises located in areas of labor surplus to hire beyond their needs. A source notes this as having occurred during the period of 1958–67 in small urban areas of the Kirgizian Republic in Central Asia; here hirings occurred beyond the enterprise plan limits.[29] Presumably, this phenomenon represents the greater power of local authorities over enterprise managements than over the geographically broader-based authorities who at that time set the plan limits for labor in the enterprises.

It is, of course, quite unnecessary for me to attempt to defend hypothesis (3.1) by the claim that there are no Soviet localities where genuine "absence of work" for women exists. I need only argue that the cases are sufficiently rare so as to come under a reasonable quantitative value of ε_1 in (3.1).

JOB RIGHTS

Much more striking than the overfull employment aspect of labor demand is the *de facto*, although not *de jure*, provision of the right of the individual to his existing job. This right goes far beyond what is found, even in periods of

---

[28] M. P. Zhemanova and S. A. Usminskaia in *Sotsial'nye problemy truda i obrazovaniia* (1969), pp. 27–30.

It is worth noting that it was also in the Urals (although in a different *oblast*) that, five years later, 54 per cent of that same year's graduates of secondary education in a small region (*raion*) were found to be working in the sector of household services, although only 4 per cent of a substantial sample had indicated as of the end of the school year a desire to do so. Of the sample, 15 per cent had desired to work in other sectors of the economy, but none had obtained jobs there. Clearly it remained difficult in this region to find desired jobs quickly (S. M. Gusev in *Trudovye resursy i sovershenstvovanie* [1975], pp. 67–70).

[29] Chernova (1970), p. 221. Such make-work hiring occurred particularly in the garment and food-processing industries of the south of the Republic, an area where there were large numbers of non-working women.

normal prosperity, in any capitalist economy. Such a job right is common in the public service in most countries, but is limited to only a small proportion of the national labor force. In Japan, this right is common in large-scale enterprises generally, but only in a modified form: it does not protect against undesired transfers within the same company or to affiliated companies. Furthermore, this job right in Japan is sharply limited as to the proportion of the national labor force covered. Not only does it fail to apply to enterprises employing the majority of the Japanese labor force, but even in the larger enterprises it excludes men over fifty-five to fifty-eight years of age – although overwhelmingly these remain in the national labor force – and almost all women. In contrast to all capitalist countries, Soviet job rights apply to the vast bulk of the labor force. Only a small number of employees specifically hired as temporary or seasonal employees, or holding particularly responsible posts such as managerial ones, or violating such Soviet mores as those prohibiting political opposition, are excluded from such rights.

Since the JROE hypothesis (3.1) of overfull employment provides no assurance of jobs other than those of low skill and with low income, it would be extremely unsatisfactory by itself. Something further is required to protect employees with work experience from suddenly being forced, if they wish to work at all, to take jobs vastly inferior to those they had been filling. If Soviet employees were to face the permanent threat of such downgrading because of general economic conditions, such threat would seem almost as serious as the prospective unavailability of any job at all. Since involuntary unemployment is not defined in terms of the unavailability of a job consistent with the individual's skill and experience, but rather is defined in terms of the unavailability of any job that the individual is capable of filling, an economic system that did no more than abolish this type of involuntary unemployment would hardly meet the social objectives of Soviet society.

Similarly, the job-rights hypothesis (3.3) alone would jeopardize whatever degree of overfull employment was created by economic "overheating" alone, since enterprise managements in the Soviet Union as elsewhere would be more reluctant to engage in new hires to the degree that they were prevented from dismissing workers. Thus the constraints of full-employment and of job-rights are complements, and careful design of institutions and policies is required to assure that both can be fulfilled simultaneously.

The JROE job-rights hypothesis offers protection against downgrading of job and income to virtually all employees other than those who voluntarily quit their job. It is stated as follows:

$$Pr\{B_i\} < \varepsilon_3 \qquad (3.3)$$

where

B_i = dismissal of individual (i) from enterprise (k), or forcing him to change jobs within the same enterprise except where these jobs differ only by substituting the characteristic (e) in the new job for (h) in the previous one (with resultant loss of earnings).

h,e = physically demanding and physically undemanding jobs respectively, as defined in (3.1).

Hypothesis (3.3) does not apply to those holding managerial positions, and may not in practice apply to those of pensionable age. Further, it does not apply to those violating political mores (e.g. applying for emigration) or, apparently, to those who act as whistle blowers and report illegal actions to higher authorities or to the press.[30]

By guaranteeing the individual against the loss of his existing job, hypothesis (3.3) combined with (3.2) also guarantees with probability $\geq \{1-[(\varepsilon_3)(1-\varepsilon_2)+\varepsilon_2]\}$ the right to an approximation of his existing monetary quasi-rents on the labor market to each individual $i_{a,b,u}$ and $i_{a,b,s}$ – where b = the branch of the economy and is $\in \{b_1, b_2,\ldots,b_V\}$, and where a and s refer to locality and to skilled jobs respectively as in (3.1).[31] This guarantee is provided subject to two limitations:

(a)   That there is no change within the particular enterprise – in reaction to variation in the relative local labor market conditions for the different trades and skills – in the average quasi-rents of the groups consisting of all $i_{a,b,u,e}$ or of all $i_{a,b,s,e}$.

(b)   That individual (i) does not opt out of this guarantee by quitting his job.

Hypothesis (3.3) not only guarantees individual (i) against income loss, but also against having his utility from work satisfaction reduced by being compelled to perform a different type of work in enterprise (k) or to transfer from enterprise (k) to another enterprise. Under Soviet law, such transfers can be forced upon the individual only for limited periods.

The reader may wonder why the Soviet leadership should try to guarantee job rights as in JROE instead of being satisfied with overfull employment alone. A partial answer may lie in the difficulties involved in

[30] For a treatment of whistle blowing, see Lampert (1985), chapter 4.
[31] The individual may be transferred within enterprise (k) from a job with characteristic (h) to one with characteristic (e) – i.e. from a physically demanding to a physically undemanding position – so long as the two jobs have the same skill characteristic and are in the same locality. Presumably the logic is that $(Y_{k,h}-Y_{k,e})$, with Y representing personal income, is not considered as a quasi-rent but rather as payment for the additional work effort required in the job with the characteristic (h).

attempting to guarantee overfull employment on a locality by locality basis if this guarantee were to be defined in terms of providing "appropriate" jobs.

If the Soviet leadership were to try to act in such a fashion that its behavior could better be described as that of providing overfull employment for each individual skill (in each locality), rather than that of providing the combination of overfull employment and job rights included in JROE, the task might well be beyond its powers. For, as long as (3.2) was maintained, the combination of (3.1')[32] – as given in note 32 – and of (3.2) would require a very high degree of concordance between the stock of skills in the labor force of each locality and the stock of skill requirements in the job market. Every time an individual with certain skills chose to migrate, a job of that skill would have to be created in his new locality.

Even if this substitute task were to prove feasible, it would presumably provide less job satisfaction to the national labor force than does the hypothesized combination of the union of (3.1), (3.2), and (3.3). For the substitute would not assure maintenance of the same primary workgroups for those who could now be dismissed, nor would it prevent the increase of commuting time for such individuals.

Although hypothesis (3.3) is intended to apply to dismissals in general, it seems essential to divide up the broad category of potential dismissal according to the justification underlying it. The workers who are the potential objects of dismissal may be:

(a) Violators of labor discipline
(b) Persons who are incapable of performing, or unwilling to perform, their existing tasks effectively
(c) Persons occupying work places that have become redundant

Soviet law treats these three sub-categories somewhat differently. But more important for our analysis, ε_3 in (3.3) seems substantially higher for an individual when he falls into the first category than when he falls into either of the other two. Moreover, those in the first category can reasonably be assimilated to workers who voluntarily quit their job and thus renounce their right to existing monetary and in-kind quasi-rents. Such assimilation would not be appropriate for those in the second two categories.

---

[32] Hypothesis (3.1') can be described as identical with (3.1) except for the substitution of Z'_j for Z_j. Here, Z'_j is defined as $(a\ s'\ h')$ with s' and h' each taking on a very large number of possible values and being defined as:

$$s' = \epsilon \{u = s_o, s_1, \ldots, s_S\}$$
$$h' = \epsilon \{e = h_o, h_1, \ldots, h_H\} \qquad\qquad (3.1')$$

Violations of labor discipline

It is worth noting that, in Soviet statistics, job-separations on this basis are combined with quits into a single term (*tekuchest'*). Dismissals on any other ground are, in contrast, thrown into the residual category of separations which includes such diverse grounds as death or retirement on the one hand and being drafted or elected to full-time public office on the other. Such combination seems to express the Soviet viewpoint that disciplinary dismissals and quits are both results of voluntary action on the part of the job holder, and that action resulting in either should be thought of as being taken in the private rather than in the social interest. Clearly the line between private and social interests is not a sharp one, and it has seemed much less so since the mid-1960s when quits began to be defended as socially useful. Nevertheless, leaving a job to begin full-time education is never attacked as socially harmful, while existing "high" quit rates are still regarded by the vast majority of Soviet writers as deleterious. Violations of labor discipline are, of course, universally deplored.

Such combination of disciplinary dismissals and of quits seems to reflect a general Soviet viewpoint that there is no reason for society to worry about the job rights of the violator of discipline. If considerable obstacles are put in the way of such dismissals, it is for reasons other than concern for the individual.

An example showing the prevailing Soviet attitude is given for work in various forestry areas where, it is said, jobs as minor white-collar employees are scarce. Unjustified absenteeism among women white-collar employees in these regions is rare since dismissal would entail either taking a strenuous manual job in forestry or in road transport or leaving the area. The difference in the degree of unjustified absenteeism among manual and white-collar female employees is explained by the author as due to labor market conditions rather than to the nature of the two types of labor force.[33]

When we turn to a quantitative appreciation of the importance of disciplinary dismissals in the Soviet Union, we find no aggregative treatments above the level of the enterprise that explicitly deal with such dismissals as a proportion of the labor force. However, we do have a number of treatments of such dismissals as a proportion of quits plus dismissals, and these allow us to make estimates related to the entire labor force. The aggregative data that I have seen permit the estimates of Table 3.2. They suggest that disciplinary dismissals have constituted something

---

[33] Smirnov (1972), p. 110.

Table 3.2 *Annual disciplinary dismissals as a proportion of the average labor force*

Year	Coverage	Percentage
1965–66	all industrial enterprises in the Russian Republic	1.3[a]
1967	all industrial enterprises in the Kirgizian All-Union Republic (in Central Asia)	2.3[b]
1967	all workers and employees in the city of Vilna (in Lithuania)	1.3[c]
1971	all those seeking jobs through employment offices in thirteen cities of the Russian Republic	1.3[d]
1971	all those working in the city of Kaluga	1[e]
circa 1978	all industrial manual workers in the Russian Republic	2.0[f]
1978–1980	all industrial enterprises in the Soviet Union	1.7[g]

[a] *Otnoshenie k trudu* (1970), pp. 9–10. I have used the 1967 figure of quits plus dismissals of industrial manual workers for the Russian Republic (L. M. Danilov in *Dvizhenie rabochikh kadrov* [1973], p. 128) and made the usual Soviet assumption that total separations are 50 per cent larger.

[b] Chernova (1970), pp. 184–86.

[c] B. P. Gailgalas in *Sotsial'nye problemy truda i obrazovaniia* (1969), pp. 54–58. The same supplementary assumption was made as in footnote (a) above.

[d] Maslova (1976), p. 179. The 1969 figure of quits plus dismissals of industrial manual workers for the Russian Republic (Danilov in *Dvizhenie*, p. 128) was combined with the Maslova data.

[e] Kaluga was then a city of 200,000, located in the Central Region of the Russian Republic. The raw data provided are the number of disciplinary dismissals (*Trud*, February 2, 1972, p. 2). Depending upon assumptions as to the size of the city's total labor force, the percentage falls within the bounds of 0.7 and 1.2 per cent.

[f] Z. V. Kupriianova in *Formirovanie* (1982), p. 214 for an indeterminate date presumably in the late 1970s, for disciplinary dismissals as a proportion of quits plus disciplinary dismissals. Quits plus dismissals in 1978 in the Russian Republic is from A. G. Sozykin in *C.D.S.P.*, XXXII, 32 (September 10, 1980), p. 20, combined with Rusanov (1971), p. 111.

[g] L. Kartashova in *P.Kh.*, 1984, 9, p. 84 combined with my estimated 18.2 per cent figure of quits plus dismissals of manual workers in the Soviet Union in 1978 (see Chapter 2).

of the order of 1 to 2 per cent annually of the industrial labor force. Although I have little confidence in any of the individual estimates – partly because they represent an uncertain combination of manual and white-collar employees as well as of industrial and other state-sector employees, and partly because only in the cases of Maslova and, perhaps, of Chernova do the original data appear trustworthy – all the estimates are both reasonably independent and consistent.[34]

[34] I must caution the reader against concluding from Table 3.2 that disciplinary dismissals had increased in importance by 1980. Kartashova, who is the basic source of the 1978–1980

Unfortunately, I know of no data for other countries that would let us view the Soviet figures in perspective. However, when one takes account both of the high rate of drunkenness in the Soviet Union, which enlarges the domain of workers liable to such dismissals, and of the fact that many of the dimissed workers presumably had multiple dismissals within the same year, the proportion of the national labor force involved seems relatively restricted. This is all the more the case when one considers that an unknown proportion of such dismissals are in fact quits – individuals who are bound to their existing job either by contract or due to state direction after their education was completed, and who can leave only by mutual agreement with their employer or by dismissal.[35]

An unexcused absence for an entire day, or drunkenness on the job, constitutes legal grounds for disciplinary dismissal. All other offenses can lead to dismissal only if they are "systematic" – this being defined as occurring, and being noted in the form of a formal reprimand or other punishment, at least twice during the same year. (Apparently, some courts have refused to accept dismissals for absenteeism unless they are similarly systematic, but this procedure runs counter to a 1967 decision of the Supreme Court of the Soviet Union.) Dismissal must occur within a specified period from when the offense was committed.[36]

That systematic disciplinary offenses must be fairly major is suggested by the complaint of one manager that there is no way to dismiss auto mechanics who take small bribes from customers or who cheat them out of sums that are too small to warrant criminal prosecution.[37]

More significant is the view that disciplinary dismissals should be accepted by the trade unions and the courts only as measures of last resort. A Soviet film of the 1970s concerns the protection by the local trade union of a perfect candidate for such dismissal; "social pressure" is

figure, describes in the same paragraph such dismissals as being 9.6 per cent of quits plus such dismissals of industrial manual workers in 1980, and as being 16.9 per cent in 1983. I find these data unconvincing because the dramatic increase indicated over a three-year period is due mainly to an implied reduction in quits by more than one third. (See the comments of R. Livshits in *S.T.*, 1982, 11, pp. 74–81 arguing for the insignificance and, indeed, ambivalent effect on quits of recent regulations.)

35 A report of an individual enterprise having to dismiss a high proportion of its assignees from vocational schools is given by Iu. N. Udovichenko in *E.K.O.*, 1980, 10, pp. 33–34. Maslova (1976), p. 165 fn. describes departures before the end of a contracted period in organized recruitment as being treated as disciplinary dismissals. On the other hand, L. A. Shishkina in *Opyt* (1969), p. 59 says that in Siberia such departures are treated as being by mutual agreement and are registered statistically as quits. Clearly, as one would expect, practice varies.

36 Nikitinskii and Paniugin (1973), pp. 49–56, and M. Pankin in *S.T.*, 1973, 1, pp. 139–40.

37 S. Petrachenkov in *C.D.S.P.*, XXXIII, 52 (January 27, 1982), p. 15.

the trade union spokesman's preferred solution. A regional police officer, writing in *Pravda* as late as 1982, is critical of enterprises that dismiss malfeasants – since such enterprises are simply throwing the burden of dealing with these people onto the shoulders of others.[38]

It is the viewpoint expressed by the last writer that seems best to express the basis for the Soviet reluctance to sanction disciplinary dismissals. It is only the most successful enterprises, able readily to attract new workers to replace those dismissed, who can permit themselves the luxury of "purifying" their own labor forces. The dismissees gravitate to the less attractive enterprises – which thus become even less successful. Moreover, and this is the special interest of the policeman, the expulsion of these individuals from a stable workgroup in which they are known increases the probability of their eventually degenerating into criminality. These grounds for restricting disciplinary dismissals are completely distinct from a job-rights ethos.

Nevertheless, whatever the reason, the ability of managers to dismiss workers on disciplinary grounds is sharply restricted. What matters here is that such restrictions are not solely those arising out of the labor market conditions, but instead are a reflection of social costs and benefits rather than purely private ones (i.e. those of the employing enterprise). It is this element that makes hypothesis (3.3) apply to disciplinary dismissals, although in a much attenuated form – i.e. with a higher probability of exception – as compared with the other two categories of dismissals.

Inability properly to perform the job

Although no statistical data exist as to the loss of jobs for reasons of incompetence, all indications are that such losses are minimal. This statement applies, at a minimum, to ordinary manual and white-collar workers after a probationary period.

As a Moldavian Republic prosecutor writes, "There is a widespread opinion that it's impossible to fire someone whose work is poor."[39] In a study that was probably conducted in the early 1970s as to the practices of various enterprises, not a single case was found of the legally permitted

---

[38] Prudinskii (1966), pp. 46–47, cites a 1965 ruling of the presidium of the central council of the Soviet Union's trade unions that factory trade union committees should only as a last resort sanction dismissal for absenteeism. See also *Sovetskie profsoiuzy*, 1965, 4, p. 30; B. A. Ruble in *Comparative Labor Law*, 2, 3 (fall 1977), p. 183; I. Serov in *Pravda*, May 3, 1982, p. 2.

[39] I. Cheban in *C.D.S.P.*, XXXII, 39 (October 29, 1980), p. 9. The 1967 letter by a chief engineer reflects this widespread opinion (quoted in Berliner [1976], pp. 162–63).

transfer of a worker to a lower-level job, with dismissal if he did not accept this demotion, due to the worker's failure to fulfill work norms because of his own fault.[40] Incompetence, as opposed to deliberate disciplinary infractions, seems well protected by Soviet custom. As Soviet lawyers hasten to point out, however, such absolute protection is not provided by law.

Certain groups are outside the protection of either the trade unions or the courts, and can be dismissed by purely managerial decision; these groups include managerial personnel down to foremen level, various senior specialists, teaching, research and creative artists subject to competitive re-evaluation, and research personnel subject to re-certification every three years. For most other groups, there is a similar absence of legal or trade union protection only during a probationary period; this period is limited to one week for manual workers, two weeks for minor white-collar personnel, and one month for most others. Most important, no extension of the probationary period is permitted, even by agreement of both parties.[41]

In fact, one suspects that even the non-protected groups are less subject to downgrading or dismissal than are similar groups in at least some capitalist countries, e.g. in the United States.

As occurs in other countries as well, people whose health permanently prevents them from continuing at their normal work are transferred to lighter work in the same enterprise. (Such transfer, however, is obligatory under Soviet law provided that such jobs exist.)[42] In a 1964 study of engineering enterprises in Novosibirsk, it was found that the lowest labor turnover was in such lighter work; the numbers of manual workers holding these jobs seemed to the researchers to be higher than dictated by production conditions.[43]

So long as they fall within the categories coming under the protection of the law, certain groups are given special protection against obligatory transfer or dismissal: youth under eighteen years, youth assigned to a factory after completing special training, pregnant women and mothers with a child under the age of one year, youth subject to military draft during the current year, and others. The remainder in the legally protected categories are still assured by law that they cannot be forced into accepting downgrading under the threat of dismissal on the basis of insufficient

[40] *Trudovoe pravo* (1972), p. 123.
[41] Nikitinskii and Paniugin (1973), pp. 11–20, 36–38, 61–63.
[42] R. Livshits in *S.T.*, 1971, 3, p. 133. Tsepin (1973), pp. 84–90.
[43] E. G. Antosenkov and T. A. Sil'chenko in *Opyt* (1969), pp. 91–92.

experience, of lack of specialized education, or of temporary health problems.[44]

Redundancy

The category of potential candidates for dismissal that is of greatest interest consists of those holding positions that have been made redundant. To cite an opinion concerning this category that is opposite to my own position, the American economist Berliner writes that substantial numbers of workers are dismissed for redundancy, and he questions whether the restraining influence on such dismissals consists of legal and moral pressures as opposed to the incentives given to managers to hoard labor.[45]

The first step in examination of the issue is to obtain some notion of the dimensions of redundancy. Soviet writers complain of the lack of clarity in the concept and of the multiplicity of definitions used, even in the same enterprise.[46] Since I know of only one Soviet study in which the term was defined,[47] and even here partly by implication, one can use Soviet redundancy statistics only with the greatest hesitancy.

The definition that was used in the above study takes the production shop as the unit of analysis. Work places that were previously occupied by a worker of a given narrow trade, but that have now been eliminated due to the installation of new equipment, a change in the production process, or rationalization are counted as "redundant." The concept is gross; it ignores any offsetting substitute increases in workers with different trades,

[44] Prudinskii (1966), pp. 63–64 and Nikitinskii and Paniugin (1973), pp. 46–48, 68–70.

[45] Berliner (1976), pp. 168–69.

[46] Redundancy may refer to reduction in number of people relative to the existing number employed, relative to the number of work positions in the table of organization, relative to the planned figure, or relative to some normative figure. It may refer to all work positions, whether or not currently occupied, or only to occupied positions. (See I. I. Matrozova, E. I. Bonn and A. N. Vukolova in *Dvizhenie rabochikh kadrov* [1973], pp. 86–87; Kheifets [1974], pp. 45–46, 57–65; V. Iagodkin and I. Maslova in *V.E.*, 1965, 6, pp. 31–2.)

The term *vysvobozhdenie* is also at times used still more broadly to refer to the reduction in the number of people employed over a particular time period compared to what would have been needed if labor productivity had remained unchanged as output grew. The breadth of this last definition, however, usually allows its use to be identified from the statistics given.

[47] This was a study carried out by the Research Institute of the State Committee of Labor of the Soviet Union, and covered thirty-nine enterprises of the automotive, tractor and agricultural equipment industry. Sixty-six production shops with some 30,000 blue-collar workers were studied. The enterprises employed one-third of the labor force of their branches, and were selected on the basis of having had the highest rates of growth of labor productivity, of the capital/labor ratio, and of the consumption of electricity per unit of product. (L. M. Danilov and I. I. Matrozova *et al.* in *Dvizhenie rabochikh kadrov* [1973], pp. 5, 89–90.)

or of the same trade in another shop of the same enterprise. On the other hand, it also ignores the effect of output expansion in the given production shop on the need for workers of a given trade who would otherwise have become redundant. All "redundant" workers either leave the production shop or work within the shop in a different trade.[48] Unfortunately, due to the basis of selection of the shops and enterprises studied, the degree of total redundancy created is of no special interest.

A broader study is that of the State Committee of Labor and the Central Statistical Office of the Soviet Union, covering about 45 per cent of all industrial employees in the Soviet Union. The enterprises and industrial associations studied were chosen on the basis of having introduced by 1980 at least some part of the Shchekinskii method of economizing on labor; thus it seems reasonable to assume that the degree of redundancy in these enterprises was greater than that for industry as a whole. While redundancy is not specifically defined, all "redundant" employees either were shifted to other posts within the enterprise or left the enterprise; thus it would seem that the definition employed was either similar to the one described above or was broader. The study's measure of redundancy appears to be a maximum estimate of the degree of redundancy in Soviet industry under the above definition.

The study showed a redundancy of 6 per cent of all industrial personnel during the five year period of 1976–80. This constitutes about 4.3 per cent of all departures from enterprises during that period and an annual rate of 1.2 per cent of the labor force; those redundant individuals who actually left their enterprise constituted some 2.4 per cent of departures for all reasons.[49] The first set of figures represents an estimate of those who could be legally compelled to change their trade or other conditions of work within the enterprise, as well as those who could be legally compelled to leave the enterprise. Like departures, it includes those who in fact died, retired, left for the military draft or for full-time schooling; those who would have left the enterprise as quits even without redundancy; and those who changed trade (and perhaps also shop) within the enterprise gladly rather than under pressure.

In order best to understand the significance of changing trade, we can turn back to the large study of 1966 that was cited earlier. The meaning of changing a trade for redundant manual workers is shown by the data of Table 3.3 for three principal categories of machinists. If we were to define

---

[48] *Ibid.*, pp. 85–87.
[49] V. Fil'ev in *V.E.*, 1983, 2, p. 59. Total departures are assumed to be 150 per cent of the rate of quits plus disciplinary dismissals for industrial manual workers in 1978.

Table 3.3 *Relocation of redundant manual workers within the enterprise*
(percentages)

Categories of those redundant manual workers who remained in the same enterprise (over half of all redundancies)	Trade at the time of redundancy operator of		
	lathe	grinder	drill
Transferred to other shops at their old trade	12	24	...
Remained as a machine operator but in another machinist trade than the earlier one	45	14	36
Became a set-up man (a more skilled level of machinist)	21	36	} 42
Became an inspector	...	10	
Became a manual worker in some other trade	12	16	
Became a white-collar employee, manager or professional	10	0	...
Total	100	100	100

Source: I. I. Matrozova *et al.* in *Dvizhenie rabochikh kadrov* (1973), pp. 95–97.

trade as a machinist or parts inspector, rather than using the very narrow Soviet definitions, only 22 per cent of the redundant lathe operators who remained in their former plant, and 16 per cent of the grinder operators, changed their trade as a result of redundancy. Taking an unweighted average of the percentages for these two trades, and applying it to the figures of the 1976–80 study, we see that redundancy defined as actual departures plus change of trade within the enterprise constituted only 2.8 per cent (rather than 4.3 per cent as above) of total departures from the enterprises.

Furthermore, when we look at those manual workers who remained in their former enterprise and changed their trade as this term is narrowly defined by the Soviet classification system, 42 per cent of them raised their skill grade as manual workers, 9 per cent became white-collar employees, managers or professionals, and only 11 per cent were reduced in grade as a result of the change of trade.[50] This low proportion of demotions is fully consistent with the fact that only about 25 per cent of these workers changed trade when this term is defined more broadly and meaningfully.

These data as to Soviet redundancies stand in sharp contrast to what is sometimes written in Western literature as to the scope of Soviet redundancy dismissals. Berliner, for example, writes of 32 per cent of the redundant workers in one plant being dismissed, and a higher proportion

[50] Matrozova *et al.* in *Dvizhenie rabochikh kadrov* (1973), p. 96.

in another;[51] but when we turn to his original sources, these constituted all those who left the plant for any reason.

Of the total number of redundant workers in the 1976–80 Soviet study cited above, 45 per cent were transferred to other positions in the same enterprise. Somewhat higher proportions are typically shown in earlier Soviet studies.[52] But there does not seem to be anything particularly striking, for a full employment economy, in such a rate of internal transfer. The only data of which I am aware that come from a developed capitalist country relate to the German Federal Republic during 1972. For a representative national sample of all employees, the employers were questioned as to whether redundancies (economizing of labor) had occurred during the previous year. It was reported that 74 per cent of their redundant personnel had been given other positions within the same enterprise.[53] Thus the very limited comparative statistical evidence available provides no basis for believing that those Soviet workers who in fact become redundant are peculiarly likely to take other jobs in the same plant.

Although, as we saw above, industrial personnel subject to obligatory change of job within the enterprise or to dismissal totalled only 5 per cent of total departures from enterprises during 1976–80, the figures may be considerably higher for special groups. It is striking that, of pension age research personnel in nine Academy of Science institutes in Moscow and Kiev studied during 1975–76, one-third of those who had actually retired gave "reduction in staff" as the reason.[54] This would suggest that pension-age personnel may be peculiarly liable to dismissal.

A second group that may have a high rate of transfer/dismissal for redundancy reasons consists of administrative staff of organizations generally. As in other countries, periodic efforts are made at a central level to reduce such overhead manning. Special privileges have been given to such personnel shifting through transfer or dismissal to production jobs; these privileges seem intended to reduce the case for local resistance that is either

---

[51] Berliner (1976), pp. 158–59. This same confusion of redundancy dismissals with total departures occurs in the article by F. Hajenko in *Bulletin of the Institute for the Study of the USSR* (Munich), XIII, 6 (June 1968), pp. 32–33.

[52] The extreme case is that of the Cheliabinsk sovnarkhoz (an area with several million inhabitants) where, during 1961, 81 per cent of all personnel who were declared redundant remained in the same enterprise (V. Iagodkin and I. Maslova in *V.E.*, 1965, 6, pp. 34–37). In fourteen Shchekinskii-experiment enterprises that were studied for the period up to January 1972, 53 per cent had remained in their enterprise (Ruzavina [1975], p. 72). In three-hundred-twenty-six such enterprises, studied in 1975 over an unspecified period, 75 per cent remained (S. Ivanov in *S.T.*, 1977, 4, pp. 13–14).

[53] Bunz, Jansen and Schacht (1973), pp. 104, 245–46.

[54] M. Ia. Sonin and K. A. Lainer in *S.I.*, 1979, 1, pp. 130–33.

based on, or rationalized by, humanitarian considerations.[55] On the other hand, there is evidence of reclassification of white-collar personnel in enterprises from administrative to non-administrative posts without any change in their function.[56] Thus, as in the case of pensioners, it is not clear whether administrative staff are in fact peculiarly exposed to managerial action on the basis of redundancy.

One problem cited by some Soviet authors in enforcing transfers/dismissals because of redundancy consists of the sharp limits placed upon payments made to workers while undergoing retraining. Within his old enterprise, an employee can be given retraining for up to six months while preserving his previous average earnings.[57] Training elsewhere normally pays only the maintenance costs customarily given young trainees.[58] In the case of coal-miners in central Russia, where redundancy occurred because of pit closings, miners in the late 1960s were given a six month retraining program outside the mines – but at a stipend that was only about 43 per cent of their previous average earnings.[59] This was regarded as a special and peculiarly bountiful arrangement. The Soviet labor expert Manevich reports the view of various enterprise managers that the lack of generous payments to workers who are made redundant is one of the important factors preventing enterprises from declaring such redundancies.[60]

A managerial expert, G. Popov of Moscow University, has suggested a system of guaranteed employment in a public works program and of minimum wage for those dismissed because of redundancy,[61] but I have seen no follow-up on this proposal during the following four years. (It is interesting that Popov was promptly attacked in *Pravda* by a lawyer who insisted that his proposed measure would be a flagrant violation both of Soviet labor legislation and of the Soviet constitution, which the lawyer

---

[55] See *S.T.*, 1970, 5, p. 145; M. Pankin in *S.T.*, 1970, 8, pp. 145–47; M. Pankin in *S.T.*, 1973, 3, p. 136; Baranenkova (1974), pp. 120–21; V. Sozinov in *S.T.*, 1976, 10, p. 94. References are made to central decrees of 1969 and 1970.

[56] Shkurko (1977), pp. 45–47 and D. Nikolaev in *Pravda*, March 29, 1984, p. 2.

[57] It is unclear, however, whether this period of retraining is not restricted to those previously holding administrative staff posts (see Pankin in *S.T.*, 1973, 3, p. 136, and Baranenkova [1974], pp. 120–21, compared with Sozinov in *S.T.*, 1976, 10, p. 93).

[58] Sozinov in *S.T.*, 1976, 10, p. 93.

[59] Maikov and Khaikin in *Sovetskoe profsoiuzy*, 1969, 15, pp. 19–20. Average earnings are assumed to be the average for manual workers in the coal industry of the country as a whole; this latter is calculated by assuming that they grew between 1966 and 1969 by the average percentage for all industrial manual workers (see TsSU, *Trud* [1968], p. 139 and *Narkhoz SSSR v 1970 g.*, p. 519).

[60] Manevich (1980), pp. 87–88 fn.   [61] *Pravda*, December 27, 1980, p. 3.

claimed guaranteed an individual the right to choose his own occupation.)[62]

A second continuing problem hindering the enterprise in declaring redundancies is that it itself is responsible for finding another position for the redundant employee.[63] Since the position need not be in the enterprise itself nor at the old trade, one may wonder why in an overfull-employment economy this requirement should be constantly cited as a major obstacle to the declaring of redundancies.[64] The only explanation would seem to be that the requirement is usually interpreted very narrowly as finding a "comparable" job – and that such comparability refers to trade, work conditions, earnings and location.[65] Given a strict enough interpretation – the extreme would be that provided for involuntary transfers within an enterprise[66] – this burden on the enterprise might be expected to be very frequently prohibitive, even under Soviet employment conditions.

A striking example of the reluctance of enterprises to declare workers

[62] V. Malakhin in *C.D.S.P.*, XXXIII, 5 (March 4, 1981), p. 23. In fact, the constitution does this only "taking account of social need."

[63] The governing legislation appears to be a decree of the People's Commissariat of Labor of the Russian Republic in February 6, 1928; presumably there were similar decrees in other republics. Decrees of the Council of Ministers of the Soviet Union on December 14, 1957, and again on December 20, 1962, transferred this responsibility to administrative levels above that of the enterprise – but the decrees are said to have never gone into force (Baranenkova [1974], pp. 113 and 151). In legal literature of 1967, for example, it is said that the enterprise must find another job in the same locality (*raion*). (See *Kommentarii k zakonodatel'stvu o trude* [Moscow, Iuridicheskaia literatura: 1967), p. 88, as cited in *ibid.*, p. 113.)

This obligation continues to be referred to in later publications (*Trudovye resursy SSSR* [1979], p. 267, and E. Manevich in *V.E.*, 1981, 9, p. 62).

On the other hand, Hauslohner (1984), p. 284, reports that he was told in a 1981 interview with a Soviet labor specialist that until 1970 – with the promulgation of a new Labor Code – enterprises had only a moral rather than a legal obligation to find jobs for redundant employees.

In 1984, the SSSR Supreme Court ruled that the enterprise does not bear a legal responsibility for finding another position for the redundant employee, changing previous legal practice due to the development of a network of labor offices (L. V. Nikitinskii, legal consultant, in *Izvestiia*, June 6, 1985, p. 3). The ruling appears to be by implication only (see *Biulleten' verkhovnogo suda SSSR*, 1984, 3, p. 27, paragraph 12). More significantly, there is no indication as yet that this ruling will have any greater effect than did the 1957 and 1962 decrees of the SSSR Council of Ministers. (I am indebted to Peter Hauslohner for calling this source to my attention.)

[64] Bliakhman *et al.* (1968), p. 10 and *Ref.*, 1981, 11, E57.

[65] E. L. Manevich in *Osnovnye problemy* (1971), p. 20 mentions trade, skill, location, etc. Baranenkova (1974), p. 113 also specifically mentions locality. However, V. Sozinov in *S.T.*, 1976, 10, p. 94 writes of movement to other regions being necessary for miners who wish to maintain their previous high earnings – twice or more that of employees elsewhere – and their special privileges such as that of early pension age. Sozinov's treatment is consistent with my job-rights hypothesis (3.3).

[66] Article 25 of the Russian Republic's Code of Labor Laws.

redundant is the case of the Shchekinskii chemical combine, that had been singled out specifically for a major experiment in rewarding the elimination of unneeded workers. During the first nine months of the experiment, 260 work places were declared redundant. But as of the end of this period, only 38 to 65 per cent of their occupants had in fact left the redundant work places. Both the original source and a Soviet commentator in 1982 find the reason in the fact that the remainder could not be found other jobs.[67] This is despite both the moral pressure that must have existed on the combine's management and trade union to eliminate workers quickly because of their plant being the prime publicity focus of the nationally reported experiment, and the fact that one reason for authorities having chosen this combine for the experiment was its favorable objective position with regard to finding other similar work for unneeded personnel; the latter was due both to the combine's own expansion and to the existence of a nearby recently built chemical fiber plant.[68]

Indeed, writing about Soviet technological change in processes, one Soviet writer comments that it has often been easier for management of enterprises to put personnel "to one side" rather than to retrain them and relocate them.[69]

Even if the enterprise management and trade union are willing to declare employees redundant, higher authorities may reject such dismissals. The émigré economist Katsenelinboigen writes of having visited the city of Gor'kii in 1954–55, when the major automobile plant there had declared redundant some 5,000 of its employees (6 per cent of the total). He reports that, since these personnel refused to move to rural areas where they were needed, there was substantial resulting local unemployment and the enterprise was obliged to rehire them. A central ministry was chastised for having originally authorized these redundancy dismissals.[70]

Indeed, Grigorii Romanov is said to be the only current Politbureau member as of 1984 who had ever given his explicit public support for actual dismissals of redundant workers.[71]

Is the dismissal constraint binding? Quit rates. A relevant issue is that of whether (3.3) has been a constraint really binding on enterprise behavior. The

---

[67] The original source gives a figure of 65 per cent (T. A. Baranenkova in *Osnovnye problemy* [1971], p. 246 fn.), but the later commentator reduces this to 38 per cent (A. M. Dobrusin in *E.K.O.*, 1982, 8, p. 130).
[68] Kheifets (1974), p. 17.   [69] *Ibid.*, p. 45.
[70] A. Katsenelinboigen in *Revue d'études comparatives est-ouest*, 9 (1978), 4, pp. 16–17.
[71] Hauslohner (1984), Chapter 5, fn. 160. The statement refers only to election speeches as published in *Pravda*.

question is most relevant as to redundancy dismissals, for it is these that are most likely to be restrained sufficiently by external conditions binding on enterprises so as to meet fully the desires of the Central authority. Furthermore, it is the hypothesized Central objective of avoiding such dismissals that would have the greatest effect on the institutional design of the economy needed to realize (3.3).

The "rival hypothesis" discussed below offers a general alternative to the hypothesis that (3.3) is not only a constraint but, more important, a binding constraint. At this point, however, a single objection will be considered. This objection is based on the high level of quits in the Soviet economy. With such a quit level, it may be argued, enterprise managers can very quickly run down their labor force in any skills and occupations where this seems desirable without having to engage in dismissals.

One answer to this objection consists of the data of Table 2.1, showing that the Soviet industrial quit rate does not appear particularly high by American standards. In the case of American employers, one would not argue that this rate is sufficient to eliminate employer desire for redundancy dismissals and layoffs. As shown below U.S. layoffs in manufacturing during 1943 and 1944 were very substantially higher than normal Soviet total dismissals despite the fact that the American quit rate in manufacturing ran in these years at an annual rate of 75–76 per cent. (Layoffs are defined as being initiated without prejudice to the worker; they thus constitute a portion of what would be treated as redundancy dismissals in the Soviet Union.)

One would still wish, however, to know something of the structure of the respective quit rates. To the degree that the American quits may be much more highly concentrated than are Soviet among certain categories of workers (e.g. youth), even a very high quit rate might not provide a satisfactory means of reducing overmanning in particular skills and occupations in the United States although it does in the Soviet Union. Unfortunately, we have no relevant data as to the structure of American quits; but we do have Soviet data, and one might suspect from these that Soviet industry does not enjoy an internationally unusual lack of concentration either among youth or among new recruits to individual enterprises.

Broad samples covering a wide range of geographic areas and years between 1963 and 1979 show that the Soviet quit rate for workers thirty to forty-five years of age is about 28 to 45 per cent of that of the twenty to twenty-nine age group, and some 55 to 65 per cent of the average quit rate for all ages. Workers older than forty to forty-five have a quit rate some 40 to 50 per cent of the average for all ages.[72]

The most recent American data as to quits that was available in the late 1970s showed that the relative quit rates for males in their twenties was much the same proportion of the rate for those in their thirties and forties as was the case for both sexes together in the Soviet Union, but that the ratio for those from their mid-forties to retirement age was a great deal lower than was the Soviet proportion.[73] These figures suggest no great difference between the two countries in the concentration of quits among youth vs. the prime age group, but a substantial difference with regard to the older generation in that the older Soviet worker participates more substantially in the quit process than does the older American.[74]

A second structural characteristic of the labor force for which Soviet data are available is that of length of employment within the same enterprise. This is clearly related to age, but is far from being simply a proxy for it; the latter is exemplified by data for the Russian Republic's food industry where only 10 per cent of the female quits in 1978 were of women with three years or more of employment in the enterprise, despite the fact that 59 per cent of all female quits were thirty years or older.[75]

The quit rate in two reported samples for those with six to ten years of employment in the same enterprise has run some 15 to 25 per cent of those with one to two years, and some 15 per cent of those with less than one year's employment.[76] In a sample of the industry of the Central Asian

[72] See, especially, Antosenkov and Kupriianova (1970), pp. 170–71; Chernova (1970), pp. 187–89; *Dvizhenie rabochikh kadrov* (1973), pp. 184–85; *Naselenie i trudovye resursy RSFSR* (1982), p. 13; *Opyt* (1969), p. 115; Vodomerov (1975), p. 72. Some of the above samples hold constant either sex or detailed industrial sub-branch.

[73] Linda Leighton and Jacob Mincer in Freeman and Wise (1982), p. 242. The original American source is the Bureau of Labor Statistics, Special Labor Force Report no. 35, *Job Mobility in 1961*.

A rough comparison of relative quit rates at different ages as between the two countries, with Soviet data being for both sexes combined and the American being only for males, is as follows:

Years of age	Index base	Soviet Union (1963–79)	United States (1961)
30–45	20–29 yrs = 100	28–45	
35–44	20–24 yrs = 100		37
over 40–45	30–45 yrs = 100	71	
45–54	35–44 yrs = 100		58
55–64	35–44 yrs = 100		23

[74] However, the comparison in the text overstates the national difference with regard to the older workers, since the Soviet retirement age is younger than is the American.

[75] *Zaniatost' naseleniia* (1983), p. 155.

[76] Antosenkov and Kupriianova (1970), p. 135; *Formirovanie* (1982), p. 279.

Kirgizian Republic in 1963, this meant that only 27 per cent of all quits had worked in that enterprise for three years or longer. In Novosibirsk samples of the engineering industries and of construction, the comparable figures were 24–26 per cent in 1964 and 35–37 per cent in 1970–71.[77]

These figures show what would be expected: that, while quits are significant for all age groups and for all periods of seniority in the individual enterprise, they are quite concentrated both among the youth and among new recruits to the enterprise regardless of age. To the degree that certain skill/occupation combinations in individual enterprises are manned primarily by workers over thirty years of age and with more than two years of seniority, the enterprise will be totally unable to reduce quickly any redundant manpower through natural wastage.

Legal restrictions on dismissals in general

The trade union local. As is the case with all labor disputes between an individual employee and the management of his enterprise or other employment unit, the last word prior to the matter being taken to court rests with the trade union factory committee of the enterprise. Moreover, the committee's decision regarding any dispute that is of a type eligible to be taken to court (this includes all post-probation dismissals of manual workers and of rank-and-file white-collar employees) cannot be reviewed and overturned by a trade union body above the level of the enterprise.[78] Nor can either the enterprise management nor the state procurator appeal to the courts as illegal the failure of a trade union factory committee to permit a dismissal.[79] Only those categories of dismissals (discussed above) that cannot be appealed to the courts are also immune from the need for prior permission from the factory committee.

It is the freedom of the factory committee from higher trade union bodies that is truly striking in the Soviet context, since it represents a denial of the basic Soviet administrative principle of "democratic centralism" according to which a hierarchically higher body can always overturn the decision of a lower unit. Labor disputes of a litigious nature represent the only area

[77] Chernova (1970), p. 179, and Antosenkov and Kupriianova (1977), p. 211.
[78] McAuley (1969), Chapter 3 and especially pp. 141 and 147. The relevant law dates from 1957–58; McAuley cites legal sources of the 1950s and 1960s for the interpretation that higher trade union authorities have no role at all in the procedure. With specific regard to dismissals, Nikitinskii and Paniugin (1973), p. 38 and Sevost'ianov (1975), p. 36 are legal sources of the 1970s that make the same point.
[79] Nikitinskii and Paniugin (1973), p. 38.

in Soviet society of which I am aware where the principle of centralism has been waived.

A second unusual feature that applies to dismissals alone is that trade union permission to management to dismiss an employee must be taken by the full meeting of the elected local factory committee; the president of the committee is not allowed to give approval on his own, with later ratification of the decision by the committee. Moreover, for permission to be granted, a two-thirds quorum of the committee must be present at the meeting and an absolute majority of those present must vote for dismissal. The factory committee's permission must be obtained prior to the issuance of a dismissal order by the management, and the ground for dismissal stated in the order must be identical with that stated in the permission. All of the above formalities have come up as issues in court appeals by dismissed workers, and violation of any of them have led to reinstatement of the employee by the courts.[80]

It is, of course, difficult to say how much genuine protection is provided to the individual employee by these procedures. Presumably, the situation differs considerably among enterprises. The only real evidence of which I am aware is the study by a British scholar during 1962–63, of the internal records of five Leningrad factories, with a combined employment of 20,000. She estimated that the trade union factory committees agreed to roughly half of the dismissal requests made by management. Moreover, all the dismissal requests seemed to this scholar to be soundly based in Soviet law, so that the employee would have had no chance of reinstatement by the courts if the factory committee had approved.[81] If these factories are at all typical with regard to the trade union role in dismissals, then the legal procedures as to the factory committee's role do offer major protection to the individual.

In any case, and whatever the practical effect may be, Soviet authorities clearly have wished, in the case of dismissals, to give powers that are most unusual – perhaps unique in Soviet society – to local elected representatives. It would seem reasonable to interpet such a desire as part of the protection opted for by higher authorities themselves under hypothesis (3.3).

The Courts. Various surveys have been conducted as to appeals to the courts by dismissed employees. It appears that one-third to two-thirds of the

[80] Nikitinskii and Paniugin (1973), pp. 32–36. B. Ruble in *Comparative Labor Law*, 2, 3 (fall 1977), pp. 182–83 cites a reversal by the Russian Republic's Supreme Court on the basis that different grounds were cited in the permission and in the dismissal order.
[81] McAuley (1969), pp. 73–77, 123, 254–55.

appeals are based on the fact that no permission for the dismissal was given by the trade union factory committee.[82] These appeals are upheld automatically; but, of course, we know nothing as to how many such dismissals are never appealed.

Of all appeals, it would appear that a bit over half are upheld.[83] It would seem that some 40 per cent of these successful appeals are based on all grounds other than the failure of the factory committee to grant permission.[84] If we consider only appeals other than those that should be granted automatically, about 37 per cent are successful.

Thus, although we have no data as to the proportion of dismissals that are appealed to the courts, it would seem from the above figures that the Soviet legal system constitutes a second major barrier to dismissals. With such a high success rate in appeals, it should not surprise us that the overwhelming majority of successful appeals seems to come from people employed in very small enterprises where there is little or no access by management to competent legal advice.[85]

If a court finds that a dismissal was illegal, the individual must be rehired. However, compensation for the illegal dismissal is minimal: it is payment of the difference between his average earnings on the job from which he had been dismissed and his actual earnings during that period, but limited to a time-span of three months.[86] No suit may be filed by the illegally dismissed individual against the person responsible for the dismissal. It is true that the manager who carried out the dismissal may be held responsible to the enterprise itself for these legally required payments, but only where the illegality was clear beforehand such as in the refusal to obey a court order to rehire.[87]

---

[82] McAuley (1969), p. 212 reports on seven such surveys for the early 1960s; six of them reported 65–88 per cent of the appeals being based on the absence of permission. For 1968, a national figure of almost 60 per cent is cited (N. N. Romanov in *Trud*, April 17, 1969, p. 2). In 1975, a national figure of 33 per cent emerges from a sample survey conducted by the Soviet Union's Supreme Court (Nick Lampert in Lane [1986], pp. 262–63).

[83] Half the claims in the early 1960s (McAuley [1969], p. 213); over 50 per cent in 1972 and 1973 (V. Kulikov in *S.T.*, 1974, 7, p. 126); 55 per cent in 1975 (Lampert in Lane [1986], p. 266); half in the Moldavian Republic in 1979 (*C.D.S.P.*, XXXII, 39 [October 29, 1980], p. 258).

[84] Data for 1972 and 1973 (Kulikov, *S.T.*, 1974, 7, p. 126).

[85] Nikitinskii and Paniugin (1973), p. 87. This is based on a survey conducted in Moscow *oblast*.

[86] During 1974, the plaintiff received damages in only one-quarter of the cases of dismissal without the permission of the trade union factory committee (Lampert in Lane [1986], p. 269).

[87] Sevost'ianov (1975), pp. 47–48, and V. Kulikov in *S.T.*, 1974, 7, p. 129. During 1974, managers were personally fined in half of the cases in which their enterprises paid damages for dismissal without trade union permission (Lampert in Lane [1986], p. 269).

Here we have what seems to be the only serious weakness in Soviet protection against dismissals. But this is not a weakness that seems to have been grossly exploited by enterprise managements.

THE RIVAL HYPOTHESIS

In its simplest form, the hypothesis that is alternative to the JROE set explains the relative security from dismissal of the Soviet worker by the conditions of the Soviet labor market. Given that the market is one of overfull employment, any employer is extremely reluctant to dismiss workers because of the difficulty of finding a replacement. If the worker is not currently needed, he is still kept on the payroll (labor hoarding) because of the possibility of his being needed in the future. This labor policy by the individual employer is primarily a response to the high cost (and uncertainty) of engaging a new worker from outside the enterprise, although it is also a response to the linkage of salaries of managers to the number of personnel in their units. The Soviet worker has the same employment security, and essentially for the same reason, as does the worker in a liberal capitalist economy in periods of high boom; job rights are quite unnecessary as an explanation.[88]

This hypothesis places all the stress upon the existence of overfull employment; job security is no more than a natural consequence of this labor market condition. In contrast, the JROE hypothesis-set takes job security as the phenomenon of prime interest, considering this as what sets the Soviet economy apart from capitalist economies in prosperous times.

The labor market disequilibrium hypothesis would not be very satisfactory if left in the above primitive form in which permanent overfull employment is treated as exogenous. Instead, it is commonly endogenized along the lines established in Kornai (1980). There exists an insatiable investment drive in the economy, existing either at the *micro level of the enterprise* (Kornai's emphasis) or at the level of the central planners or both. This drive is treated as exogenous. It leads to an insatiable demand for production inputs, of which labor is one. At the micro level, there is an absence of the "hard constraint" upon such demand by the enterprise that would arise in a capitalist economy from the fear of illiquidity and bankruptcy. This absence of a hard financial constraint is one of the basic

There is also a provision for criminal penalties in case of illegal dismissal for "personal motives," but a British scholar thinks that this provision has little practical import (*ibid.*, p. 261).

[88] See Berliner (1976), pp. 168–69, and Philip Hanson in Lane (1986), pp. 85–86.

hallmarks of the system; it is an observed phenomenon and is left exogenous to the theory. Given the unconstrained insatiable labor demand of enterprises, overfull employment is the inevitable consequence.

As was discussed at the end of Chapter 2, this approach has the problem that Kornai also views the enterprise as subject to the hard constraint of the wage fund in the shortrun. What Kornai stresses is that the enterprise's requests to the Center with regard to future years are unconstrained. Since it is assumed that the Center will grant the requests made (although, perhaps, in reduced form and with time lags), the absence of constraints that are internalized to the enterprise and restrict the making of such requests is the basis for the view that the longrun effective demand for labor is insatiable. In fact, however, it is only the yielding by the Center to requests that causes labor demand for future periods to be unconstrained.

This brings us full circle to the question of why the Center should yield to the demand of enterprises for larger employment in future years. Given that the Center's concern is macroeconomic, its interest in expanding gross national product and investment is no explanation. Financing of unrealizable demand for labor, or of new capacity when the total resulting capacity has manpower requirements exceeding the labor supply available nationally, is unlikely to have positive macroeconomic effects. Presumably, a successful answer to this question posed by the labor market hypothesis is most likely to be obtained by pursuing the institutional lines suggested in connection with sequential and multi-level decision making above the enterprise level.[89] At present, however, a convincing institutional treatment has not, to my knowledge, been provided.

Even more of a problem is that of answering how it is possible for the Center to be unrealistic in its manpower planning (granting enterprise requests, the sum of which are unrealizable), while at the same time it is realistic in its planning of nominal earnings per employee. This is particularly a puzzle since, as we saw in Chapter 2, the operational form of permitting more manpower to be engaged is that of increasing the enterprise's wage fund, and this increased wage fund can be used by the enterprise to raise average nominal earnings when it is not needed to employ the planned growth of manpower. Yet the Soviet record of wage inflation has been very good, at least until the late 1970s.

Of course, what matters for wage inflation is the macro planning by the

[89] See D. M. Nuti in Lane (1986), pp. 115–19. Michael Marrese earlier pioneered along these lines in a working paper. One of the more interesting efforts to work out this approach as applied to fixed investment is by T. Bauer in "Investment cycles in planned economies," *Acta Oeconomica*, 21, 3 (1978), pp. 243–60.

Center of per employee earnings as embodied in the total national wage fund. This could well be higher than the implicit average embodied in the sum of the enterprise and ministry plans of manpower and wage funds, since the Center's expected amount of total employment could be below the summation of employment incorporated in the approved micro-level plans.[90] But if the Center is institutionally capable of having a "hidden" over-all plan for average earnings that is different from what is implied by the total of the unit plans, why should it not be similarly capable of having such a hidden plan for manpower? Why is it incapable of restraining aggregate enterprise labor demand to a realizable level, if only by holding down job-creating types of investments? In short, why should it allow the observed overfull employment to occur?

These problems in explaining both why and how the Center acts as hypothesized do not arise in the JROE hypothesis-set. There, the Center's desire for overfull employment is assumed, and is taken as exogenous. Given this desire, the Center is treated as being successful in achieving the labor employment effects that it desires. This is consistent with the Center's apparent success in achieving its objectives with regard to average nominal earnings per employee.[91]

Modification of the rival hypothesis

The hypothesis of labor market disequilibrium might be modified so as to eliminate the need for miscalculation by the Center in its manpower planning. Instead, we might place the emphasis upon the desire and ability of enterprise management to thwart the intentions of the Center, with managers achieving a higher level of employment and a compensatingly lower average level of manual-worker earnings in the enterprise than was intended by the Center. Here, the emphasis would be upon the unavailability to the Center of instruments sufficient to carry out its policy. I myself find this form of the hypothesis more attractive than the one presented above.

[90] Indeed, we are authoritatively told that this occurred in 1976, and that in "recent years" (as of early 1978) the planned national wage funds were based on manpower estimates by the State Planning Commission of the Soviet Union that were one and one-half to two million persons lower than the sum of the enterprise plans (L. A. Kostin, A. V. Bakhurin, and E. P. Voronin and V. G. Kostakov in *Trudovye resursy SSSR* [1979], pp. 21–22, 39, and 265). Similar differences between estimates by Gosplan SSSR and enterprise plans for 1971 and 1975 are shown in E. Voronin in *S.T.*, 1977, 1, p. 30.

[91] The JROE hypothesis-set must explain why individual enterprises use their allotted wage funds to maintain overfull employment, rather than maximizing current earnings per employee by restraining new hirings. This task will be postponed to Chapter 8.

Managers of enterprises attempt to maximize a combination of the likelihood of plan fulfillment over the long-term and of the discounted value of the wage fund plus material-stimulation fund per standardized member of the labor force. These two arguments of the managers' objective function are non-competitive.   (3.4a)

The wage fund available in (t) is constrained by the planned wage fund of (t) and by the ratio (achieved output/planned output) during (t).
                                                                           (3.4b)

In order to retain manual workers with enterprise-specific skills, the enterprise must pay higher earnings than would be necessary to recruit workers from outside. Thus, by accepting a higher quit rate of manual workers and a lower level of enterprise-specific skills than had been assumed by the Center, management can use a given size wage fund in (t) to employ a larger labor force of manual workers.   (3.4c)

At the achievable rate of hiring of manual workers, there exists the inequality

$$\frac{\partial o_t/\partial l_{u,t} + \partial \sum_{i=1}^{\infty} o_{t+i}(1+r)^{-i}/\partial I_{u,t}}{\partial o_t/\partial l_{ss,t}} > \frac{\partial W_t/\partial l_{u,t}}{\partial W_t/\partial l_{ss,t}}$$

                                                                           (3.4d)

where $\partial \sum_{i=1}^{\infty} o_{t+i}(1+r)^{-i}/\partial l_{u,t} =$

$$\left[\frac{W_{ss,t}/l_{ss,t}}{W_{u,t}/l_{ut}} - 1 \right] \left[\frac{\partial \sum_{i=1}^{\infty} WF_{t+i}(1-k)^i}{\partial l_{(u+ss),t}} \right] \left[\sum_{i=1}^{\infty} \frac{\partial o_{t+i}(1+r)^{-i}}{\partial WF_{t+i}} \right]$$

and o = the managers' objective function

W = total wages paid to manual workers

l_u = number of manual workers without enterprise-specific skills

l_{ss} = number of manual workers with enterprise-specific skills

W_u = total wages paid to manual workers without enterprise-specific skills

WF = planned wage fund of manual workers

k = rate of decay of effect of l_t on WF_{t+i}

r = managers' subjective rate of time discount

In hypothesis (3.4), (a) represents a combination of career and bonus effects on managerial income. The material-stimulation fund makes its primary contribution to per capita white-collar earnings rather than to manual-worker earnings; thus it is ignored in (d); (b) and (c) are results from Chapter 2.

The critical part of the hypothesis is (3.4d). It postulates that, as a border condition within the domain of achievable inflow of new workers into the enterprise, and with the enterprise constrained by its current wage fund for manual workers, the managers' objective function would always be increased by substituting new hires for existing manual workers – thus increasing the total number of workers at the expense of their skill level. This effect is due to a combination of the postulated ratio of marginal productivity to wages for the two types of workers, and of the positive effect of the total number of workers in period (t) on the planned wage fund for $(t+i)$. The latter results from the fact that the Center plans from the "achieved level" (of manpower in this case) and that it does not treat enterprise-specific skills as a characteristic of the workforce that requires specific attention in planning the wage fund. The result is that the enterprise is always ready to recruit more labor than it can.

A problem posed by (3.4d) is that of why we do not find an equilibrium attained at least in industry by means of recruitment of unskilled personnel from other urban sectors of the economy where earnings are lower. (The limitations on recruitment of rural labor can be explained by the need to provide housing.) A defender of the hypothesis would have to point to the low quality of most of this labor (in terms both of low education and relatively high age), and thus to the unattractiveness to industrial enterprises of employing such workers to fill the jobs of machine operators, an occupational category where labor scarcity is particularly acute.

Confrontation of the rival hypothesis with labor market observations

In addition to the absence of indication that Soviet frictional unemployment is peculiarly low by the standards of post-war Western Europe prior to the first oil crisis, one may point to the following observations:

Experience of other socialist countries. As was pointed out in the Introduction, an explanation of labor market phenomena in the Soviet Union should ideally be applicable to other socialist countries where the same characteristics are observed. China and Yugoslavia, both countries in which one finds job rights but not overfull employment, are the appropriate test cases in this regard.

The JROE hypothesis can explain the maintenance of job rights in these two countries. In contrast, neither the overheating hypothesis, nor its modification in terms of hiring problems within a fixed wage fund, apply.

Mix of hirings. While (3.4d) predicts that the enterprise is always desirous of hiring more labor than is available to it, the observation made in the mid-1970s by one of the leading Soviet labor economists suggests that this is, at best, a gross exaggeration. Of the personnel voluntarily coming in search of employment to the municipal employment offices, and sent by them to would-be employers who had indicated job openings, about one third are *rejected by the employers* (enterprises).[92] This high proportion of rejects is not what one would expect in a labor market so overheated that enterprises accept any warm body.

Dismissals. As was observed above, the hypothesis of labor market disequilibrium finds it unnecessary to offer any special explanation of the low rate of dismissals in the Soviet Union. This low rate is regarded simply as a by-product of overfull employment. International comparison would seem to be called for at this point.

For Soviet manual workers in industry, we have seen that disciplinary dismissals constitute annually some 1 to 2 per cent of the labor force, redundancy dismissals from the enterprise constituted 0.67 per cent during 1976–80 in a group of enterprises where it might be expected to have been higher than average, while dismissals for poor job performance were probably negligible. Since the figure of redundancy dismissals includes individuals who in fact quit, retired, were drafted into the military forces, etc., we would seem safe in considering total actual dismissals as falling within an upper limit of 2 to 2.5 per cent annually of the Soviet industrial labor force.

For comparison, let us look at dismissals in American manufacturing during the five years of 1930–74 when they were at their lowest as a proportion of the labor force. For comparison with the Soviet Union, we would seem entitled to include all "layoffs" – defined in the American statistics as suspensions without pay that last or are expected to last more than seven consecutive calendar days and are initiated by the employer without prejudice to the worker. All other dismissals are hidden in the

---

92 Maslova (1976), p. 191. The one-third reject figure has the individual job referral as its unit.

category of "other separations," which is the residue from total separations after deduction of quits and layoffs. Not surprisingly, four of the five years when such figures were lowest fell during the Second World War. One would seem entitled to treat these years as those of overfull employment.

Placing the American Bureau of Labor Statistics data on an annual basis,[93] these categories were the following proportions of the manual labor force in manufacturing:

	1941	1942	1943	1944	1973
layoffs	19.2	15.6	8.4	8.4	10.8
other separations	8.4	22.8	19.2	14.4	12.0

No matter how low a proportion of the "other separations" category should be considered as constituting dismissals, we would seem to be dealing with total-dismissal figures that in the lowest years were more than five times as high as the Soviet figures.

It is true that Soviet establishments are on average much larger as measured in workforce than are American, and thus that there are greater possibilities for transfers of individuals within Soviet than within American establishments. However, it must be remembered that obligatory permanent transfers in the Soviet Union are legally constrained equally with dismissals. Although we have no data as to the degree of constraint in practice, there seems no reason to believe that it departs from the legal situation. In order to explain by relative size of plant the difference in dismissal rates between the Soviet Union and the United States in years of peak overfull employment, we would have to depend upon Soviet temporary transfers alone. Such transfers, which are also legally constrained, appear to the writer to be unable to bear the weight of explaining a five to one difference.

Quits. An approach that explains dismissals by the degree of employment existing in a country might reasonably be expected to explain worker quits in the same fashion. Indeed, as is not surprising, quits in American industry are much higher in boom than in recession years. Following this approach, we would expect the average Soviet quit rate to be considerably higher than the average in capitalist economies.[94] Table 2.1 permits comparison of the Soviet quit rate with that in the United States and in

[93] U.S., B.L.S. *Employment and Earnings, 1909–75.*

[94] It is true that such an expectation would be modified by the barriers to intercity mobility stemming from shortages of housing and from restrictions on entry to various larger cities. But the force of these considerations should not, in my view, destroy the above expectation.

Australia; the Soviet quit rate is not particularly high by that comparison. Data as to total separations during prosperous years in the United Kingdom and in the German Federal Republic also do not suggest especially high Soviet quit rates.[95]

Absenteeism. Just as quits might be expected to be peculiarly high in an overheated economy, so too might absenteeism. However, as will be seen in Chapter 8, the Soviet rate of industrial full-day absenteeism seems to be in line with data from Western countries when one takes account of the degree to which such absenteeism is paid by the employer. (Absenteeism is here defined as constituting all absences from the job other than paid vacations and recognized holidays.)

Investment by the center in human capital. Hypothesis (3.4d) suggests (although it does not assert) that the marginal productivity relative to earnings of workers with enterprise-specific skills is not high compared to the same ratio for those newly hired into the enterprises. If this should hold, we might think of extending this assumption to other dimensions of worker skills.

Indeed, Soviet data suggest some confirmation. Sociological studies are said to show that only half as many manual workers are occupied in work of high skill as have the appropriate training. Most junior colleges are described as, in fact, being primarily trainers of manual workers, despite the fact that such preparation is not intended for them at all.[96]

The question then arises: Why do Soviet planners spend large sums providing vocational education that exceeds the demand for its graduates by the Soviet economy as it is currently constituted? Here would seem to be a misinvestment that cries for explanation.

The hypothesis of labor market disequilibrium provides no explanation; these facts are outside of its domain. As we shall see in Chapter 7, the JROE hypothesis has implications that include such educational "over-investment."

Quantity of hirings. The planned wage funds of individual enterprises must, from time to time, suffer decline as a result of shocks that lead to reduced

---

[95] Other separations data (for Canada, France, Sweden, Italy, Japan, and Great Britain) are provided in Roger T. Kaufman, "An international comparison of unemployment rates," Ph.D. dissertation (M.I.T., 1978), pp. 49–52 as quoted in Hauslohner (1984), Table 8.2. These data, covering the years 1953–1975, also suggest nothing peculiar about the Soviet Union.

[96] F. Filippov in *Sovetskaia Rossiia*, January 22, 1984, p. 1.

production plans. These enterprises cannot respond through dismissals, but they can engage in fairly rapid labor force attrition by not replacing workers who have quit. If local overfull employment is not to be jeopardized, other enterprises in the locality must respond by increasing their own labor force. Similarly, enterprises engage in hirings in order to maintain what are labor "surpluses" when judged from their effect on labor productivity, but which are necessary to attain plan fulfillment in the face of stochastic disturbances in supply and in production targets.

Such hiring, however, must reduce the average wage fund per employee (for a homogeneous labor force) in these enterprises due to the effect on labor productivity of diminishing returns with constancy of other factors. The question then arises: Why do we not see resistance on the part of the mass of the labor force in these enterprises to such hirings?

As in the case of investment in human capital, the hypothesis of labor market disequilibrium offers no explanation. The JROE hypothesis (see Chapter 8) does provide one.

Conclusion

Although comparative international data of dismissals and quits have indicated difficulties in reconciling the labor market disequilibrium hypothesis with observed labor market facts, this case cannot be pushed too far. International data as to dismissals and quits are too scanty and of too poor a quality to allow us to draw strong conclusions. Furthermore, no effort has been made to attempt to consider the effects of other factors (e.g. age of the labor force – particularly important, as we would expect juveniles in any country to have especially high rates) on these international comparisons.

Thus, while I would suggest that the weight of the empirical evidence is disfavorable to the labor market disequilibrium hypothesis, this evidence is certainly not strong enough to lead us to reject it. In order to test the two hypotheses against one another, one must take a different route as indicated in the Introduction. The treatments above of investment in human capital and of the quantity of hirings are examples of the path to be followed: that of examining the breadth of domain of the two hypotheses.

Part 2

4

Maximization model for testing the JROE hypothesis-set

This chapter develops a model that will be used throughout the remainder of the book as the basis for testing the JROE hypotheses. As was described in the Introduction, the model has two components. Model A consists of an objective function and a set of constraints that together guide the behavior of the Center both in institution creation and in policy choices. However, the JROE hypotheses are not included in Model A's objective function. Model B has the same objective function and constraints as does Model A, but in addition it adds the JROE hypotheses as lexicographically preferred arguments into the Center's objective function. Our concern is with seeing which stylized facts of the Soviet economy are explained by maximization behavior on the part of the Center under Model B, but not under Model A.[1]

Both Models A and B are treated heuristically rather than being given the string of strong assumptions that would be needed in order to solve mathematically problems of maximization under constraints. Thus mathematical language is in this chapter always used heuristically for descriptive purposes, rather than being intended as a formal treatment for purposes of proof. Since even Model A is extremely broad in its coverage, it seems to me that rigor would add nothing to the likelihood of convincing the reader of my case; the variety and breadth of special assumptions required would leave the reader in as much doubt as does a heuristic method. Given this choice of approach, it is unnecessary to build uncertainty models; for the sake of simplicity, it will usually be assumed that results from the Center's choice of behavior are non-stochastic – aside from those stated in (3.1) ... (3.3) and the use by the Center of Bayesian priors. However, no assumption is made as to full information.

---

[1] A different form of such modelling, using a set-theory approach, was presented by Granick in Zimbalist (1984).

EXTENSIONS OF THE NEOCLASSICAL APPROACH

The approach taken is neoclassical, in the sense that all economic actors are decision makers who maximize objective functions under constraints. Furthermore, no decision makers below the level of the Center are altruistic: i.e. they maximize their own utility functions, and these do not contain as arguments the utility of other actors. The Center's objective function can be interpreted either in the same fashion or in terms of the Center's altruism; the choice between these interpretations has no significance for the results obtained.

The principal extension of the usual neoclassical approach is with regard both to the decisions of the Center as to normal policy issues (e.g. what proportion of national income should be devoted to investment) and as to the creation of institutions. The most fundamental maintained hypothesis in this chapter consists of the following twin propositions:

All Central decisions represent maximization under constraints of a single objective function.   (4.1a)

Economic institutions are created, or at least preserved, by decisions of the Center.   (4.1b)

Thus there are no coalitions involved in the generation of decisions by the Center. Furthermore, all institutions that have existed for a considerable time period are assumed to be appropriate to the Center's maximization process; inconsistencies that are found compel re-evaluation of the formulation of the Center's objective function, of the constraints, or of both.

The concept of a single objective function for the Center is old fashioned in terms of the history of political science writing about the Soviet Union. It is in the spirit of the totalitarian model of Soviet society, rather than reflecting the concept of pluralistic elites.[2] Its great virtue comes from the power of simplification. It allows us, using a mode of analysis analogous to revealed preference, to treat the question of whether a particular Central action is consistent with a hypothesized objective function, or whether instead a revised hypothesis as to the objective function is required. If instead we were to treat Central decisions as generated by changing

---

[2] See Hough (1977), chapters 4, 8, and 10 for a powerful argument in favor of such pluralism. On the other hand, Hough (1969) undercut much of Western thinking as to the pervasiveness and strength of institutional vested interests in the Soviet Union, specifically as to regional Communist Party institutions compared to state-administered industrial organizations. The notion commonly cited in the West of Brezhnev having acted as a mediator among opposing groups, and for this reason stalemating the Politbureau against any bold decisions, also reflects the concept of pluralistic elites.

coalitions, we would, so far as I can see, be unable to deal with this question.

Fortunately, proposition (4.1a) is not only essential for my purposes, but can also be defended as fairly realistic within the context that I shall use it. First, the Soviet elite at its very highest levels appears to be much more unified, and less pluralistic in terms of special interests, than are counter-part elites in developed democratic capitalist countries where personal backgrounds, ideologies, and personal vested interests are more variegated.[3] Second, to the degree that the political elite is free from the need to form changing electoral majorities, it is relieved of much of the pressure to form coalitions that would exist if political decision makers were chosen by a wider strata of the population.

Third, the elements of the Center's objective function that are needed for purposes of my modelling are those that are likely to be least controversial among Soviet elite groups. (The same applies to those of the constraints affecting the Center that are ideologically determined, and so could alternatively be treated as lexicographically preferred arguments in the objective function.) Differences of opinion on such important matters as the proportion of growth of national income to devote to consumption, the proper degree of income egalitarianism, and the appropriate role of nationality policy in determing the location of investments are irrelevant. Naturally, the less sensitive the model is to such important potential differences in the Center's objective function, the less objectionable is the assumption of a single objective function common to all groups in the Center.[4]

One might suspect that a trade-off would be needed between the objective of "extensive" growth – defined as the rapid growth rate of inputs in general – and that of "intensive" growth, where the latter is defined as achieving the maximum ratio of outputs to inputs consistent with the given level (but not change in level) and composition of inputs. Such a trade-off would exist if the economic mechanisms required for efficient use of inputs are inconsistent with those required for the rapid growth of such inputs. In this treatment, "extensive growth" implies a low level of X-efficiency.[5]

---

[3] See Hauslohner (1984), p. 58 for the view that it is not particularly controversial among Western scholars that the Soviet elite is characterized by a high degree of consensus when judged by the standard of elites internationally.

[4] The irrelevance of such potential arguments in the objective function follows from the nature of the stylized facts that we will be able to explain by Model B but not by Model A. As we shall see in later chapters, this distinction in the explanatory ability of the two models is independent of whether such potential arguments are included in the Center's objective function in both models.

[5] The terms "intensive" and "extensive" growth are usually used very loosely, and my definitions of these terms may well differ from what is meant by some users. An alternate

In our period, however, extensive growth cannot refer to the mustering of labor resources because of the already achieved high participation rate in the labor force. Instead, it must be limited to the pursuit of a high rate of net capital investment.

The pursuit of a high rate of capital investment may well be promoted through "priority" methods of plan enforcement by the Center that are inimical to efficiency since they lead to uneven degrees of plan fulfillment for different sectors. Priority sectors receive their full planned allotments of materials inputs, while shortfalls are concentrated upon non-priority sectors. If our model were intended to deal with the move away from priority towards "balanced" methods of plan enforcement, we might be compelled into making such further specification of the Center's objective function. For our purposes, however, this represents a degree of detail in planning and administration with which we need not be concerned.

Proposition (4.1b) finds its justification in the planned (or administered, if one prefers) nature of the Soviet economy. Planners concerned with the effective achievement of their goals will presumably attempt to design institutions that are appropriate for this. The incessant Soviet tinkering with at least minor aspects of institutions, and of regulations and incentives for coordinating their activities, suggests a conscious and active policy in this regard.

Proposition (4.1b) also finds support in the fact that the Soviet leadership – like that of modern societies in general – is highly rational in Max Weber's sense of the word, not being unduly restricted by a felt-need to follow time-hallowed or family-promoting ways. Equally important, it is a leadership that follows traditional Marxism in its evaluation of economic progress; it has never rejected the view that any socioeconomic system shows its progressivity in its given historical context by the rapidity of its economic development, since a progressive system is one that has removed the weights on the economy that would otherwise hamper its technological progress. The international ideological struggle thus finds its reflection in the Center's urge for rapid economic growth.

Another maintained hypothesis that I shall require is one that will allow me to follow an economic as opposed to a political-science approach.

Relevant Central decisions in the period under study, including those as to the creation/preservation of institutions, are not substantially influenced by considerations of power-preservation for the decision makers.

$$(4.2)$$

definition of intensive growth refers to a high rate of growth of factor productivity, and ignores the issue of X-efficiency. In any case, it is the potential trade-off rather than the use of terms that is relevant here.

The key term in (4.2) is "relevant decisions."

Specifically, I wish to be able to discuss the fact that only a very minor role is provided for markets and money in the Soviet economy, with the very major exceptions of the labor market and of the market for final consumer goods, without having to deal with the following proposed explanation. Namely, that the current non-market system preserves a role for the lower and medium-level Party functionaries who would find their power evaporating in a society whose economy was not physically planned. This explanation continues with the argument that, for this reason, these Party functionaries would force from power Central decision makers who attempted to change the economy substantially away from physical planning.

I find both the Yugoslav and Hungarian experiences difficult to reconcile with the above hypothesis. Both countries have now had experience over a considerable time in operating with relatively little central physical planning; but I see no basis for believing – and I am not familiar with any arguments to this effect, although they may well exist – that the Communist Party functionaries at regional and lower levels in these countries have less power today than they did prior to the expansion of the role of markets. However, this is a large subject and it seems best to deal with it as an assumption of the model.[6]

THE OBJECTIVE FUNCTION AND CONSTRAINTS IN MODEL A

Model A excludes the JROE hypotheses, both as lexicographic arguments in the Center's objective function and as constraints within whose bounds the Center makes decisions. As such, the model represents my effort to depict heuristically the remainder of the relevant goals and pressures that jointly determine Soviet Central decisions.

The objective function

The objective function will be kept as simple as possible, consistent with the modelling objective of showing that there are stylized facts compatible with maximizing behavior under Model B but not under A. At this point, I shall simply assert the irrelevance to this objective of the inclusion of other likely candidates as arguments in the function. As we come to individual

---

[6] Hauslohner (1984), pp. 23–24 presents an interesting argument for why regional Party functionaries should not be treated as having homogeneous interests in this respect, and for why many might well have no such vested interest as called for in the hypothesis. As Hauslohner points out, no serious empirical data are available for the Soviet Union that bear on the hypothesis.

stylized facts in Chapter 5, the issue of such irrelevance will be examined in a fashion that is readily expandable to the stylized facts of the later chapters.

Thus we assume that

> The Center's objective function consists of the growth of the Soviet Union's per capita final product (consumption plus military/economic power) over a long period. This growth is discounted by the Center's rate of time preference. The relevant concept of final product is one in which individual product groups, aggregated to a level at least as high as that used in Soviet annual physical planning, are weighted by their shadow prices equal to their marginal contributions to the Center's objective function. (4.3)

It is assumed in (4.3) that investment does not enter directly into the Center's objective function. Since investment differs from usual intermediate products only with regard to the time dimension, keeping investment out of the objective function amounts to no more than making the assumption that the Center is rational. During a particular short period, of course, the Center may quite reasonably set a high value on the growth of investment as a proxy for future growth in final product.

The Center's rate of time preference is also left unstated. Given the method of weighting employed in (4.3), the significance of time preference lies in the fact that it restricts the Center in its choice of the "turnpike" approach (of emphasizing investment, up to a point set by technical considerations of complementarity, at the expense of current final product) to reaching the product mix ultimately desired.[7]

The advantage of this choice of function – provided, of course, that it turns out to be sufficiently complete for my purposes – is that it incorporates all trade-offs and weighting among desiderata.

In this treatment, it is assumed that the welfare of final consumers is embodied as an argument in the Center's objective function, and thus that individuals' utility functions affect not only the pricing system used in weighting the different components of GNP but also the Center's rate of time preference. An alternative procedure would be to eliminate the welfare resulting from final consumption from the Center's objective

---

[7] I am here assuming the existence of a turnpike. The rate of time preference used in the objective function may differ from one period to another, and this may so restrict the acceptable growth path that no turnpike exists.

If for the above reason no turnpike exists, my emphasis upon the importance of the rate(s) of time preferences chosen is only further strengthened. Reference to the turnpike is heuristic.

function, and instead to introduce it as a factor in the country's production function.[8] For our purposes, the two treatments are equivalent, and the present one is chosen for reasons of convenience.

The constraints

No mention will be made of the physical constraints that are involved in such a problem of maximization under constraints. These are obvious enough.

I shall also not specify other constraints that may be thought of as psychological and sociological. Examples are the following: The fact that economic actors operating below the level of the Center are thought of as responding to plans and other orders of the Center, as well as to requests for information, in terms of maximization of their own private utility, rather than simply by execution as would be the case in a Weberian model of bureaucracy. The fact that there exist limits on the amount of information that the Center can process. The presence of problems of operating large organizations of the sort epitomized in the "span of control" literature. The quantitative dimensions of marginal rates of preference between leisure and money income that exist among different segments of the population. The historical experience of the Soviet labor force that leads to particular reactions to words or actions by the Center which may be different from the reactions to be expected from a population with a different history.

The amalgam of the above physical, psychological and sociological constraints constitute a set that is certainly highly constraining on the Center's decisions. My failure to specify them would be inexcusable in a rigorous model. In this heuristic model, however, such specification would only divert attention from matters of interest. Instead, I shall concentrate on a very limited number of constraints affecting the rules and institutions of economic coordination and incentives. These constraints could be categorized as falling within two groupings: those determined by ideology and those determined by Bayesian priors.

---

[8] The treatment in Hauslohner (1984), Chapter 7 of the Ufa-Kaluga experiment (compelling all hires in these two cities to be carried out through the local labor exchanges) is particularly revealing in this regard. See especially pp. 602–05 and 630–33.

See also W. Schrettl in *Verein* (1984), pp. 158–59 for a presentation of the second procedure, with an argument that it is more faithful to Soviet reality. Schrettl treats output as a function of capital and of labor effort, while labor effort is a function of the difference between the consumer goods supplied and the aspiration level of the labor force for consumption goods.

Two preliminary remarks are needed here. First, it is difficult to see how ideology can be completely eliminated as a constraint, particularly in view of the way that the Center's objective function was defined. Without the use of ideology as a constraint in the model, we would – for example – have to explain the Soviet retention of public ownership of most means of production purely on the basis of a belief that it furthers the rate of growth of GNP subject to the other governing constraints. While one might try to make such a case, such an effort would take us far afield.

On the other hand, once we admit ideology as a constraint, we have a *deus ex machina* which can be used to explain almost any behavior. Moreover, Soviet leaders have historically shown a willingness to throw overboard at least minor ideological prejudices when these have been seen as obstacles to Central goals that were considered important.

It seems to me that we should adopt the position of a Chinese commentator in explaining the anti-ideological aphorism of Deng Xiaoping that a cat of any color is good if it catches mice. The commentator pointed out that it still did matter, however, that the mechanism used for catching mice be a cat. "For us, a cat means socialism," he said.[9] My interpretation of this position for our purposes is that some concepts of socialism should be taken as ideological constraints, but that these should be developed as little as possible and postulated as explanatory variables only where unavoidable.

The second remark concerns the use I shall make of Bayesian priors as constraints. In a world in which it is difficult to evaluate the true effects of alternative policies, decisions makers are bound in many areas to operate on the basis of their subjective priors as to the results of policies. While indeed these priors should be altered as evidence comes in regarding actual effects, such evidence may be so weak and subject to such different interpretations that the Bayesian prior remains relatively unchanged over a long period even when in reality it is in substantial conflict with the facts. There is no reason to expect that Bayesian priors will be the same in different cultures, and still less that the priors will constitute rectangular distributions, assigning equal probability to all possible outcomes of a given decision. An example of what I interpret as the lasting nature of such priors is the different treatment of natural monopolies (nationalization vs. regulation) on the European Continent and in the United States.

One might, of course, subsume many particular Bayesian priors under

---

[9] The commentator was Professor Su Shaozhi, director of the Institute of Marxism-Leninism and Mao Zedong Thought (C. S. Wren, New York Times Service, in *International Herald Tribune*, December 29–30, 1984, p. 1).

the rubric of "ideology;" indeed, I believe that one could reasonably interpret a good part of ideology as consisting of a series of Bayesian priors. But there is little point in such treatment for our purposes.

I recognize that the concept of Bayesian prior is almost as subject to abuse as that of ideology. But here, fortunately, we do have a control; we can inquire as to how good is the actual evidence on the relevant subject, since good evidence would have caused virtually any true prior to evolve substantially over the course of Soviet history toward a true model. It is this feature of Bayesian priors that represents a link between my use of such priors and analysis on the basis of rational expectations. The Bayesian priors that I shall use as constraints can be interpreted as informing Soviet Central decision making within a rational expectations framework under condition of poor information that do not improve markedly over time.

Constraints affecting economic coordination. The first constraint reflects traditional socialist, as opposed either to individualistic Lockean or to syndicalist, ideology.

Means of production are to be "owned" by the national government. Ownership refers both to control over usage of the property, and to receipt of the income created by it. (4.4a)

Quasi-rents may be enjoyed by the contemporary employees of an enterprise operating a bundle of such means of production. But such quasi-rents must be quite short-term. (4.4b)

The only major exception to (4.4a) consists of the private plots of agricultural employees; even here, significant restraints are imposed on the enjoyment of private property. It seems generally accepted, at least by Western scholars, that the collective farms and state farms have both evolved so that there is now little difference between the two forms of property with regard to national vs. collective (syndicalist) "ownership."[10]

Constraint (4.4b) prohibits the emergence of a system like the Yugoslav, in which the personnel of different enterprises – although with identical skills, and in the same branch and locality – can earn very different incomes over a long time period. The success of a given enterprise can yield only very short-term advantages to its employees. For this reason, a meaningful system of workers' control over enterprises is also taboo; this is due to the fact that, since an individual enterprise cannot significantly influence the long-term earnings of its employees, a utility maximizing

[10] K. E. Wädekin in *Studies in Comparative Communism*, XI, 1 & 2 (Spring, Summer 1978), especially p. 119.

workers' control would seek to minimize (within whatever constraints exist) the work effort of these employees.

Thus (4.4) assures the existence of a central administrative system in which the Center appoints and removes the managers of individual enterprises. It also requires that, at least periodically, earnings per worker in an enterprise be determined absolutely without regard to enterprise performance or, at a minimum, that they be linked to the relationship between performance and potential rather than to the relationship between performance in the current period and performance in some past period. If a given enterprise has established a better internal organization, lower quit rate, superior top management, better relations with its suppliers, etc. than had its neighbor, these achievements of one period should be regarded as fixed productive factors for the next period. The quasi-rents earned by these factors cannot be enjoyed for long by the narrow circle of enterprise employees, but must instead be passed on to the state.

Since potential must be measured, this implies that it is the performance/plan relationship that alone can be allowed – at least in the longrun – to change an enterprise's actual per capita wage fund from the average for the branch and locality.

The second major limitation on the set of acceptable methods of coordinating the economy is that these methods must provide for detailed Central determination of product mix.

> The national product mix both of final and of intermediate products, the latter aggregated to the same level as in (4.3), is to be determined by the Center. (4.5)

Here is a constraint that has been removed, in principle completely and to a large degree in practice, from the Hungarian economy since the 1968 reforms. It is the lifting of this constraint which is probably the main factor of differentiation between the current reformed economy of Hungary and the Soviet economy. In the Hungarian economy, the degree of aggregation of final products is much coarser (consumer goods as a whole constitute little more than a single aggregate) and, in principle, intermediate products do not enter at all.

Constraint (4.5) is accepted partly on ideological grounds and partly on the grounds of a Bayesian prior. The ideological basis is the distrust of consumers' sovereignty as the appropriate principle for determining either the current mix of consumers' goods or the medium-term future mix to the extent that this will be influenced by the pattern of current investment. The Center does fundamentally accept consumers' choice: the right of the individual to determine the product mix of his own personal consumption, subject to the constraints of income and of the prices that are determined by the Center. But the total output of each group of consumers' goods is to be determined by the Center; the reconciliation of consumers' choice and planners' sovereignty is intended to be achieved through differential sales taxes levied on the various product groups.

Equally and perhaps even more important as the basis for (4.5) is a Bayesian prior to the effect that coordination of those production units that are technologically linked through an input-output matrix is more efficiently done through a system of central planning than through a market mechanism. Given this prior, it is natural that the Center should attempt to determine both production and consumption of intermediate products on a relatively disaggregative level.

It should be pointed out that constraint (4.5) might be realized by the Center through the direct setting of either prices or quantities. The Central determination of both, as is done in the Soviet economy, introduces redundancy into the control system.[11] If we think of a non-stochastic system (the assumption of my model), there is no theoretic preference as between controlling through prices combined with a rule for profit maximization by the enterprises, or of controlling through quantities of output targets and material-input allocations. One is the dual of the other. In a stochastic world, it is the curvatures of the total social cost and social benefit functions that determine which control method is more effective.[12]

Although (4.5) applies both to products and to the factors of capital and land, it does not apply to labor inputs entering production. The empirical basis for this restriction on (4.5) was presented in Chapter 2; the Center does not control either the prices or quantities of particular kinds of labor within individual enterprises – and such absence of control at this level has an inevitable ripple effect on the degree of control by the Center over labor usage as between enterprises and industries. The justification for this restriction might be found either in the value system of the Center, in the Center's belief in the inefficiency (for motivational reasons) of labor allocation either directly or through labor prices that are sticky over the period of a decade or more[13] or, most likely, for both reasons.

[11] As we shall see in Chapter 5, there is not really this redundancy in the Soviet system because quantities and prices are set at different levels of aggregation.
[12] M. L. Weitzman in *R.E.S.*, 41, 4 (October 1974), pp. 477–91.
[13] It is assumed here that the Center would be prohibited, for reasons of administrative workload, from setting labor prices more frequently than it currently sets wage rates in the Soviet Union.

There should be no direct quantitative determination by the Center of the amount of labor with particular aggregated skill qualifications to be used in producing specific aggregates of goods in a particular period. In other words, labor should not be allocated. (4.6)

Given that labor allocation is to be determined by labor force reaction to market-determined prices, it does not seem unreasonable to think of the Center as accepting consumers' choice as constituting, for incentive reasons, a necessary concomitant of this method of labor allocation.

The mix of consumer goods provided to the individual consumer in exchange for money is to be determined primarily according to the principle of consumers' choice, although not according to consumers' sovereignty. (4.7)

The final constraint on the set of methods of economic coordination stems from the limitation of resources available to the Center for the processing of information.

Whether prices or quantities are used by the Center as its means for directing the economy, these must be changed frequently. As a result, the number of product groups that can be singled out is limited. While some of these groups may be chosen so that each constitutes a set with only one member – a highly critical and bottleneck product – the vast majority of product groups must be aggregate sets of goods with very many members. (4.8)

Thus, in the Soviet Union, where it is quantities that are used to direct the economy, these are set annually at an aggregative level. Annual planning and distribution of products have been in aggregates described as ranging from 16,000 to 67,000 depending on the period and source, while the number of individual industrial items produced are said to range from 12 to 25 million depending on the source.[14]

Together, Constraints (4.4) and (4.5) in particular dictate economic coordination by one or more members of a class of administrative systems that includes the Soviet type of central planning. The description in result (4.9) of the features of this class shows the richness of the consequences of these two constraints.

[14] Berliner (1976), p. 64 gives the figure of 16,000 for 1968. I. Kalinin in *P.Kh.*, 1980, 8, p. 38 gives a figure of roughly double this for the early 1980s. O. M. Iun' in *E.K.O.*, 1983, 8, p. 26 suggests a figure climbing up to 67,000. The figures as to the number of individual items come from Iu. V. Subotskii in *E.K.O.*, 1981, 11, p. 18 and from D. Ukrainskii in *P.Kh.*, 1984, 2, p. 39.

A hierarchical organization of the economy is required, with the Center appointing and dismissing managers of lower units. Not only is workers' management excluded, but so also is the larger set of management systems that consists of independent decision making by individual enterprises.

(4.9a)

Detailed input-output relations must be analyzed by the Center, either as a guide to quantity targets or to price determination. This is required in order to provide consistency between the sums of sources and of uses of each aggregate of intermediate products, since there is no feedback mechanism available in the shortrun that reflects enterprise-level supply and demand.

(4.9b)

The calculation burden on the Center is very great simply in order to achieve consistency. If the Center's calculations were also intended to take account of efficiency considerations, especially given that they also are used to set a standard of performance for individual enterprises, then the burden would become overwhelming.

(4.9c)

If the Center wishes to motivate the labor force of individual enterprises by distributing a portion of the quasi-rents earned by the enterprise, but to do this as per (4.4b) for only a limited period after the relevant factors of production are put into place, then the standard of enterprise performance must be a Plan rather than being performance in a previous period.

(4.9d)

If quasi-rents are distributed as per (4.9d), lower units have incentives to provide misinformation to the Center.

(4.9e)

Constraints affecting incentives. In contrast to the constraints affecting economic coordination, those affecting incentives appear to have no ideological basis. They represent the Bayesian priors of the Center as to the principles of an efficient motivational system for people working in a very large organization, and specifically for a labor force with the historical experience of the Soviet population. These priors appear to have remained unchanged since the beginning of the 1930s.[15]

The constraints on the incentive system employed in economic organizations are as follows:

The entire labor force of an enterprise should be covered by an incentive system that links earnings to results. Incentives should not be restricted to managers and professionals or to particular categories of manual employees such as piece-workers.

(4.10)

[15] See Granick in Guroff and Carstensen (1983).

Incentive rewards should be attached to the performance of the smallest feasible group of employees, so as to provide the greatest incentive to the individual.   (4.11)

Incentives should be for performance during a brief and recent period, certainly not longer than one year. The reason for this restriction is the presumption of a short memory on the part of the labor force as to precisely which of their actions resulted in the incentive payments received.   (4.12)

In order to be credible to the entire labor force, incentives should be linked exclusively to measurable performance.   (4.13)

Constraints (4.10) ... (4.13) arise from an extension of the philosophy underlying the work of the American, Frederick W. Taylor, at the turn of the century, work that was directed explicitly to unskilled labor. All personnel in the enterprise, from unskilled workers with only incomplete primary education to top professionals and managers, are viewed as subject to similar economic motivational principles. For all of them, including managers, the most important goal of a proper incentive system is to increase effort and the effective use of it in an X-efficiency sense. Proper choice of trade-off ratios among the various dimensions of enterprise performance is desirable, but comes second to technical efficiency in an almost lexicographic ordering. Given that the world is stochastic and that the entire labor force is risk averse, an appropriate form of bonus (or piece-rate) will yield a higher payoff to the Center than could be attained through the use of any straight wage or salary.[16]

For those agents of the Center such as managers, whose product consists largely of decisions and whose performance can only be measured by group results, the risk-averse character of their utility functions requires that their reward function be known beforehand by the agents if the reward is to be effective motivationally. The agents' positive rates of time preference, assumed to be strong, require that the measurable performance of period (t) should be rewarded fully in (t), and that (t) should constitute as short a period as feasible.

An important limitation on the definition of incentive in (4.10)...(4.13) lies in the exclusion of career advancement from the incentive system. This is developed in the context of an agent-principal model, in which each

---

[16] For the last point, see Tracy R. Lewis in *Bell Journal of Economics*, 11, 1 (spring 1980), pp. 292–301. Lewis' result would apply to a wider class of bonuses than the one he discusses.

enterprise employee (including top managers) attempts to maximize his own utility function $U(Y_t)$, where

$$Y_t = \sum_{t=1}^{N} f(B_t, C_t)/(1+r)^t$$

and Y_t=the agent's discounted earnings earned in period (t); B_t=bonuses received in period (t); C_t=career level attained as of period (t); r=the rate of time preference of the agent[17]; and N=the expected number of periods before retirement of the agent. B_t, C_t, and N are each functions both of the behavior of the agent and of choice variables determined by the principal, while r is a choice variable of the agent. U of the agent would be an arbitrary constant if the agent were risk neutral.

Let us now consider a matrix (C) whose rows represent all of the individuals (L) who can be viewed as having at some time been potential candidates for more responsible agent positions in the enterprise as of period (t), and whose columns represent the career posts held by the individual candidate in period $C_{t-m}, C_{t-m+1}, \ldots, C_{t-1}$. For each individual, these career posts are linked in a Markov chain.

Following from the above equation, and from the fact that the matrix C [with dimensions $L \times (m-1)$] determines who are the particular agents in more responsible positions in the enterprise during period (t), we obtain

$$F_t = \gamma \{U(Y_t) \quad C\} \text{ subject to constraints} \qquad (4.14)$$

where F_t = enterprise actions in period (t).

The Center's problem is to obtain from the enterprise that set of $\sum_{t=0}^{T} F_t^*$ which maximizes the Center's objective function.

A significant assumption affecting incentives, particularly those of upper managers, is that the Center as principal uses its power to determine the individual manager's C_t with the exclusive purpose of using (4.14) directly to influence $\sum_{z=1}^{\infty} F_z$, where $z=t+1$. The significance of this assumption is that the Center renounces the use of C_t as a means of influencing Y_t in the previous equation. This is a strategic choice of the Center, which can be described as the decision to use the Center's power to appoint managers solely in the interest of selecting those managers having the greatest X-efficiency[18] rather than in order to provide incentives for managers or as a mixed strategy.

---

[17] Due to the lack of opportunities for the Soviet consumer to lend and borrow on a significant scale, the interest rate is not used here. It is assumed that the rate of time preference of the agent is constant over the range of inter-temporal trade-offs open to him; but this assumption is not necessary since one could use an expected r_t rather than an r common to all periods.

[18] The word "solely" refers to the absence of incentive criteria in career decisions by the Center, rather than to the absence of political criteria, nepotism, etc.

Career advancement should not be considered as part of the incentive system. The former should be based upon consideration of the individual's potential for future performance in the new post. The latter, in contrast, is based exclusively upon performance in the immediate past.

(4.15)

The constraints (4.10)...(4.13), in conjunction with the promotion principle (4.15),[19] explain an important characteristic of the Soviet economy: namely, the inability of the Center to internalize into the utility function of enterprise managers a wide range of important Central objectives. Such objectives of the Center are externalities to the enterprise. These externalities include both the introduction by existing enterprises of new major products and processes in production operations, and the improvement of the quality of output.

The Center is incapable of internalizing into the utility function of the agent (enterprise managers) any objectives of the Center whose fulfillment cannot be measured within a period of one year from fulfillment.

(4.16)

The existence of such externalities, considerably wider in extent than is typically found in enterprises of developed capitalist countries, places the Center in the situation of having no instruments available to pursue some of its highest-priority goals.

Nor is it feasible for the Center to use political criteria in its choice of enterprise managers as a means of internalizing such objectives. We have assumed that the manager's utility function $U = U(Y_t)$. Suppose instead that it equalled $U'(Y_t D_{u,t})$, where $D_{u,t}$ = the aspects of enterprise performance in period (t) that are unmeasurable in (t) but are nevertheless of importance to the Center. So long as the utility function of the rest of the labor force in the enterprise was characterized by $U = U(Y_t)$, constraint (4.10) would prevent the manager from giving much weight in his decision making to $D_{u,t}$. A manager who built into his decision-making process objectives that were externalities to his labor force would soon find that his enterprise was non-competitive in the competition for obtaining labor. The quit rate of his labor force would be high, and the ability of the enterprise to

---

[19] The Bayesian priors are enunciated on the basis that they are all beliefs that could be held by reasonable men (whether or not they are correct as hypotheses concerning the real world of the Soviet economy), and that together they lead to the bonus policies that can be observed. It is not asserted that Soviet administrators hold these priors in the forms outlined, but only that they act as though they do.

attract outside labor would be low. Such a manager would be unlikely to be considered successful by the Center.

The outcome of heuristic maximization

A process of heuristic maximization within the confines of Model A results in a number of major malfunctions of the economic system. These malfunctions are consistent with the stylized facts of the Soviet economy as shown both in the Soviet and in Western literature. Since Model A is intended to include the constraints most directly related to economic coordination and to incentives, we would indeed hope that it would have such explanatory power.

These malfunctions will simply be listed here. Result (4.9), stemming from constraints (4.4)...(4.8), represents the basis commonly provided by Western students for problems of coordination in centrally planned economies. The significance of incentive constraints (4.10)...(4.13) and (4.15) have been treated in somewhat greater depth by Granick in Guroff and Carstensen (1983) and in Zimbalist (1984).

Inconsistency, as defined in input-output, is inevitable among the various aggregates in which planning (whether through setting outputs or prices) is carried out. (4.17)

Given the above inconsistency problem, the attention of the Center is concentrated on obtaining as much consistency as is possible within the limitations of its information processing resources. The search for efficiency, as defined by the equating of marginal rates of substitution between input aggregates in the production of different output aggregates, is sacrificed in the interest of maximizing the degree of feasibility contained in the national plan. (4.18)

There is inefficient choice by the Center as to the product aggregates chosen for import as opposed to export. This foreign trade inefficiency in achieving comparative advantage results from the Center's preoccupation with problems of feasibility. (4.19)

Each enterprise determines its input mix in the light of its production isoquants and of its input availabilities. In a system of quantity planning by the Center, input availabilities are determined as a first approximation by input allocations. In a system of planning through price setting, the inconsistencies of (4.17) would lead to informal rationing as between enterprises and thus would have a similar effect.

Considering the enterprise's determination of input mix for its individual products as a programming problem, individual enterprises will be faced with very different relative shadow prices for identical input aggregates, even in the production of common output aggregates. This implies that the marginal rates of substitution between input aggregates will differ considerably not only in the production of different output aggregates, but also as among enterprises producing the same aggregates. (4.20)

As a result of (4.18) and (4.20), a semi-legal barter economy is created for exchange of goods among enterprises. Not only are production inputs bartered for one another, but also above-plan outputs are bartered for inputs available to other enterprises. (4.21)

Enterprise managers are provided with incentives to misinform the Center as to their production capacities. Such misinformation is always in the downward direction. Avoidance of any substantial overfulfillment of current plans is one tactic employed in this misinformation campaign. (4.22)

In order to assure the determination of the national product mix by the Center (4.5), the opportunity cost to ministries and/or enterprises of receiving investment resources must be sufficiently low so that they apply for these resources. (If planning should be carried out through the setting of prices rather than quantities, the inconsistencies of [4.17] would also prevent the requests for investment resources from exactly equalling the amounts that the Center desires to provide.) Should the opportunity cost to the ministry/enterprise of investment be allowed to rise above the marginal benefit to such a unit, the Center would lose control over the allocation of investments.

The Center is subject to considerable pressure to overcommit the resources that it has decided to allocate for total national investment. This pressure arises particularly from the existence of information at the ministry/enterprise level that is not available to the Center. The consequence of such overcommitment is a stretch-out of construction periods leading to a very high ratio, by international standards, in the value of unfinished investment projects to annual investment expenditures. (4.23)

As a result of the operation of the incentive system, major objectives of the Center remain externalities to the enterprise and thus are subject to neglect. Such externalities include both the introduction by existing enterprises of new major products and processes into production operations, and the improvement of quality of output. (4.24)

MODEL B

Model B contains the same argument in the objective function and all the constraints of Model A. In addition, it adds the lexicographic arguments of JROE to the objective function. These were presented in (3.1)...(3.3) and will not be repeated.

All the results (4.17)...(4.24) of Model A remain undisturbed in Model B. In addition, other stylized facts are explained by Model B. These will be developed in the following chapters.

5

Fixed prices and JROE

This is the first of the chapters that tests the explanatory power of the JROE hypothesis within a wider domain than the bare facts of the labor market that were its origin. The domain examined here is that of pricing of products, a field of investigation that one might expect (particularly with regard to the aspects investigated) to be far from that of labor markets. It is suggested that the alternative labor market hypothesis has no application to this domain, and is in this respect a theory inferior to the JROE one.

Here we shall examine the use in the Soviet economy of both Centrally determined prices and quantities, in contrast to the Western theoretic models of central planning that treat prices simply as the dual of the quantities. Given that quantities are determined by the Center, Central determination of prices as well in the Soviet Union is found both to compel some relaxation of either or both constraints (4.5) and (4.7) and seriously to reduce the value of the objective function that can be attained in Model A.

A mechanism is proposed that would permit the combination of market-determined prices with Central determination both of quantities and of average prices for each of thousands of aggregates of goods. This mechanism leads to a result that, within the context of Model A and from the viewpoint of the Center, is considerably superior to that attained by current Soviet practice. However, the proposed mechanism is inconsistent with the JROE lexicographic arguments in the objective function of Model B. It is suggested that such inconsistency provides an explanation for the failure of the Soviet leadership to adopt a mechanism of the proposed type.

THE PROBLEM

Modern modelling of socialist allocation of resources began with an approach in which the Center sets parametric prices and the rules of behavior for enterprise managers, and in which these managers decide on physical outputs and inputs as a function of such prices and rules.[1] The implications of this approach with regard to socialist managers' behavior was worked out in some detail by Abram Bergson.[2] The principal line of such modelling has continued along this path, substituting incentive systems for rules of behavior. An efficiency objection to such allocation through pricing instruments is that of Weitzman.[3] But the basic objection to such theoretic development of the use of the "dual" is that of irrelevance: in no socialist economy has the Center in fact attempted to control the socialist sector of the economy in this fashion.

The alternative approach has been to model an allocation system in which the Center determines directly, through one or another iterative approach, the outputs of all products.[4] On the face of things, this approach would appear to be much more relevant to the working of the Soviet economy.

In fact, however, this planning-through-quantities approach of Malinvaud has no greater direct application to the Soviet economy than has the planning-through-prices approach of Lange. For both, in contrast to (4.8), assume that planning by the Center can be done at the level of the individual product. Yet Soviet planning is carried out in terms of product aggregates that number well under 100,000, and probably less than 50,000, although these aggregates cover some twelve to twenty-five million individual products. The limitation of information-processing resources available to the Center would appear to prohibit any direct application of either the Malinvaud or Lange approach to a modern economy.

Since Soviet coordination of the various productive units in the economy is implemented through quantitative planning, such planning is done in terms of product aggregates. Annual output and materials-allocation plans at the level of the enterprise are said to be established using the same aggregates,[5] a reasonable enough procedure if national sources and uses are to mesh. In contrast, prices are set by individual product.

[1] O. Lange in *R.E.S.*, 4, 1 and 2 (1936–37).
[2] "Socialist Economics" and "Socialist Calculation" in Bergson (1966).
[3] M. L. Weitzman in *R.E.S.*, 41, 4 (October 1974).
[4] E. Malinvaud in Malinvaud and Bacharach (1967).
[5] See O. M. Iun' of Gosplan SSSR in *E.K.O.*, 1983, 8, p. 26. However, it is not clear whether such identity in aggregation procedures occurs, as one would expect, at each balancing level. In 1977, the Council of Ministers and the State Planning Commission of the Soviet Union approved over 3,500 product aggregates in output for purposes of bonus calculations (*S.T.*, 1977, 6, p. 4). For allocation purposes, sources refer to only 2000 aggregates being approved at these levels in 1966, 1977, and in the early 1980s (Berliner [1976], p. 64; O. D. Drotsenko and D. I. Soloveichik in *E.K.O.*, 1977, 2, p. 39; and Iun' in *E.K.O.*, 1983, 8, p. 26). On the other hand, a leading Soviet academic referred in 1984 to Gosplan SSSR

Prices can be determined at this level of complete disaggregation only because they are not used to direct the economy. For this reason, prices can and do remain fixed for long periods of time. Over-all changes in the wholesale prices charged by producers occurred during the last thirty years only in 1955, 1967, and 1982. Although changes in the prices of particular major groups of products did occur between 1967 and 1982, such changes appear to have typically occurred only once for any particular group; in the case of rolled metal, changes occurred twice (in 1972 and 1976).[6] For consumer goods, there is one Soviet statement that some 200,000 retail prices are approved annually for new products; but this price setting reflects mainly a comparison with existing analogous products. It is at best only at a time of general price revision for at least an entire category of goods that the balancing of supply and demand seems to be seriously considered in price setting.[7]

The post-war years have had one period (1949–54) of annual changes (reductions) in prices charged to consumers, and one may wonder how the Center was administratively capable of determining these frequent price changes. The answer, not surprisingly, is that each change was at a unified percentage for all goods in a particular group;[8] thus these frequent changes were done according to aggregates in the same fashion that planning by quantities has continued to be carried out.

Indeed, the price-setting task is even more burdensome than is suggested by the twelve to twenty-five million products for which wholesale prices must be set. Retail prices are also established for consumers' goods in general. This task requires the determination of the particular one of the existing multitudinous rates of sales tax that is to be applied to the individual product. In addition, a third price system exists and applies to all goods: this is the system of constant prices. Although the constant-price system requires no additional price setting beyond what must already be done for the determination of current wholesale prices, it does require keeping records of two different enterprise wholesale prices for each product. "Constant prices" do not necessarily change less frequently than do "current prices"; the timing of their changes, however, is not the

doing its planning in terms of about 4,000 aggregates whose weights are in physical terms (N. P. Fedorenko in *E.K.O.*, 1984, 12, p. 7).
[6] Rzheshevskii (1975), p. 41; editorial in *P.Kh.*, 1977, 9, p. 4; A. Akhmeduev in *V.E.*, 1980, 3, pp. 17–18; and Iu. Iakovets in *V.E.*, 1983, 8, p. 29.
[7] See V. T. Poliakov in *V.M.U.*, 1974, 1, pp. 58–59. The 200,000 figure seems high in comparison with a figure of 135,000 new prices for all types of products in 1968 (Berliner [1976], p. 364). It also seems very high in the light of P. Lokshin in *P.Kh.*, 1981, 8, p. 51.
[8] *Dokhody* (1973), pp. 34–35.

same.[9] An effort to eliminate the system of constant prices, and to replace it with a system of price indices, was made during 1948–49; but the effort was renounced on the basis both of complexity and inaccuracy.[10]

None of the three price systems incorporates changes (except for new products and for particularly grievous cases) with sufficient frequency so that relative prices can reflect either the current objective function of the Center or, for intermediate products, the shadow prices consistent with carrying out the Center's desires. Thus none are used directly to manage the economy. But all three have important economic effects.

Consumer demand schedules are functions of the individual retail prices. Enterprise cost and profitability results are functions of the current enterprise wholesale prices, while their production and labor-productivity results are most frequently functions of the constant enterprise wholesale prices. These functional relations cause the material-stimulation fund to be a function of both types of wholesale prices. The wage fund that is paid out by the enterprise seems most frequently to be a function of the constant enterprise wholesale prices.[11] From the above we can see that retail prices are important in determining the desired expenditure patterns of final consumers, while the two types of wholesale prices are important in

---

[9] For new industrial products, the constant price appears generally, but not always, to be the same as the original enterprise wholesale price (P. Krylov in *P.Kh.*, 1977, 9, p.64). Constant prices for a given sector are set not only at times of general national price revisions, but also during intermediate periods. For industry, constant prices of 1926/27 were used until 1952; then prices of 1952, of 1955, of 1967, of 1975 and of 1982 (*ibid.*, pp. 60–71 and B. Plyshevskii in *V.E.*, 1981, 2, p. 18). Despite the general change in current wholesale prices in January 1982, constant prices of 1973 were still being used in agriculture at least as late as 1983 (see *Narkhoz SSSR v 1983 g.*, p. 207).

[10] Krylov, *P.Kh.*, 1977, 9, p. 61.

[11] An enterprise's production may be evaluated in value terms measured in constant prices, in value terms measured in current prices, or in natural units. The 1965 reform is said to have represented a movement from measurement in constant prices to measurement in current prices, with the principal types of products being measured in natural quantities for purposes of product-mix planning (A. Bachurin in *P.Kh.*, 1976, 3, pp. 13–14). On the other hand, the growing importance of the Five Year Plans after 1970 meant that production measured in constant prices had to again become more vital (see V. Ivanchenko in *V.E.*, 1975, 1, p. 10).

Prior to 1980, "production" as the numerator in labor productivity was normally defined in value terms; it was only in the unusual industry, such as coal and lumber, that it was defined in natural units. Thereafter, the definition was to be determined by the individual branch, and the same definitiion of production used for labor productivity was to control the determination of the relationship between the actual and the planned wage fund in a given period (M. Rogovskii in *S.T.*, 1980, 2, p. 10). An official of Gosplan SSSR informed his readers in 1984 that control over plan fulfillment, both that of the enterprise and of the ministry, is exercised primarily in value terms rather than in natural units (D. Ukrainskii in *P.Kh.*, 1984, 4, pp. 52–53).

their effect on the incentives of enterprises in making production decisions.

Consumer goods

In order to assure Central control over product mix in the production of consumer goods (4.5), and at the same time to assure consumers' choice (4.7), one would wish to ensure the following equality:

$$Q^S_{i,t} = \sum_{n=1}^{N} Q^D_{i,n,t}$$

where i=a group of consumer goods, aggregated at the level used by the Center in planning, n=the individual consumer, and Q_S and Q_D are supply and demand respectively. Since it would appear that Soviet leaders have always preferred to see demand exceeding supply for each product group[12] so long as the excess is not very great, let us instead express the desired equality as

$$Q^S_{i,t} = (1-\sigma_i) \sum_{n=1}^{N} Q^D_{i,n,t} \tag{5.1}$$

with δ_i small and positive, and with Q^S being set autonomously by the Center and Q^D adjusting to it.

However, the total quantity of group (i) demanded by customers in the economy is a function of nominal disposable income, its distribution among individuals, retail prices, and consumer tastes (consumer wealth will be neglected). Thus

$$\sum_{n=1}^{N} Q^D_{i,n} = g(Y_1, \ldots, Y_N, T_1, \ldots T_N, P_1, \ldots, P_S) \tag{5.2}$$

where y_n=the income of the individual, T_n=the tastes of the individual, and P_s=the average retail price of a particular product in any one of the aggregate groups of consumer goods.

One must now ask what instruments are available to the Center in order to prevent σ_i from becoming uncomfortably large in absolute value (with perhaps an undesired negative sign). Consumer tastes can be affected by advertising, but relatively little effort is devoted to this in the Soviet Union. Through the Center's control both over the planned wage fund and planned material-stimulation fund in the state sector, and over the prices paid by the state to collective farms for agricultural products, the Center has the instruments to maintain a reasonably good control over $\sum Y_{n,t}$. As

---

[12] But see *Organizatsiia i metody* (1971), pp. 9 and 241–42. At the 1969 conference reported on there, a deputy-minister of trade for the Soviet Union stated that the basic position of the Ministry of Trade was that consumer goods production should grow more rapidly than demand. This view was attacked by a representative of Gosplan SSSR, who insisted that they should grow proportionally.

was seen in Chapter 2, its control over income distribution is considerably poorer; but instruments for this do exist both in the form of setting wage rates (particularly the minimum wage) and in the determination of the total planned wage fund available to each organizational unit.

The serious problem for the Center lies in the determination of $P_{i,t}$. Only at sporadic intervals can the Center change the prices whose average constitutes P_i; the only control over $P_{i,t}$ that can be exercised is through the pricing of individual products that are both newly introduced in year (t) and that constitute part of the aggregate Q_j. It is true that there have been numerous statements in recent years that new products are introduced in the Soviet Union at higher prices than their existing counterparts, and it is also true that one might expect reduced resistance on the part of the Center to local efforts to raise prices for new products within those aggregates for which consumer demand is greater than supply. Yet we are told by one Soviet author that the prices for new products are not normally set in consideration of supply and demand factors, and I know of no evidence disputing him.[13]

In essence, therefore, it is at best only at times of broad price changes that the Center is in a position to assure (5.1) without adjusting Q^S to Q^D.[14] The fact that the demand functions for different consumer-good aggregates have sharply varying income elasticities, and that real per capita income and income distribution typically both change substantially during the periods between price revisions, would alone prevent unchanging retail prices from being consistent with this desideratum of the Center. Even assuming that the principle of consumers' choice as enunciated in (4.7) relates to product aggregates rather than to individual products, the

[13] V. T. Poliakov in *V.M.U.*, 1974, 1, pp. 58–59. See Berliner (1976), Part II for a comprehensive treatment of the pricing of new products in the Soviet Union; the only reference that he makes to the role of supply and demand being used as a criterion in the setting of such prices is with regard to the sharing between user and producer of monetary gains from replacement of older products with new and improved ones (pp. 316–19). Even here, it is the supply and demand situation for the individual new product, rather than for its product aggregate, that matters.

[14] One means does exist for the Soviet Center to exercise this form of planner's sovereignty, but it is a means which it has never employed. Rather than fixing the prices of individual consumer products at the time of a price reform, it might at that time fix the ratios of prices of all products within a given consumer-goods aggregate to the average prices of that aggregate. The Center could then annually change the average price of each such aggregate at the same time that it fixed the output plans. This mechanism for liberating the central planners from the constraint of consumers' demand would appear to be administratively practical, since there are only a limited number of consumer-good aggregates which would require such annual repricing. (This mechanism is an elaboration of a suggestion by Herbert S. Levine.)

Center is unable to meet both of the constraints (4.5) and (4.7) except possibly at such moments of price change.[15]

One result of this tension between two constraints is that σ_i in equality (5.1) becomes quite large in absolute value for some product groups, and that it is also negative for some. Negative values of σ_i are, of course, always regarded by Soviet leaders as malfunctions of the system. Although large positive values are accepted for certain products (e.g. housing and cars), their presence for a substantial proportion of all product groups could not help but have significantly negative incentive effects on the labor market.

The alternative for the Center to accepting such labor disincentives is to renounce some of its decision-making power over the relative production of different categories of consumer goods. Through its control over monetary income going into the hands of the public, the Center can assure a reasonable degree of equality between $\sum_{i=1}^{I} Q^S_{i,t}$ and $\sum_{i=1}^{I} Q^D_{i,t}$ – at least in periods when the stock of liquid funds in the hands of consumers is not excessive – for any desired $\sum_{i=1}^{I} Q^S_{i,t}$. Thus loss of control by the Center over the determination of $Q^S_{i,t}$ represents no threat to its continued control over the total amount of resources to be devoted to all consumer goods.

If it is to avoid an excessive degree of tension in the fulfillment of constraint (4.7), it is thus suggested that the Center is at best free in determining most $Q^S_{i,t}$ only at the moment of general price changes. In all intermediate years, it is the Center's plan for $Q^S_{i,t}$ that must be adapted to whatever value of $Q^D_{i,t}$ is forecast, given the Center-imposed constraint of $\sum_{n=1}^{N} Y_{n,t}$ together with an acceptable positive value of $\delta_{i,t}$. This necessity, as it applies to the value of $Q^S_{i,t+i}$ that is projected during the planning period $(t-1)$, implies that the Center is similarly constrained with regard to the distribution made among product groups of the total investment resources intended for the consumer goods sector. Thus, there follows the result that

The mix of aggregates of consumer goods provided in exchange for money must, at least between periods of revision of retail prices, reflect a good deal of consumers' sovereignty as well as of consumers' choice.

(5.3)

In the above statement, it is the determination of quantities rather than of prices which is regarded as the feature of importance to planners, and "a good deal of consumers' sovereignty" is regarded as simply the obverse of

15 I am not asserting here that the Center does better in meeting both constraints at times of price changes than at other periods; I know of no evidence to indicate this. The issue is simply that the Center does have the necessary instruments at such moments; whether it is in a position to use them effectively, or even seriously to attempt to do so, is another matter.

planners' sovereignty in this respect. As D. M. Nuti has pointed out to me, true consumers' sovereignty would require that consumers' preferences affect relative prices as well as quantities. But planners' sovereignty is not rescued by the pricing limitations upon consumers' sovereignty that exists in the Soviet economy.

Result (5.3) follows from the combination of (4.7) and (4.8). It is an analytic conclusion that I think is new in the literature, and it represents a significant modification of the classic treatment by Abram Bergson of the Soviet economy as one with consumers' choice but without consumers' sovereignty. It is difficult not to believe that Soviet central leaders view (5.3) as a regrettable consequence forced upon them by systemic pressures.

Producer goods

In the case of producer goods, i.e. capital goods and intermediate products, the Center controls not only $Q^S_{i,t}$ through the production plans that it hands down but also $Q^D_{i,t}$ through the materials allocations provided to users. Since it is materials allocations rather than the availability of financial funds that determine the effective demand for producer goods, no difficulty arises – as it does in the case of consumer goods – in maintaining the Center's exogenous control over the product mix produced at the level of aggregation of Q_j.[16]

Nevertheless, the problem for the Center in the case of producer goods is even more pronounced than it is for consumer goods. The Center may view with equanimity the fact that supply and *ex ante* effective demand do not match for individual products within each consumer goods aggregate $Q_{i,t}$, and that they match *ex post* only because consumers shift their demand within $Q_{i,t}$ to individual products that are available to them. However, the Center is unlikely to be so nonchalant with regard to the equating of effective demand and supply for individual producer goods. Here, for efficiency reasons, its concern goes down to the level of the individual product.

Whatever its degree of concern, the Center has no instruments available to influence either the supply or demand of producer goods below the level

---

16 It is assumed throughout that product groups (i) and (j) do not overlap, whether for purposes of production plans or of materials allocation. This assumption is not strictly true; a user for whom the consumption of an item that normally falls into (i) is insignificant, compared to his total materials inputs, may presumably have his allocation of it lumped together with other items falling into (j). The quantitative dimensions of such overlapping of product groups appears, however, to be small enough so that it can be ignored both here and in the proposal to be presented below.

of aggregation Q_i (see 4.8). Neither production plans nor materials allocations can be expressed in terms of more disaggregated units. Within an aggregate Q_i, both supply and effective demand functions will have arguments that include the relative current prices, constant prices, and units in natural terms (e.g. tons)[17] of the individual products within the aggregate. As pointed out above, the necessarily stable character of these prices puts them outside the control either of the Center or of the direct producers/purchasers except in periods of price changes. Although barter and grey markets (e.g. the use of steel pipe as a form of "cigarette money" among enterprises) does permit the change of relative implicit prices for producer goods, such trade exists only among users. Thus the "implicit price" does not reflect the relative cost structure of producers. For any given year (t), the explicit prices – which affect producer choices as between commodities – must be considered as exogenous. No forces exist that tend toward an equilibrium of supply and demand for individual products.

Conventional wisdom, as expressed both in Soviet and in Western writings, is that purchasers exercise little more control over the composition of products within an aggregate than does the Center. Presumably this is because of the fact that, although users collectively may originally be given only the same volume of materials allocations for $Q_{i,t}$ as are included in the output plans of producers, users are prevented from using such mutual dependence with producers by threatening not to purchase their total allocation if provided only with individual products they do not want. For if producers are left with products unsold through the allocation system, it would seem that additional allocations are provided to other users.[18] There is no evidence available to me that would cause me to dispute this conventional wisdom on the subject.

The implication is that within a given aggregate, producers choose the proportion of different products as a function of the marginal rates of product transformation of such products (on a particular product transformation curve, given not only the producer's existing capacity but also the allocation that he has received of inputs), of current prices of purchased inputs, and of the current enterprise wholesale prices, constant prices, and

---

[17] Production is often expressed in terms of natural units rather than (or as well as) in constant prices. This leads to a relative weighting of individual products within a given aggregate which is virtually outside the control of the Center at all times rather than only in years between prices changes.

[18] See E. Manevich in *V.E.*, 1973, 12, p. 32 and G. Zhuk in *P.Kh.*, 1984, 2, p. 44. Manevich, writing about above-plan production, says that the producer enterprise is guaranteed that it will automatically sell everything it produces.

expression in natural units of each of the products.[19] Thus both the producer's production function and the fixed prices are taken into account in determining the mix within an aggregate; what is ignored is the relative marginal value of product to the user of each of these alternative products. The above statement concerning mix of producer goods also applies to consumer goods.

From the point of view of the user and, more important, from that of the Center, the mix within any given planned aggregate is determined anarchistically. From the point of view of the producer, on the other hand, a utility maximizing choice is involved.

The results of this inequality of supply and demand for producer goods at the level of the individual product within a given aggregate consists not only of the fact that

Inequality of Q^D_1 and Q^S_1 results in static inefficiency due to the inequality of the marginal rate of product transformation and of the marginal rate of substitution for Q_1 and Q_2 within aggregate Q_i.

$$(5.4)$$

This inequality also seems to bear the prime responsibility for the high degree of vertical integration in the Soviet economy, and for the excessive costs associated with such integration.

It is true that vertical integration is promoted by lack of balance of supply and demand – i.e. as between production and materials allocation – of producer good aggregates. Integration occurring for this reason results from (4.17). But it seems likely that the principal problem for enterprises in receiving allocations is not the imbalance in the supplies they receive of different aggregates of materials, but rather consists of disproportions at the level of individual products.[20]

There is an extreme degree of vertical integration at the enterprise level, developed to a large extent with the purpose of reducing dependence upon suppliers for the desired mix within an aggregate Q_i that would otherwise be allocated to the enterprise. The cost to the economy of this

[19] This implication ignores qualitative considerations such as the "political credit" that may be obtained by management from better satisfying users. Such considerations must have their effect; but they are disregarded here in the interest of having a simple neoclassical maximization model.

[20] See Granick (1967), pp. 166–67 for the suggestion that the much heavier use of castings as opposed to rolled metal in Soviet machinebuilding than in American machinebuilding, with the concomitant greater weight of transport equipment and of Soviet machinery, is in part a result of this imbalance at the level of the individual product within the materials allocation of rolled metal.

development consists both in the failure to realize economies of scale in production, and in the need for individual enterprise managements to supervise the use in their plant of an excessively wide range of technologies.   (5.5)

Vertical integration within ministries and their subdivisions (*glavki* and all-Union *ob''edineniia*) have developed for the same reason as has integration within an enterprise. An enterprise is more likely to receive the desired mix within an allocation of Q_i if it is dealing with another enterprise within its own organization than if it is dependent upon a "foreign" organization.

A major malfunction arising from such integration consists of extensive transportation crosshauls.   (5.6)

Containment of the dimension of the problem. In order to provide creditability to the reader, I would like to suggest how the dimensions of the problem of "anarchy" in microeconomic product choice is reduced to a level with which the Center can, although most uncomfortably, live.

One might expect the product mix within each subaggregate – whether of producer or of consumer goods – to evolve during the interim between price changes in the direction of a single product. Suppose that a given enterprise were to begin by producing a wide range of products, all included within the same aggregate and thus subject only to a joint output-plan minimum constraint, with each product produced at constant returns and using an identical proportion of inputs of different types (including capital capacity). In this case, one might expect the enterprise to cease production of all those products within the aggregate whose price/cost ratio is less than the highest ratio found among these products.

Of course, the conditions above are quite strong. Normally, one would expect different enterprises to have varying relative cost structures, and individual products within a given aggregate to incur changing marginal costs in a specific enterprise as their relative outputs varied. Second, one product may be favored by the use of current prices, a second by the use of constant prices, and yet a third by the use of natural units. The relative importance of these three different product-evaluations can change from year to year (e.g. through alteration by the Center of the definition of production or of the relative weight in the enterprise reward function of labor productivity versus profitability); thus there may be annual changes as to the particular products within the given aggregate which the producer prefers. Third, labor inputs are paid for at market-determined prices; for this reason, different products within a given aggregate that require the use of different types of labor may have changing relative profitability, and may make changing contributions to output and to the factory's labor productivity index for a given usage of the constrained total wage fund. These considerations suggest both that the production of a mix of products – rather than a single product – within an aggregate may well be dictated by the consideration of maximizing the producing enterprise's objective function, and that this mix is likely to change over time.

The same conclusion arises from the influence on product mix of uncertainty in the receipt of supplies. (This has been pointed out to me by Gary Krueger.) To the degree that different outputs require different current material inputs, and that there is uncertainty as to the receipt by the enterprise of the allocated amounts of each, a maximizing enterprise management whose objective function includes as arguments not only the expected value but also the variance of the reward function will be likely to produce more than one product within a given subaggregate.

However, although the analysis up to this point suggests that there should be some mix of products within a given subaggregate, it provides no reason why such a mix, or the direction of its temporal variation, should be at all influenced by demand.

One redeeming element of the situation consists of informal "barter" arrangements. These apply most readily when two enterprises each supply goods to one another, and thus can directly trade favors with regard to product mix within different subaggregates; but clearly such barter arrangements may be more complicated and involve triangular trade. Bribes, either in the form of allocated inputs received by the purchasing enterprise from other sectors, or in the form of money, may also reduce the dimensions of such anarchy.

The principal saving feature, however, seems to be administrative. Producing and purchasing units are expected in the Soviet system to negotiate among themselves as to the product mix within each aggregate that is specified both in the producer's output plan and in the purchaser's materials-allocation plan. The negotiations result in a contract. Arbitration exists not only as to the carrying out of the contract, but also as to the original negotiation of the contract itself. While it is true that the producer has the whiphand not only in negotiations but also in arbitration,[21] the negotiating power of a non-monopolistic supplier is at its greatest when his reputation with purchasers, relative to the reputation of possible alternative suppliers, is high. It is under these conditions that purchasers are

[21] Kurotchenko (1975), pp. 164–65.

most willing to accept without appeal to higher authorities producer decisions as to product mix, packaging, delivery dates, etc.

It is because of this system of pre-contract and post-contract arbitration that the medium-run objective function of the Soviet enterprise should include as an argument its reputation with purchasing organizations. It is here that we find some constraint on the purely supply-directed narrowing and shifting of product mix that would otherwise occur within any given aggregate. A parallel in capitalist economies is the constraint on the speed and degree of change of relative prices among products within a given product line of a company; under conditions of imperfect competition, capitalist competition is multi-dimensional and includes competition with regard to reputation for price stability.

A PROPOSED SOLUTION FOR PRODUCER GOODS

The proposed solution takes the form of the use of two vectors of enterprise wholesale prices of producer goods, just as is currently done in the Soviet Union. One vector is specified by the Center; the second is set on the market-place. As is currently the case, both output plans and allocations are given in terms of aggregates. What is new here is that market-determined prices are to be the key parameters used by the producer in deciding as to the relative production of different goods within any aggregate. The Center, having control at the level of the aggregates, loses no authority compared with the current situation. The gain is that the mix of products within aggregate Q_j are now determined by a process that – subject to a border condition – virtually equalizes the producer's rate of product transformation with the user's rate of technical substitution.[22]

Two different sub-solutions will be proposed, depending on whether or not production planning targets are expected to be extremely taut. The Center's considerations should be twofold: the first is to assure that the product mix within aggregate Q_j is chosen by the producer/user enterprises so as to be most consistent with macroeconomic efficiency. The second consideration is to assure the Center's control over the average current price within each aggregate, although control over the vector of prices of the individual products must be renounced.

What is meant here by taut production plans can best be defined in terms of the two ends of the continuum. Viewing targets as a set of

---

[22] The assumption made in all the various alternatives of the proposal is that the bonus scheme for enterprises and their managers is such as to conform to lexicographic ordering of fulfillment of the output plan over pursuit of the remaining arguments in the enterprise's maximand. This would probably require some change from most of the bonus schemes currently in force in the Soviet Union; but it is in their spirit.

constraints on enterprise behavior, within which the enterprise management attempts to maximize a reward function, the "loose" end of the continuum is one in which output targets are always non-binding constraints. The "taut" end is one in which there is no room for any process of maximization by the enterprise management. When targets are taut, we would expect that many organizations would fail in their efforts to remain within the targeted constraints. None would be able to exceed them.

When production planning is taut, the Center should evaluate fulfillment by a ministry or enterprise of its production plan for the aggregate Q_i in terms of prices determined frequently (e.g. annually) and *ex post* by the Center, while the allocation plan for Q_i is established in terms of current prices determined on the market-place.

Center-determined prices are to reflect relative one-period-lagged current prices of the products (m) within aggregate Q_i, as well as the average price increase of products within Q_i that is desired by the Center and that has served as the basis for selecting the planned volumes (expressed in market-determined prices) of Q_i for each user. Center-determined prices are to be set according to the formula

$$\hat{P}_{m,t} = P_{m,t-1} \left\{ \eta_{i,t} \left| \frac{\sum_{m=1}^{M} P_{m,t-1} Q_{m,t-1}}{\sum_{m=1}^{M} P_{m,t} Q_{m,t-1}} \right. \right\}$$

or the same formula with quantity weights of period (t), where $\hat{P}$=Center-determined price, P=market-determined price, $\eta_{i,t}$=average price change for Q_i desired by the Center in period (t) [$\eta_{i,t}=1$ if desired price increase is zero], and Q_m= the quantity of each individual product within Q_i.

(5.7)

This solution is to be modified as follows when production planning is not taut:

With planning not taut, the Center should follow the same procedure as in (5.7) of setting the production plan for Q_i in terms of Center-determined prices, and the allocation of Q_i in terms of market-determined prices. The difference in procedure is with regard to the establishment of Center-set prices.

Center-set prices should be determined in the same fashion as currently, i.e. without any necessary relationship to relative prices as reflected in the market-place. They need be set with no greater frequency than is currently the practice in the Soviet Union.

(5.8)

Using the assumption that all actors are price takers

This assumption allows us to analyze the effects of the proposals, within a given planning aggregate of products, under conditions that are analogous to those of perfect competition. Thus it provides a good starting point.

Assuming that all production plans are taut. Assuming the existence of only two products within Q_i, the problem for the producer can be stated as being that of solving the following Lagrangian:

$$L_P = \text{Maximand} + \lambda_1[X^\circ - h(Q_1\,Q_2)] + \lambda_2[S_p - (\hat{P}_1 Q_1 + \hat{P}_2 Q_2)]$$

where X°=fixed inputs (plant and equipment, allocated materials, and planned wage fund), S_p=the producer's production plan of Q_i stated in Center-determined prices, and $\hat{P}$=the Center-determined price.

However, the assumption of tautness implies that the producer can at best satisfy the stated constraints and that the maximand can be ignored. Thus the problem can be restated as:

$$L_P = \hat{P}_2 Q_1 + \hat{P}_2 Q_2 + \lambda_1[X^\circ - h(Q_1\,Q_2)]$$

with
$$\hat{P}_{1,t}/\hat{P}_{2,t} = P_{1,t-1}/P_{2,t-1}=\text{ratio of market-determined prices} \qquad (5.9)$$

Given the usual convexity assumptions, and differentiating with respect to λ_1 and to the producer's choice variables Q_1, Q_2, we obtain the condition that $\hat{P}_1/\hat{P}_2=h_1/h_2$=the producer's rate of product transformation.

The problem for the user is to maximize his own production, subject to his allocation of materials ($Q_1\,Q_2$).

$$L_u = f(Q_1\,Q_2) + \lambda_3[S_u - (P_1 Q_1 + P_2 Q_2)] \text{ with } f[\cdot] \text{ being the user's pro-}$$
duction and S_u being the user's allocation of Q_i stated in market-determined prices $\qquad (5.10)$

Following the same procedure as we did for the producer, we obtain the result that $P_1/P_2=f_1/f_2$=the user's rate of technical substitution.

Since market prices are functions of $Q_1{}^*$, $Q_2{}^*$ determined by the simultaneous solution of the two maximizing solutions, the resulting prices yield the same optimal static efficiency result, although only in equilibrium where relative product prices are stable over time, as is found in perfect competition. Namely:

$$\hat{P}_1{}^*/\hat{P}_2{}^* = P_1{}^*/P_2{}^* = h_1/h_2 = f_1/f_2 \tag{5.11}$$

The difficulty with this proposal is that the Center is obliged to reset all $\hat{P}$ at frequent intervals (e.g. annually), and one might ask how this could be technically feasible. There are two answers. The first is that the Center need only determine $\eta_{i,t}$ (in 5.7), with the remaining price-setting procedure being purely mechanical. The second is that there will not be many (if any) product aggregates Q_j for which production planning will be truly taut in the sense defined above unless the Soviet Center drastically changes its existing planning practice.[23] Thus the pricing burden for the Center should not be severe.

Assuming that production plans are not taut. For the producer, the problem can be stated as the meeting of Kuhn-Tucker conditions in maximization under inequality constraints.

Maximize $P_1 Q_{1+\delta_1} + P_2 Q_{2+\delta_2}$

Subject to:

$$\begin{aligned}
h(Q_1\ Q_2) &\leqslant X^\circ \\
Q_1, Q_2 &\geqslant 0 \\
-(\hat{P}_1 Q_1 + \hat{P}_2 Q_2) &\leqslant -S_p
\end{aligned}$$

$$L_p = P_1 Q_{1+\delta_1} + P_2 Q_{2+\delta_2} + \lambda_1 [X^\circ - h(Q_1\ Q_2)] \\ + \lambda_2 (-S_p + \hat{P}_1 Q_1 + \hat{P}_2 Q_2) \tag{5.12}$$

If the third constraint is binding, then there are two possibilities. The first is that either there exists only one combination of Q_1, Q_2 that needs the two constraints (i.e. that the production plan S_p is tangent to the producer's production frontier) or that no combination does. In this case, there is no maximizing problem. The producer either chooses the constraint-satisfying combination, or he chooses the combination that comes as close as possible to satisfying the third constraint (i.e. to fulfilling the plan S_p). Clearly this is a case of taut planning, and would better have been treated by the Center under (5.7) instead of under (5.8). But the Center may make mistakes in judging whether or not a plan is taut.

[23] See D. Granick in *J.C.E.*, 4, 3 (September 1980), pp. 261–63 and A. C. Gorlin and D. P. Doane in *J.C.E.*, 7, 4 (December 1983), pp. 415–31. These data indicate the existence of very little tautness in Soviet industry at the ministerial level. Of course, even in ministries that do not fulfill their output plans, many individual enterprises overfulfill theirs. The data refer to plans as they existed at the end, rather than at the beginning, of the planning period. Since it is the level of these end-year plans that determines whether enterprises are in a position to consider their maximands or only their constraints, they are the relevant data for this section.

The second possibility is that S_p intersects the production frontier curve either at one or two points. In this case, only part of the set of combinations of Q_1, Q_2 that lie on the producer's production frontier will meet the constraint of fulfilling the production plan. From the subset of combinations that meet his three constraints, the producer will choose that combination that comes as close as possible to what he would have chosen if the plan constraint had not been binding. Here we have a border condition of maximization. The producer chooses that combination which minimizes the absolute value of $(P_1/P2 - h_1/h_2)$.

If the third constraint is not binding, we have what amounts to a Lagrangian maximization problem with one constraint. In this case

$$\partial L_p/\partial Q_1 = \partial L_p/\partial Q_2 \qquad = 0$$
$$\partial[X° - h(Q_1\ Q_2)]/\partial\lambda_1 \qquad = 0$$
$$\lambda_1 \qquad\qquad\qquad > 0$$
$$\partial(-S_p + \hat{P}_1 Q_1 + \hat{P}_2 Q_2)/\partial\lambda_2 > 0$$
$$\lambda_2 \qquad\qquad\qquad = 0$$

This gives us the result that $P_1/P_2 = h_1/h_2$.

The user's maximization problem is precisely the same as it was in (5.10), and his solution is once more that $P_1/P_2 = f_1/f_2$.

Thus, under the condition that the constraint of meeting his production plan is not binding on the producer, the results amount to the same as given in (5.11) for the case of taut planning.

$$P_1*/P_2* = h_1/h_2 = f_1/f_2 \tag{5.13}$$

For $(P_1 Q_{1+\delta_1} + P_2 Q_{2+\delta_2})$ to be a function that the producer can maximize, it is essential that it can be different from the $(P_1 Q_1 + P_2 Q_2)$ allocated in rubles to the user. The need for this potential difference is a result of the fact that prices $(P_1\ P_2)$ move freely during the planning period, and that the allocation $(P_1 Q_1 + P_2 Q_2)$ is a single ruble figure expressed in market prices. Thus producers as a group would always receive the same number of rubles in market prices, whatever their production of $(Q_1\ Q_2)$, so long as they are allowed to sell only to users having allocations and so long as these allocations are not increased by the Center. [We can assume that users will always wish to use their allocations fully, whatever the relative volumes of $(Q_1\ Q_2)$ they can obtain; the products can be used for barter purposes if for nothing else.]

The necessary distinction between the maximand and $(P_1 Q_1 + P_2 Q_2)$ is provided by the following rule that applies to the planners:

(a)   Once $(\hat{P}_1 Q_1 + \hat{P}_2 Q_2)$ has been produced, additional allocations

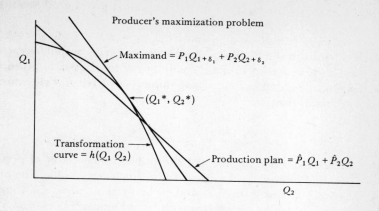

Producer's maximization problem

Q_1

Maximand $= P_1 Q_{1+\delta_1} + P_2 Q_{2+\delta_2}$

$(Q_1{}^*, Q_2{}^*)$

Transformation curve $= h(Q_1 \, Q_2)$

Production plan $= \hat{P}_1 Q_1 + \hat{P}_2 Q_2$

Q_2

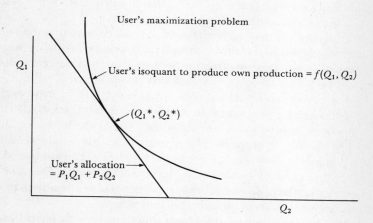

User's maximization problem

Q_1

User's isoquant to produce own production $= f(Q_1, Q_2)$

$(Q_1{}^*, Q_2{}^*)$

User's allocation $= P_1 Q_1 + P_2 Q_2$

Q_2

Figure 5.1   Non-taut planning with all actors being price takers

denominated in rubles at market-determined prices are given to users.

(b)   These allocations are based on estimates of future plan overfulfillment during (t) of $(Q_1 \, Q_2)$, and are calculated at those $(P_{1,t} \, P_{2,t})$ prices already established in the market-place in the sale of the planned quantities $(Q_{1,t} \, Q_{2,t})$.   (5.14)

This solution creates less of a burden on the Center than does that for taut planning, since it requires no change in the existing pricing practice of the Center in the Soviet Union. Center-determined prices need be set no more frequently than is done at present.

Note that the producer's maximand $(P_1 Q_{1+\delta_1} + P_2 Q_{2+\delta_2})$ in (5.12) can be given either its straightforward interpretation of gross output, or can be interpreted as profits earned under conditions of fixed costs imposed by materials allocations and a planned wage fund (the latter being close to the actual wage fund spent).

Using the assumption that producers set prices

In the previous section, we adopted the pricing assumption of perfect competition and arrived at the usual static efficiency results. The only exceptions were the cases of taut and partially taut plans. Of course, nothing is contributed by the scheme with regard to assuring efficiency as to quantities of the aggregates Q_i and Q_j produced; the efficiency results hold only within the compass of a given aggregate.

But the assumption that the Soviet producer will be content to be a price taker is no more realistic than the counterpart assumption made for the capitalist enterprise. It is true that the Soviet producer is operating under the condition where his total planned production – $(\hat{P}_1 Q_1 + \hat{P}_2 Q_2)$ – is allocated to users whose allocation – $(P_1 Q_1 + P_2 Q_2)$ – is expressed in market-determined rather than in Center-determined prices. (Let us ignore above-plan production at this point.) Given the above equality, enforced by the Center through its planning system, the producer can do nothing to increase the average price of the planned aggregate Q_i and, by this means, to increase the value of his maximand in (5.12). This is one of two reasons that the proposed scheme expresses the production plan and the materials allocations in terms of different prices.

Nevertheless, the producer does have a preference with regard to the combination of Q_1 and Q_2. He would like to produce those relative quantities that equate P_1/P_2 with h_1/h_2, unconstrained by the necessity that these ratios also equal the user's f_1/f_2. This would allow the producer, given his capacity, to achieve a higher output and profit measured either in the Center-determined prices of (5.9) in the taut planning scheme, or in the market-determined prices of (5.12). By maximizing L_p in (5.12) through differentiating by λ_1 and all three choice variables (Q_1, Q_2, and P_1/P_2), the producer attains the ratio $h_1 = h_2$. Thus we will have set $\partial X^o/\partial Q_1 = \partial X^o/\partial Q_2$. This is precisely the result that occurs under the present pricing mechanism in the Soviet Union, where the Center influences the product mix through its choice of a set of fixed prices. Here the

Center would be limited to defining the fixed units in which the individual Q_m are to be measured.

If there are many producers and users of the same Q_j aggregate, and if users are not bound to a single producer, those producers choosing the above pricing strategy will be viewed by the users as suppliers of last resort. Despite this, since there is equality of the sum of all output plans for Q_j with allocations, some users with materials allocations will eventually be forced to purchase from the maximizing producer. If specific users are assigned by the Center to a given producer, then the same result would ensue; the only difference would be the speed of convergence to this result.

This leaves the Center with the need for a means of restraining producers from determining the ratio P_1/P_2 in the manner indicated. (Note, however, that this "worst case" is no different than the situation existing under the system actually used in the Soviet economy.) Not surprisingly, what is required is that the hand of the user be strengthened relative to that of the producer.

Such strengthening is exactly what is accomplished by the proposed scheme in which materials allocations and production plans are expressed in different prices. So long as production can be sold only to allocation holders, the problem disappears of excess effective demand for the planned output quantities of producer goods. Any such excess as might exist at prevailing market-determined prices would have its effect directly on these prices – thus automatically reducing the purchasing power of the original allocations to the level of the available planned production. No longer could the Center be pressured to create excess effective demand by issuing excess allocations so as to ensure that no production goes unsold. The days of excess effective demand for producer goods (for which the binding constraint consists of allocations rather than money) would be over.

A problem does remain, however, as to above-plan production. For such output, the producer's maximand is expressed in market-determined prices and is unconstrained by any limitation expressed in prices set by the Center. Since materials allocations would also be expressed in the same market-determined prices, no automatic restraining influence would exist to prevent producers from raising prices sharply for this output. Such price increases would reduce the cost of production incurred in obtaining a fixed gross revenue from users who had received the additional allocations issued to cover the expected above-plan output.

A partial solution to this problem lies in State regulation prohibiting market prices charged for above-plan production of any given item from being higher than had been the price (e.g. the annual average) charged for the same item by the same producer in disposing of his planned output of the aggregate Q_j. This, however, leaves the problem that a producer may set a very high price for product (m) from the beginning – thus selling almost none of it from his planned production of Q_j – so that he could concentrate his above-plan production of Q_j upon product (m). Presumably, one important criterion for choosing (m) would be that it be a product for which, if its producer-determined price were such that $h_1/h_m = f_1/f_m$, $|dQ_1\hat{P}_1/dQ_m\hat{P}_m| > |dQ_1 P_1/dQ_m P_m|$. Given this condition, the production of (m) would make less of a relative contribution to plan fulfillment than it would to planned output measured in market prices. The raising of the market price of (m), so that the demand response would cause $h_1/h_m > f_1/f_m$, would then have the advantage to the producer that a higher proportion of his total output would be above plan.

I have no answer to this problem, but it is unlikely to be overly serious in Soviet conditions. Generally, above-plan production is too small a proportion of planned output to make it worth the while of the producer to engage in manoeuvers that might be exposed. At least as important, the belief by Soviet producers that planning is based on the ratchet principle would make it improbable that a dynamic maximizer would attempt to expand his above-plan output in that fashion.

The setting of allocations

Beyond the critical question of allocating material allocations and production plans in terms of different prices, the only other important consideration is to continue current Soviet practice of permitting producers to sell above-plan production only against materials allocations. This is vital since materials allocations would be unnecessary if there were not considerable excess monetary demand for producer goods – demand which is ineffective only so long as allocations are required for purchase of such products, regardless of their source.

Additional allocations beyond those originally granted should be given late in the year (as seems now to be done) in an amount equal to the expected overfulfillment of production plans for aggregate Q_j. Since I have suggested earlier that prices for these additional quantities of products be frozen at the levels that had existed for planned production, the automatic balancing of supply and demand within aggregate $Q_{j+\delta_j}$ would not exist. It is unlikely that the results would be overly serious, however, both because of the relatively small proportions of above-plan output to planned output and because of the fact that the frozen relative prices should be reasonably similar to what market-equilibrium ones would have been.

One might ask how the material allocation of aggregate Q_j for a particular user can be reasonably determined when it is to be expressed in prices to be set on the market-place only in the future. How can the user make his application or the granting agency its decision?

The answer is straight forward: the problem is merely that of finding an index number. So long as there is a prior Central decision as to the summation of production plans (in prices set by the Center) and of allocations (in market-determined prices) for aggregate Q_j, the Center has available a conversion factor. One might proceed, for example, by having the applicant assume the conversion factor of the previous year, and by the Center automatically adjusting all applications to the current year's situation before considering them.

It is true that this index-number approach will be unsatisfactory for users interested only in particular products within the Q_j aggregate. But their dissatisfaction should be considerably less than that felt under the existing Soviet system where they cannot be assured of receiving such individual items at all whatever their allocation of Q_j may be.

These original allocations of Q_j should be set at a level equal to the summation of the production plans as they are expected to stand at the end of the planning period rather than at the beginning. Although there are many differences between these two at the level of the individual enterprise, these differences may not be great at the aggregate level of Q_j and the Center may choose to disregard them.[24] In any case, errors will affect primarily only the average price level in market-determined prices for Q_j.

THE PROPOSED SOLUTION FOR CONSUMER GOODS

This represents a relatively minor modification of the proposal concerning producer goods. Although the Soviet Center would among other things be interested in a better match of supply and demand for consumer goods at the level of the individual product, our attention will be concentrated upon the presumed objective of rescuing planners' sovereignty in the determination of the size of aggregates of consumer goods. See (5.3).

Production plans would be set in terms of Center-determined enterprise wholesale prices as in the previous proposal, and organizational recipients (mostly wholesalers and retailers) of these goods would receive their

[24] See the writings of V. P. Shaikin for Soviet research on the subject. His article in *Ekonomika i Matematicheskie Metody*, 1974, 1, pp. 98–109 is a good example of this work.

allocations in market-determined wholesale prices. The only difference from the scheme for producer goods is as to how the Center decides on the proper conversion rate to use for each aggregate as between Center-determined and market-determined prices.

As discussed in the first section, the problem for the Center is to be able to change the relative average price of different consumer good aggregates at frequent intervals without having to make changes at the level of the individual product. This can be done in this scheme through the determination of the total annual allocation in market-determined prices to the sum of all organizational recipients of each aggregate. A weighted average of the wholesale prices of the individual products within that aggregate in the coming year will result from a comparison of such allocation with the production plan for the aggregate. Sales-tax rates on the different products, as well as authorized trade markups, should remain unchanged. In this fashion, the Center will be free to set the quantity supplied of each aggregate as it wishes – and without violating constraint (4.7).

The above scheme can be stated more precisely in the following terms:

Plan given to the producer $= \hat{P}_{i,t} Q_{i,t}$

Allocation F given to the trade organization $=$

$\sum\limits_{i=1}^{I} A_{i,t}$ expressed in rubles

Task facing the planner:

To set $\hat{P}_{i,t}$ so that $Q_{i,t}{}^S = (1-\sigma_i) \sum\limits_{n=1}^{N} Q_{i,n,t} D$

given

$Q_{i,t}{}^S$ and σ_i as the planner's choices,

$Y_1, \ldots, Y_N, T_1, \ldots T_N$, and the consumer demand

function (5.2)

Task facing the sales (or profit) maximizing trade organizations:

To set the vector $(P_1, P_2, \ldots, P_T)$, given $T_1, \ldots, T_N$ and the demand function (5.2), so that

$$P_1 Q_{1,t} + P_2 Q_{2,t} + \ldots + P_T Q_{T,t} = \sum\limits_{i+1}^{I} A_{i,t}$$

It is clear that this proposal involves the Center in the counterpart of annually setting prices (i.e. in the setting of conversion factors) for consumer goods. But the number of such prices is equal only to the number of aggregates whose production and distribution is planned, rather than to the total number of consumer products. The number of aggregates is said to be only about five hundred,[25] and establishing prices annually for such a small number should be a feasible task for the Soviet Center.

---

[25] P. Lokshin in *P.Kh.*, 1981, 8, p. 51. These are the total number of aggregates confirmed by any of the following: Council of Ministers SSSR, Gosplan SSSR, Gossnab SSSR, and both Union and Union-Republic ministries.

THE PROPOSED SOLUTIONS AND THE MODELS

Consistency with Model A

The proposed solutions do not appear to present any problem as to inconsistency with the constraints incorporated in Model A. In fact, the solution proposed for consumer goods permits a full realization of both constraints (4.5) and (4.7), rather than the compromise between consumer choice and planner's sovereignty embodied in the actual Soviet system. See (5.3).

The solution proposed for producer goods permits the Center to reach a higher maximand (4.3) because of improved static efficiency in the macroeconomic production of goods. It is irrelevant with regard to satisfying the constraints.[26] In both respects, this is the opposite of the situation emanating from the solution for consumer goods.

We should, of course, ask whether Model A should properly be extended to include other constraints, or other arguments in the objective function, that have particular relevance to the proposed solutions.

First, one might ask whether an ideological constraint unmentioned in the model prohibits the use of market prices. Although there is certainly suspicion by the Soviet Center of market-formed prices as lending themselves to "speculation," the long existence and continuous significance of collective-farm markets[27] would seem to push a supposition of the existence of such a constraint to the limits of creditability. This is all the more so since the proposed solutions do not diminish any aspect of the Center's power to coordinate the economy in as great detail as the Center is otherwise capable of doing.

Second, one might ask whether the model's neglect of the issue of intensive versus extensive growth, with the latter perhaps being promoted through the use of "priority" methods of plan enforcement by the Center, creates consistency problems as between the proposals and Soviet constraints. It seems to me that no problem exists here; it is difficult to see how priority methods of plan enforcement can be used to any great extent at a level of product disaggregation that goes below the units in which the

---

[26] Materials allocation is retained in the proposal so as to avoid violating constraint (4.5). The user can substitute Q_1 for Q_2 since both are within product group (i), but he cannot substitute Q_1 for Q_3 that is in group (j).

[27] Between 1965 and 1983, some 4.2 to 5.3 per cent of all Soviet retail trade in foodstuffs (with no trend in these figures) was carried out at market-formed prices on the collective-farm markets. Using the same weights for all kinds of retail trade in foodstuffs regardless of the channel, these figures were 2.2 to 3.8 per cent (with a downward trend). The ranges for a fixed but unspecified market basket of foodstuffs were 8.1–11.0 and 4.6–5.5 per cent respectively (*Narkhoz SSSR 1922–82*, pp. 466–67 and *Narkhoz SSSR v 1983 g.*, pp. 457–58).

Center itself calculates. If an individual product were at any time given sufficiently high priority to matter significantly, one would expect it to be raised to the level of one of the tens of thousands of aggregates used in Soviet planning.

Third, one might ask whether it is only the primitive statement of the objective function as being in terms of the rate of growth of (gross national product) GNP (4.3) that permits my conclusion that the proposal concerning producer goods unambivalently leads to an increase in this function, and that the one with regard to consumer good leads to no reduction. Since neither the distribution of income nor the distribution of GNP at levels of aggregation at least as high as the Q_j aggregate are affected, and since the decision-making powers of the Center are enhanced rather than diminished, it is difficult to see why this definition of the objective function should be a problem.

Consistency with JROE in Model B

Of the three JROE constraints, (3.1) ... (3.3), it is (3.2) that creates the consistency problem. The overfull employment constraint (3.1) could be met by vigorous macroeconomic policies, and (3.3) could be enforced by administratively limiting enterprise (k) to maximum annual dismissals of $\varepsilon_{3,kj}$ employees with the skill characteristic (j) – with $\varepsilon_{3,kj}$ being a fixed percentage of (kj), identical for all (j). But the guarantee of individual (i) against excessive unwanted idleness within his current enterprise is a more serious problem. The reader will recall the importance of this constraint (3.2) if the individual is to be guaranteed more than a minimum income, and if the emphasis is to be placed upon the social rather than the economic aspects of an employee's property rights to his existing job.

The difficulty is that "unwanted idleness" is not a phenomenon observable by higher authorities. Such idleness need not take such crass forms as that of being sent home from the place of employment, or of being placed in a special recreation room in the factory. It may be reflected in nothing more concrete than the pace of work set for the employee. Furthermore, this pace must not have been voluntarily chosen by the employee. Thus constraint (3.2) can be respected only if the parameters of enterprise decision making are such as to lead management to wish to meet this constraint without its ever having to be stated formally by the Center, and without anyone checking later as to whether the constraint was indeed met.

For the Center, this problem can be stated as being that of choosing (g) and $(w_1 \ w_2)$ below so that the enterprise management, in maximizing its own reward function subject to meeting Kuhn-Tucker conditions, will freely select values of its choice variables that lead to $Pr(A_i) < \varepsilon_2$ for a value of $(y_2 \; \varepsilon_2)$ that is exogenously but realistically chosen by the Center. The problem of maximization under inequality constraints is the following:

Maximize $\qquad\qquad g(W_1 Q_1 + W_2 Q_2)$

Subject to:
$$h(Q_1 \; Q_2) \qquad\qquad \leqslant X^\circ$$
$$Q_1, Q_2 \qquad\qquad\qquad \geqslant 0$$
$$-\varepsilon_2 \qquad\qquad\qquad \leqslant -Pr(A_i)$$
$$L_m = g(W_1 Q_1 + W_2 Q_2) + \lambda_1 [X^\circ - h(Q_1 \; Q_2)] + \lambda_2 [-\varepsilon_2 + Pr(A_i)]$$

$$(5.15)$$

where L_m = management's Lagrangian, W_1, W_2 are relative weights for Q_1, Q_2 in the enterprise management's reward function, and the other symbols are the same as those used in (3.2) and in (5.12).

In other words, management must be motivated to choose such a product mix as not to keep workers unwillingly idle despite the fact that the enterprise cannot dismiss workers. The factor that eases the Center's problem is that the expected value of the proportion of workers being separated during the year other than by dismissal is at least some 25 per cent. Of course, however, the proportion of non-dismissal separations will be a great deal lower for particular trades in particular enterprises.

Now there are two reasons that Soviet enterprise managers might wish to hold workers idle. The first is that, for a given maximizing choice of $(Q_1 \; Q_2)$ on the part of management, the isoquant of shortrun adjustment, that is drawn on the j-axes, of j different kinds of labor occupations/skills is sufficiently close to being right-angled that there is no effective way to employ all of the available workers of a particular occupation/skill even though the saving in wage fund from keeping some of them idle is nil.

The second reason is that idle employees need not be paid as much as those working at a normal pace. If they are piece-workers, for example, their earnings will automatically be less. Thus the management economizes on its wage fund, and it can use the saving to increase the earnings of other employees with occupations/skills required for the given product mix. This redistribution of wage fund places the management in a better position to retain employees of the desired occupations/skills and to hire new ones.

Leaning on the results of Chapter 2, one might argue that this second reason cannot be of much importance; this is because the enterprise management can achieve the same redirection of the wage fund through the appropriate apportionment of bonuses, and without resorting to enforcing idleness on some employees. But, first, such opportunities are limited in the years immediately following a major increase in wage rates. Second, occupational/skill differences in piece-rate earnings usually constitute a major means of redirecting the wage fund – a means whose potential use would be greatly expanded if some workers could be made idle. Third, redirection of an enterprise's wage fund through the normal means available to Soviet managers cannot be an instantaneous process, for it requires the overcoming of social resistance by that portion of the enterprise labor force to be disadvantaged. The process of redirection could be speeded up substantially through enforced idleness.

The aspect of income maintenance in the no-idleness constraint (3.2) still permits enterprise managers to change the relative earnings of workers with different occupations and skill levels. Such change is essential if the labor markets for heterogeneous types of labor are to clear under the condition of given total wage funds for individual enterprises. What (3.2) does do, however, is to ensure that such changes in relative income occur exclusively for reasons other than enforced differential degrees of idleness. Such idleness refers to what occurs with the existing enterprise product mix and factor proportions, rather than to what would occur with the proportions that would be preferred by enterprise management if it were not for the existence of institutions designed to enforce the inequality (3.2).

To what degree does the existing Soviet system lead the maximizing enterprise management to select during period (t) those values of its choice variables which lead to $Pr(A_i) < \varepsilon_2$ in (5.15)? Presumably, the management had previous to (t) engaged in a hiring policy that was appropriate to its then existing product mix; a high $A_{i,t}$ would be appropriate for management only if there were to be fairly sudden changes of some sort. Such changes, leading to sharp variation in the desired occupation/skill mix within the enterprise's labor force, could be due to:

(1) Variations in the relative size of the output targets given by the Center for various aggregates whose production requires different types of labor. Here, it is the Center that must exercise self restraint if constraint (3.2) is to be met.

(2) Changes in the production functions applicable to existing enterprises for the individual products Q_1 and Q_2. Such changes lead both to a shift in the desired amounts of labor for the production of each of these individual products, and to shifts in the optimal combination of $(Q_1 \ Q_2)$ within Q_j.

It is now well established in the Western literature that the Soviet economy is relatively slow by international standards in introducing technological change into production.[28] I explain this phenomenon here as being primarily a result of the externalities problem described in (4.16), that itself arises from the Center's Bayesian priors concerning incentives. Particularly if one assumes[29] that technological change is especially slow in existing enterprises, no great pressure to violate constraint (3.2) arises out of technological change.

(3) Changes in the optimum combination of different types of labor in the production of the individual products Q_1 and Q_2 due either to economies of scale or to movement along the learning curve by the individual enterprises.

(4) Changes in relative earnings of different occupation/skills within a given enterprise, and variations in quit rates for different types of complementary labor. These disturbing features of a free labor market cannot be eliminated so long as constraint (4.6) is respected by the Center.

The potential effect of the above four types of changes in leading to violation of (3.2) is mitigated by the natural wastage of the existing labor force. So long as the Center exercises self restraint in its change of relative production of aggregates, one would not expect major difficulties to arise. Nevertheless, these changes impose lower limits on $(y_2 \, \varepsilon_2)$ in (5.15) and in (3.2).

Under the proposed solutions, on the other hand, the stability of $(W_1 \, W_2)$ in (5.15) would end; the W would now consist of market-determined prices that would change with shifts in demand for Q_1 relative to Q_2. I would expect the changes in relative prices to be much sharper than the changes in relative wages of (4) above. If one can assume that the preferred occupation/skill combinations differ considerably as between these products, and that the relevant shortrun-adjustment isoquants are reasonably close to being right-angled, then it would seem likely that the maintenance of constraint (3.2) would be jeopardized in many enterprises.

The significance of the use of market-determined prices as the W would depend heavily upon the degree of difference in preferred occupation/skill combinations for the different products within a given aggregate Q_j. Unfortunately, no quantitative information is available as to this key issue. However, products are aggregated by the Center not only with regard to substitutability of products in production, but probably even to a great degree in accord with their substitutability in use (since the aggregates

---

[28] The literature on this is extensive. See especially Amann *et al.* (1977).
[29] No data exist as to this question, to my knowledge.

serve as the basis for materials allocation). Thus, it is difficult to believe that products within a given aggregate could generally be produced with very similar preferred labor combinations.

Of course, there exists a problem of the need for complementarity between existing industrial equipment within a given enterprise and the management's choice of occupation/skill mix in the labor force. Here it is important to note that Soviet industrial establishments are extremely large in comparison with those of developed capitalist countries.[30] Furthermore, Soviet establishments are also probably more variegated (only partly because of size) with regard to their capital equipment.

It would seem that considerable slack in capacity utilization exists widely in Soviet industry, and that it has been growing over time. The best indicator of this is the fact that, within the industry of the Russian Republic, the proportion of manual workers who were employed outside of the main shift used in their plant declined from 33 per cent in 1965 to 26 per cent in 1981, a reduction of 22 per cent in sixteen years.[31] In the Ukraine, the decline was from 37 to 32 per cent between 1965 and 1975, a reduction of 13 per cent in ten years.[32] For the Soviet Union as a whole between 1965 and 1972, the annual percentage decline was an identical 1.2 per cent; moreover, of the changes indicated between 1965, 1969 and 1972 for seventeen branches, thirty-three of the thirty-four changes were declines.[33] By 1983 or 1984, the total economy in the Soviet Union as a whole showed only 12 per cent employed outside of the main shift.[34] Combining the existence of such slack in the use of plant with the existence of variegated equipment at an establishment level, we may conclude that the problem of complementarity between equipment and what would be desired as an occupation/skill mix if unconstrained by the equipment available in the factory is much less severe than might at first impression have been thought.[35]

[30] In the early 1960s, Soviet industrial establishments averaged seven times the number of employees in West German industrial establishments, twelve times the number in American, and were even larger in relationship to England, France, and Japan. Only 30 per cent of the number of Soviet industrial establishments had one hundred or less employees, compared to 86 per cent in West Germany and 92 to 98 per cent in the other countries (Ia. Kvasha in *V.E.*, 1967, 5, pp. 26–27). The Soviet data refer to enterprises rather than to establishments, but at that time the first was a very good proxy for the second.

[31] A. E. Kotliar in *Zaniatost' naseleniia* (1983), p. 22.   [32] Dolishnii (1978), p. 62.

[33] Kostin (1974), p. 155.

[34] Iu. Charukhin in *S.T.*, 1984, 9, p. 15.

[35] Contradictory data exist in the periodic one-day censuses conducted by the SSSR Central Statistical Administration as to the use of mainline production equipment in engineering industries. Comparison of five such censuses between 1967 and 1982 (*V.S.*, assorted issues)

It is here that we have the principal justification for the critical assumption as to relative elasticities of marginal rates of substitution that is made in the JROE explanation of fixed prices. It is assumed in this explanation that, in the production of subaggregate Q_j by an individual enterprise, the elasticity of substitution of Q_1 for Q_2 is comparatively high. This contrasts with the inelasticity of substitution between different types of labor factors in producing Q_1 and Q_2 individually. The assumption is based on the existence of considerable excess equipment of different types at the level of the individual enterprise, so that capital is a slack variable in the production function. It is this observed phenomenon which makes possible high elasticity of substitution between Q_1 and Q_2. A second contributing phenomenon is the widespread reliance upon general-purpose as opposed to specialized equipment in manufacturing.

One may ask, however, whether the use of market-determined prices for inputs would not constitute an offsetting advantage with respect to satisfying constraint (3.2). Namely, that the product mix of inputs within an aggregate of materials allocation would be much closer than it is

shows neither a deterioration in the number of hours out of twenty-four that such equipment is used, nor an increase in the share of equipment-idleness that is due to the absence of the required machine operators.

In my opinion, this evidence should be discounted for two reasons. The first is that such one-day census data contain a great deal of noise. Partly this is because enterprise management know the day of the census ahead of time, and consciously organize their use of equipment so as to set a good record at the expense of work in the surrounding days. (See G. V. Davydova and I. Ia. Kriukov in *E.K.O.*, 1980, 3, pp. 76–77 for supporting data from four factories.) Partly it is because of the absence of any standardized definition in factory practice as to the equipment that is to be counted; there were enterprises where over half of the equipment in the mainline production shops was ignored in the 1980 census, and on average 22 per cent of metalworking equipment was ignored in that census (N. Konovalova, a section leader in an organization attached to the SSSR State Planning Commission, in *P.Kh.*, 1983, 11, p. 42).

The second reason is that there is independent Soviet evidence as to a sharp decline in utilization of equipment. This evidence is presented for Soviet industry as a whole, using the author's candidate as the broadest measure of capacity utilization: kwh. of electricity used per annum per kw. of industrial capacity of electric motors and of electrical apparatus separately. These figures show 13 and 18 per cent decline respectively between 1961 and 1977 (D. Palterovich in *P.Kh.*, 1979, 10, p. 110). Using other measures, similar declines are shown between 1965 and 1975 for metalworking equipment in engineering and metalworking industries, between 1960 and 1977 in the weaving industry, and in other sectors (*ibid.*, pp. 111–14). Another author similarly speaks of the importance of the reduction in equipment utilization in the economy as a whole, and points particularly to the engineering industries in which the one-time censuses had shown no decline (V. Krasovskii in *V.E.*, 1984, 5, p. 42).

Thus it would appear that the absence of trend in the Central Statistical Administration one-day censuses is not only the result of considerable noise (which by itself would be a major damping factor), but also of bias.

currently to the mix desired by the user, and that this better fit would reduce obligatory idleness in the user enterprise.

This argument would seem insubstantial for two reasons. The main one is that it is not the closeness of the fit of the input mix to the user's desires that matters, but rather the stability of the input mix. Since the mix within an aggregate is determined in the existing Soviet system primarily by the equality of the producer's marginal rate of product transformation with the stable price ratio, there seems no reason to expect that there is room for major improvement in the degree of stability.

The second reason is that, to the degree that the input mix desired by the users is price elastic, a new source of instability on the input side would be introduced by the proposals. At least the possibility of substantial price elasticity is suggested by the fact that, in 1983, only 14.3 per cent of all industrial costs – measured at the level of the enterprise (i.e. of the decision making unit under the proposals) – consisted of wage and social security payments, while 68.0 per cent were accounted for by purchases of materials.[36] These relative proportions should make efforts (under the proposals) to economize on the cost of materials per unit of output seem particularly attractive to enterprises; this result would hold regardless of whether the objective function consisted of output (with fixed inputs) or of profits.

Still a further question that might legitimately be raised with regard to the likely effect of the proposals upon inputs is that of whether regularity of deliveries within the planning period would not be substantially improved. This should occur because market-determined prices would presumably take account of such delivery conditions. Would not such increased regularity of deliveries reduce the "normal" idleness forced upon workers in Soviet enterprises because of the unavailability of materials on particular workdays, and thus make it easier to respect constraint (3.2) for any $(y_2 \, \varepsilon_2)$ selected by the Center?

Here, we return to the logic underlying (3.2): that of protecting the employee's human dignity, to use Kornai's expression, as well as his income. The employee who is paid during part of the month while he is in fact idle, but then works overtime (often without hourly pay) or at a stressful pace at other periods in the month, is unlikely to perceive the situation as one of net idleness. Since the justification for introducing (3.2) as a constraint was both social and economic, the employee's perception of what is enforced idleness is important. Both for social and economic reasons, idleness should be treated as a net rather than a gross concept.

[36] *Narkhoz SSSR v 1983 g.*, p. 148.

The upshot of this section is the conclusion that introduction of the proposed solutions into the Soviet economy would be quite likely to introduce inconsistency with the JROE constraint (3.2). This stands in contrast to the existing Soviet system of fixed prices that leads to respect by the enterprises for this constraint. It is this inconsistency property that is proposed as the basic explanation of why the Soviet Center has not developed a pricing mechanism along the lines of the proposed solutions.

The term "explanation" is here being used in a particular sense that I believe is appropriate to theoretic hypotheses. It is not assured that Soviet leaders have at any point explicitly considered proposals similar to those made in this chapter, and that they have rejected them for the reason suggested above. Rather it is suggested both that they have acted as though they had undertaken such a thought process, and that such a thought process is a rational one of maximization under constraints. This interpretation of the word "explanation" as it applies to hypotheses has a long history in the discipline of economics.

ALTERNATIVE EXPLANATIONS OF THE EXISTENCE OF SOVIET FIXED PRICES

In turning to alternative explanations for why nothing resembling the proposed solutions has ever been adopted in the Soviet Union, I shall be primarily examining only alternatives that have occurred to me. I have had the advantage of only one explanation offered by others who were convinced of its usefulness.

Alternative 1: Proposals of this type have never been considered at an appropriate advisory or decision-making level in the Soviet Union.

(5.16)

Certainly it is possible that there has been such complete absence of consideration, although it would be a bit strange given the fact that the Soviet economy has suffered for over half a century from the ills that these proposals would correct. However, such a completely *ad hoc* explanation should be ruled out of court in any theoretic analysis. Certainly it would be completely in contradiction to the spirit of rational expectations analysis.

Alternative 2: The administrative complexity of implementation prevents the adoption of these or similar proposals. (5.17)

In the case of non-taut planning, the adoption of solution (5.8) for producer goods would make no demands on the Center beyond those that exist currently. It is true that it would be more difficult than it is at present for the Center to defend its having given a specific materials allocations of Q_j to a particular recipient but, as discussed above, this issue should not be determinant.

It is indeed the case that, in the instance of taut planning, solution (5.7) does require the Center to calculate annually a complete new set of prices. This is a real burden, although purely of a computational nature for producer goods (since η in [5.7] can be given the same value for all product aggregates). In the light of other such burdens that Soviet planners are willing to shoulder, it seems doubtful that proposals would be rejected simply because of the need for such additional computations; but I must admit that it is possible.

In any case, if (5.8) were adopted for all goods, the results would be no different for all enterprises whose plans were taut than those of the current system. In dealing with such enterprises, there would be neither gain nor cost to the Center. For all other enterprises – and these must have been a high proportion of the total at all peacetime periods in Soviet history after the early 1930s – the Center would reap gains at no cost.

For consumer goods, there is the additional requirement that the Center fix the average price of Q_j at frequent intervals. Since such determination of relative prices of aggregates requires decision making rather than simple computation, it does represent a burden of different sort than exists for producer goods. But the number of aggregates that must be considered is tiny by current Soviet standards of price setting. In any case, the producer-good solution could also be adopted for consumer goods if the pricing burden were felt to be too great.

One can be sure that additional administrative difficulties that have not been thought of would arise in the process of implementation. But this is true of all proposals. No unusually severe problem of this type appears to be involved in dealing with these specific pricing proposals.

Alternative 3: Soviet central planners have an ideological commitment to keep relative prices stable. Freely changing prices are viewed as immoral. In short, Center-determined prices are lexicographically preferred over market-determined prices in the planners' social welfare function.   (5.18)

As expounded in "The Constraints" section of Chapter 4, ideology is a *deus ex machina* which can be used to explain almost any behavior; thus it should be appealed to as rarely as possible. Nevertheless, it cannot be eliminated.

With regard to the specific ideological issue raised, one might wonder why market prices for consumer goods are accepted in collective farm markets (even if such market-determined price making has been limited by recurrent local efforts at restriction) in view of such asserted lexicographic Central preference. One might also wonder why the relative prices of intermediate products and capital goods should be regarded as a moral issue.

Alternative 4: The proposals are based on the assumption that all goods are allocated. For non-allocated items, the proposals place no lid on market-determined prices.   (5.19)

The principal non-allocated industrial producer goods seem to be those produced for local use.[37] In the case of housing and other non-factory construction – which would appear to be a particularly appropriate place to use such products – an official of the national State Planning Commission has recognized that an enterprise that has money for such activities, but that receives no materials allocations because the activities are not included in the state plan, has only a pious hope of being able to carry out the construction.[38]

In the case of consumer non-durable goods, no more than 70 per cent of the orders (*zaiavki*) placed for shoes by the national Ministry of Trade are filled.[39] For seven broad types of consumer durables described in 1979 and 1981, there were three observations (out of fourteen by category and year) in which over 90 per cent of the orders placed by trade organizations of the Russian Republic were accepted by industry; five observations in the 80–89 per cent range; three in the 70–79 per cent range; two in the 60–69 per cent; and one at 54 per cent. Much of even those orders accepted were not filled.[40] Furthermore, the sources do not indicate whether the orders were fully disaggregated or whether they themselves represented product-aggregation at some level. Clearly, it would normally be hopeless for trade organizations to attempt to order from industry goods for which they had no allocations.[41]

Thus it would appear that the non-allocated category of goods is miniscule. It could well be handled in the standard Soviet fashion, with all prices being set by the Center at long intervals, with little harm to the overall Soviet economy.

[37] Berliner (1976), pp. 64 and 87–88.   [38] V. Rzheshevskii in *S.T.*, 1980, 5, p. 17.
[39] S. E. Sarukhanov, a vice-minister of the Ministry of Trade SSSR, in *P.Kh.*, 1984, 4, p. 45.
[40] V. Shimanski, minister of trade of the Russian Republic, in *P.Kh.*, 1981, 9, p. 34.
[41] See the discussion in Hanson (1968), pp. 185–88 and Berliner (1976), p. 210.

Alternative 5: Lower and medium-level Communist Party functionaries at regional level derive much of their power from the ability to intervene in determining the composition and distribution of the Q_i aggregate as between Q_1 and Q_2. The constraint on the Center that prevents the adoption of the proposed changes is a political constraint, growing out of the relationship between top national Party leaders and low/medium level Party functionaries.   (5.20)

This explanation was ruled out of bounds in the maintained hypothesis (4.2) in order to keep the analysis outside of a political-science framework in which power is the fundamental maximand of the Center. But, of course, the mere statement of a maintained hypothesis is no basis for rejecting the factual appropriateness of Alternative 5.

The discussion of (4.2) in Chapter 4 provides a modest empirical basis for rejecting this Alternative. Nevertheless, I find Alternative 5 to be a serious competitor with my JROE explanation.

It seems striking that of the alternatives examined, the first four are at best *ad hoc*, while the fifth grows out of a theoretic structure foreign to the discipline of economics. In any case, and this is what matters, all five of these alternatives are quite unrelated to (3.4) – the "rival hypothesis" to JROE in explaining the labor market phenomena observed in the Soviet Union.

6

Fixed investment and JROE

This chapter attempts to explain why the Soviet economy appears in recent years to have received such low returns from its heavy investments in fixed capital. Many of the observed phenomena are equally well interpreted as resulting from the incentive constraints of Model A as from the JROE constraints of Model B. But certain phenomena seem poorly explained by Model A alone. It is on this basis that it is argued that Model B finds support in this area of investigation.

DATA EXPLAINED BY EITHER SET OF CONSTRAINTS

Both Soviet and Western scholars are agreed that the Soviet economy has been receiving significantly deteriorating returns during recent decades from its investments in fixed capital. Although both groups have concentrated their attention on industry, the problem appears to be general throughout the economy.

Quite different techniques have yielded similar results in this regard. Cobb-Douglas functions have shown steady declines (aside, perhaps, from the second half of the 1960s) in the rate of improvement of factor-productivity.[1] Constant elasticity of substitution functions with Hicks-neutral technological change have not indicated any such worsening in this rate, but they have shown a very low elasticity of substitution between fixed capital and labor. Since capital has been growing much more rapidly than the labor force, this has implied a sharp decline in the return on capital.[2] Soviet marginal capital/output ratios have also shown substantial

---

[1] See, among others, A. Bergson in Bergson and Levine (1983), pp. 35–44 for total gross national product and for all material sectors taken together, and M. L. Weitzman in *ibid.*, pp. 179–86 and P. Desai in *J.C.E.*, 9, 1 (March 1985), pp. 1–23 for industry.
[2] M. L. Weitzman in *ibid.*, pp. 187–88 for industry.

Table 6.1 *Annual rates of increase in the Soviet capital/labor ratio*

Sector	Period				
	1950/51–1960/61	1960/61–1965/66	1965/66–1970/71	1970/71–1975/76	1975/76–1980/81
All material production other than agriculture	. . .	. . .	5.3%	6.1%	5.8%
Industry	7.7%	7.0%	6.2%	6.9%	6.0%

Note: Capital figures are as of the end-of-year, relate only to fixed production capital, and are measured in 1973 prices. Labor figures refer to the number employed, and are averages for the year; thus the average is taken for the year of the capital data and for the following year. The number employed in industry excludes those in auxiliary operations such as restaurants and clinics within industrial enterprises; thus these data are comparable in coverage to the capital figures. For the remaining material production sector other than agriculture, labor data include those employed in such auxiliary operations; the degree of incomparability with the capital data should not, however, be great.

These data should be considered as representing only a rough calculation. They take no account either of the decline in the working day during the second half of the 1950s and first years of the 1960s, or of the apparent inflation in the capital figures. Stanley H. Cohn estimates capital inflation as being less than one per cent per annum (unpublished supplement to his paper in *J.E.C.* [1979]).

Source: Narkhoz SSSR, various issues.

deterioration over time.[3] All of these results held well before the late 1970s, let alone in the relatively catastrophic recent years.[4]

Throughout the post-war period, Soviet net investment has been high and the capital/labor ratio has risen sharply as can be seen in Table 6.1. The annual increase of five to eight per cent in this ratio represents a major challenge with regard to capital absorption. This is so not only as it relates to the completing of construction projects within a reasonable period, to the maintaining of sectoral balance as defined in an input-output sense, and to the expansion of the managerial organization at a sufficient pace so as effectively to operate the increased capital capacities. Rather, the challenge that is interesting for us at this point is the necessary reorganization of production processes in order to adapt to the changing relative availabilities of capital and labor.[5]

[3] See A. Notkin in *V.E..*, 1981, 9, p. 93.

[4] For a summary of the above literature on production functions, see J. S. Brada in *Osteuropa Wirtschaft*, 1985, 2, pp. 116–22.

[5] The assumptions made in these various production functions and throughout this chapter are that technological progress is Hicks-neutral and that there are no net economies of scale. S. Gomulka has pointed out that the above CES production function result does not necessarily follow from heavy investments if technological progress is of the labor-augment-

To the degree that this necessary reorganization has been unsuccessful, we would expect to see such failure reflected in the production function. If a constant elasticity of substitution production function with Hicks-neutral technology is fitted to the data, one would expect the function to show a low elasticity of substitution between capital and labor.[6] If a Cobb-Douglas function were fitted, with its presumed incorrect assumption of an elasticity of substitution of unity, the rate of factor-productivity improvement should be low and declining steadily. Nor is there reason to be surprised at the rise in the marginal capital/output ratio since, despite the relative ineffectiveness of the substitution of capital for labor, such substitution is nevertheless still occurring.[7]

That the above statistical phenomena are not inevitable results of a rapid change in the relative availability of capital to labor is demonstrated by the post-war experience of the Japanese economy until the first oil crisis of the early 1970s.[8] Although Japanese industry had at least as rapid a rate of capital growth as did Soviet industry, the two economies have differed markedly in the quality of their respective responses to the challenge represented by such growth.[9] Partly this is the case because of the much more rapid change in the inter-sectoral composition of industry in Japan; but it is also due to a major difference in the rate of technological change within individual sectors.

ing type. In that case, Gomulka's work on statistics of Soviet industry indicates that the sum of squared errors is insensitive to the assumed elasticity of substitution.

 However, as Gomulka has also pointed out, if the capital/labor elasticity of substitution is low and if technological change constitutes a mix of capital-augmenting and labor-augmenting innovations, then the challenge described in the text can be interpreted as that of shifting the mix of innovations diffused throughout the Soviet economy in the direction of the labor-augmenting type (Gomulka [1986], pp. 105, 113, and 151). This interpretation would be sufficient to bear the weight of the analysis of this chapter under conditions of labor-augmenting technological progress. A low elasticity of substitution is independently suggested by the reduction in the number of hours of daily usage of capital equipment within Soviet industry (see Chapter 5) as the capital/labor ratio has risen.

6 Since growth in the Soviet capital/labor ratio has been relatively stable over a thirty year period, and thus the reorganization problem has been of a reasonably constant dimension, there is no reason why different elasticities should necessarily be shown in the various sub-periods. Thus the above explanation of low elasticity is not in conflict with the finding that the identical function can be fitted for industry in the sub-periods 1950–63 and 1964–78 (Weitzman in Bergson and Levine [1983], pp. 187–88).

7 There has also been deterioration in the average shift coefficient of capital equipment in industry, as well as a shift in the inter-sectoral structure of investment in a capital intensive direction. These are clearly also contributing factors.

8 The rate of factor-productivity improvement, based upon an enlarged Cobb-Douglas function, was virtually the same during 1961–71 as it had been in 1953–61 (Denison and Chung [1976], p. 38).

9 See Stanley H. Cohn in *J.E.C.* (1983), Part 1, pp. 173 and 183–84.

Various studies have been made by Western writers, all indicating that the Soviet diffusion rate of technological innovations in civilian sectors during the post-war years has been slow in comparison with that in developed capitalist countries.[10] Although the record of Soviet basic and applied research does not receive particularly high marks, it seems clear that the essential Soviet problem with innovation does not lie there. Instead, it rests in the inability or unwillingness to introduce change in a timely fashion at the factory level – whether this change be of product or of process. The bottleneck both to pushing outward the Soviet production frontier in individual sectors, and to adapting to changes in relative scarcities of factors, lies primarily in the implementation of ideas for change rather than in the creation (or transfer from abroad) of such ideas.[11]

One might reasonably expect to see a positive partial correlation between the speed of implementation of technical innovation (i.e. shifting of isoquants) and the rate of change in the occupational structure of the economy. The assumption made here is that change in technology is accompanied by variations in the types of worker skills required in production. Operating in the opposite direction in its effect on Soviet occupational structure should be the positive partial correlation between the rate of increase in the capital/labor ratio (i.e. appropriate point of production on a given isoquant) and the degree of alteration in such structure. The rate of change in occupational structure in the Soviet Union compared with that in other developed countries should reflect (or be reflected in, depending on the direction of causation) the relative strength of these two forces.

Various measures of occupational change are possible. However, with an eye to the JROE hypotheses, the measure selected consists of the number and importance of those occupations whose membership declined between occupational censuses. This choice is motivated by the belief that a decline in the absolute number of people employed nationally within a

---

10 Perhaps the earliest of such studies is that of Michael Boretsky in *J.E.C.* (1966). The most full-blown and convincing is the book of Amann *et al.* (1977). A guide to German-language literature, extending such comparison to socialist and capitalist developed countries in general, is found in Armin Bohnet and Mihaly Laki in *Verein* (1984), p. 82.

11 Polish experience, which is presumably also relevant to the Soviet Union, suggests that implementation of technical change does occur frequently and rapidly in one area: that of overcoming supply difficulties. This is described as the "innovation of poverty" – the substitution of one material for another, with necessary accompanying design modifications of the product, due to temporary supply difficulties in a particular factory rather than as a response to relative scarcities existing at a national level. (See *ibid.*, pp. 111–12 with references to articles of S. Gomulka [1977] and L. Balczerowicz [1980].)

given occupation can serve as a reasonable proxy for the degree of difficulty in maintaining the right to the given job in the given enterprise for those employed in that occupation at the beginning of the period. The major exception to this link exists where a particular occupation is unattractive to potential entrants and, in particular, where many original members of the occupational group are anxious to leave it when and if opportunity occurs.

Soviet occupational change between 1959 and 1970

The Soviet population censuses of January 1959 and 1970 record the occupations of individuals, who were asked both as to the occupation and economic sector in which they were currently working.[12] The eleven year period between these two censuses (unfortunately, the only two post-war ones for which such data have been published) roughly corresponds to the ten year period between the American 1960 and 1970 censuses which also give occupational data. Thus comparison of change in occupations between the two countries over the same time period is possible.

Occupations examined here are those that are defined as, or that can be grouped to be, comparable between the two countries, that are blue-collar, and that are not specifically agricultural. (Agricultural occupations are omitted partly because of the extreme difference in the proportion of the labor force engaged within this sector in the two countries, partly because of the effect of changes in collective-farm pension legislation in the Soviet Union (see Note *a* of Table 6.3), but also because occupational definitions – reflecting the distinctive national realities of occupational breakdown within agriculture – are radically different.) The number of occupations examined include 64 that are directly comparable; in addition, there are 14 groupings of occupations for which the individual groupings are comparable.

Table 6.2 provides a comparison of the occupational change in the two countries during the 1960s. We can see from the table that 49 per cent of the sample of blue-collar non-agricultural occupations declined over the ten years in the United States, versus 38 per cent during eleven years in the Soviet Union. The decline in the labor force within such occupations was also higher in the U.S.: a compound annual rate of 0.8 per cent versus 0.6 per cent in the USSR. Furthermore, the Soviet capital/labor ratio increased at two and one-half times the American rate; this last fact, *ceteris paribus*, should have caused the Soviet figures referred to earlier to have

---

[12] Military personnel are included, and classified according to their last civilian job. For an analysis of the two occupational censuses, see Rapawy (1976), pp. 12–15.

Table 6.2 *Labor-force reductions during the 1960s in the Soviet Union and the U.S.*

(blue-collar occupations that are not specifically agricultural)

	U.S.S.R. (1959–1970)	U.S. (1960–1970)
A. *Occupations in the sample*		
Number of sample occupations as given in the censuses	135	128
Labor force in these sample occupations as a percentage of the total blue-collar and white-collar labor force in non-agricultural occupations (1959–60 censuses)	37%	25%
Sample occupations whose labor force declined between censuses		
Number of declining occupations	51	63
Declining occupations as percentage of all sample occupations	38%	49%
Inter-census decline in labor force in declining occupations as percentage of the total labor force in all sample occupations as of the time of the earlier census		
Total	8.9%	7.8%
Total excluding persons listed as employed in the agricultural sector	7.0%	7.8%
B. *Capital/labor ratio (compound annual rate of increase)[a]*		
All materials sectors except agriculture	4.9%	
All non-farm private business		2.0%
C. *Labor force (compound annual rate of increase)*		
Total labor force	1.4%	1.8%
Total non-agricultural labor force[b]	3.3%	2.2%
Total non-agricultural blue-collar labor force[b]	2.8%	
Total in sample occupations and not employed in the agricultural sector[b]	2.9%	0.6%

Notes: I am indebted to my former research assistant, Edward Albertini, for having carried out the necessary classifications of occupations and for doing the calculations.

[a] The sectors covered in the two countries are fairly comparable, since trade is included in the Soviet definition of a material sector.

[b] For the Soviet Union, persons who are in the sample occupations, but who are also listed as employed in the agricultural sector, are excluded. Such exclusion raises the Soviet figures by 0.5, 0.2, and 0.3 per cent respectively.

Sources: Soviet labor data are taken from TsSU, *Itogi perepisi 1970*, Vol. 6 (1973), Tables 2 and 34, and from TsSU, *Itogi perepisi 1959* (1962), Table 44. Soviet capital data are for fixed capital, and are taken from Stanley H. Cohn's unpublished appendixes to his paper in *J.E.C.* (1983). American labor data are from the 1960 and 1970 Censuses of Population; the capital data are from the *U.S. Statistical Abstracts 1982–83* and are left undepreciated so as to conform with the Soviet treatment.

Table 6.3 *Proportions of all Soviet manual labor-force reductions in declining occupations, by category of occupation (1959–1970)*

Category of those occupations showing a decline in absolute numbers	Blue-collar occupations outside of agriculture (4.4 million in declining occupations)	Blue-collar occupations within agriculture[a] (13.7 million in declining occupations)	All Blue-collar occupations (18.1 million in declining occupations)
Occupations embodying no skill[b]	54.1%[d]	83.6%	76.4%
Three specified occupations[c]	14.2[d]	3.9	6.2
Other agricultural occupations	0	12.5	9.5
Sub-totals	*68*	*100*	*92*

Notes:

 [a] Much of this decline is due to the change in pension law covering collective farmers. The share of pensioners in the collective-farm population rose from 3.2 to 24.2 per cent over this period. Furthermore, most pensioners in agriculture who did continue working were excluded from the census definition of labor force (Rapawy [1976], p. 14).

 [b] This category is narrowly defined. In agriculture, it consists of all those without specified occupations. In transport, it refers to carters, loaders, porters, and the like. In construction, it covers pick-and-shovel navvies. Warehouse workers constitute another category, and janitors and watchmen the final one.

 [c] Blacksmiths, carpenters, and loggers cutting and stripping trees.

 [d] Blacksmiths are not included here; their decline was limited to the agricultural sector.

Sources: TsSU, *Itogi perepisi 1959* (1962), Table 44, and TsSU, *Itogi perepisi 1970*, Vol. 6 (1973), Tables 2 and 34.

been substantially higher instead of lower than the American ones. These results correspond well with what might have been predicted from what we know about relative rates of diffusion of technical innovations.

Unfortunately, the data as to growth of the labor force muddy the picture. No problem arises if we look at total labor-force growth; American growth was somewhat faster than Soviet during this period, which should have had the effect of reducing the number of declining occupations in the United States versus the Soviet Union. But the relative growth rates reverse sharply if we look only at the non-agricultural labor force, and even more if we restrict ourselves to the sample occupations. Since it is not clear which of these comparisons is more relevant to the probability, *ceteris paribus*, of a particular occupation declining in absolute number over the relevant period, we must be cautious in drawing conclusions from Table 6.2.

Let us turn to examining the nature of the Soviet occupations in which declines in employment occurred between 1959 and 1970. Here I will use the full Soviet occupational-census data for all blue-collar workers, rather than a sample of these data as was used in Table 6.2. This analysis yields Table 6.3.

Looking at the total number of lost jobs in those blue-collar occupations that declined during 1959–70, we observe that they constituted 22.6 per cent of all blue-collar jobs in 1959 – a loss rate of 1.9 per cent per annum. But if we deduct those occupations without skills, the loss over eleven years falls to 5.3 per cent. If we further proceed to deduct all other agricultural occupations in which the number of jobs declined – basing such exclusion partly on the change in pension legislation noted in Table 6.3, and partly on the argument that, generally speaking, agricultural workers were glad to move to other, better paid sectors – the loss figure falls to 3.2 per cent over the period, or 0.3 per cent per annum. It is this 3.2 per cent over eleven years that is probably the upper limit of the lost jobs in declining occupations which were regarded by any workers as constituting a reduction in desirable work opportunities.

Turning to declining blue-collar occupations outside of agriculture, job losses here constituted 9.6 per cent of all jobs existing in non-agricultural, blue-collar occupations in 1959.[13] When we exclude the occupations with absolutely no skill, the proportion falls to 4.4 per cent over the period, or 0.4 per cent per annum. It is this figure which is of the greatest relevance to the issue of employers being able to respect the JROE constraint with regard to dismissals or forced occupational changes.

Of these remaining job losses outside of agriculture, 31 per cent were in two occupations. Roughly half were loggers cutting and stripping trees, seasonal work linked fairly closely to agriculture in its source of labor supply. The 38 per cent decline in such jobs must have been influenced by the change in pension legislation for collective farmers that was noted earlier and, due to the exclusion from the census definition of labor force of pensioners who are working seasonally, is partly a statistical artifact. It is at least possible that the genuine portion of the decline was not greatly regretted by many workers, given the nature of the work. The other half of the job losses consists of carpenters (but not cabinet makers), whose numbers declined by 22 per cent. Since the number in this occupation increased slightly in the United States in the comparable period, and since the Soviet 1959 figure was 172 per cent of the American 1960 statistic, it seems likely that the Soviet definition in 1959 was much broader than the American "carpenter and carpenter's helper" and included many workers with little skill. These suppositions should be taken as no more than that.

[13] This figure contrasts with 7 per cent in the sample data of Table 6.2.

What is clear is that there was considerable concentration of the job losses of non-agricultural blue-collar workers with some skills into two narrow occupational categories.

Summarizing the above data, the minimum that can be said is the following:

Despite the rapid growth of the capital/labor ratio in the Soviet non-agricultural economy, the breadth of those blue-collar occupations whose labor force declined absolutely during the 1960s in the United States was far from matched in the Soviet Union.

Two-thirds of the decline in blue collar, non-agricultural occupations in the Soviet Union was concentrated in those either entailing no skills or in two narrow occupations.[14]

(6.1)

Explanations of these Soviet occupational data

Explanation in terms of Model A. The Model A explanation assumes that the causal relationship is expressed by $\dot{S}=f(\dot{D}, \dot{k})$ where $\dot{S}=$the rate of change in the occupational structure of the economy, $\dot{D}=$the speed of diffusion of technical innovation, and $k=$the rate of growth of the capital/labor ratio. It concentrates upon the explanation as to why $\dot{D}$ is low in the Soviet economy.

The principal feature of this explanation is the incentive problem faced by the Soviet Center: namely, that the Center is incapable of internalizing into the utility function of enterprise managers objectives whose fulfillment cannot be measured within a period of one year from such fulfillment. (Result [4.16] from constraints [4.10]...[4.13] and promotion principle [4.15].) Since costs are generally higher than returns during the first year of implementation of a technical innovation, such implementation is properly regarded by enterprise managers as representing an externality from the viewpoint of the enterprise. Efforts by the Center, inaugurated particularly during the 1960s and 1970s, to change this calculation by subsidizing part of the costs of innovation implementation have not been successful.[15]

[14] However, the percentage decline compared with their 1959 numbers was just the same in these occupations as in the residual of all declining occupations: 32 per cent.

[15] See Berliner (1976), Parts 2 and 3 for a treatment of the history of such subsidization, and for an analysis of the incentives of the enterprise.

There is a suggestion that, at least in the engineering industries, the speed of implementation of new products actually deteriorated between 1967 and 1978 (D. Palterovich in *P.Kh.*, 1980, 9, p. 105 fn.). A 1982 pricing revision was accompanied by a Soviet analysis acknowledging that the subsidization system of the second half of the 1960s and of the 1970s had been unsuccessful. The replacement system would appear to be highly

The second feature of this explanation rests upon constraints (4.5) and (4.8) that lead to allocation of materials in the form of aggregates rather than individual products. Implementation of innovations in the form of either product or process frequently requires changes in the mix of materials used. However, potential implementing enterprises have standing relations with suppliers who provide, within the allocated aggregate, a customary mix of items to which the user has adjusted his production process. The request for a change of mix to meet new needs may lead to major supply difficulties.[16]

Aside from explaining why $\dot{D}$ should be low, we must also ask of an explanation that it account for the structure of the occupational declines which occurred. Why has the enterprises's choice of innovations to be implemented been such as to economize primarily upon totally unskilled labor? Presumably, an explanation in terms of Model A should be expressed in a cost-benefit analysis for enterprise management.

Such an explanation starts from the changing labor-supply situation facing the enterprise over the 1960s. As the educational level of the labor force improved, it became increasingly difficult for management to find the previous number of workers willing to carry out completely unskilled work. This must have been particularly true where such work was poorly paid. Because of the large numbers of such unskilled jobs within the relevant enterprises, managements could respond only to a limited degree by raising the relative earnings of such workers out of their constrained wage funds. (The decline in the number of transport and warehouse workers did not occur in industry; presumably, industrial enterprises were better able than others to bid for the available types of labor.) Thus the combination of quits and of inability to recruit sufficient replacements explains the decline of these occupations. Management had no choice but to adjust.

One form of adjustment has been dependence upon local authorities to obligate other enterprises to send members of their labor force on temporary assignment to do precisely this type of work.[17] While no data are available as to its dimensions, such dependence has been of growing significance. No technical innovation at all is needed for this type of adjustment.

inflationary, and is to be limited only to products embodying "very effective new technology." (L. I. Rozenova in *V.E.*, 1984, 2, pp. 24–26).

16   The explanation resting upon the desirability of unchanged supply mix is related to the concept of "vegetative mechanisms" in Kornai (1980), pp. 147–49.

17   See Chapter 2, pp. 38–40. Mobilization in urban areas for both unloading and warehousing connected with agriculture, and for urban street and building maintenance, has been specifically noted in the Soviet literature.

The innovative type of adjustment rests upon work reorganization and, probably more significantly, on capital/labor substitution. Where the first form of adjustment is unavailable or insufficient, this second type can have a high pay-off to the implementing enterprise.

The difficulty with the above supply-oriented explanation is the period which it addresses: the 1960s. The national labor force outside of agriculture grew at virtually as rapid a rate in the 1960s as it had in the 1950s. Moreover, only half of the 1960s expansion, as contrasted to all of that of the 1950s, came from teenagers who might be expected to be the age-group most reluctant to accept such poorly paid work without a future. During the 1960s, almost half of the labor-force expansion came from the increased labor-force participation of women. What is striking about this development for our purposes is that the rate of increase in female participation over the decade is positively correlated with the age of the cohort (see Table 2.3). Moreover, it is worth noting that the extent of compulsory temporary mobilization for work in agriculture increased by only 20 per cent during the 1960s, as compared with 150 and 117 per cent respectively during the 1950s and 1970s.

Despite the above empirical problems, it may well be that supply difficulties in such unskilled work did increase in the 1960s to the degree suggested by the Model A explanation. But I would be happier if the data to be explained were of the 1970s instead.

Explanation in terms of Model B. Model B, resting on the JROE constraints, reverses the causality relationship provided in the previous explanation. $\dot{D}$ becomes the dependent variable, with $\dot{S}$ and $\dot{k}$ the independent ones. $\dot{D} = g(\dot{S}, \dot{k})$.

Here, the problem for the Center can be stated as:

Maximize $\dot{Y}(\dot{S}_1, \ldots, \dot{S}_j, \ldots, \dot{S}_J, \dot{k}, \dot{L})$ subject to:
  $\dot{S}_j{}^*$ is chosen so that constraint (3.1) holds where
    $V_{z_j} = \gamma(\dot{S}_1, \ldots, \dot{S}_j, \ldots, \dot{S}_J)$
  and so that constraint (3.3) holds where
    $B_i = \beta(\dot{S}_1, \ldots, \dot{S}_j, \ldots, \dot{S}_J)$
  and so that constraint (3.2) holds where
    $A_i = \alpha(B_i, \dot{S}_1, \ldots, \dot{S}_j, \ldots, \dot{S}_J)$
  $\dot{k}{}^*$ is chosen subject to the Center's rate of time discount, the production function, $\dot{L}$, and $\dot{S}_1{}^*, \ldots, \dot{S}_j{}^*, \ldots, \dot{S}_J{}^*$

where $\dot{Y}$ = rate of growth of per capita final product
       $\dot{k}$ = rate of growth of the aggregate capital/labor ratio
       $\dot{S}_j$ = the rate of change in the number of people
            working in occupation (j)
       $\dot{L}$ = rate of growth in the labor force   (6.2)

The maximand and the last constraint together represent the objective function (4.3). The other three constraints are those of full employment, no dismissals and no obligatory idleness in the JROE set. $\dot{L}$ is here treated as exogenous. $\dot{S}_j$ and $\dot{k}$ constitute the Center's choice variables. The Center must solve simultaneously for $\dot{S}_j^*$ (k) and for $\dot{k}^*(\dot{S}_j)$. It then attempts to promote the maximum rate of diffusion of technical innovation, $\dot{D}^*$, that is consistent with $\dot{S}^*_j$ and $\dot{k}^*$. It is assumed that the Center is able to achieve a rate of diffusion at the factory floor that is satisfactory to it – given the upper-bound on an acceptable $\dot{D}$ that results from $\dot{S}^*_j$ and $\dot{k}^*$.

In this explanation, given the concentration of declining occupations in the unskilled category of labor, it is clear that the constraint (3.1) of full employment must be treated as having been non-binding during the 1960s on the choice of $\dot{S}_j^*$. This is because those workers with skills could always take unskilled jobs if other posts were not available, while the counterpart statement as to unskilled workers is not true. It is the non-idleness and non-dismissals constraints (3.2 and 3.3) which alone were binding.

This explanation is quite consistent, as was that of Model A, with the restricted breadth of declining occupations and with the slow speed of diffusion of technical innovations. In this explanation, it is the requirement of sharply limiting dismissals or forced job changes within each individual factory (and even, to a lesser degree, each shop) that compels considerable caution on the part both of the Center and of individual enterprises in allowing the absolute numbers within a given occupation to decline. This is not only because the occupational declines treated in Tables 6.2 and 6.3 are aggregated at a national level rather than constituting the sum of all declines occurring at an enterprise level, but also because each occupation itself is an aggregation of many *"spetsial'nosti"* used in the definition of job retention.

Another aspect of the problem of declining occupations is exemplified by the experience of the Shchekino chemical combinat, the national show-piece of labor reduction during the late 1960s and first half of the 1970s. The combinat apparently handled the problem of combining job reduction with no dismissals by virtually ceasing new hirings during a period of fifteen years. As a result of the consequent aging of the labor force, the combinat had by the early 1980s incurred a bad production reputation, and it was said to be no longer popular to speak publicly of the experience of this combinat.[18]

Furthermore, Model B does as well as Model A – but no better – in explaining the concentration of declining occupations among the unskilled working in low-paying jobs. In both cases, the explanation is supply oriented; for Model B, it is the high quit rate that might be expected in such jobs as better ones become available. The year 1970 differed from 1959 in that the labor force was better educated, and thus that a higher proportion of any given age group were qualified for more than unskilled work. The difficulty with the Model B explanation is that one wonders why the full-employment constraint (3.1) did not become binding during the 1960s, and prevent a reduction in such unskilled occupations. After all, this was the decade when a major increase occurred in the number of older women participating in the labor force; many of them must have been unqualified for other than unskilled work.

A minor and quite different use of Model B is to provide a better basis for the explanation offered by Model A as to the reluctance of enterprises, based on expectations of additional difficulties in obtaining materials supplies, to implement technical innovations. Model B was the source of the hypothesis, provided in Chapter 5, for why the Center does not combine Center-determined and market-determined prices in such a fashion as to cause the actual product mix within an allocated aggregate of materials to reflect user preferences. If such a pricing system were utilized, the supplies-based component of the explanation offered by Model A would become less plausible.

DATA EXPLAINED ONLY BY MODEL B

Evolution of unskilled workers in industry alone

This section deals with the essentially unskilled component of the materials-handling and warehousing workforce within Soviet industry alone. The total labor force engaged in such movement of materials was said to constitute some 14 per cent of all Soviet industrial manual workers[19]

[18] Knishnik and Levikov (1983), pp. 27–28. Although published in German only (but in Moscow), the authors are journalists of the Soviet weekly *Literaturnaia Gazeta*.

[19] Both here and throughout the book, the term "manual workers" is used as a translation of "*rabochie*," and is synonymous with "blue-collar." The term is somewhat narrower than the comparable American term, usually excluding apprentices, janitorial personnel and

Table 6.4 *Unskilled materials handlers, warehousemen and packers in Soviet industry (000)*

Category	1948	1954	1959	1962	1965	1969	1979
Loaders, carriers, and unskilled personnel loading and unloading processing machines	1,215^a	1,793^a	1,675^a	1,701^a	1,888^a	1,643^a	
			1,562^c		1,919^c	1,985^c	
					1,322^d		2,500^e
Storeroom keepers, warehousemen, packers	133^a	273^a	334^a	429^a	522^a	500^b	1,900^e
Total of internal transport, warehousemen and packers						2,692$^{d\,e}$	4,500^f
Sum of unskilled sub-categories on the assumption that their percentage of the third-row total was the same in 1979 as it was in 1969						1,822^d	3,046

Notes: Data through 1969 are taken explicitly from the period counts of the number of manual workers in industry within given trades. It is claimed that coverage in the counts is over 90 per cent. Data problems are suggested by the fact that the 1965 count (of August 2nd) shows 13 per cent fewer manual workers in the engineering industries, and 22 per cent fewer in light industry, than do the official data of the average for the year (Krevnevich [1971], p. 239). The 1979 data are also presumably from the same source; clearly the sub-totals for this year are too high, seemingly because they include almost all drivers, crane operators, and other materials handlers.

Many of the storeroom keepers are skilled personnel. But the category that includes warehousemen and packers must be overwhelmingly unskilled.

One author, presumably on the basis of these same data, says that ten per cent of the total increase of manual workers in industry between 1962 and 1969 occurred in internal transport and warehousing. Assuming (the article is unclear in this regard) that his various percentages apply to the whole Soviet Union and not simply to the Russian Republic, this would suggest that the number of such workers increased by 744,000 – or 38 per cent – over this period. Furthermore, the substantial sub-category of totally unskilled workers loading and unloading processing machines (*podsobnye rabochie*) was said to have increased in numbers during these years by a slightly higher percentage than did the aggregate of all industrial manual workers (L. M. Danilov in *Problemy ratsional'nogo* [1973], p. 116). These calculations cast further doubt on the table's indicated decline in absolute numbers between 1965 and 1969.

Sources:
^{a} *Narkhoz SSSR 1965*, pp. 569–70.
^{b} Shafranova (1972), p. 55.
^{c} Calculated from percentages given by A. Zdravomyslov in *Kommunist*, 1971, 13, p. 29. This source is quoted as authoritative by Omel'ianenko (1973), p. 24.
^{d} Shafranova (1972), pp. 55 and 59.
^{e} Sub-categories are summed by me so as to be most comparable with the stated definition of the data of 1979.
^{f} A. I. Kovalev in *E.K.O.*, 1979, 10, p. 55. However, Kovalev's 18 per cent figure for the total as a proportion of all manual workers implies 5,261.

in 1975 and 18 per cent in 1979, in contrast to a bit under nine per cent in American industry in the early 1970s. In the Soviet case, 29 per cent of total manual-worker manhours were described as being used in such work when one counts the time spent by production workers as well.[20] Materials handling is an activity whose lack of mechanization in Soviet industry is well recognized both by Soviet and Western students. It is a field in which the substitution of capital for labor is relatively straightforward and uncomplicated, but in which such substitution has progressed only slowly.

Table 6.4 presents the available data from the various periodic counts by the Central Statistical Administration of the number of people working in industry within given trades. The 1979 data, and probably the 1969 to a lesser degree, contain serious problems of definitional comparability with the earlier data. The table shows a major increase in the absolute numbers during 1969–79; but an expansion of the degree indicated is difficult to credit. The conclusion that I draw from this table is that, although there was a steady decline in the proportion of the industrial manual labor force engaged in these activities until 1969, there were no significant declines over the entire period 1948–79 (except possibly during 1965–69) in the absolute numbers employed. Such absence of reduction in absolute numbers is described as continuing into the 1980s.[21]

Given the poor quality of the figures in Table 6.4, it seems worth while to provide independent supporting evidence for the conclusion drawn. A variety of types of evidence exist.

During 1971–75 in all engineering industry existing on the territory of the Russian Republic, internal-transport shops and warehousing operations increased their numbers employed by 147 per cent of the rate of growth that occurred in the industrial branch's auxiliary shops as a whole. Although we have no data as to the growth of employment in auxiliary vs. productive shops in engineering as such, the ratio for all industry in the Russian Republic during these years was 225 per cent.[22] In the republic of Azerbaidzhan during 1966–75, the number of materials-handlers working without mechanized equipment increased more rapidly than did the number working with such equipment.[23]

---

guards. In 1979, manual workers constituted 80 per cent of all industrial employees; if one were to use the term in the wider sense, the figure rises to 83 per cent.

[20] A. I. Kovalev in *E.K.O.*, 1979, 10, p. 55, and M. L. Shukhgapter in *E.K.O.*, 1979, 10, pp. 46–47. The Soviet data for 1979 are presumably taken from that year's count of people in different trades in industry, conducted by the Central Statistic Administration.

[21] N. A. Petrunina in *Formirovanie* (1982), p. 297. The group described in this source consists of unskilled and semi-skilled blue-collar workers, which is essentially the same category.

[22] N. Zenchenko in *P.Kh.*, 1977, 6, p. 66.   [23] S. Divilov in *P.Kh.*, 1978, 4, p. 105.

During 1976–80, the average annual rate of increase in the production of materials-handling equipment in Soviet industry was only 28 per cent of that of engineering production as a whole.[24] As of the end of 1978, despite a Central decree of 1973 ordering the expansion in plant capacity for building such equipment, not one of the new factories stipulated in the 1973 decree had been brought into operation.[25] Nor did matters improve during the 1981–84 period.[26]

A very broad and heterogeneous category, which includes the group of interest to us here, is that of "auxiliary" as opposed to mainline-production manual workers. This category grew from 46 to 49 per cent of all industrial manual workers between 1965 and 1972.[27] During the late 1970s and early 1980s, the category was said to have increased by 6 per cent while the number of mainline-production workers declined by 1 per cent.[28] In Estonian industry during 1971–75, there was a similar increase in auxiliary workers and decline of those in mainline production.[29] These changes are in contrast to the situation in the United States where auxiliary workers, grouped according to the Soviet definition, are said to have constituted only one-third of all industrial manual workers in the early 1970s, and where the proportion had remained virtually unchanged since the middle 1950s.[30]

These disparate developments in the number of auxiliary vs. mainline-production workers are given significance by data as to average earnings in Soviet industry as a whole. During the years 1970–80, auxiliary workers received only 64–66 per cent of the per capita earnings of mainline-production manual workers.[31] Although auxiliary workers do include a substantial number of highly skilled ones (e.g. in maintenance and set-up),[32] the figures of relative earnings suggest that Soviet literature is correct in

24 *Pravda*, April 20, 1981 as quoted by A. M. Dobrusin in *E.K.O.*, 1982, 8, p. 125.
25 Brezhnev in November 1978, as quoted in Hauslohner (1984), pp. 432–33.
26 A. Shadyev and P. Krylov in *P.Kh.*, 1985, 6, p. 79.
27 Kostin (1974), p. 129 and Shafranova (1972), p. 51.
28 Data for 1977–81 for all Soviet industry in N. Safronov, Ia. Shagalov and A. Shirov in *S.T.*, 1983, 7, p. 16. B. Tsvetkov (in *S.T.*, 1980, 3, p. 73) writes that evaluations in Soviet economic literature generally hold that the first category is growing twice as rapidly as is the second.
29 E. Vitsur in *Kommunist Estonii* (in Russian), May 1978, pp. 55–64 as translated in the U.S. Joint Publications Research Series Translations on U.S.S.R. Economic Affairs, Nr. 844.
30 M. L. Shukhgapter in *E.K.O.*, 1979, 10, pp. 46–47 and S. A. Kheinman in *E.K.O.*, 1979, 10, p. 24.
31 M. E. Belkin and V. A. Volkonskii in *E.K.O.*, 1982, 10, p. 116.
32 Repair and set-up workers in 1979 in Soviet industry as a whole constituted twice the number of those workers who were operating mainline production machine tools (A. G. Zelenskii in *E.K.O.*, 1983, 2, pp. 76 and 83).

stereotypically treating these workers as being largely unskilled. It is this fact that makes notable their sharp relative expansion within industry.

Still another category, manual workers who do not use mechanized equipment, is much studied both by Soviet and Western writers commenting on Soviet industry. It overlaps very heavily with the "auxiliary worker" category.[33] Although this group is also very heterogeneous,[34] what is significant for our purposes is the part of this group that is described as unskilled; this sub-category increased somewhat in absolute numbers in industry between 1970 and 1972, and continued increasing in the 1980s.[35]

Indeed, it seems likely that the actual amount of unskilled work performed in industry has grown more rapidly than has the amount performed by unskilled workers. There are complaints that an increasing number of skilled personnel in industry are used, for part of their time, to do unskilled work, although at least as early as 1971 there were complaints of such usage that was even then explained by a shortage of unskilled workers.[36] Thus, despite the fact that technology is changing so as to reduce the relative amount of such unskilled work that is needed, the change is occurring even more slowly than is shown by the proportion of unskilled workers to the total industrial labor force.

Explanations of the evolution. (1) The first possible explanation is that unskilled labor has not been in short supply in the Soviet economy, and thus that it has not been worth the while of the Center to allocate investment resources to substitute for such labor in industry. Given the ruble-cost relationship between carrying out unskilled work with labor versus equipment, this argument implies that the opportunity cost of unskilled labor has been substantially less than its wage cost.

This is indeed an argument that I myself have made as applying to the period through roughly the middle 1950s. But it would not seem to apply to the present or to the recent past. Using a constant elasticity of substitution production function with Hicks-neutral technological change, the imputed labor share of industrial income created – which represents the opportunity cost of labor – rose steadily from 21 per cent in 1950 to 52 per cent in 1956,

[33] B. Tsvetkov in *S.T.*, 1980, 3, p. 73.

[34] Krevnevich (1971), pp. 21–24 considers it to be so heterogeneous as to be useless for analytic purposes.

[35] V. P. Skaldina in *Trudovy resursy: sotsial'no-ekonomicheskii* (1976), p. 142, and L. Chizhova in *V.E.*, 1983, 5, p. 63.

[36] G. Sergeeva and L. Chizhova in *S.T.*, 1981, 4, p. 118, and A. Sh. Tashbulatova in *Sotsial'nye problemy truda na promyshlennykh predpriiatiakh* (1971), p. 55.

60 per cent in 1970 and 73 per cent in 1978.[37] In Chapter 5 we saw that there has been a steady decline in the intensity with which the capital stock of industry is used; in the Russian Republic, the proportion of manual workers employed outside of the main shift used in their plant fell between 1965 and 1981 by 22 per cent, while in the Ukraine the decline between 1965 and 1975 was 13 per cent.[38] Robert Campbell believes that such Soviet intensity of capital use in industry is now below that of "any industrial developed country."[39] One author, head of a section in the Institute of Economics of the Soviet Union's Academy of Science, views the decline in intershift and intra-shift usage of capital equipment as the single most important cause of the increase in the capital/output ratio in the economy.[40] The reason for such decline has been a shortage of labor, and not at all a changing preference on the part of the Center for single-shift operations.[41]

In the case of new industrial plant brought into operation in the Russian Republic during the years 1971–75, some 19 per cent of the workplaces were unfilled as of 1976, and some eight per cent still in 1978. In reconstructed enterprises, the comparable figures were seven and 4.3 per cent.[42] Capacity usage (undefined) of Soviet industry as a whole is described as having fallen from 91.5 to 80 per cent between 1975 and 1979, with the explanation offered consisting of the fact that one million work places had been added without the manpower being available to fill them.[43] The chairman of the State Committee on Labor claimed that in Soviet industry as a whole in 1975 there existed 12 per cent more working places than workers.[44] For lack of complementary labor needed to man it, part of the investment in industrial plant and equipment is simply wasted.

[37] M. L. Weitzman in Bergson and Levine (1983), p. 187. Such an increasing imputed value follows from construction in the CES function when the capital/labor ratio rises secularly.

[38] A. E. Kotliar in *Zaniatost' naseleniia* (1983), p. 22, and Dolishnii (1978), p. 62.

[39] R. W. Campbell in Byrnes (1983), p. 90.

[40] V. Krasovskii in *V.E.*, 1984, 5, p. 42.

[41] See the December 1983 plenum of the Central Committee of the Communist Party of the SSSR as reported by N. Paneleev in *P.Kh.*, 1985, 2, p. 107.

[42] R. Tikizhiev in *P.Kh.*, 1981, 12, pp. 45–46. It is to be presumed that the data for reconstructed enterprises come from a study by the SSSR Central Statistical Administration of virtually all enterprise reconstruction projects that were carried out during 1971–75 (see E. Ivanov in *E.G.*, 1977, 21, p. 12).

[43] N. Safronov, Ia. Shagalov and A. Shirov in *S.T.*, 1983, 7, p. 8. Data presented for 1982 show, as one would have expected, that a decline in capacity use of these dimensions during such a short period was not due only to labor shortage; disproportional investment as between processing industry on the one hand, and the mining industry and iron and steel on the other, was also important (see V. Kirichenko in *V.E.*, 1984, 11, p. 7).

[44] N. Pantelev in *P.Kh.*, 1985, 2, p. 107.

A diversion of some of this investment to pure labor substitution would presumably lower rather than raise the marginal capital/output ratio.

Moreover, the explanation for such unbalanced investment does not seem to lie in the need for more investment in the development of natural resources. The engineering branch has accounted for an ever-increasing proportion of investment in total industry (Soviet definition, which includes mining and gas-oil lifting, but not pipelines). This proportion has risen from 18.8 per cent during 1966–70 to 22.4 per cent during 1971–75 to 24.6 per cent during 1976–80.[45] Investment of such magnitude in this branch seems difficult to explain as being no more than what has been required to wrestle with bottlenecks.

These data relate to the hypothetical plenitude of labor in general in Soviet industry. But they do not address the issue of unskilled labor in particular. For this we must appeal to the rapidly changing educational level of the Soviet labor force: between the 1959, 1970 and 1979 censuses, the share of the urban labor force with no more than primary education fell from 43 to 25 to 14 per cent.[46] It was expected that 47 per cent of those reaching pension age between 1975 and 1980 would have only this minimal educational level.[47] This change finds its reflection not only in specific findings of shortage of unskilled labor,[48] but more impressively in the increase of earnings of unskilled relative to skilled workers,[49] as well as in the possibly greater equality of earnings than of wage rates among industrial manual workers.[50] It is also reflected in the complaints, noted

[45] G. Ia. Kurbatova in *E.K.O.*, 1982, 3, p. 73.

[46] TsSU, *Itogi vsesoiuznoi perepisi 1970*, Vol. 3, p. 408, and *V.S.*, 1983, 9, p. 68. Such education is defined as being anything less than seven years of studies prior to 1962, and eight years thereafter.

[47] *Trudovoe resursy: sotsial'no* (1976), p. 95.

[48] In a 1979 study conducted in twelve leading industrial enterprises of the Gor'kii region, it was found that jobs in the lowest blue-collar skill grades exceeded the number of such workers by 50 per cent. On the other hand, there were only half as many jobs in the highest blue-collar skill grades as there were workers in these plants who were qualified to fill them (T. V. Riabushkin in *S.I.*, 1980, 4, p. 21).

[49] See Ia. Gomberg and L. Sushkin in *E.N.*, 1982, 1, p. 61 for a comparison between 1966 and 1976 of the earnings of the 10th and 90th percentiles of manual workers in three major industrial branches.

[50] In what appears to be a 1976 study conducted shortly after the introduction of new wage rates, little systematic bias was found when using an unweighted average of industrial branches in comparing the relative earnings to relative wage rates of the highest and lowest skill-grade manual workers. However, the engineering industry – with one-third of all industrial blue-collar workers – was counted as a single branch in this study. Here, relative earnings were more egalitarian than relative wage rates despite the fact that the average percentage of overfulfillment of output norms in this branch increased with the skill level of the worker (Kunel'skii [1981], pp. 149–151).

On the other hand, another Soviet author, largely on the basis of a 1978 study of

above, as to the need for increasing use of the work time of skilled personnel to perform unskilled work in industry.

(2) The second possible explanation is that of Model A: namely, the slow rate of diffusion of technical innovation. But this explanation is also difficult to credit.

The technology most relevant for materials handling received its first major international introduction into industry some sixty years ago. The widespread introduction of such equipment into industry, with major effects on labor productivity, occurred in the United States during the 1920s and 1930s. Delayed by the Great Depression and then by the war, it became widespread in Western Europe in the 1950s. What could have been the innovation obstacles to the diffusion of such a well-established technology in Soviet industry during the following quarter of a century?

Indeed, the case against this explanation is reinforced by the fact that enterprises using such technology have a technically simple adjustment problem that can be rapidly resolved. What is required is little more than the receipt of the necessary equipment. Since such equipment could be produced in the Soviet Union in standard form and using mass production methods, it would seem to constitute the type of product group which is most susceptible to development on command from the Center. One can only surmise that such command has not been given, at least with serious intent.

Yet the pay-off period for investment in materials handling and warehousing work in Soviet conditions is less than one year.[51] Soviet sources, ranging at least from 1970 through 1982, state that capital expenditures needed to reduce manpower requirements in industry by a given amount would be only one-third to two-fifths as high if these expenditures were concentrated in auxiliary production instead of in mainline production.[52] Data from an engineering industry study of fifty shops, which were chosen because they neither changed product mix nor reduced output volume over the three year period analyzed, show the same figures specifically for materials-handling and warehousing operations in comparison with mainline production.[53] Despite such potential gain, even

time-paid blue-collar workers, holds that there is less equality of earnings than of wage rates in industry (L. Kheifets in *V.E.*, 1982, 6, pp. 37–38).

[51] Calculations of the Institute of Economics of the Siberian Section of the SSSR Academy of Science (S. Divilov in *P.Kh.*, 1978, 4, p. 105).

[52] I. Maslova in *S.T.*, 1970, 7, pp. 109–110 and S. A. Shalaiev in *C.D.S.P.*, 35, 11 (April 14, 1982), p. 7. A still lower estimate of 20–25 per cent is made by E. Manevich in *V.E.*, 1978, 8, p. 43.

[53] Studies conducted by the Labor Research Institute (A. N. Vukolova, I. I. Matrozova and A. V. Shteiner in *Problemy ispol'zovaniia* [1973], pp. 105 and 114).

in the 1980s only one-fifth of the capital funds allocated for mechanization in industry went to all of auxiliary production.[54]

(3) A third explanation refers to a misplaced success indicator for enterprises. Managerial pay is related to the number of "working places" within the administrative unit, even when the personnel needed to man these places cannot be recruited. Thus management's incentive is to have the maximum number of "working places" that it can persuade higher authorities to authorize; it should have no desire to reduce this number through mechanization of unskilled jobs.[55]

The objection to this explanation is that it is completely *ad hoc*. It leaves unexplained why such a misplaced incentive is allowed to remain in place despite complaints in the Soviet Union about it over a period of years.

(4) Model B offers the fourth possible explanation: the JROE constraint against dismissals or obligatory job transfers. Unskilled occupations in industry are quite distinct from their counterparts in most of the remainder of the urban economy in that they provide considerably higher earnings. The number of unskilled workers in industry is large, but is not such a high percentage of all industrial employees that the enterprises are unable to bid up the price of such labor out of their wage funds. The situation is different for the enterprises' counterparts in agriculture and commerce, for municipal warehouses, and probably for transport units such as ports and railroad stations. In these organizations, earnings are effectively set by Central authorities through the allocation of wage funds; the units are unable to bid for labor on the market-place. This is why such units have increasingly had to be supplied with labor on loan from other enterprises in order to carry out unskilled jobs, while industrial enterprises have been able to meet their needs for this kind of labor on the normal labor market.

Here is the explanation as to why people in these trades who are themselves uneducated and unskilled[56] are much less likely to quit jobs in

[54] S. A. Shalaiev in *C.D.S.P.*, 35, 11 (April 14, 1982), p. 7.
[55] V. Boldyrev in *Pravda*, May 25, 1972, p. 2 and I. Malmygin in *Pravda*, January 15, 1984, p. 2, as referred to by Philip Hanson in Lane (1986), p. 88 and fn. 18, p. 108.
[56] One also finds people in such occupations who are recent migrants from rural areas, as well as those who have completed secondary education and who are attending higher educational institutions at night or in correspondence courses, or who are studying to retake competitive entrance examinations for full-time higher studies. (See, for example, T. V. Riabushkin in *S.I.*, 1980, 4, p. 23.) Presumably, as in Western countries, youth wishing such education take these jobs because they are easy to obtain, have hours that fit into their educational needs, and are undemanding so far as mental effort is concerned.

industry than they are, for example, in commerce. The market for their services is sharply segmented.[57]

The Soviet Union's Labor Research Institute conducted a study of manual workers who were forty years of age or older and who were engaged in non-mechanized work in industry. In the thirteen enterprises (of various branches) that were studied, 39 per cent of those who had been forced to leave their previous non-mechanized work because the workplace was abolished suffered a reduction in earnings; the proportion was the same for those who were given another non-mechanized job as for those who took mechanized work. Questioning of manual workers who continued in their non-mechanized jobs, although others in the same enterprise had lost theirs, revealed that 22 per cent of those aged forty to forty-nine years, and 42 per cent of those fifty years or older, would wish to continue in non-mechanized work rather than take training for a mechanized job if they were forced to change their workplace. The authors of the article interpreted this response as constituting a rejection of work change even when accompanied by paid retraining.[58]

One writer, describing the engineering industry of the West Siberian Altai region in the late 1970s and 1980s, pointed to the older age and low general educational level of unskilled workers in non-mechanized work. She felt that these factors, combined with the comparatively high earnings received in their current jobs, made it practically impossible to attract them to other work if they were unneeded in their present posts.[59]

In still another article, it was pointed out that women will constitute 72 per cent of those reaching pension age during 1981–85. The authors commented that this natural process of the change of generations makes easier the task of net redistribution between occupations of the female labor force, "in so far as it does not much affect the interests of the population that is currently working."[60] Model B would suggest that the amount of investment in industrial materials handling and warehousing has been

---

[57] It has been suggested to me that enterprise managements might be able to "buy out" such unskilled industrial workers so as to persuade them to quit. Special housing and privileges in being sent to vacation homes are two of the possible payments.

One could indeed envision such side-payments which would be to the mutual benefit of all parties. Presumably, bodies above the level of the enterprise would have to provide the resources for such side-payments, or this buying-out procedure would be unacceptable to the other workers in the enterprise and, in all likelihood, to the local trade union branch that would have to give its approval.

No information is available as to the existence of such possible side-payments. It seems unlikely that they are made on any large scale.

[58] L. Danilov and V. Arev in *S.T.*, 1983, 5, p. 101.

[59] N. A. Petrunina in *Formirovanie* (1982), p. 297.

[60] S. Sergeeva and L. Chizhova in *S.T.*, 1981, 4, p. 120.

kept low up to the present so that its timing may coincide with retirements of unskilled workers from the industrial labor force.

The above argument as to segmented markets for unskilled labor, accompanied by higher earning rates in industry than in certain other segments of the urban economy, raises the question as to why industrial enterprises do not fully satisfy their labor needs from what should be a perfectly earnings-elastic unskilled labor supply.[61]

One possible answer is that of the wage fund constraint with which they are faced. Central authorities, realizing the implications of such additional hiring in industry at the expense of other sectors, prevent such hiring by refusing the necessary funds to industrial ministries and thus indirectly to their enterprises.

A second possible answer is that the combination of education and age (and, to some degree, sex) of such unskilled labor in non-industrial sectors makes the employment of these workers inappropriate for filling such jobs as machine operators in industry. But this second answer would return us directly to the issue raised earlier: namely, is there then no shortage of the relevant type of unskilled labor, and thus no economic reason to substitute capital for this type of labor in industry?

Since it is the Center that controls the amount and mix of investment in new equipment, the issue of labor shortage must be examined from the viewpoint of the Center. If the materials handling and warehousing processes in industry were mechanized under conditions of no job rights, the present workers in these occupations could be attracted (for lack of job alternatives) to similar unskilled tasks in the remaining urban economy and conceivably even to some degree in agriculture. This would permit a reduction of the calls upon industrial enterprises to make temporary loans of personnel to poorly paid urban sectors and to agriculture. Currently, industrial enterprises lend people of all skills, since they are incapable of satisfying the demands made upon them solely from their own unskilled personnel; this is due to their being restricted in the amount of such temporary duty that they can require from any individual. Thus a reduction of such enterprise loans would amount on a national level to a substitution of unskilled for semi-skilled personnel in the carrying out of identical tasks with identical complementary resources in these poorly paid sectors. As a consequence, shift utilization of capital equipment in industry could be increased.

It is job rights alone which could prevent the Center from indirectly

[61] I am indebted to Paul David for raising this question.

Table 6.5 *Retirement rates for fixed assets in the economy as a whole*
(retirements as percentage of capital stock at the beginning of the year)

Country	Retirements		
	Producer durables	Non-residential plant	Annual rates of growth of capital stock in manufacturing (1969–73)
Germany	10.2	3.7	6.0
France	12.5	5.7	6.5
Italy	11.1	4.0	...
Canada	9.0	4.2	4.7
U.K.	7.3	2.5	3.2
U.S.	8.5	3.3	2.7
Unweighted average of above	9.8	3.9	4.6
U.S.S.R.	4.1	1.5	9.0

Sources: Retirements: Stanley H. Cohn in *J.E.C.* (1983), Part I, p. 181 Capital growth: Economic Commission for Europe (1985), p. 35, and S. Cohn, unpublished appendix to his article in J.E.C. (1983), Part I.

substituting capital in this fashion for the types of labor of which industry is short.

Equipment replacement and maintenance workers

Extent of retirements of equipment. The estimation of the average lifetime of capital equipment is a difficult problem in any country, and the evaluation of Soviet equipment lives suffers as much from the unreliability of international standards[62] as from problems with the Soviet data themselves. However, I shall accept the estimates of Stanley Cohn that reflect the "accepted wisdom" both in the Soviet Union and in the West; in the West, Cohn has been the leader in creating such accepted wisdom.

Cohn's data are for retirement rates and seem to reflect conditions in the 1970s in the economy as a whole. They are shown in Table 6.5 and indicate Soviet rates that are less than half of those found in Western Europe and North America. I know of only one author, Soviet or otherwise, who

[62] See, for example, the revisions in the United Kingdom official estimates for industry on the basis of "discussions with some larger undertakings" by Central Statistical Office staff (United Kingdom Central Statistical Office, *National Income and Expenditure*, 1983 edition, p. 114, as quoted in Economic Commission for Europe [1985], p. 30, fn. 20).

Fixed investment and JROE 195

considers the rate of scrapping in the Soviet Union as adequate; he offers no international comparisons, and uses a retirement figure for 1962–72 that is little higher than the comparable estimate of Cohn.[63]

Furthermore, the relative Soviet retirement rates would probably be substantially lower if agriculture and construction were omitted; it is said that the retirement percentages in the Soviet Union in these two sectors are high due to poor maintenance both in operation and in the repair process itself.[64]

Although there is no empirical evidence for the belief that Western practice is appropriate for Western conditions (profit maximization combined with the survivor principle do provide a theoretic reason), I shall assume that it is appropriate so that I can concentrate upon differences between Soviet and Western conditions while making a normative evaluation of the Soviet policy of capital retirements. In my discussion, I shall limit myself to equipment retirement, making the assumption that retirement of non-residential plant is closely linked to this.[65]

There are three reasons why Soviet conditions should dictate a lower rate of retirement of equipment than is found in the West:

(1) The Soviet capital stock has been growing more rapidly than has Western, and thus a lower retirement rate would coincide with an identical average lifetime. This argument has significance when the standard of comparison for retirement rates is the United States or England; it is not so important in relation to the other four countries treated in Table 6.5.

(2) Since there is less frequent change of product in Soviet manufacturing, there should similarly be less frequent retirement of special-purpose equipment that is unusable in manufacturing the new product.

(3) Existing Soviet equipment appears typically to embody considerably less technological backwardness compared to its available replacement

---

[63] Boris Rumer in *Soviet Studies*, 26, 2 (April 1984), pp. 258–59. There is no indication in the original source that the higher estimate of the Soviet author Fal'tsman that Rumer uses for 1971–75 refers to retirements. (See Cohn in *J.E.C.* [1983], Part I, p. 181 for a treatment of the coverage of the "bulk of Soviet estimates of replacement investment." Fal'tsman himself does not indicate the coverage of his figure.)

[64] D. Palterovich in *P.Kh.*, 1980, 9, p. 103. Cohn in *J.E.C.* (1983), Part I, p. 180 gives sectoral estimates for the Soviet Union. For industry, the producer durables estimate is 3.68 per cent, while for plant it is 1.15 per cent.

[65] Rebuilding or replacement of buildings often seems appropriate in order to use new equipment effectively. An example is the historic movement in American factories to one-story design so as to simplify materials handling. In the case of replacement of Soviet textile equipment during the 1970s, the new spinning and weaving equipment increased in size more than it did in productivity. (This seems to be true internationally.) Thus buildings also had to be altered or replaced. (See T. Khachaturov and P. Sedlov in *P.Kh.*, 1981, 10, p. 74.)

than is the case in Western industry. If one takes this as an exogenous "fact of life" in determining appropriate retirement rates, retirement for reasons of obsolescence should occur less frequently in the Soviet Union than elsewhere. Writing about the economy as a whole, one Soviet author evaluates the retirement of equipment for reasons of obsolescence as currently not exceeding 1.3 to 2 per cent annually, and thinks that it should be double that.[66] Judging by the figures of Table 6.5, his "doubling" statistic is probably quite low by the standards of continental Western Europe. But it may be quite reasonable under Soviet conditions. This obsolescence argument is the only one of the three given above on which I would place substantial quantitative emphasis.

To counterbalance the above three arguments, there are two suggesting that higher rates of retirement in the Soviet Union than elsewhere would be appropriate.

(4) It seems probable that a lower proportion of capital equipment that is retired by its current owner is physically scrapped in the Soviet Union than elsewhere. Of retired assets in industry during 1965–73, only some half to two-thirds were scrapped.[67] Although it is true that second-hand markets for capital equipment do exist in Western countries, their dimensions seem much smaller than the combination of Soviet transfers without charge plus sales. It is scrapping, rather than retirements, that is relevant for the determination of service life.

(5) Both ordinary maintenance and, particularly, major repair of equipment is substantially more expensive relative to the cost of new equipment in the Soviet Union than elsewhere. This is because spare parts are normally unavailable either from the original producers or from specialized producers of parts, and must instead be produced by the user enterprises themselves. Similarly, the user enterprise must normally do its maintenance and repair work itself, being unable to purchase this service from specialized enterprises. Such high cost of maintenance should make the appropriate service life shorter in the Soviet Union than in the West.

It is impossible to say whether the effects of the above five factors effectively cancel one another. But since there seems no strong reason to predict that their net effect is to lengthen the appropriate service life in the U.S.S.R. vs. the West, and since the differences shown in Table 6.5 are more than two-to-one, it seems reasonable to conclude that service lives of equipment – relative to what would be appropriate under national

[66] V. Krasovskii in *V.E.*, 1984, 5, p. 42.
[67] S. Cohn in *J.E.C.* (1979), p. 236. D. Palterovich in *P.Kh.*, 1980, 9, p. 106 suggests a figure of some 87 per cent about 1977; but he is not explicit as to the sector treated.

conditions – are indeed longer in the Soviet Union. The fact that this is the virtually unanimous opinion of all students of the matter adds weight to the result. Thus I shall treat this conclusion as a "stylized fact" of Soviet economic life.[68]

Extent of Maintenance Work. In the light of the slow rate of technological progress embodied in Soviet production equipment, the main opportunity cost of long service lives can probably be considered as consisting of the resulting high maintenance costs. Such cost, however, seems to be considerable in terms of the use of skilled manpower.

In 1969, roughly some 3.1 million equipment-maintenance workers were shown in industry in what appears to have been that year's one-time count by occupations; these constituted 14 per cent of all industrial blue-collar workers according to this count. The 1972 count showed 3.2 million. In both years, only 10 per cent of these maintenance workers were employed in enterprises specializing in the repair of industrial equipment and in the production of spare parts, although it is true that such enterprises did a much larger share of the work.[69] Five years later, a reliable Gosplan official reported that 18 per cent of all industrial blue-collar workers were engaged in the maintenance of equipment.[70] For the early 1980s, data of the Central Statistical Administration were said to indicate that there were 3.9 million in industry working in major repair alone (i.e. 13 per cent of the industrial labor force).[71] None of these figures include maintenance employees or producers of spare parts who were in branches of the economy other than industry.

Some impression of the contrast with Western countries is given by a

[68] Scrapping in Soviet industry is said to run some 2.4 to 2.5 per annum, compared with an optimal scrapping rate as estimated by the SSSR State Committee on Science and Technology of 5.6 per cent (N. Safronov, Ia. Shagalov and A. Shirov in *S.T.*, 1983, 7, p. 9). For scrapping rates of individual types of equipment in 1980, both in industry and in other sectors, see V. Fal'tsman and A. Ozhegov in *V.E.*, 1983, 6, p. 57.

I have previously suggested (NATO [1978], p. 75) that a substantial and growing portion of equipment stock may be obsolete for purposes of the enterprises in which it is housed, and that it is kept by them unused rather than being scrapped. This suggestion was almost certainly incorrect. Three one-time censuses of four different types of equipment for mainline production in engineering enterprises of engineering ministries show that the total number of units held in reserve (long-term) or that were obsolete ranged only between 1.4 and 2.8 per cent of all installed equipment. Partial data for auxiliary production in the same enterprises suggest that the figures there are probably not much different. (Data are for 1969, 1975 and 1982. See *V.S.*, 1970, 8, pp. 89–91; 1976, 4, pp. 93–94; 1983, 4, pp. 68–69.)

[69] Shafranova (1972), pp. 55–56, and Kostin (1974), pp. 133–34 and 142.
[70] N. Rogovskii in *P.Kh.*, 1977, 9, p. 20.
[71] N. Safronov, Ia. Shagalov and A. Shirov in *S.T.*, 1983, 7, p. 9.

comparison of the distribution of all metalcutting machine tools in the economy as of 1958. In the U.S.S.R., 31 per cent of these had been installed within the metalworking industries themselves and were used for purposes other than the maintenance of equipment in the same plant. In the U.S. in the same year, the comparable figure was 59 per cent.[72] A comparison of these national figures can be used as a proxy for a comparison of the relative number of workers engaged in the production of equipment compared to its maintenance. There is no reason to think that the relative proportions have changed since.

It would be wrong to look at the relative lives of equipment as constituting the prime explanation of this national discrepancy. Much more important is the inefficiency of the maintenance function in the Soviet Union because of the felt need for enterprise-level self-sufficiency. But it is hard to doubt that the relative length of life of equipment makes a significant contribution to the discrepancy.[73]

Explanation. The explanation for the average long life of equipment in sectors other than agriculture and construction (where bad maintenance practice is the dominant influence) lies partly in the slow tempo at which technical progress is embodied in new equipment models. This presumably makes for less obsolescence than in Western countries (judging obsolescence against the standard of available alternatives) and thus, *ceteris paribus*, makes a longer life appropriate.

As we have seen in the first Section of this chapter, either Model A or the JROE considerations of Model B can explain this slow technical progress. But when it comes to changes in the physical models of similar equipment, I believe that Model A does better. This is because much upgrading of equipment calls for no significant changes in the skills of personnel either producing or using such equipment. Yet there is no indication that Soviet technical progress in these sorts of models is rapid.

Model B comes into its own in explaining the "stylized fact" of the long life of equipment after taking account of societal differences in the rate of obsolescence. This JROE explanation is in terms of the preservation of jobs for the large labor force of equipment-repair men and spare-parts producers scattered throughout Soviet industry and, indeed, throughout the Soviet economy. A determined increase in the rate of scrapping would have

[72] Calculated from Kheinman (1961), pp. 169–70.
[73] See the fairly typical statement by G. Ia. Kurbatova in *E.K.O.*, 1982, 3, pp. 67–68. She points out that, although equipment often is subjected to three, four or more major repairs before it is retired, experts (her specific reference is to D. M. Palterovich) believe that only the first major repair is cost effective.

the effect of making many of these jobs unnecessary. Moreover, since such posts are generally skilled and appear to be attractive, it is difficult to phase out the need for such protection in timing with the retirement of poorly educated generations, in the way that one should be able to do for unskilled jobs.

Model B also does well in explaining what the Hungarian economist Bauer describes as the absence of any cyclical variation in the degree of scrapping during swings in the investment cycle. In the Soviet Union, according to Bauer, upswings are reflected in the rate of growth of investment commitments and of the stock of investment projects in progress, but not in investment expenditures.[74] Such a "cyclically" changing investment pattern does not increase the short- or medium-term need for equipment-repair workers, although it does presume – if successful – an enlarged complementary requirement for labor in general in the near future. An expansion in the scrapping rate would reduce with a lag the need for repair workers, and thus would provide the additional industrial labor needed as the new investment facilities come into operation in a lumpy fashion. But such cyclical expansion of scrapping does not occur in the Soviet Union because it would have a negative effect on the possibility of maintaining the current jobs of the army of repair workers.

Capital/labor substitution in general

We have seen that neither unskilled (materials handling and warehousing) nor skilled (equipment-repair) jobs have been phased out of Soviet industry through the readily available possibility of capital investment in labor substitution. The broad range of industrial blue-collar jobs seems to be covered by the generalization that such substitution has at best (in the case of unskilled labor) been limited to a relative but not to an absolute reduction in the number of workers in capital-substitutable jobs. This is despite the shortage of labor that has been felt increasingly in industry and has left capital equipment idle. In these major respects, the opportunity to use reallocation of capital investment within industry as a means of pursuing the Center's often repeated goal of "intensified growth" has been totally ignored. I have offered the JROE set of constraints as the explanation.

Both the replacement of unskilled industrial materials handlers through the substitution of equipment for non-mechanized manpower, and the replacement of skilled repairmen by an increase in the rate of scrappage of

---

[74] T. Bauer in *Acta Oeconomica*, 21, 3 (1978), pp. 256 and 259.

existing equipment, would have required diversion of gross investment to these objectives. Thus the failure to have seriously tackled either one, but not the other, would be fully consistent with a policy of pursuing under constraints the substitution of capital for labor in industry. But the failure to tackle either task is inconsistent with such a policy. Given the constraint on the economy arising out of the supply of labor, this failure to reallocate investment appears to lead to lower total output than is feasible with the given capital stock and annual total gross investment. For, as Krasovskii pointed out in 1984,[75] capacity usage is constantly declining and this is *the* major source of the increasing capital/output ratio in industry. The reason for the trend in capacity usage seems similarly clear: it is the scarcity of the complementary factor of labor.

One might choose to explain through time-lags in response the failure of Soviet central authorities to reallocate capital investment in such a way as to come to grips with these well- and long-recognized facts of Soviet industrial production. Labor shortages in industry began really to bite only in the late 1960s and early 1970s, and it could be argued that the period since then has not been sufficiently long to have awakened a serious response by the Center.

This explanation might be reinforced by the common view among both Western and Soviet observers that Soviet investment policy in industry has always been bifurcated, promoting capital intensity in mainline production processes and labor intensity in auxiliary processes.[76] A long-continuing strategy takes time to change. Calls by authoritative Soviet figures for labor-saving investment in auxiliary processes can be viewed as efforts to awaken a response by a slumbering Center rather than as indications of a desire by the Center for such reallocation of investment if only accepted constraints did not prevent this.

Such an explanation involving lags in response is difficult to refute. Nevertheless, the length of the hypothesized lag – and the absence of any

[75] V. Krasovskii in *V.E.*, 1984, 5, p. 42.
[76] As I have argued at length elsewhere (Granick [1967], Chapter 6), this interpretation of Soviet investment policy conceals more than it reveals. I interpret Soviet policy as having historically promoted an allocation of investment within any given industrial sector in such a way as to obtain the highest possible output for the given total investment on the assumption that complementary labor would be available within the sector. Thus labor-substitution types of investment were eschewed, whether in mainline production or in auxiliary operations. *De facto*, most of the recognized opportunities were in auxiliary work; but assembly and foundry work were important mainline production activities in which mechanizing investment was avoided, and so too was metalcutting at least during the years of 1929–33 (*ibid.*, pp. 182–89).

The above description of Soviet investment strategy can be substituted for the one in the text without in any way changing the argument underlying the text's lag explanation.

basis for it except bureaucratic inertia – make such an explanation unsatisfactory.

Thus it is my contention that the JROE constraint against dismissals is a more acceptable explanation for the failure of Soviet central authorities to reallocate capital investment.

7

Education and JROE

The fundamental assumption made in this chapter is that the amount of education provided in the Soviet Union, and its mix between levels as well as between types within a given level, is determined by economic considerations. Education is here viewed as a form of investment, and the amount provided is determined by a comparison of the return to investment in human capital with the return obtained from investments made in material forms of capital. Since our interest is in the provision of education, rather than in the demand by individuals for different types and amounts of education, it is the social rather than the private return that is relevant.

Within this context, JROE performs well in reconciling the facts of education and of labor usage. At the end of the chapter, there will be an examination of the explanatory power of other theories that combine non-economic explanations of the amount and type of education with a neglect of JROE considerations.

SOVIET EDUCATION AS INVESTMENT IN HUMAN CAPITAL

The approach to education as an economic investment by society is rooted in the earliest days of Soviet history. First in 1918–1919, and then again using a much larger sample in 1929, the prominent economist Strumilin measured the rate of return per year of primary education. Using the total increase in lifetime earnings of the individuals as his measure of gross return to society, Strumilin argued that the Soviet government could undertake no better investment than in major extension of primary and early secondary schooling. A circumstantial case can be made that his publication of 1930 had an important effect on the timing of the universalizing of primary education during the first five year plan – a period during which investment resources were in particularly short supply.[1]

[1] Enrollments in the first four years of education increased by 53 per cent during three years. (See D. Granick in *l'Actualité économique*, July–September 1977, pp. 482–84.)

It is true that such studies of education appear to have ceased thereafter in the Soviet Union – perhaps having served their purpose – and were taken up again only in the 1960s after the theme of investment in human capital was resurrected by the Chicago school, using a refined version of Strumilin's methodology although with an entirely different rationale. Even afterward, such studies play no great role in Soviet economic literature. A Soviet writer in 1983 was apparently forced to go back to books published in 1968 and 1969 for estimates as to the social return on investment in education.[2]

Nevertheless, it is significant that education beyond the secondary general education level always has been, and continues to be, considered as vocational in the Soviet Union.[3] (The virtual universalization of such secondary education was, on the other hand, debated only partly on the basis of its constituting necessary pre-vocational training.)[4] A fixed number of entrance slots in each field and educational institution are determined each year; the basis for the division is, in theory, the expected demand in the economy for such graduates. While such demand predictions may, of course, be in serious error, and indeed other (JROE?) considerations may enter into the determination of the numbers, there are no indications that the preferences by field of would-be students play any significant role. The competition among individuals for entrance slots is conducted primarily on the basis of the expected economic return to society from educating one person versus another,[5] although it is true that non-economic considerations also enter into decisions.[6]

If one accepts the proposition that post-secondary education is viewed as vocational, one is faced with the puzzle that the use of Strumilin's methodology, when modified to take account of lost earnings during the

[2] L. S. Sbytova in *Problemy povysheniia effektivnosti* (1983), pp. 111–12.

[3] This is, of course, generally much more the rule than the exception on the continent of Europe.

[4] The early and middle 1970s had seen a dispute among sociologists and economists as to whether secondary education was being extended too rapidly. The argument was to a large extent conducted in terms of economic pay-off on the investment, but it also included references to the social pay-off in terms of the ability to participate effectively in non-economic aspects of social life. (See Shkaratan [1978], pp. 143–45.)

[5] Thus grades and examinations serve as the primary basis for determining admissions. In medical schools, where there has been discrimination in favor of males, a rationale given has been the greater number of expected hours worked by males during a lifetime (Vasil'eva [1973], p. 60).

[6] For example affirmative action in favor of various national minorities, and admission of some current blue-collar workers into preparatory classes – a practice which allows them to escape the higher educational competitive examinations that are open to all. Socially disapproved considerations such as bribes also play a role, but they are not of relevance here.

Table 7.1 *Annual graduations*

Level and type of education	Compound annual rate of growth (percentage)			Graduations as percentage of age group[a]			Stock of graduates as percentage of the labor force[b]	
	1951–60	1961–70	1971–83	1960	1970	1983	1970	1979
Eighth grade	4.8	6.9	−1.1	72.3	105.9	98.1		
Tenth grade, academic, plus vocational school[c d]	14.0	9.4	4.0	32.0	58.7	105.8		
Of this, tenth grade academic[d]	14.0	9.4	2.7	32.0	58.7	89.6		
Junior college[e]	4.4	7.9	1.6	11.9	30.2	29.8	10.5	15.6
Higher education (called "university" hereafter)[f]	6.9	6.3	2.3	8.4	18.4	20.0	6.5	10.0

Notes: Eighth and tenth grades are both end-points in Soviet education. However, all pupils going further are included in the eighth grade graduations. As to the degree of overlap between junior college and higher education students, 17 per cent is probably a somewhat high estimate. In 1977, junior college graduates constituted some five per cent of applicants for full-time and 35 per cent of those for part-time education, and thus were 17 per cent of all applicants (A. V. Kinsburskii in *S.I.*, 1979, 2, p. 101).

[a] The relevant age group is taken as one-fifth of the fifteen to nineteen year olds for eighth and tenth grade graduations, and as one-fifth of the twenty to twenty-four year olds for junior college and higher education graduations. Age groups for 1960 and 1970 are taken from the population censuses; 1960 graduations are compared with the 1959 age group.

[b] Data are from the population censuses. Students and a portion of working old-age pensioners are excluded, while the military are mainly included.

[c] The first pupils in vocational schools offering complete secondary education as part of their program graduated in 1971. The number of such graduates grew very rapidly thereafter. (Geliuta and Staroverov [1977], p. 49.)

[d] The percentage of eighth graders proceeding to the full-time academic ninth grade rose from 40 per cent in 1965 to 61 in 1975, and remained at 60 per cent in 1980. The percentage proceeding to full-time vocational school for secondary education was 10 per cent in 1975 and 19 per cent in 1980. Thus the total proportion proceeding directly in full-time secondary education beyond the eighth grade doubled between 1965 and 1980, reaching 80 per cent in this latter year. (M. N. Rutkevich in *S.I.*, 1984, 4, p. 24.)

[e] This translation is used for "specialized secondary education."

[f] This translation is used for the Russian term *vuzy*. The higher educational program is normally five years. Degrees beyond the basic one are excluded from the statistics.

Sources: Narkhoz SSSR, various issues; TsSU, *Itogi perepisi 1970*, Vol. 2, pp. 12–13; TsSU *Narodnoe obrazovanie* (1977), p. 93; *V.S.*, 1983, 9, pp. 68–80; and *V.S.*, 1984, 11, p. 49. All data were published by the SSSR Central Statistical Administration. The same age groups as described above are calculated for 1983 from the estimates in M. Feshbach in Bergson and Levin (1983), pp. 104–05.

Table 7.2 *Full-time students as percentage of all graduates*

Level of education	Graduations in the year							
	1950	1955	1960	1965	1970	1975	1980	1983
Eighth grade	91.2	93.0	89.1	86.2	91.2	97.6	97.2	97.6
Tenth grade, academic	80.3	85.6	67.2	68.1	76.2	76.2	68.8	66.3
Junior college	88.9	89.0	72.0	53.5	58.3	65.0	65.4	64.7
Higher education	82.5	72.9	66.6	55.7	53.1	60.7	63.4	64.2

Source: Narkhoz, SSSR, various issues.

period of study, probably yields a negative marginal social return to current human-capital investment in higher education. This is because of the narrow income differential between blue-collar workers and those employees with higher education.[7] Although I suspect that the actual non-discounted marginal social return can be fairly represented as negative, a methodology that assumes that the gross social return is equal to the gross private return is disputable.

It is to avoid this methodological problem that I shall abandon at this point all calculations of rates of return. Instead, I shall deal with data at an earlier stage of processing; for example, with the jobs held by people having different educations. But it is reassuring that a return-on-capital calculation is not inconsistent with these more primitive results that will be presented below.

SUPPLY AND DEMAND CONDITIONS FOR DIFFERENT LEVELS OF EDUCATION

Tables 7.1 and 7.2 present an overview of what has been happening in Soviet education during the post-war years. Eighth grade education (ending at fifteen years of age if the pupil is on track) had been virtually universalized by 1970, while complete secondary education expanded enormously both during the 1950s and the 1960s. What changed in the

[7] One report presented at a conference that occurred about 1974 calculated the non-discounted, private return to higher education, where the only investment consists of lost earnings (minus expected value of stipend) during five years as a student, as being nil in the city of Tartu in Estonia (O. M. Raiu in *Vosproizvodstvo* [1975], pp. 78–79). My recalculations from the data presented yields a positive, non-discounted private return; but it is only 0.6 per cent per annum for men, and 0.3 per cent for women.

1970s was that the proportion of completions of secondary education that occurred within the vocational schools grew sharply: from 0.4 per cent in 1970, to 5.4 per cent in 1975, and to 12.6 per cent in 1980.[8] Nevertheless, the proportion was still small in 1983 (15.3 per cent), and some 30 per cent of the 1970–83 growth had been offset by the decline in the proportion of entrants into the junior colleges who had not previously completed secondary education. As of 1983, complete secondary education was not only almost universal, but in the process of expansion it had retained its character of being overwhelmingly academic.

When we ask what is unusual by West European standards about the Soviet educational developments shown in Table 7.1, the first item which strikes one's eye is the abbreviated schooling period scheduled for completion of secondary education: ten years after primary education begins at the age of seven. This contrasts with twelve years in France and in the United States and thirteen in the German Federal Republic and the United Kingdom, although it should be said that schooling in the first three of these latter countries begins at the age of six, and in the last at five, rather than at seven as in the Soviet Union.

International differences in the period of schooling required to complete secondary education make it even more difficult than would otherwise be the case to compare countries with regard to the scholastic level attained at the end of such schooling. Perhaps there is greater homogeneity at the time of completion of higher education, with the five year period of university education in the Soviet Union (versus three in England, for example) compensating for the briefer earlier education. The conclusion that I wish to draw from the various periods of education ending with complete secondary is that we should be careful in looking for a West European comparison with the Soviet junior college (or "specialized secondary education", as the Russians call it); the German *Fachhochschule*, for example, is probably at a higher level. Thus I would not emphasize the fact that some 30 per cent of recent Soviet age cohorts have completed such education.

Similarly, I would not stress the fact that 20 per cent of recent age cohorts have completed higher education. The great Russian expansion in higher education (called "university" hereafter) occurred during the 1950s and 1960s while the West European explosion took place in the 1970s. By the 1980s, the Soviet proportion of the latest age cohort with completed

---

[8] TsSU, *Narodnoe obrazovanie* (1977), p. 93; *V.S.*, 1982, 12, p. 71; *V.S.*, 1984, 11, p. 49.

higher education was 84 per cent of the American figure[9] and was 180 per cent of the West German.[10]

But comparisons of the level attained are difficult. Total Soviet education is one year shorter than the American, but begins one year later. The standards for graduation from the poorer American colleges are worse than those from the poorer Soviet ones. On the other hand, total Soviet education through university is three years shorter than that of the German Federal Republic. International standards are too diverse for us to be able to judge the Soviet Union as being either high or low in its proportion of university graduates.

What is most unusual, however, is that *academic* complete secondary education covers almost some 60 per cent of the age group in the Soviet Union.[11] This situation can be contrasted with that of West Germany, where one-fifth of the age cohort receives the *Abitur* degree of academic secondary completion.[12] Although the Russians have indeed been diversi-

---

[9] In 1978 in the United States, 23.8 per cent of the twenty-five to twenty-nine year age cohort had completed four years or more of college (U.S. *Economic Report* [1980], p. 130). Another 6 per cent of the age cohort was still attending college as undergraduates (R. T. Reynolds in *American Demographics*, June 1979, p. 38).

If one should view the European and Soviet first degree as equivalent to the American Master's – a view common in Europe – then the United States falls out of first place in its current provision of higher education to the relevant age cohort.

[10] *Stat. Jahrbuch für die B.R.D.* (1984), pp. 61 and 357. The West German figure is intermediate between the British and the French. The Soviet proportion is 140 per cent of the British.

[11] It is not intended to overlook the "polytechnical" (i.e. practical) side of Soviet general education. Expansion and contraction of this element have gone through phases, with considerable expansion at the end of the 1950s, and then contraction by 1966 back to the 1955 stage when tenth grade education had been intended solely as a preparation for higher education. Renewed expansion occurred during the second half of the 1970s, with work training in enterprises and farms provided to 85 per cent of all ninth and tenth grade pupils in 1979/80, to 96 per cent in 1980/81, and to 98 per cent in 1983/84. (See Matthews [1982], pp. 21–55, and *Narkhoz SSSR*, assorted issues.)

But what is significant is that all pupils take the same program, and that the overwhelmingly dominant function of this program in the senior secondary years has throughout Soviet history been to fit pupils for higher education. Electives were introduced for the first time in 1966 from the seventh class on, and they were restricted to some six per cent of the hours of all ten classes combined – implying about some 15 per cent of the time in the upper classes. But by 1978, the number of elective hours had been reduced by one-quarter although the number of total school hours did not change. (Matthews [1982], pp. 51–54, and M. Matthews and J. Dunstan in Tomiak [1983], pp. 16 and 73.)

It is this overwhelming presence of academic secondary education, combined with the unimportance of electives within this program, that most differentiates the Soviet educational system from the American. However, in both of these regards the Soviet system is only a weaker form of the Japanese.

[12] In 1982, the figure was 21 per cent (*Stat. Jahrbuch für die B.R.D.* [1984], pp. 61 and 363).

fying the last two years of secondary education away from a universal academic model by introducing vocational school secondary education – which has a different content than the normal academic program[13] – this still constitutes only a small proportion of the total.[14]

Of course, this pattern of academic education for a majority of the age group has quality costs. One can see this in the proportion of pupils left back to repeat a class: only 1.4 per cent already in the school year 1970/71 and 0.5 per cent in 1975/76.[15] One may contrast this with Germany, where 24 per cent of that select group entering (in their fifth year of studies) the academic Gymnasium in 1975/76 had transferred out by the end of the tenth year.[16] In France, the time-honored figure of one-third failure rate of the state examination for the academic secondary school diploma (*baccalauréat*) by a similarly select group continued into the 1980s. In the Soviet Union, in contrast, the 1981 figure of completions of tenth grade without receiving a graduation certificate was only 0.3 per cent.[17]

Junior college level

This education (often described incompletely in Soviet sources as *tekhnikumy*) is offered on the basis of competitive examinations both to graduates of incomplete (eighth year) and complete (tenth year) academic secondary schools. The program consists of four years for the first group, and three years for the second. Prior to 1950, incomplete-secondary graduates (at that time seven years of total schooling) were numerically overwhelmingly dominant among the students. These were said to have fallen to 75 per cent of the total number of junior college entrants in 1954 and to 34 per cent in 1956.[18] But either the 1956 figure is a mistake or the proportion quickly rose once more. Tenth year graduates constituted only 26–27 per cent of entrants in 1964–65 and 44 per cent in 1970–71. By

---

[13] Sonin (1980), pp. 166–67.
[14] It increased between 1965 and 1980 from zero to 19 per cent of the sixteen to seventeen year age group completing eighth grade, while academic education increased from 40 to 60 per cent. In 1983, however, a leading Soviet academic writer on educational matters advocated the German model; he thought that the above proportions should be almost reversed, with complete academic secondary education covering only 25 to 30 per cent of the age group (M. Rutkevich in *Sovetskaia Rossiia*, September 21, 1983, p. 3).
[15] *V.S.*, 1980, 7, p. 64 and *Narkhoz SSSR 1922–82*, p. 501.
[16] *Süddeutsche Zeitung*, June 7, 1985, p. 34. Presumably, these data refer to Munich.
[17] M. A. Prokoviev, Minister of Education of the Soviet Union, in *C.D.S.P.*, XXXIV, 15 (May 12, 1982), pp. 8–9.
[18] De Witt (1961), p. 168.

1981, however, their proportion had reached 64 per cent.[19] Thus junior college education by the 1980s was largely a complement to, rather than constituting partly as substitute for, academic secondary education.[20]

The junior college system is organized to produce technicians. In the case of industry, the training of junior college graduates is such as to make them intermediate between skilled blue-collar workers and engineers; they are both traditionally and still today officially expected to fill jobs in the "professionals and managers" category. Just as in the universities, full-time students are normally provided with stipendia.

The system, unlike vocational school education, is (or at least was at the beginning of the 1970s) fairly prestigious and has enjoyed popularity with students. In 1972, there were 2.1 competitors with incomplete secondary education for each entrance place available to them, and 2.6 for graduates of tenth year education.[21] In the same year, eighth and tenth year students in one small region (*raion*) in the central Urals were questioned on the day before their final exams as to what they wished to do next. Of the eighth graders, 30 per cent wanted to enter a junior college; but in the event, only ten per cent were admitted. In contrast, 29 per cent of them wished to go on to the ninth year of the academic secondary school, but 45 per cent in fact did so. Of the tenth graders, the percentages of those wanting to go to junior college and of those actually admitted were virtually identical with those of the eighth graders.[22]

This program may have enjoyed considerable prestige with the state (as shown by its continuing expansion despite the high cost of such three year education on top of normal complete secondary education), and have been popular with prospective students; but it has suffered from an ever-increasing shortfall of demand for its graduates. At least, as we shall see, this is the case within industry. That industry is probably reasonably typical in this regard is suggested by the fact that the mix of students within the junior colleges has shifted only moderately. The proportion of all entrants into

---

[19] E. Zhil'stov and V. Zuev in *Obrazovatel'naia* (1975), pp. 19–20 and 46, and A. Umanskii in *S.T.*, 1983, 8, p. 53.

[20] In 1959 (by implication, these figures are from census data), people having completed junior college had an average of 12.0 years of schooling versus 15.0 years for those having completed university. In 1970, the respective figures were 12.7 and 15.2 years (Sonin [1980], p. 165).

[21] D. Ziuzin in *Obrazovatel'naia* (1975), p. 39. These figures average approximately the same as those for universities, where in 1970 the number of applicants per place available was 2.43 (A. V. Kinsburskii in *S.I.*, 1979, 2, p. 102). Examinations in the Soviet Union are timed so that students can only exceptionally apply to more than one institution in the same year (see G. Zabulis in *C.D.S.P.*, XXXII, 1 [February 6, 1980], p. 22).

[22] S. M. Gusev in *Trudovye resursy i sovershenstvovanie* (1975), pp. 64–72.

junior colleges who were in industrial and construction specialties fell only from 42 to 40 per cent between 1960 and 1975, and to 37 per cent in 1983. In absolute numbers, the admissions to such specialties were stable from 1970 on.[23]

The extent of the shortfall in demand by industry is shown by the proportion of the junior college graduates in industry as a whole who work there as blue-collar workers. This has risen from only a few per cent in 1952[24] to 20 per cent in 1968, and then steadily to 33 per cent in 1975.[25] There are no indications in the Soviet literature that an inordinately high number in this group are graduates, in specialties such as education, agriculture or health, who have abandoned their original fields without having skills relevant to industry. By 1984, a prominent sociologist could write that most industrial junior colleges were currently engaged primarily in training pupils who would ultimately become blue-collar workers.[26]

Some Soviet writers implicitly try to explain the high proportion of junior college graduates in industry who are working as blue-collar workers by the greater attractiveness to them of such jobs than of the industrial white-collar posts for which these workers had been trained. Others (or the same) write of the growing needs for such training among highly skilled blue-collar workers. But it would seem that one should not take seriously such rationalizations.

If one considers the total number of graduates of junior colleges and of higher education working in industry, and divides them by the total number of managerial and professional posts existing in the same year, the resulting proportion increases from 87 per cent in 1965, to 128 per cent in 1975, to 150 per cent in 1983.[27] Even if we were to evaluate these figures only as an index rather than as absolute percentages, the dimensions of the development are clear. It would have been impossible by the 1970s and 1980s for all junior college graduates to have obtained posts appropriate to their education.

In the current handbook of skills and blue-collar trades, only thirty-nine trades out of about seven thousand are listed as requiring knowledge by the worker at the level of that intended to be obtained at the time of

[23] *Narkhoz SSSR 1983*, p. 501.
[24] Study of the Central Statistical Administration, reported in *V.S.*, 1974, 7, p. 92.
[25] Geliuta and Staroverov (1977), pp. 74–75.
[26] F. Filippov in *Sovetskaia Rossiia*, January 22, 1984, p. 1.
[27] *Narkhoz SSSR 1975*, pp. 210 and 552, and *Narkhoz SSSR 1983*, pp. 40 and 132. The methodology is that used by I. I. Ivanov in *S.I.*, 1978, 2, p. 49. It is possible that the statistics in the numerator have a broader industrial coverage than do those in the denominator, although Ivanov describes their coverage as identical.

graduation from junior college. A 1981 source, however, states that the actual number of such trades are about three hundred and fifty. A study conducted in two engineering plants of Novosibirsk during 1980–81 indicated that only 10 to 14 per cent of the junior college graduates working as blue-collar workers were in jobs on the latter list.[28] A 1979 sample study of industrial blue-collar workers in Gor'kii showed that the proportion of workers with junior college education or higher was little more for those in highly skilled posts than for all manual workers (15 vs. 11.3 per cent).[29]

A further indication of the ever growing over-supply is the apparent fact that plants were authorized in the late 1970s or early 1980s to use as blue-collar workers those junior college graduates who are assigned to them for an obligatory work period.[30] Yet the courses of the industrial junior colleges have continued to be modelled on the university engineering program, producing what is called a cheaper edition of an engineer.[31] Moreover, the projected educational reform as of early 1984 proposed continuing and perhaps even strengthening this tendency.[32]

Given the dim prospect for an appropriate job, why has the demand by pupils for places in the junior colleges been maintained? Can such continued demand be reconciled with the data reported above?

First, there are occasional suggestions that demand by pupils has indeed declined. But second and more significantly, the relevant school competitor for the pupil is the vocational school, and pupil applications for places there have continued to expand. Given that an adolescent decides to opt for an education as a skilled worker or technician, it is not surprising that many should prefer the school that offers at least the possibility of a post as technician.

If we include differences in the nature of future working conditions as part of the returns to private investment in education, expected marginal discounted private returns must always be greater than zero or the individual will not make the investment. For at least junior college education, the marginal social return in the Soviet Union seems to be negative. The distinction lies partly in the fact that the state meets a large part of the opportunity costs of this education, but secondly in that the difference in working conditions for the individual enters into expected private returns but not into expected marginal social return.

If the current junior college student has a 50 per cent chance of becoming

[28] V. M. Moskovich in *Proizvoditel'nost'* (1982), p. 257; Kunel'skii (1981), p. 117; E. M. Bezrodnyi in *S.I.*, 1982, 1, p. 102.
[29] T. V. Riabushkin in *S.I.*, 1980, 4, p. 23.
[30] G. Kulagin in *C.D.S.P.*, XXXIII, 52 (January 27, 1982), p. 11.
[31] *Ibid.*   [32] This is implied by F. Filippov in *Sovetskaia Rossiia*, January 22, 1984, p. 1.

a white-collar technician as a result of his studies, the likelihood should be factored into the expected marginal private return. This is because the individual student's chances are stochastic. But for the state, there is nothing stochastic in this aspect of the expected marginal social return. If one could confidently predict that only half of the junior college students will eventually be placed in jobs that use their education, the expected marginal social return would have to be based on a zero probability that the education will be used.[33]

Higher education

There are no indications that the Soviet graduate of a higher educational institution (called university here, as the reader will remember) has a similar problem to that of the junior college graduate in finding a position which is at least nominally consistent with his education. In what was presumably the middle to late 1970s, the number of university graduates working in industry as technicians constituted only some four per cent of a single year's university class in industrial and construction academic specialties.[34] Nor have there been reports of any significant number of engineering graduates working as blue-collar workers except in temporary postings.

There has indeed been great wastage of vocational educational skills both among those with teaching and with agricultural specialties. Taking the universities and junior colleges together as of 1980, graduates of the last nine and six graduating classes (of 1972–80 and of 1975–80) respectively would have been sufficient, if they had stayed in their fields, to have manned the total number of posts available in teaching and agriculture. It seems likely that there has been similar movement out of the field for graduates of universities alone in these two broad areas.[35] But there is no suggestion that the reason for such wastage is the lack of demand in education and agriculture; rather it is the unattractiveness of such work, particularly in rural areas.[36]

[33] I am indebted to Volkhart Vincentz for this analysis.
[34] D. N. Karpukhin in *Trudovye resursy SSSR* (1979), p. 167.
[35] N. A. Aitov and R. T. Nasibullin in *S.I.*, 1980, 2, pp. 107–11, and comparisons with *Narkhoz SSSR*, various issues.
[36] During 1973–77, 11 per cent of the graduates of a dairy university either never arrived at the jobs to which they were assigned or "didn't stick around for long." This university is said to have by no means the worst record in this regard (Rector V. Lobanov in *C.D.S.P.*, XXX, 21 [June 21, 1978], p. 7).
    As to primary and secondary school teachers, it is true that the proportion of rural teachers with higher education rose from 44 per cent in the 1970/71 school year to 64 per

However, it would not seem that there is much wastage among the other 65–75 per cent of university graduates. A recent sample study in smaller central Russian cities showed that, although one-third of all university graduates were currently working in specialties other than the narrow one (*spetsial'nost*) for which they were trained, 70 to 80 per cent were in the same scientific discipline as that which they had studied at university. With regard to engineering graduates from the Ufa Aviation Institute, those working in narrow specialties other than their own were rated by specialists as having somewhat greater knowledge and experience, as well as superior personal qualities, compared with those who had not changed field. Furthermore, 59 per cent of those changing their narrow specialty had received an increase in earnings as a result of the change, while the earnings of another 30 per cent were unaffected.[37] Thus change of speciality should not be taken as a proxy for wastage.

All this leads one to believe that, from the point of view of the formal jobs that university graduates are engaged in, there has been no more wastage of state investment in vocational skills than is inevitable in a mobile society with a distaste for rural living. It is otherwise, however, with regard to the content of work done.

One finds various Soviet studies showing that occupants of many engineering jobs feel that university education is not needed in order properly to carry out their duties.[38] Young male engineers seem often to be viewed by their enterprises as prime candidates for temporary duty as unskilled labor in agriculture, city services, and other work to which the enterprise is obliged to send personnel. Such usage is explicitly linked by Soviet authors to the "overproduction" of engineers.[39] Low earnings of the young engineer compared to his contemporary who is a skilled manual worker are noted in sociological studies.[40] While figures of earnings across organizations cannot reasonably be taken as an indication of relative labor scarcity, since these are determined by the wage funds allocated to the individual enterprises or administrations, earnings comparisons within

cent in 1977/78 (A. A. Utukov in *S.I.*, 1980, 2, p. 115). Nevertheless, data of the 1980s show no indication of catch-up in the quality of education in rural versus urban areas; nor is it suggested that there has been any between different regions of the Soviet Union (F. P. Filippov and V. A. Malova in *S.I.*, 1984, 2, p. 64).

[37] Aitov and Nasibullin in *S.I.*, 1980, 2, pp. 106–11.

[38] Mangutov (1980), pp. 142–45. Although not enough is said about these studies to allow one to form any judgment as to their quality, it should be noted that this source is cited approvingly on these matters by A. Merson in *S.T.*, 1982, 9, p. 98.

[39] G. Kulagin in *S.T.*, 1980, 1, p. 96, and *C.D.S.P.*, XXX, 20 (June 28, 1978), pp. 20–21.

[40] M. N. Rutkevich in *S.I.*, 1984, 4, p. 26. This source gives a figure of earnings only two-thirds as high for beginning engineers as for skilled workers of the same age.

individual organizations can be used as such an indicator (see Chapter 2).[41] The low earnings of teachers and physicians fall into the first category. But engineers are in the second category, since they are used in enterprises everywhere.

Indeed, in looking at the number of university graduates produced in different fields in the 1980s, one author believes that the current rates of graduation are needed only for primary- and secondary-school teachers and for agriculture, and that the rest could be cut.[42] Yet these "needed" occupations are precisely those where shortage arises from the wastage of those so trained, and whose percentage of all university graduates has steadily and substantially declined.[43] Thus it would seem that we can think of university education in general as being over-developed when judged purely from the standpoint of the creation of human capital through vocational training.

Vocational education (PTU)

Pupils completing vocational education in schools (whether or not such education has included the completion of secondary education, or even if entrance into vocational training has been only after such completion) grew by 4.2 per cent compounded annually during 1951–60, by 5.0 per cent during 1961–70, and by 3.4 to 5.6 per cent during 1971–82/83.[44] When we compare these growth rates with those of other types of education (see Table 7.1), one can see that these were the lowest of all during the 1950s and 1960s, but were the highest in the 1970s and early 1980s. The temporal difference, however, is mainly due to the slowing down in the 1970s of the rates of growth of other types of education. In contrast to their variation, vocational education has shown a modest and relatively steady rate of growth.

Another view of the same development examines the proportion of

---

[41] Two Soviet authors, in explaining the steady decline in relative average earnings within industry of managerial and professional personnel compared to blue-collar workers from 146 per cent in 1965 to 115 per cent in 1980, state that "Economic laws are beginning to operate here independently of human will" (G. Kulagin and E. Khabarin in *S.T.*, 1982, 6, pp. 88–90). Although the data refer to a much broader group than engineers alone, the Soviet source applies the statement specifically to engineers *inter alia*.

[42] N. Denisov in *E.N.*, 1984, 6, pp. 69–76.

[43] From 52 per cent in 1950 to 40 per cent in 1960 to 33 per cent in 1965 and 29 per cent in 1983 (*Narkhoz SSSR*, various years).

[44] Novgorodskii *et al.* (1973), p. 49; M. Sonin in *Obrazovatel'naia* (1975), pp. 3–11; Iu. Iakobets in *S.T.*, 1984, 1, p. 9, and *V.S.*, 1984, 11, p. 49. Figures from different sources differ significantly only for 1982/83; it is unclear which figure for this year is more appropriate to use for comparison with the 1970 statistics.

secondary school students who proceeded directly to full-time vocational education:[45]

	On Completion of	
	Eighth grade	Tenth grade
1965	12.3%	...
1975	31.6	12.9%
1980	33.1	26.9
1983	28	37

The evolution of these latter figures are, however, somewhat misleading with respect to graduates of the eighth grade. As of 1970, vocational training for thirty per cent of all trades required a minimum age of sixteen and a half to seventeen and a half, while the standard age for graduating eighth grade was fifteen years. Presumably, numerous graduates entered later when they were eligible. (In 1968, virtually half of all entrants into vocational education were other than those just completing either eighth or tenth grade.)[46] But by 1975, fifteen year olds could enter directly all vocational schools providing secondary education.

Vocational education has always been overwhelmingly full-time[47] although, of course, involving production work. In 1968, before completion of secondary education began to be combined with vocational education, 47 per cent of all full-time vocational programs lasted less than one year, 51 per cent were one to two years, and only 2 per cent were two to three years.[48] Thus Soviet vocational training is considerably shorter than apprenticeship programs found in other countries. Even after its widespread development by the 1980s, the Soviet system cannot be compared with the German apprenticeship system in which, as of 1970, over 60 per cent of all industrial employees had gone through apprenticeship programs, and where these programs generally exceeded two years.[49]

A major *de facto* social function of Soviet vocational education has been to serve as a way-station for rural youth in their entrance into urban jobs. As of 1970, some 57 per cent of all youth admitted to vocational education came from rural areas, although about 30 per cent of this rural contingent

[45] See M. Rutkevich in *Sovetskaia Rossiia*, September 21, 1983, p. 3, and F. P. Filippov and V. A. Malova in *S.I.*, 1984, 2, p. 65.

[46] Krevnevich (1971), pp. 365 and 373–74.

[47] For annual 1966–75 data, see *Sotsial'noe razvitie* (1977), p. 240. Data of 1960 are in *V.S.*, 1975, 8, p. 91, and of 1982 in *Narkhoz SSSR 1922–1982*, pp. 409–11.

[48] Kostin (1974), p. 193 and Krevnevich (1971), p. 373. The 1972 figures were 51, 35, and 14 per cent respectively.

[49] Maurice *et al.* (1982), especially p. 22.

studied in urban vocational schools.[50] This compares with 51 per cent of
the ten to fourteen year age group (the most comparable one for which
census data are available) that was rural. In 1968, some 51 per cent of the
Soviet Union's total number of vocational trainees were said to have been
trained for agriculture and have been sent there after graduation.[51] Of
those trained for industry either on-the-job or in school, only about 15 per
cent were given vocational school training; in agriculture, in contrast, the
figure was 58 per cent.[52]

But such vocational training for agriculture in fact served primarily as
preparation for urban jobs. Vocational training for agriculture must have
been essentially of "mechanizers" (drivers and operators of agricultural
equipment such as tractors, combines, and also excavators). The number
of such mechanizers trained during the twenty-two years between 1950 and
1971 in the Soviet Union was five and a half times the net increase of such
mechanizers engaged in agriculture. In the Russian Republic during
1965–69, the comparable statistic was 24 times.[53]

In one sense, one could argue that the vocational training of rural youth
represented for the state more of a negative than a positive investment in
human capital; after all, Soviet policy has been to attempt to slow down the
migration of rural youth to the cities, and such training undoubtedly
speeded it up. But taken in a wider context, this position is unfair. Given
the government's broader policies, there was probably little that it could
have done about rural migration; it could only have made the transition
easier or more painful, and rendered the factor contribution of labor to
urban production greater or less. In this wider sense, one might well
maintain that vocational education for rural youth served primarily as a
socializing process, while urban youth could just as well obtain through
on-the-job training the purely job-learning aspects of such education.

A second social function, developing since the early 1970s, is to provide
(along with the junior colleges) some relief from a single-track system of
upper secondary education. This was not necessary in the 1960s when only
half of an age cohort completed any type of secondary education; a single
academic track was then still feasible. But as complete secondary edu-

---

[50] E. V. Klopov in *Sotsial'noe razvitie* (1977), pp. 78–79 and 240, and *Narkhoz SSSR 1970*,
p. 528.

[51] Calculated from Krevnevich (1971), pp. 311–12. Lower figures are given in other sources,
but never less than 34 per cent through 1974.

[52] Similar figures are given for all skilled workers in different sectors of the economy in 1976
(N. Rogovskii in *Kommunist*, 1976, 16, p. 58).

[53] A. I. Arkhipov in *Osnovnye problemy* (1971), p. 105, and P. Taov in *S.T.*, 1972, 5, p. 130. The
same pattern for 1960–79 is observed in Kazakhstan (T. M. Renner in *Problemy vosproizvodstva* [1981], p. 210.)

cation has been universalized, a vocational educational system that offers its own diverging version of senior secondary education can be thought of as very useful.

A third social function may have applied in a few cities such as Moscow and Leningrad where a very high percentage of youth went on to university and junior college studies.[54] A 5 per cent sample of the 1963 graduates of the tenth grade in the city of Leningrad showed that 82 per cent were still studying at a university in 1968 or had completed studies there, and 6 per cent more were in the same position with regard to junior colleges.[55] Commenting on an earlier version of these figures, one prominent Leningrad sociologist asserted that it was only the extension of vocational training that kept any Leningrad youth oriented toward a blue-collar career.[56]

Aside from these important sociological functions of vocational training, what can be said as to the pay-off on the educational investment in comparison with the alternative of on-the-job training? Soviet comments have been favorable as to the existence of a gross benefit to formal vocational training (measured in terms of the rate of promotion, the direction of school leavers to industry in contrast to trade and public catering and, in a single study, in a lower level of occupational change), but even as to this the evidence is mixed.[57] The main problem is that what has

[54] Sixty per cent of a very large sample of the tenth grade graduates of two sectors (*raiony*) of the city of Moscow in 1981 were admitted to full-time university education in the same year; this contrasted with 15 per cent for the Soviet Union as a whole (I. E. Zalavskii, V. A. Kuz'min, and R. T. Ostrovskaia in *S.I.*, 1983, 3, p. 132). A sample of the total employed population of Leningrad proper (without its suburbs) in 1974/75 showed 24 per cent as having complete university education (Vasil'eva [1978], pp. 200–06), compared with 10 per cent in 1979 in the country as a whole.

[55] Vasil'eva (1973), p. 54.   [56] Shkaratan (1978), pp. 150–51.

[57] For direction of school leavers, see Breev (1977), pp. 115–16. For degree of occupational change, see A. Bulgakov in *C.D.S.P.*, XXIX, 26 (July 27, 1977), p. 5. For promotions, see N. A. Aitov in *Druzhba Narodov*, 1974, 6, pp. 230–31, A. E. Kotliar and M. I. Talalai in *E.K.O.*, 1977, 4, p. 34, and Shkaratan (1978), pp. 147 and 152–53.

In contrast, L. S. Dorokhova and G. I. Shinakova in *Sotsial'no-ekonomicheskie voprosy* (1974), pp. 83–84, report on a study of factory recruits in 1962 to a prestigious Moscow auto. plant. Of the 1962 recruits as a group, 25 per cent still remained in early 1968; but all of the vocational trainees had left by the beginning of 1967. The explanation given is that these trainees had a low level of general education, could not be promoted because of this lack, and thus were dissatisfied.

Of all these studies, only the ones reported in Shkaratan attempt to hold other factors constant, and the results there are mixed as to whether or not vocational education provides any gross benefit at all. The treatment in Matthews (1982), p. 86 is decidedly on the negative side in this respect.

Nowhere is any consideration given as to the extent to which observed gross benefit reflects only the added information (particularly with regard to rural youth) that is

been studied is principally the zero-coefficient of an implicit regression equation, rather than the partial coefficient. Sex, for example, is not held constant; this must bias the results in favor of formal training since Soviet girls eschew or are kept out of vocational schools.[58]

I have seen only one Soviet study that goes beyond the issue of gross benefit to the examination of a rate of return. This study consists of a comparison of machinists, spinners and carders working in the Moscow region who had received their training during 1974–78. The sample consists of 1,000 individuals, divided into two groups depending upon whether or not their training was through vocational education. Costs ignore foregone earnings of the worker while training, and gross returns are taken as total earnings during the first four years of work at the trade. The relative undiscounted return to training is only 15 per cent as high in the engineering trades, and 32 per cent as high in the textile trades, when the training is in vocational schools as opposed to on-the-job. Thus the social rate of return, by this measure, is negative.[59]

Two sociologists report that, in a 1983 study conducted in Moscow, one-third of the vocational pupils changed their narrow specialty within the first few years after completing their training. This contrasts with another statement of one-seventh.[60] But no such figures would be too meaningful, since specialties studied are very narrow and skills are transferable.[61]

A more significant problem of vocational education arises from the military draft. Males have constituted three-quarters or more of all entrants into vocational education,[62] and it is exaggeratedly complained that they "usually" change their work specialty from that learned in vocational education to that learned in the army. Thus, it is asserted, the return on their vocational education is negative.[63]

A second problem arises out of the "compulsory" assignment to their first job of graduates of such vocational education as is given in schools not attached to individual plants. One author complains that almost all such

provided to the employing enterprise by the fact that an individual has chosen to take a vocational course.

[58] McAuley (1981), pp. 150–51 provides the documented second interpretation.
[59] V. G. Aseev and E. N. Pugacheva in *Professional'naia* (1980), pp. 158–63.
[60] F. P. Filippov and V. A. Malova in *S.I.*, 1984, 2, p. 65, and S. Ia. Batyshev in *Sotsialisticheskaia Industriia*, February 15, 1975 as quoted in L. I. Lebedeva (1977), p. 24.
[61] F. O'Dell in Tomiak (1983), p. 133 says that the vocational schools attempt to provide a training that is transferable.
[62] Data for 1950–70 in *Narkhoz SSSR 1970*, p. 528. A later figure is in Tarasov (1979), p. 35.
[63] E. V. Kasimovskii in *Problemy ratsional'nogo* (1973), p. 43. A similar sort of complaint is voiced by I. S. Poltorak and Iu. E. Shul'ga in *S.I.*, 1984, 2, p. 79.

graduates leave within their first five years of work the plant to which they had been assigned, and she explains this fact by the observation that the trades studied frequently do not correspond to the needs of the plant. Thus they are given heavy, unskilled work – and quit.[64]

Much more significant is the view that only half as many blue-collar workers in the 1980s are in fact occupied in work of high skill as those that have the appropriate training. It is no secret, reported a prominent professor, that as a result some managers draw the conclusion that they "do not recognize skills acquired in school or in 'foreign' (i.e. not their own) vocational training."[65] This would suggest that some of the current vocational training, even if it should be highly successful in creating skills, is unnecessary given the existing structure of the Soviet economy and its skill requirements.

EXPLANATIONS OF THE EXCESS SUPPLY OF HUMAN CAPITAL

The last section has presented the case for the view that Soviet educational expansion has been excessive when judged strictly as an economic investment by the state. Of the four types of education examined, the case for over-expansion is strongest with regard to junior colleges. But it also applies to the strictly academic side of complete secondary education, to the universities, and even to vocational education. Our purpose now is to explain the "over-expansion."

This over-expansion is not something observed when comparison is made with international standards (except for the purely academic stream of secondary education); rather, its existence arises from the inability of the Soviet economy to adjust the composition of its jobs to the rapidly shifting educational level of Soviet youth. The fundamental reasons for such failure to adjust were discussed in Chapter 6, and the JROE objectives were there seen to play a significant role. But a secondary cause is the weak development of the tertiary sector of the economy in comparison with what has occurred in Western developed countries. Such weak development does not appear to be a Soviet desideratum, but is rather the result of the Center wanting a secondary (mainly industrial) sector that is somewhat on the high side by West European standards, while at the same time

[64] Z. P. Kupriianova in *Dvizhenie rabochikh kadrov na promyshlennykh predpriiatiiakh* (1974), pp. 237–38. The assignments are "obligatory," but there are probably no legal penalties for refusal.

[65] The excess of supply over demand for skilled workers is a conclusion drawn from sociological studies in White Russia, the Gor'kii region, and in other unspecified areas (F. Filippov in *Sovetskaia Rossiia*, January 22, 1984, p. 1).

authorities are forced to maintain a primary (mainly agricultural) sector that is very large.

The economic appropriateness of the size of the Soviet educational effort must be judged in terms of the capability of the Soviet economy usefully to absorb the product. If the Soviet economy has lower needs in terms of the quality of the labor force than do other developed countries, then international comparisons as to the absolute level of education of youth are beside the point.

Explanation in terms of Model B

Here I propose the hypothesis that the degree of expansion is rational in terms of maximizing the growth objective (4.3), subject both to the lexicographic JROE objectives of (3.1)...(3.3) and to the constraints of Chapter 4. What is irrationality (in terms of economic investment) without consideration of the JROE objectives of the Center is turned, through the JROE hypothesis, into rational behavior on the part of the Center.

By sharply restricting the ability of enterprises to dismiss individuals, (3.3) makes natural wastage of labor virtually the only means of providing flexibility in the composition of the enterprise's labor force. Soviet scholars estimate that two-thirds of such wastage occurs through quits which are motivated by the hope of finding a better job.

If such labor turnover is to represent more than the mere reshuffling of workers among a set of job-slots that remains unaltered, workers must possess the ability to change their occupation at the same time that they change jobs. Presumably, the higher their level of general education, the greater is their ability to adapt to changing occupational requirements. Furthermore, and at least as important, a higher level of general education should provide individuals with increased confidence in their own ability to so adapt, as well as with greater willingness to make the effort in order to enjoy the potentially enhanced job satisfaction that can come from fuller use of their abilities. Of course, and this is essential, there are also economic incentives for Soviet workers to shift through labor turnover to jobs where there is a more substantial demand for recruits than is the case for their old occupations.

This role of labor turnover exists in most modern societies. The point here is that the Soviet economy must trust to it far more than do other economies because of the Soviet inability to compel people – either through dismissals or through obligatory job changes within a given enterprise – to make such occupational changes. Since the incentive effect must be relied upon virtually exclusively, it is peculiarly important to remove psychological barriers to job change.

The general issue is that, in order to achieve equal performance of the economy, the Soviet Union would require a higher educational level in its labor force than would a capitalist country with an identical technology and rate of technological change. This is because, in the capitalist economy, the particular individuals who are to undergo occupational changes can be selected by the employer through the process of dismissal or of compulsory job change within the economy. It is not necessary for society to have previously ensured a psychological readiness on their part. Since actual ability to adapt to occupational change is considerably higher than self-perceived ability (if only because the latter, in contrast to the former, must discount for the risk of failure), a capitalist economy need not provide education solely for the purpose of overcoming psychological obstacles.

In the Soviet Union, in contrast, the individuals involved in occupational change are self-selected. Due to the fact that the size of this labor pool is relatively limited, the average degree of change required of its members would be larger than that demanded from the much larger pool in an otherwise similar capitalist economy. Yet at the time of the education of a given generation, little information is available as to the individuals' future psychological characteristics which will make them more or less ready to accept change. Thus a substantial multiple of the proportion of the workforce expected to self-select into the Soviet pool must be given an education appropriate for such adaptability.

Finally, the Soviet situation could be expected to grow more critical during the 1980s and 1990s than it had been earlier. This is because of the fact that the greater is the annual percentage gross intake of youth into a country's labor force, the higher is "natural adaptability" coming from people looking for their first job, as well as from those under roughly thirty years of age and by whom change is accepted as a normal phenomenon. However, we should largely exclude the Central Asian native youth from having such adaptability; they have shown themselves to be largely unwilling to leave the rural areas of their native republics.[66]

If we consider the gross intake of sixteen year old youths in the Soviet Union excluding Central Asia and Kazakhstan, and divide each decade's intake by the labor-age population in the Soviet Union as a whole at the

[66] M. Feshbach in *J.E.C.* (1979), pp. 656–709.

beginning of the decade, we see that the gross intake percentage may be expected to decline by about one-third between the 1970s and the following two decades.[67] Thus adaptability must depend to a sharply increased degree upon the mature worker, and the economic case for more educational investment is strengthened.

A second consideration is the overfull employment objective in each locality as presented in (3.1). With a large number of placements required each year because of the substantial quit rate, one might suspect that the employment objective would be impossible to realize if workers did not possess considerable potential flexibility. Since workers are assured only of a job that they can fill, rather than of one which uses all of their skills, overfull employment at the level of disaggregation of the individual locality can be realized more readily the higher the general educational and skill levels of the workers seeking employment.

It is for the above reasons that one may argue that Soviet educational expansion has been rational as a purely economic investment if one takes account of the JROE lexicographic objectives – although not otherwise.

The same may also apply to the expansion of an area of major employment of Soviet engineers and physical scientists: namely, organizations of applied research and industrial design. The issue is not particularly the absolute size of the labor force employed in such work, but rather the relative ineffectiveness of this activity in the light of the substantial obstacles standing in the way of successful implementation of applied research and new product design (see Chapter 4). In view of such obstacles, and of the inability of Soviet leaders to remove them, why has the applied research and design staff been allowed to develop to a size where its product is well beyond what can be absorbed by the economy?[68]

Part of the explanation presumably lies in the high demand by graduate engineers and junior college graduates for employment in this sphere rather than in production. Demand for such jobs may create its own

---

[67] See M. Feshbach in Bergson and Levine (1983), Tables 3.11 and 3.13. The annual rate of such gross intake is calculated as 2.7 per cent in 1970–79, 1.9 during 1980–89, and 1.9 during 1990–2000. Sixteen years is taken as the relevant age for measuring intake because it is the beginning of "labor age" as defined in the Soviet Union; average age of joining the labor force must now be two or three years older.

[68] As of the end of 1968, only 58 per cent of engineers worked in some production branch of the economy. In industry at the beginning of the 1970s, the net increase of engineers with higher education, and of *tekhniki* (junior college graduates with engineering specialities) working as managerial and professional employees, was occurring primarily in design organizations and in factory administration rather than in production shops (Komarov [1972], pp. 169–70).

supply.[69] But it seems unlikely that this phenomenon by itself can explain more than a portion of the excess.

More fruitful as an explanation is the combination of this high demand for such employment with the JROE restriction on dismissals. Since demand by qualified personnel for research and design positions seems to exceed considerably the number of available posts, we would expect (although I do not know of any available data) that the voluntary turnover from such posts would be low. Thus the achievement of a major reduction of posts within any given research or design organization must be very difficult.

Here we have an explanation for the phenomenon observed by Julian Cooper: that the pattern of change of the Soviet distribution of scientific personnel among different branches of the economy is conservative in comparison with that of the American distribution. Cooper explains this evolutionary rather than abruptly discontinuous pattern by the fact that Soviet research organizations, once established, remain in operation and continue to expand even under circumstances in which they would be disbanded in the more ruthless conditions of the American economy. "One could summarize," writes Cooper, "by saying that in the USA the old is replaced by the new; in the USSR the new supplements the old."[70]

The JROE objective of non-dismissal provides the Center with a positive incentive for such maintenance of organizations at full size. We need not depend for explanation, as does Cooper, simply on the unavailability of those market pressures in the Soviet Union which would compel the reduction of staff and even the elimination of organizations as a whole.

Finally, the JROE objectives provide an explanation as to why almost two-thirds of Soviet university graduates are full-time students, and why this ratio was allowed to rise sharply during the 1970s (see Table 7.2).

Part-time education offers significant cost advantages to the state. It is considerably cheaper per student taught, since part-time students do not receive stipends (although they do receive some partially paid time off from work for examinations and their preparation), and since the student/

---

[69] For such a view, see G. Kulagin in *S.T.*, 1980, 1, p. 97. The high demand is exemplified in a study carried out in 1977–78 among foremen (the group within which one would least expect to find it) with higher education working in Leningrad factories. About half of them wanted to work in a research organization (V. P. Klimonov in *E.K.O.*, 1980, 5, pp. 133 and 137–38).

[70] Julian Cooper, "Scientists and Soviet industry: a statistical analysis," *CREES Discussion Papers*, Series RC/B17, No. B, November 1981.

teacher ratio is higher.[71] Moreover, although there is less competition among would-be part-time students than among those trying to enter full-time education, such competition is still substantial and must be sufficient to permit selection by the universities.[72] The dropout rate during the 1980/81 school year was 11 per cent for evening, 8 per cent for correspondence, and only 4 per cent for full-time students. Grades were also substantially better among full-time students. However, the proportion of students in the three types of educations who received a grade of good or excellent for their diploma projects was much the same for all types of education: some 38 to 40 per cent.[73] One cannot regard part-time university education as so inferior that it represents simply a waste of state resources in comparison with full-time education.

Nevertheless, it is not the cost savings but rather the gross benefits which are really of importance. We have indications of this with regard only to engineering education, but there is no reason to believe that this field is peculiar either as to its proportion of part-time students or as to the benefits.

Part-time engineering students are supposed, during the last half of their studies, to be working in jobs connected with the specialty that they are studying. When they have in fact been placed in such jobs, they seem to be regarded as having, on graduation, an unquestionable advantage in obtaining line management posts. Their speed of advancement is said to be two to three times as rapid as that of former full-time students.[74] Even more to the point, graduates of part-time education appear to be much more willing than do full-time students to take such jobs rather than to aim for functional positions off the shop floor.

The need by enterprises for such line management personnel is shown by

71 The student/teacher ratio in the 1980s was set at ten to one in full-time university education, twenty to one in evening education, and fifty to one in correspondence courses (I. G. Reznik in *E.K.O.*, 1983, 6, p. 87). Although differential course-repeat and dropout rates must be taken into account as offsets, a Soviet study conducted in the middle 1960s found that university correspondence courses are still less than half as expensive to the state as are full-time courses (J. Tomiak in Tomiak [1983], pp. 262–63).

72 In 1970 for all universities in the Soviet Union, there were 2.11 applicants for each opening in part-time education compared with 2.69 applicants in daytime education. (These figures are calculated from A. V. Kinsburskii, in *S.I.*, 1979, 2, p. 102). It is true, however, that the average academic quality of the two sets of applicants must be different. In 1977, of that portion of the year's crop of graduates from full-time academic secondary education who took any examination for university entrance, only 11 per cent took an exam for a part-time university program (*ibid.*, p. 101). This figure should be viewed in the light of the fact that 40 per cent of all admissions to universities in that year were for part-time education.

73 I. G. Reznik in *E.K.O.*, 1983, 6, p. 85.

74 Bliakhman (1978), pp. 103–04 and Shkaratan (1978), pp. 146–47.

the relative earnings of lower-level line personnel (below shop superintendent) compared with engineer-designers in the engineering industry of Leningrad. In 1970, the "foremen" earned an average of 26 per cent more than did the engineer-designers. If one assumes that "foremen" earnings rose between 1965 and 1976 at the same rate as did that of higher line management extending from shop superintendent through enterprise director, then the foreman/designer ratio of average earnings rose from 120 per cent in 1965 to 126 in 1970 to 139 in 1976.[75] This was at a time when the proportion of part-time junior college and university graduates was falling nationally.

Why, then, do we not see a reversal of the ratios of Soviet students graduating from part-time versus full-time university programs, at a minimum in engineering? Use of the JROE hypothesis suggests that the reason is the advantage to the Center arising out of the greater generality of the full-time engineering program, and its superior theoretic preparation. This permits more flexibility of daytime students as between work at various engineering specialties, and provides them with enhanced psychological willingness to change specialty when opportunities become better in a new field.

It is true that this interpretation runs counter to the fact that Soviet engineering education as a whole is organized into very narrow specialties. But this traditional Soviet organizational pattern appears today to be relatively inconsequential for full-time students. The assignment of graduating engineers to their first job is a process which applies only to those completing full-time education; here we are told that both the planning and execution of such assignments largely ignores the subspecialties into which the teaching programs have been organized.[76] Almost every rector is said to proclaim that the university he heads produces engineers with broad general training.[77] The sample study referred to earlier in this chapter showed what a high proportion of all university graduates work outside the specialty in which they were trained, and with what success for the graduates of at least one engineering university.[78] Thus, with regard to

[75] Shkaratan (1978), p. 167 and Trufanov (1973), pp. 57 and 61–62. The "foreman" category presumably includes not only chiefs of white-collar sections but also charge hands. In 1970, the "foremen" earned 88 per cent of what the higher managers received. The enterprises in the sample had been chosen in 1965 to be representative of the total labor force of Leningrad engineering with respect to earnings, age, skills, and total period in the national non-agricultural labor force.

[76] A. Grigorev in *C.D.S.P.*, XXXIII, 23 (July 8, 1981), pp. 1–2. But one must add that only one to two per cent of the university study time is devoted to such sub-specialties in at least some universities (Matthews [1982], p. 119 and M. Matthews in Tomiak [1983], p. 19).

[77] Grigorev, pp. 1–2.   [78] Aitov and Nasibullin in *S.I.*, 1980, 2, pp. 106–11.

full-time engineering education, we need not take the narrow specialization seriously. On the other hand, the weaker theoretic grounding provided in part-time education[79] must make the educational specialization there much more significant as a limitation on later change.

It has been suggested to me that the posited willingness of Soviet leaders to promote the versatility both of manual workers and of white-collar employees through costly educational investments is in contradiction to what we know of these same leaders' attitudes toward labor turnover in general. Such versatility is useful primarily as a means of encouraging job change (frequently, but not necessarily, between enterprises). Yet job change has been discouraged in the 1980s through the increase in the length of the period required for notice, and its potential advantages have been undermined by reducing the period of job search permitted without loss of the privileges of continuous work service (see Chapter 2). Can the posited motives of the Soviet leaders in promoting formal education be reconciled with their observed behavior in this related area?

I believe that there is no difficulty in such reconciliation. As was discussed in Chapter 3, quits are quite concentrated – although apparently less so in the Soviet Union than in the United States – within the youngest age group and among those with the least seniority in their present enterprises. The vast bulk of job changes involve no substantial alteration in job characteristics, although very frequently they are accompanied by departure from a given trade specialty as indicated by the exceedingly narrow set of Soviet definitions. Political leaders might well wish to discourage this type of job change, while at the same time desiring to encourage the sort of job wastage which investment in education can promote. There does not appear to be any contradiction involved here.

Explanation in terms of promoting class mobility

The Soviet government has traditionally shown a strong attachment to promoting equal opportunity for different nationalities and social groups in the population. It has expressed this concern through active discrimination against portions of the population whose share of upper status positions – and of the education normally required in order to be a proper candidate for such a position – is higher than the average. In this regard, Soviet policy has been a forerunner of the American affirmative action doctrine of legislatures, executive branches and judges as expressed during the latter 1960s and the 1970s.

[79] Ia. Dovgalevskii in *C.D.S.P.*, XXVI, 19 (June 5, 1974), pp. 1–2.

One may, of course, dispute the notion that the Soviet government has been concerned with equal opportunity *per se*. Its long-term discrimination in university admissions in favor of Central Asian Muslim nationalities, and its discrimination against Jews in recent decades,[80] can be explained by other motivations. So, too, can its effort to increase the share of university admissions going to blue-collar workers and to peasants; such effort is in line with long-term class ideology. But the fact remains that Soviet discrimination has never yet succeeded in reversing a situation where the groups discriminated against have enjoyed more than their proportional shares of higher education.[81]

Soviet sociological studies of the 1960s and 1970s document the unsurprising fact that children coming from families with more education receive better school grades at all levels including university.[82] This can be readily explained by the influence of the home environment which is expressed not only in a direct intellectual and motivational fashion, but also through the provision of better study space at home to the pupil.[83] Moreover, these studies also demonstrate that children tend to follow occupations requiring similar education and skill to that of the occupations of their fathers.[84]

What is unexpected, however, is what shows up in one study. Here, continuity between the social position of the respondent at the time of questioning and the social position of his/her father at the beginning of the respondent's work experience is seen to be transmitted much more strongly through the respondent's educational level than is the case in either the

---

[80] See for example, N. Kravetz in *Comparative Education*, 16, 1 (March 1980), pp. 13–24 as cited by N. Grant in Tomiak (1983), pp. 36–37, and Grant's comments.

[81] Even during 1935, when formal quotas were still in existence on admissions to higher education of youth of white-collar parentage, the Soviet government did not achieve equality let alone reverse the traditional inequality. Thirty per cent of entrants to engineering faculties were of such families (Granick [1960], p. 55 and M. Burakovskii in *Za Promyshlennye Kadry*, 1935, 21, pp. 34–37).

For 1973/74 data, see G. Avis in Tomiak (1983), p. 227. For a national sample of entering university students, some 45–50 per cent of the fathers and 75 per cent of the mothers held white-collar jobs.

[82] Vasil'eva (1973), pp. 16, 21, 41–42, 61–63; V. A. Kutsenko in *S.I.*, 1977, 2, pp. 79–80.

[83] Vasil'eva (1973), p. 23.

[84] The 1974 study of inter-generational occupational mobility in the city of Kazan, conducted by the careful sociologist O. I. Shkaratan, showed that 34–37 per cent of the two relevant age groups under forty years of age began their work career in a job requiring higher education provided that the father had started his career in a similar job. When the father had begun as a skilled or highly skilled blue-collar worker, 46–55 per cent of the children in all four age categories under fifty years of age also began work in the same occupational category. (Vasil'eva [1978], p. 98.)

United States or Japan.[85] It thus appears that it has been the relative failure of the Soviet Union to achieve equal opportunity of education as between social classes, when such achievement is judged by the standards of either the United States or Japan let alone by any absolute standard, that has been the force constraining inter-generational social mobility. At least this was the situation shown by one sample taken in the middle 1960s.

There is no indication that the continuity between the education of Soviet workers and the social position of their fathers is due to lack of desire for more education on the part either of Soviet youth or of their parents. A study in the early or middle 1960s, while indeed demonstrating the expected existence of differential class desire for advanced education, nevertheless indicated that 36 per cent of collective farmers and 65 per cent of blue-collar workers wanted their children to receive higher education.[86] A very large study carried out in 1983 by the Soviet Central Statistical Administration among pupils in the last year of rural academic secondary schools showed that 63 per cent of them wished to continue their studies full-time. Some 31 per cent wished their education to be continued at a university.[87]

Rather than lack of desire as the causal factor for unequal education among Soviet social classes, we should look partly to the unequal school preparation as among different regions of the country and as between rural and urban areas.[88] But to an equal degree, we must hold responsible the uneven performance in the primary and secondary grades that was noted above as existing between social classes within the same region.

Government measures adopted both in the late 1950s and in the late

---

[85] The simple correlation between the social positions of the respondents and their fathers is described by the Soviet authors as being similar for the Soviet Union, the U.S., and Japan, although the data presented in fact seem to show the Soviet correlation as relatively somewhat low. But partial correlation in the Soviet Union of the two social positions is low compared with those in the other two countries. The partial correlation between the education of the respondent prior to his first work experience and the social position of the father is the same as in the other two countries, while the Soviet partial correlation of the respondent's social position at the time of the interview and his own pre-work-experience education is higher. (O. I. Shkaratan and V. O. Rukavishnikov in *S.I.*, 1974, 2, pp. 46–48.)

The Soviet data come from a one per cent sample of the employed labor force in Kazan in 1967. The city is described as having at that time been a typical Soviet city of the size-category 250–500,000 population. The tables of page 47 contain several misprints, but it is clear from the accompanying text how the material should read.

[86] The study was conducted in the Sverdlovsk region (*oblast*). See Ia. M. Tkach in *Protsessy* (1967), p. 145.

[87] *V.S.*, 1984, 9, p. 64.

[88] F. P. Filippov and V. A. Malova in *S.I.*, 1984, 2, p. 64. They refer to sociological studies as showing no diminution of the rural–urban inequality.

1960s were intended, among other objectives, to favor university admission to applicants from manual (and thus educationally disfavored) backgrounds. The measures of the late 1950s made two years prior work experience obligatory for most entering university students. In full-time divisions of six Sverdlovsk university institutions, the proportion of first year students coming directly (or almost so) from secondary school fell from a high of 79–91 per cent during 1953–56 to 17–19 per cent during 1961–63.[89] This result was viewed as favoring children of blue-collar workers and collective farmers.[90]

The 1950s regulations were for the most part abandoned in the mid-1960s, although remnants continued through 1969. At that time, they were replaced by the creation of one-year preparatory sections for universities. Graduates would automatically be accepted into the full-time programs of the universities in whose preparatory sections they had trained. Students admitted to such preparatory sections must normally either have worked as manual workers in production branches for at least one year or be demobilized soldiers, and an applicant must have the recommendation of his/her workplace manager or military commander. In the first year of the program, 89 per cent of the students came from production (one quarter of these being from farms); six years later, the figures were 66 per cent with 30 per cent of these coming from farms.[91] With regard to the promotion of class mobility, the farm figures are particularly impressive; children of intellectuals, if working in production at all, would be much more likely to have taken urban jobs.

Furthermore, the preparatory divisions provide a substantial portion of the intake of the universities. In 1977 (the last year for which such data are available to me), the graduates of these divisions constituted about 15 per cent of the freshmen university class for the country as a whole. (This compared with 3 per cent after the first year of the program.) Since the original decree creating the preparatory divisions envisioned a maximum of roughly the 1977 figure, we might guess that the proportion has stabilized around that level.

Although, as one would expect, there are Soviet comments that many of the preparatory division students – including those coming from manual jobs rather than from the military – are from white-collar families and have

[89] M. N. Rutkevich and R. R. Filippov in *International Journal of Sociology*, spring–summer 1973, p. 248. These figures probably also include those who went directly from secondary school into the military, and then directly into a university program.

[90] Vasil'eva (1973), p. 66.

[91] George Avis in *Soviet Studies*, XXXV, 1 (January 1983), p. 25. Except where otherwise noted, this is my source for all information as to the preparatory divisions.

held manual jobs in production solely in order to obtain special educational privileges for university admission, it seems hard to doubt that at least a large number must come from underprivileged educational backgrounds. We see this in the dropout rate during the year of study within the division; this has been 12 per cent or higher – several times the rate for all full-time university students – despite the fact that the universities were under pressure to fill a given quota of their freshman places with graduates of their own preparatory division. In addition, the preparatory division graduates received poorer grades and had a higher dropout rate in the universities than did the direct entrants.[92]

On the other hand, the importance among the preparatory division students of children of intellectuals is suggested not only by direct Soviet comments but also by the fact that, in 1978 in the White Russian state university, competition for places in the law and history sections of the preparatory division was sharp, while there were only half as many applicants as places in the applied mathematics and chemistry sections.[93] A study of 1976–78, covering the Russian Republic and Estonia, similarly showed that the preparatory divisions play a larger role in filling first-year university positions in the humanities than in the sciences. This is despite the fact that, in the university graduating classes, children of collective farmers, and one would imagine of manual workers, are particularly poorly represented in the humanities sections.[94]

What we have here is a very mixed bag. The measures taken both in the late 1950s and in the late 1960s seem to have had both the function and effect of improving the opportunities of social groups that are educationally disadvantaged. A price – both in dropout rates and in the quality of students eventually entering the regular university courses – has been knowingly paid as a result of the measures adopted. However, additional objectives of the measures – particularly (according to George Avis) the leavening in the 1970s of the university student body with a group that was expected to be both more mature and more activist – were also important. Without such supplementary objectives, more effective approaches might

---

[92] V. Slobozhanin and I. Novikov (in *C.D.S.P.*, XXXII, 51 [January 21, 1981], p. 10) describe the situation in the White Russian Republic where 25 to 54 per cent of all students in chemistry, mathematics, mechanics and physics dropped out of the preparatory divisions during 1970–77, and where another 11 to 22 per cent of the graduates in these subjects dropped out during the first regular year of university study.

[93] *Ibid.* Here, the term "university" is used in reference to the Soviet institution of that name, rather than in reference to higher education as a whole as is usual in this chapter.

[94] F. R. Filippov in *S.I.*, 1980, 2, pp. 87–91. See also Vasil'eva (1973), pp. 45 and 70, and Avis, *Soviet Studies*, p. 32.

Table 7.3 *Probability of a pupil continuing education beyond secondary level, depending upon parental occupational position*

Category of parents	Secondary school graduates of 1963, five years later (percentage)		
	Full-time student (1)	Part-time student (2)	Part-time as proportion of all students [3:2/(1+2)]
High skilled white-collar	81	12	13
Average skilled white-collar	57	24	30
Blue-collar and white-collar in posts not requiring special education	48	30	38

Notes: Data are from a five per cent sample of all pupils graduating from complete secondary school in Leningrad in 1963. Columns (1) and (2) refer to current status in 1968, or to the fact that the student has already graduated from junior college after following the indicated type of study program. Over 90 per cent of these post-secondary studies were in universities. Both columns (1) and (2) reflect the atypicality of the city and of the period, but there is no reason why column (3) should be so affected.
Source: Vasil'eva (1973), pp. 61–62.

have been taken to concentrate the positive discrimination upon the groups that are truly of manual worker and peasant parentage.

All this is consistent with the thesis that the Soviet government has viewed inter-generational social mobility attained through education as an important objective for which it was willing to pay the costs. This hypothesis would explain why education has been expanded beyond what would be appropriate as a purely economic investment; for, assuming that children of manual labor families have on average a poorer educational background than do others, they will presumably be disproportionately affected by the size of the total national educational investment. But while the data are not inconsistent with the hypothesis of social mobility as the explanation for educational expansion, the case for the hypothesis does not seem particularly impressive.

A sharper test of the hypothesis is its ability to explain the fact that only about one-third of both junior college and university education is part-time, and that this percentage has shown no tendency to increase during the post-war years. As seen above, part-time education – at least in engineering – seems to offer net advantages to the state both in cost and in benefit when these are viewed in purely economic terms. The Model B hypothesis can explain why full-time education should nevertheless be given preference. Can the social-mobility hypothesis also do so?

Only one set of which I am aware is relevant here.[95] This is a 5 per cent sample of the pupils graduating from the tenth class in Leningrad during 1963, with the sample divided into three categories according to parental background. The result found (column 3 in Table 7.3) is that, for those who five years after graduation were studying at, or who had completed junior college or university, the probability that they were studying or had studied part-time rose consistently as the educational level of the parents fell. This finding is in line with qualitative Soviet statements, and is what we would expect for modern industrialized countries in general.

The data of Table 7.3 are inconsistent with the social mobility thesis. Since youth whose parents worked in lower status positions went much more heavily into part-time rather than into full-time post-secondary education, expansion of the former type of education might be expected to promote social mobility. But no such relative expansion occurred. This sphere of part-time versus full-time education is the only one in which the social mobility hypothesis yields a different prediction than does the Model B hypothesis. The result favors the Model B hypothesis.

Other explanations

Meeting desires of would-be students and parents. A third possible hypothesis is that the Soviet government views education as a consumer good for the public rather than as an investment good, and that education has been expanded in all areas simply because the country was growing wealthier and could afford it. This is not a view of Soviet education that I have seen put forward either by Soviet or foreign authors, but it is nevertheless a conceivable hypothesis. It is also one that we can crudely test and reject.

As in other countries, fashions as to preferred subjects of study change among would-be university students. During the 1970s and early 1980s, Soviet accounts are in accord that engineering became a less attractive field and was replaced in popularity by the humanities and medicine.[96] This

[95] As a rule, Soviet data as to social class of students in junior colleges and in higher education combine information as to the social category of the student himself and that of his parents. Indeed, this is the official categorization system (M. N. Rutkevich and F. R. Filippov in *International Journal of Sociology*, Spring–Summer 1973, p. 245). Such data are useless for our purposes.

[96] For data as to the number in 1970 and in 1975 of applicants by field for a place in the full-time faculties of universities in the Soviet Union as a whole, see N. S. Bolotin in *S.I.*, 1979, 4, p. 128. For data as to the White Russian state university's preparatory division in 1978, see V. Slobozhanin in *C.D.S.P.*, XXXII, 51 (January 21, 1981), p. 10. For general

had gone so far by 1981 that, as of June, Bauman University – the M.I.T./Cal. Tech. of the Soviet Union – had not been able to fill all of its freshman openings.[97]

However, when we examine the number of university students according to an eight-way breakdown by field, we see virtually no change. Between 1970/71 and 1983/84, engineering actually increased infinitesimally from 43.7 to 43.8 per cent of the total student body. Students of the universities (in the Russian sense) and fine-arts students – i.e. the closest we can come to the contingent growing in popularity – fell from 8.4 to 8.0 per cent, while medicine rose from 7.2 to 7.4.[98] There is nothing in these figures that reflects the apparent major changes in student taste that had occurred.

Education desired for its own sake. This hypothesis holds that the State invests in education beyond the point warranted by purely economic considerations because such public education enters directly into the Center's welfare function. A minor variant of this is that it enters indirectly through being a necessary condition for "good citizenship": participation in social activity, in the relations within the work collective, and in "management of the enterprise."[99] The choice of type of education is similarly determined by the Center's welfare function, and need not reflect changes in the desires of would-be students or of their parents.

This hypothesis can only be mentioned, but not considered. For a national society like the Soviet Union, in which the total amount of education provided exceeds what is warranted as an economic investment, this hypothesis would seem to be irrefutable and thus untestable.

Expectations by the Center as to future economic development. To this point, all of this Section dealing with alternative hypotheses has taken as its starting point the evidence that the Soviet educational effort has been excessive when judged solely as an economic investment by the state. The reason for considering the younger generations of the Soviet population as being over-educated by this standard is the inability of the Soviet economy to

comments, see F. R. Filippov in *S.I.*, 1980, 2, p. 92; Iu. Medvedev and R. Shcherbakov in *C.D.S.P.*, XXXIII, 23 (July 8, 1981), p. 2; G. Kulagin in *C.D.S.P.*, XXXIII, 52 (January 27, 1982), p. 11.
[97] Iu. Medvedev and R. Shcherbakov, *op. cit.*   [98] *Narkhoz SSSR 1983*, p. 495.
[99] This seems to be the principal justification used by one Soviet sociologist for his own support of providing complete academic secondary education for blue-collar workers, although he also gives prominent attention to economic pay-off (Shkaratan [1978], p. 145).

adjust its composition of available jobs to the changing education of its labor force.[100]

But investments in education have a long time horizon; the educational composition of the Soviet labor force thirty to forty years from now will be affected by decisions as to the amount and types of junior college and university education to be provided today. Soviet leaders might rationally accept the notion that the economy has been and still is severely constrained in the degree to which there can be change in the educational requirements of jobs offered to would-be workers, and yet believe that such constraints will be broken during the coming quarter of a century. Given sufficient optimism in this regard, the application of a low enough rate of time discount, and a sloughing over of the problems of obsolescence of underutilized training, Soviet leaders could believe that today's educational effort is justified purely as an economic investment.

The requirements cited as needed to justify such a belief are indeed substantial. But they are not impossible, although the condition concerning obsolescence does border on infeasibility. The much-used Soviet rhetoric as to the "scientific revolution" currently said to be in progress lends support to the hypothesis that such expectations may be held by the Center.

Thus I consider this hypothesis, regarding the Center's expectations, as constituting the prime competitor to the Model B hypothesis in explaining the observed facts of Soviet education. However, like the previous hypothesis, it would seem to be untestable from the information available to students of Soviet education. It is also, of course, a completely *ad hoc* hypothesis.

---

[100] The recognition of such inability of adjustment, at least over the shortrun, to current educational levels is expressed by V. Kirichenko, director of the research institute of the SSSR State Planning Commission, in *V.E.*, 1984, 11, pp. 9–10, as well as by V. Churbanov in *Molodoi Kommunist*, 1972, 6, pp. 64–71 as quoted secondhand by G. W. Lapidus in Byrnes (1983), p. 209.

8

The labor market and JROE

This chapter considers two aspects of the Soviet labor market which were not treated in Chapter 3, and proposes a sub-model of the JROE hypothesis to explain one of them. This sub-model contains the JROE assumption that overfull employment on a locality level is a lexicographic argument in the Center's welfare function. These aspects of the labor market serve as a further domain for testing the Model B hypothesis.

PHENOMENA TO BE EXPLAINED

The presence of overfull employment in the face of frequent shocks

The Model B hypothesis, containing the JROE assumption, has the task of explaining how overfull employment at the level of the individual locality (3.1) can be attained. What is the reason for such Soviet macroeconomic success compared with developed capitalist economies?

The "rival hypothesis" of Chapter 3, both in its simplest treatment and in its modified forms of (3.4), has no difficulty in explaining this stylized fact. By assumption, the individual enterprise is always willing to increase the total number of workers that it employs, even given the constraint of its existing wage fund. The border condition of the maximum achievable gross inflow of new workers prevents the enterprise from ever reaching equilibrium in the use of its wage fund. Under this assumption of permanent excess demand, unemployment can be only frictional.

In contrast, the Model B hypothesis does not treat the labor market as being characterized in general by excess demand. Within its wage fund constraint, enterprise management equalizes (in 3.4d) its marginal gain from employing additional workers with the gain from paying its existing workers more and thus restraining their quit rates. Thus the Model B hypothesis has the problem of showing how, in the light of frequent shocks both to the demand and supply schedules of labor, unemployment can be avoided.

Soviet economists would, at least officially, explain the avoidance of unemployment by the centrally planned nature of the Soviet economy. But certainly planning cannot result in the absence of exogenous shocks; if nothing else, unexpected weather conditions operate as a major source of shock because of the importance of agriculture and agrobusiness. Nor would the most Panglossian Soviet economist deny that significant planning mistakes occur which themselves create imbalances in the economy. Finally, Soviet planners do not have a peculiarly good record in predicting behavior controlled by individuals; in the field of regional labor markets, the projected net labor force movement to Siberia and the Far East during the 1950s and 1960s was doomed to serious disappointment. Rather, the claimed effect of central planning can only refer to the absorption and offsetting, rather than to the avoidance, of shocks.

Although these shocks are frequent, they can come from many different direct exogenous sources that are often correlated with one another. Weather, for example, will represent a shock of the same type to many different enterprises in a given region, although mediated by changes in the supply of different sorts of raw materials for the various enterprises. It is partly for this reason that shocks are not fully offsetting. In addiiton, it is at the level of the individual locality that overfull employment must be maintained; thus shocks would have to offset one another within each community individually in order to satisfy (3.1) through purely stochastic processes.

Part of the absorptions by the Soviet economy of exogenous shocks occurring continually in different localities is explained by the combination of hiring obligations laid upon enterprises with regard to people entering the labor market[1] and of sharp restrictions upon the right to dismiss unneeded personnel. But far greater absorptive ability is required. There is no legal obligation placed upon enterprises to hire healthy workers other than youth leaving school, yet some one-fifth of the former voluntarily quit their existing job each year.

The sort of shock that I have in mind here is one in which the labor requirements of a given enterprise decline;[2] for example, because the

---

[1] This applies to youth (*Normativnye akty* [1972], pp. 522–29), but not to women returning to the labor market after raising children.

[2] Shocks that cause an increase in the labor needs of an individual enterprise, and where there is an accompanying increase in wage funds, further overheat the local labor market and are likely to lead to increases in earnings per worker as a result of competition for labor among

enterprise's planned output and/or its available raw materials are less than in a previous period. With its production falling, its wage fund will go down similarly; the enterprise management will be compelled either to reduce staff or to reduce per capita earnings (by cutting incentive payments). Although management cannot normally react through dismissals or lay-offs, it has no obligation to replace those workers who quit.

If we think of one enterprise reducing its gross intake of labor through wastage, local unemployment will occur unless other enterprises of the same locality increase their gross intake in compensation. This is because the number of gross exits from the locality's enterprises taken as a group remains unaffected by the sort of shock to labor demand posited above, and thus the gross intake must be similarly unchanged.[3]

It would be far-fetched to imagine that it is planning that leads to the absorption of what would otherwise be a local labor surplus: i.e. that other enterprises in different sectors, but within the same locality, are given higher production plans – accompanied by larger materials allocations and wage funds – at the expense of enterprises of their sectors situated in localities with stochastic labor shortages. Soviet planning is organized primarily on a sectoral rather than a regional basis, and Soviet sectoral planning is not sufficiently fine-tuned to be able to respond to short-term shifts in labor conditions in individual localities.

The importance of the rate of gross hires for unemployment in capitalist economies is shown by 1967–69 national data for Great Britain. During these thirteen years, the stock of unemployed as measured by the Unemployment Register stayed within a narrow range of 425–483,000 during five years, while it was above 850,000 during another five. Yet the gross inflows onto the Unemployment Register were very similar as between these sets of years: 206–250,000 per annum during the first set, and 236–264,000 during the second.[4] The differences in the annual stock of unemployed are accounted for primarily by the variation in the number of gross hirings each year.

enterprises. Since these shocks represent no threat to the maintenance of overfull employment, they will be ignored in the following treatment.

[3] It is true that there will in fact be some likely reduction in the volume of gross intake required locally. New hires may be sufficient to avoid any rise in local unemployment, yet offer on average less attractive jobs than they had previously. As this becomes known to the local labor force, the quit rate is likely to decline, and presumably there will also be a net movement of labor toward other localities.

Nevertheless, we would expect that the sum of the hirings of all local enterprises not subject to shock must still expand. For this reason, I shall henceforth ignore the above caveat that eases the quantitative dimension of the puzzle to be explained.

[4] R. B. Thomas in Creedy (1981), p. 24.

On the basis of such data, one may conclude that only a small proportion of the Soviet problem of absorption of the effect on unemployment of random shocks is likely to be explained by the obstacles placed in the way of dismissals; the bulk of the absorption must be accomplished by positive hiring action. Model B must offer an explanation as to why the enterprises that are not subject to shock, increase their hirings in the fashion indicated.

The Shchekino movement and its failure to develop

The Shchekino experiment, which began in 1967, was intended to increase labor productivity through an improvement of incentives. The critical feature of this experiment[5] was the setting in year $(t-1)$ of the planned wage fund of a given enterprise for year $(t+m)$ where $m=0$, 1, 2 to 4, irrespective of whether the number of personnel was reduced, so long as increased labor productivity compensated for the decline in the size of the labor force. In this fashion, the ratchet effect in planning was to be restricted. Workers in enterprises that had entered into the experiment were to reap Schumpeterian rents during the predetermined period of wage fund stability; only after the expiration of this period was the per capita wage fund to be reduced to a normal Soviet level.

In the original Shchekinskii chemical combinat, the total of six per cent increase in earnings per capita between 1966 and 1970 (over and beyond

[5] See Shkurko (1971), pp. 22–23 for the clearest statement of this view. Other Soviet writers have instead stressed the taking on of planned objectives for labor productivity improvement by the enterprise, and in particular the working out of detailed measures for realizing such goals. Still others have stressed the right of Shchekino enterprises to provide special bonuses out of the wage fund; but in fact these were already available to all enterprises even prior to their official expansion to them in 1973 (see L. S. Kheifets in *Izv. AN SSSR*, 1978, 1, pp. 53–54), and even prior to the creation of the Shchekino experiment in 1967 (Dubovoi and Zhil'tsov [1971], p. 61). In a *Pravda* round table, emphasis is placed upon the need for having all of these elements combined together in a scheme; "Those who implement only individual elements make a lot of noise but do little good." (G. N. Grotseskul in *Pravda*, June 14, 1982, p. 3; see also T. A. Baranenkova in *Problemy povysheniia effektivnosti* [1983], p. 73.)

Peter Rutland in *Soviet Studies*, XXXVI, 3 (July 1984), pp. 345–65 presents what may be a different viewpoint. Certainly, he offers another perspective in his conclusion where he writes that "... the Shchekino method has been ... tied up with routine, detailed and at times obscure policy trends. ... Rather than see Shchekino as part of a wave of reform, one should see it as yet another example of the 'exchange of experience of leading factories' which clogs the pages of the Soviet press, year after year." (p. 361) This perspective seems to me to be only one possible interpretation even of the material he presents, and to be fundamentally erroneous. I view incentives as the heart of the experiment, and the stability of the wage fund as the only meaningful new incentive. In this insistence on the importance of the wage fund's stability, I echo the view that is standard both in the Soviet Union and in the West.

the average wage increase in industry as a whole) that was noted in Chapter 2 reflects a fair approximation to the relevant incentive, since 1968–70 were the years in which wage fund stability was to be maintained. Taking a more extended perspective, average earnings in the combinat rose between the years 1967 and 1981 by exactly the same percentage as they did in Soviet industry as a whole.[6] This long-term development is fully consistent with the concept underlying the experiment; namely, that the gains in earnings to the individual worker were to last long enough to provide the stimulus that monopoly profits do in Schumpeter's scheme of economic development, but that they were nevertheless to be temporary.

In view of the fact that this experiment has been universally praised in the Soviet Union, it is remarkable how slowly (even though steadily) it has developed. Beginning in 1967, and starting to spread only in the 1970s, it included a bit over 0.5 per cent of the industrial enterprises of the Russian Republic in 1975, 2.1 per cent in 1978 and 4.5 per cent in 1980 of all those in the Soviet Union, and 6 per cent of those in the Russian Republic in 1982.[7] Although the movement exists in non-industrial branches of the economy as well, its importance there seems to be minimal.

Indeed, not even all of the Shchekino enterprises are in fact able to keep their wage funds intact during the guaranteed periods. The Shchekinskii combinat itself had its wage fund lowered both during the 1971–75 and during the 1976–80 periods – although stability had been guaranteed each time.[8] A July 1979 decree of the top organs of the Communist Party and Government called for fixed, long-term wage costs per ruble of output (i.e. for a fixed wage fund in the sense used here). But a characterization three

---

[6] *Pravda*, June 14, 1982, p. 3 and *Narkhoz SSSR*, various issues. End-years of the 1967–1981 period examined seem more likely than not to have favored a rapid growth of earnings in the combinat, since average earnings there were the lowest for all enterprises in the branch in 1966 (Kheifets [1973], pp. 15–16), while the combinat won a Red Banner awarded by central authorities for its results in 1981 (*Pravda*, June 14, 1982, p. 3).

[7] Unfortunately, data exist only as to the number of production units and not as to the number of employees; one would guess that the latter percentage is larger. See I. Dorokhova and T. Doroshenko in *S.T.*, 1980, 4, pp. 96–97; lead editorial in *S.T.*, 1980, 9, pp. 3–4; V. Fil'ev in *V.E.*, 1983, 2, p. 59; A. L. Mirgaleev in *Pravda*, June 14, 1982, p. 3.

   Data given for those enterprises and production associations fully using the Shchekino method (note 5 above documents the view that only these should be counted) are compared for 1978 and 1980 with the total number of industrial production units having independent balance sheets as shown in *Narkhoz SSSR*, various issues. It is not certain, however, that this is the appropriate comparison. The 1975 and 1982 percentages for the Russian Republic are taken directly from the sources.

[8] N. R. Melentev, director of the combinat, in *Pravda*, June 14, 1982, p. 3. However, V. K. Moskalenko of the Soviet Union's State Planning Commission, interjected the comment "That's an extraordinary case" (*ibid.*).

years later of how the decree was being carried out was "slowly and half-heartedly."[9]

In view of the problems faced by the Soviet economy in mustering worker and managerial effort for the improvement of productivity, it seems remarkable on the face of things that more has not been done with a movement to improve incentives by reducing the force of the ratchet effect in planning. This very slow development, in the absence of any serious criticism either in the Soviet press or scholarly journals, requires explanation.

A JROE MODEL EXPLAINING CONTINUOUS OVERFULL EMPLOYMENT IN THE PRESENCE OF SHOCKS

The model starts from the position developed in Chapter 2 that productivity improvements for an enterprise as a whole yield only a very short-term increase in earnings. I hypothesize that such an increase is insufficient to make attractive to the labor force those sorts of productivity changes that are achieved by additional effort (as opposed to those attained purely through improved machinery or organization), since the additional effort must be maintained in the future without the supplementary compensation. Moreover, the labor force does not object to a single-year reduction, within limits, of earnings that are above base wages when this is accompanied by a reduction of work effort. It is this last phenomenon that comes into play when some enterprises are forced to cease their hirings because of external shocks and which allows others of the region to expand their hirings abnormally out of the ever-revolving group of frictionally unemployed. Given that enterprise management has a motivation for such hirings that for the moment we will treat as exogenous, the model explains the absence of resistance to such hirings. The model should be interpreted as applying particularly to the potential resistance of blue-collar workers, although it can be applied to white-collar employees as well.

We set forth the following notation, similar to what was used in (2.1):

E_t effort per man in period t
$\bar{E}$ normal effort per man
i the individual worker
G the group
N_t number of workers in the group in period t

---

[9] *Ibid.* Both here and earlier, the English translation is taken from the *C.D.S.P.*, XXXIV, 24 (July 14, 1982), pp. 10–11.

$w_{1,t}$ $=WF_t/N_t=$ monthly pay earned and received by individual (i) in period (t)

$w_{2,t}$ discounted monthly pay earned by (i) in (t) but received during t, $t+1,\ldots,\infty$. This is the amount earned and received today for today's effort, minus the negative effect on tomorrow's earnings of today's effort being greater than some minimum that is less than $\bar{E}$ for the group of all (i) in the enterprise

For simplicity, but with no loss of generality, we assume that each worker receives during a given period an income which is purely a function of his effort. (This is an idealized piece-work wage system.) His wage is $w_{1,t}$, and $\partial(w_{1,t})/\partial(E_t)$ is idealized as being a constant by the assumption that, within the relevant domain of $N_t \cdot E_t$ around (planned N_t) $\cdot$ ($\bar{E}$), a given percentage change in effort per man around normal effort results during the same period in an equal percentage change in the wage fund around the planned wage fund.[10] Workers are treated as homogeneous, although this treatment is modified in the discussion.

In the following periods, however, $w_{1,t+m}$ is a declining function of the per-man effort put forth by the group as a whole during period t. This decline is a result of how the wage fund for the group is planned, the Center

---

[10] Employing a notation in which WF is the actual wage fund and $\widehat{WF}$ the planned wage fund, Q and $\hat{Q}$ are the actual and planned output, j is a function for which $dj/dQ \lessgtr 1$ when $Q/\hat{Q} \gtrless 1$, and $a_{1,t}$ is average earnings per unit of effort, we note that $a_{1,t} \overset{\mathrm{d}}{=} W_{1,t}/E_t = WF_t/(N_t \cdot E_t)$, while the percentage change in the total wage fund available to the enterprise $[(WF_t - \widehat{WF}_t)/\widehat{WF}_t] = j\{(Q_t - \hat{Q}_t)/\hat{Q}_t\}$. Let us now set the ratio by which actual is greater than planned output of the enterprise $[(Q_t - \hat{Q}_t)/\hat{Q}_t] = \theta \{N_t[(E_t - \bar{E})/\bar{E}]\}$. We thus arrive at $a_{1,t} =$ weighted average of $\widehat{WF}_t/(N_t \cdot \bar{E})$ and of $\tau(\cdot)$ where

$$\tau(\cdot) = \frac{j(\cdot)\,\theta(\cdot)}{[(E_t - \bar{E})/\bar{E}]\,N_t}. \text{ Our idealizing assumption is that}$$

$\tau(\cdot) = \widehat{WF}_t/(N_t \cdot \bar{E})$ within a domain around $\bar{E}$.

Since $d(\theta_t)/dE_t < 0$ in the relevant domain because of diminishing returns to a single factor of production (labor), and since $d(j_t)/dE_t$ is also normally < 0 when $Q_t/\hat{Q}_t > 1$, our assumption requires empirical justification. Such justification is found in the fact that, when $Q_t/\hat{Q}_t > 1$, it is essentially only the blue-collar workers of the enterprise who share in the increment of $(WF_t - \widehat{WF}_t)$, while the white-collar collar personnel are rewarded out of the material-stimulation fund which is separate from the wage fund although similarly planned. Thus the N_t which is relevant for the division of a positive $(WF_t - \widehat{WF}_t)$ is considerably smaller than the N_t relevant to the division of $WF_t \lessgtr \widehat{WF}_t$.

The argument would be only slightly affected if we were to use W (wage fund plus material-stimulation fund) and $\hat{W}$ in lieu of WF and $\widehat{WF}$. The function j would be then roughly equal to 1, or slightly larger; the relevant N would include all white-collar personnel; and returns would diminish less rapidly than in the previous case because of the indivisibility of portions of the white-collar labor force.

This is the justification for conducting the discussion in the text in terms of actual and planned wage fund alone.

having insufficient information to be able to distinguish between those labor productivity improvements that are due to increased work effort and those that have other causes and are thus deemed inappropriate to reward. $w_{2,t}$ incorporates into the payment for work done in (t) the negative effect on future earnings by members of the group of that part of group effrot that in (t) may be above some minimum.[11] Assuming that there are a large number of workers in the group,

$$\partial w_{1,t+m}/\partial E_{1,t} = 0 \qquad m>0 \qquad (8.1)$$

The two different expressions for wages and the worker's utility can be described in functional form as follows:

$$w_{1,t}=f(E_{i,t}) \text{ where } f_1 > 0 \qquad (8.2)$$

f_1 is the change in the pay earned and received in a given period as individual effort changes marginally

$$w_{2,t}=g(E_{i,t}, E_{G,t}) \text{ where } g_1> 0, g_2 < 0 \qquad (8.3)$$

g_1, g_2 are the partial derivatives of $w_{2,t}$ with respect to its first and second argument respectively. In view of (8.1), $g_1=f_1$.

g_2 is the change in the discounted monthly pay, earned in the current period but received both then and over the indefinite future, as per-worker average group effort changes marginally.

$$\text{utility } _{i,t}=u(w_{2,t} [E_{i,t}, E_{G,t}] \quad E_{i,t}) \text{ where } u_1 > 0, u_2 < 0 \qquad (8.4)$$

here, $w_{2,t}$ is used as shorthand for the expected value at period (t) of $w_{2,t}$. $-u_2$ is the opportunity cost of effort for the individual worker

[11] An example of $w_{2,t}$ can be given for our idealized piece-work system, where $w_{1,t}$ is, in the relevant domain, a linear function of $E_{i,t}$ that passes through the origin. For such a linear function, $w_{1,t}/E_{i,t} = \partial w_{1,t}/\partial E_{i,t}$. If, in addition, the ratchet effect of E_t on the Center's granting of wage fund in period $(t+m)$ begins at $\bar{E}$ and is the same for every additional unit of E_t, then

$$w_{2,t}=w_{1,t}+(E_t-\bar{E}) \left\{ \frac{\partial[\sum_{m=1}^{\infty} \sum_{i=1}^{N} W_{1,t+m}/(1+r)^m]}{\partial(\sum_{i=1}^{N} E_{i,t})} \right\}$$

where $\partial(\cdot)/\partial)\cdot) < 0$, and $r =$ the workers' rate of time preference.

Production, under a concavity assumption, occurs where average product per unit of E_t $\geq$ marginal product per unit of E_t. This is because profit-maximizing enterprise managers expand employment for a homogeneous labor force, subject to a wage fund constraint, until $w_{1,t}/E_t$ equals the marginal value of product per unit of effort. (If managers are not profit maximizers, they do the same in terms of shadow prices that express their objective function.) In the interest of efficient production, planners provide the enterprise with a wage fund that permits employment sufficient to attain the specified domain of $N_t \cdot E_t$. Although $Q_t/(N_t \cdot E_t)$ is a declining function of E_t, $\partial w_{1,t}/\partial E_t$ is a constant as E_t changes, for the reasons given in the preceding footnote.

We now introduce the following assumption, which amounts to assuming that the group can act as a cartel in fixing the individual member's effort during period (t), but that it does not have unrestrained power over its members. The group's mechanism for action is social pressure, used the world over to limit the emergence of "rate busters."

Group social pressure can constrain $E_{i,t} \leqslant \bar{E}$, but it cannot compel the individual to supply $E_{i,t} < \bar{E}$.

(8.5)

The second part of assumption (8.5) can be defended on the basis that not only is f_1 [in (8.2)] $\geqslant$ the opportunity cost of effort for the individual worker at $E_t = \bar{E}$ (and thus, with a utility concavity assumption, also at all $E_t < \bar{E}$) – if not, the effort exerted would always be less than $\bar{E}$ – but also that $\partial w_{1,t+m}/\partial E_{i,t} = 0$

$$u_1 \cdot g_1 = u_1 \cdot f_1 \geqslant -u_2, \text{ given } E_{i,t} \leqslant \bar{E}$$

(8.6)

Thus each individual worker has an economic stake, both shortrun and longrun, in resisting the reduction of his own $E_{i,t}$ below $\bar{E}$. As in any cartel, a reasonable criterion of success over an extended time period is not the setting of those output levels for the individual cartel members which maximize the average utility of these members, but rather the enforcement of a satisficing solution intermediate between the non-cartel and the cartel utility-maximizing solutions. One would expect such a satisficing solution to have to be a prominent one, and $\bar{E}$ is the only such which appears in our model.

With the group maximizing its members' welfare subect to the above constraint on group behavior, and letting $N_t \cdot w_{2,t} = h(E_{G,t})$, $u(h_1)$ – the utility of marginal group earnings per unit of effort – $\leqslant -u_2$ [in (8.4)] (the worker's opportunity cost), given E_t. This relationship holds because the group is able to increase E_t if that would improve group welfare, while it is powerless to reduce E_t below $\bar{E}$. Note that $h_1 = f_1 + \partial[\sum_{m>0} w_{1,i,t+m}/(1+r)^m]/\partial E_{G,t}$

We now further assume that

$$u(h_1) < -u_2, \text{ given } E_t.$$

(8.7)

(Note that this still allows $u_1 \cdot f_1 \geqslant -u_2$, given E_t, a condition that is necessary in our approach for explaining any positive value of E_t.) This strict inequality arises from the following empirical phenomena:

(a) The virtual obligation placed on all urban able-bodied and labor age personnel to work full-time in the socialist economy. Particularly in the light of the opportunities for work in the second economy, where one may presume that the risk-discounted reward for effort is greater than h_1 (even if perhaps not greater than f_1), one would expect many workers to wish to divert effort from the socialist sector to the second economy. Mapping this empirical situation into our hypothesized case of homogeneous workers, it might be expected that our average worker's opportunity cost would satisfy (8.7).

(b) The Center's search for equity among different groups in its planning of group wage funds, and its inability to identify that part of group labor productivity which is due to effort, cause it to give a large negative value to the effect on tomorrow's earnings of today's effort exerted by the group of all (i) workers. Indeed, this negative effect can be treated as so great that, in future periods, workers must maintain whatever increase in group effort occurred in (t) in order to obtain a w_t in these periods which is equal to what it would have been at $(\bar{E}-\varepsilon)$ if $E_{G,t}$ had been no greater than $(\bar{E}_t-\varepsilon_t)$.[12]

(c) As we shall see below, it is important for the Center, in order to be able to absorb employment shocks without incurring strong worker resistance, to maintain the inequality expressed in (8.7).

Given (8.7), workers in enterprise (k) do not resist the hiring of unneeded workers when another enterprise is forced by an exogenous shock to reduce its normal hirings from the ever-revolving group of frictionally unemployed in the locality.[13] Such additional hirings in enterprise (k), by reducing the feasible E_t there,[14] bring the workers as a group closer to their equilibrium effort given h_t. Here we are assuming that, in the *group* response to such potential hirings by management:

The group is reacting to h_t rather than to f_t.   (8.8)

Of course, we have not explained why the management of enterprise (k) should wish to engage in such hirings. What we have explained is only the absence of worker resistance to the hirings.

If E is not to decline secularly under the pressure of such exogenous

[12] This can be stated, under the assumptions of the previous footnotes, as $\partial(\Sigma w_{i,t+m})/\partial(\Sigma E_{i,t})-\partial(\Sigma w_{i,t})/\partial(\Sigma E_{i,t})=0$

[13] Of course, the issue of such resistance would not arise at all if new workers were paid a time wage equal only to their marginal product under existing employment conditions, with the E_t of existing workers being maintained at $\bar{E}$. However, although modest seniority payments are frequently made to workers, discrimination between old and new workers of the dimensions suggested above has never been introduced in the Soviet Union. It would amount to a *de facto* renunciation of a meaningful overfull employment policy.

[14] Since factors of production complementary to labor are limited in their availability to enterprise (k), and since elasticities of substitution in the relevant shortrun are likely to be low, one might think of enterprise management as organizing production in the shortrun so that it cannot use more than a given amount of labor inputs ($N_t \cdot E_t$). Thus, with given inputs of raw materials and increased N_t, the efforts of workers to maintain their previous level of E_t would simply lead to the exhaustion of materials stocks prior to the end of the working period – and thus to obligatory idleness implying a reduction in E_t.

shocks until a point is reached at which the inequality set forth in (8.7) no longer holds, then E must rise in the following period $(t+1)$ in enterprise (k) when either the excess workers can be worked off through non-replacement of those quitting, or when complementary materials supplies can be obtained. Our explanation is again managerial, since this involves moving the workers in the direction away from their group-equilibrium position of equality between $u(h_1)$ and $-u_2$ [in (8.4)]. But here it is important to note the following:

Assuming the ineffectiveness of possible group resistance to the increase of E_{t+1} above the E_t level which had been the maximum feasible in the presence of excess workers, each individual worker will be motivated to exert at least his earlier effort $\bar{E}$. This is because, by concavity, $u_1 \cdot f_1$ [in (8.6)] $> -u_2$, given that $E_t < \bar{E}$. (Note that $f_{1,t+1} \geq f_{1,t}$ for a given E.)

(8.9)

A slight extension of assumption (8.5) suggests that the group is unable to act to keep E below $\bar{E}$. (8.10)

The active role in this model with regard both to the absorption of employment shocks, and to the increase of worker effort to its normal amount in the following period, is taken by management. The labor force is reactive. One might then ask why the Center should choose our modelled situation in which the labor force is happy to see the enterprise absorb unneeded workers in case of shocks, but is resistant as a group (although not as individuals) to the following period's increase in effort per man to its normal level, in preference to a situation in which h_1 is higher and the labor force resistance to the two changes is reversed. My answer lies in the following two assumptions, the second of which is suggested by the immediately preceding paragraphs:

In choosing between models of managerially determined decision making, the Center prefers the model that minimizes worker resistance.

(8.11)

The worker-group welfare evaluation of the vector $(h_{1,t} \quad E_t)$ is discontinuous at $\bar{E}$. The absolute value of d(group welfare function)$/d(E_t)$ is substantially more when E is decreasing from $\bar{E}$ than when it is increasing to $\bar{E}$. (8.12)

The absolute effect on the group welfare function of a change of average effort is substantially more during the first period of labor expansion through taking on surplus workers than it is in the second phase of contraction of the labor force. (The direction of relative effect follows from the usual assumption of concavity of utility with respect both to income and effort.) Since this effect is positive in the first period and negative in the second, the enterprise's workforce is a net gainer over the two periods taken together in comparison with a situation in which the size of the enterprise's labor force would have been stable throughout. This pleasant result would not occur if $u(h_1) \geqslant -u_2$ at $\bar{E}$; in this case, the workforce would be a net loser from the change in the size of the labor force over the two periods.

We should also note that if the Center were to choose the alternative to our modelled situation, it might well be unable to satisfy inequality (3.2). Namely, if $u(h_{1,t})$ were greater than the worker's opportunity cost $(-u_{2,t})$, given that $E_t < \bar{E}$, all work carried out where E_t was $< \bar{E}$ would have to be defined in (3.2) as constituting "idleness."

As yet we have said nothing as to why the management of enterprise (k) should wish to take the active role indicated in hirings in year (t), and then in allowing manpower to run down in $(t+1)$. As to the hiring, we can picture the locality's Communist Party committee – acting as the prefect of the Center – exerting the necessary pressure in the interest of the Center's overfull employment objective. Furthermore, such pressure is virtually costless to the local Party authorities, since hirings will have no opportunity costs in terms of local output and there are no net financial costs to the State.

What is significant here is that very little pressure is required; management offers no resistance, and has no reason to delay action. If such hirings were to encounter worker opposition, there might be reason for management's own behavior to reflect it. But, as we have modelled the situation, this is not the case. Plan fulfillment in (t), and thus the criteria by which enterprise management is evaluated by its ministerial authorities who have different interests than those of the local Party authorities, is affected only with regard to labor productivity. Although this latter has been an important plan criterion since the early 1970s, the justification has been that of labor shortage as well as of inflation control through holding down wage payments per unit of output. Where, as in the present case, neither of these reasons apply, it would seem likely that the local Party authorities and enterprise management combined would encounter little difficulty in persuading the ministry to revise downward the enterprise's labor productivity plan for year (t).

Indeed, enterprise management even gains from such hirings. Other things equal – as they are in this case – plan fulfillment in (t) is easier and more certain with a larger labor force. Labor productivity in (t) that is depressed compared with what it would otherwise have been may lead to a lower labor productivity plan for $(t+1)$ than would normally have been set. But I would not make much of these potential gains. They are offset by the equally minor future costs that management will encounter in $(t+1)$ when it must raise E_{t+1} to the old level of $\bar{E}$. The point is that enterprise management is essentially indifferent to the hirings, and thus is ready to yield to the slightest pressure from local authorities.

What happens in $(t+1)$ when the local labor surplus has disappeared? For this, I make what seems to be the reasonable assumption that

The individual worker (i) makes his decision to quit enterprise (k), or to hire-on there from some other enterprise, in terms of $f_{\mathrm{I},t+1}$, in (8.2) rather than $h_{\mathrm{I},t+1}$.

(8.13)

But we know that in the original state, without labor surplus, $u_{\mathrm{I},t-1}(h_{\mathrm{I}}) \cdot f_{\mathrm{I},t-1} \geq -u_{2,t-1}$, given the worker's effort of $\bar{E}$ in that period. Since now $E_{i,t} < \bar{E}$, the usual concavity assumption also ensures that the opportunity cost given $E_{i,t}$ is less than the opportunity cost given $\bar{E}$. Thus, *ceteris paribus*, the individual will prefer to work in an enterprise where he is allowed to exert effort $\bar{E}$ rather than only $E_{i,t}$.

Thus the management of (k) is compelled in period $(t+1)$ to raise the average effort per worker back to $\bar{E}$, under penalty of losing on a net basis substantial parts of its labor force whose members are comparing $u_{\mathrm{I}} \cdot f_{\mathrm{I}}$ with their opportunity cost and who, now that the local labor surplus has disappeared, have the alternative of working elsewhere in the locality. (Of course, management is also motivated by the labor productivity plan-criterion incentive to act in this way.) It is true that this managerial attempt must overcome group resistance of the labor force, which calculates in terms of a comparison of $u(h_1)$ with $-u_2$. But such group resistance is not likely to be great [see (8.9) and (8.10)].

Obligation to participate in the socialist labor market

The work obligation, which is certainly binding at least on healthy males and unmarried young women, must create a situation where f_1 is less than the opportunity cost of effort of some workers. These are people who feel called upon to hold a job only so as to avoid being labelled as parasites, and who put forth the minimum effort needed so as to avoid being dismissed. What is the effect of this phenomenon on the analysis presented above?

The answer is: not much effect. Analytically, the relationship between $u_1 \cdot f_1$ and the opportunity cost is significant only for (8.9), by extension for

(8.10), and for (8.13). These, in turn, affect the argument for effort returning from E_t to $\bar{E}$ in the following period. Thus, if $u_1 \cdot f_1$ were lower than the opportunity cost of all workers at $\bar{E}$, the ability of the model to bring the local labor market back to equilibrium of individual effort at $\bar{E}$ would be destroyed. But it is the potential quit and hire-on actions of the individual worker that are really critical, and in this respect the analysis requires only that a reasonably substantial marginal number of workers have an opportunity cost less than $u_1 \cdot f_1$ and that their $E_{i,t}$ be restricted to less than $\bar{E}$.

In fact, of course, it is only a small minority of Soviet workers who work in the socialist sector solely because they are legally or socially obliged to do so. "Parasites" in the Soviet Union are reported to be estimated by the Soviet procuracy as 500,000;[15] to pick an arbitrary number, let us assume that would-be parasites constitute four times that figure. This would be very substantial in absolute terms, but still less than two per cent of the labor force working outside of the collective farms. It is true that we would expect such people to seek out those jobs and organizations which require the least effort on the job in order for the worker to avoid dismissal and keep out of trouble; for this reason, they should constitute far more than 2 per cent of the labor force of some organizations. But even if their numbers were to reach 50–60 per cent in such organizations, this would still be insufficient to affect the argument. In fact, of course, we would expect unwilling workers to congregate in those non-industrial, budgetarily financed organizations in which employee earnings are close to the fixed wage rate; the model does not apply to such organizations, and here E_t would have to be raised back to $\bar{E}$ by other means.

Consistency with data as to absenteeism

Soviet data as to full calendar day absences from the job of industrial blue-collar workers can be compared with that of Western countries. For these purposes, only holidays and fully paid annual vacations are excluded. Since in any country categorization of absences depends partly upon the national policy of payment for different kinds of absences and upon their relative social acceptability, it seems best to add together the various Soviet subcategories.

Official Soviet data for 1950 through 1974 show 18.3 days of annual absences in 1950, an increase to 21.1 days in 1965, and then a steady

---

[15] *Le Monde*, October 20, 1984, p. 6.

decline back to 18.7 in 1974.[16] A prominent labor economist reported in 1981 a figure of about 20 days, adding that not all absences were recorded.[17] Between May 1975 and May 1982, of all mainline production equipment in the engineering industries that was idle for one or more shifts on the survey day, the proportion accounted for by excused absence of the operator declined by percentages varying between 3 and 9 per cent, depending on the type of equipment.[18] These latter data cast doubt upon the hypothesis suggested by the previous figures of marked increase in absenteeism between these years. All in all, it would seem that we can consider nineteen to twenty days of recorded annual absences as a reasonable approximation both for the 1970s and for the early 1980s.

Figures for other countries seem to be for wage and salary employees combined and in all sectors of the economy. Data for 1981 and 1983 show the Netherlands and Italy to have roughly the same degree of absenteeism as the Soviet Union had in 1974, West Germany to be 83 to 97 per cent of the Soviet figure, Sweden to be 150 per cent, but the U.S. to be only 40 per cent.[19]

Data for 1972 and 1973 for West Germany, the Netherlands, and Italy are all reported as being substantially higher than those for the Soviet Union, while American data through 1978 are less than half of the Soviet level.[20]

The Soviet data are overstated relative to those of other countries by the fact that they exclude white-collar employees, whose absentee rate in the United States is substantially less than that of blue-collar workers,[21] as well as excluding absentees due to plant idleness. On the other hand, Soviet data include only full-day absences, while at least American data include part-day absences. One may wonder as to the comparability of the data among the various countries used as a basis of comparison. But there is nothing in this medley of material to suggest that Soviet full-day absentee-

---

[16] Soviet absentee data include sicknesses, pregnancy and post-natal leave, absences due to fulfilling state and social obligations, other absences with the permission of the enterprise management, idleness of the workplace equipment for a full shift or more, and absences for "other reasons." Data are from *Narkhoz SSSR 1922-72*, p. 148; *Narkhoz SSSR 1973*, p. 93; and *Narkhoz SSSR 1974*, p. 189. No later official data are available.

[17] E. Manevich in *V.E.*, 1981, 9, p. 59.

[18] *V.S.*, 1976, 4, pp. 93-95, and *V.S.*, 1983, 4, pp. 68-70.

[19] Salowsky (1983), especially p. 17, and the Cologne Institut der deutschen Wirtschaft, Information Service Nr. 37 of September 13, 1984, p. 3. A Japanese figure of 22 per cent is also cited, but the Japanese study from which the figure is taken excludes illness from the definition of absenteeism (see *Japan Economic Journal*, September 21, 1982, p. 3).

[20] D. E. Taylor in *Monthly Labor Review*, August 1979, p. 49.   [21] *Ibid.*, pp. 50-51.

ism is peculiarly high by the exceedingly heterogeneous standards of developed capitalist economies.[22] This is particularly the case when comparison is made with the Netherlands, Italy, and West Germany, the countries with which the Soviet Union is most comparable as to the degree to which excused absences are paid.[23]

This finding is contrary to what is frequently assumed in Western literature about the Soviet Union.[24] It is more certain for the period through the mid-1970s than later, while it is during the later years that one might hypothesize that absenteeism would rise because of increased disequilibrium between supply and demand of consumer goods. Nevertheless, what I shall take as the fact to be explained is that there is nothing unusual about the degree of blue-collar absenteeism in the Soviet Union.

Such normal or below-normal absenteeism is what might be expected from our model. Although $u(h_1)$ in (8.7), is less than the opportunity cost of effort, given $\bar{E}$, this is not the case for $u_1 \cdot f_1$, in (8.6). The individual, in determining whether or not to work on a given day, makes his decision in terms of f_1 – which is here the change in pay both earned and received in the month as his work-time changes by a day. For the average Soviet worker, $u_1 \cdot f_1 \geqslant -u_2$, while in a perfectly competitive economy without state intervention the wage = the opportunity cost.

An alternative analysis which ignored group social pressure, and thus contained no distinction between w_1 and w_2, would have difficulty reconciling the stylized fact of a low level of effort by the Soviet worker ("They

[22] Part-day absences may well be higher in the Soviet Union than elsewhere because of the difficulties of shopping, receiving medical care, and carrying on business with official government offices outside of working hours. In Moscow oblast, questionnaires answered by 30,000 employees of two-hundred-forty-five industrial enterprises indicated that 73 per cent of the respondents take time off work for such purposes; the Soviet author blamed such absences primarily upon the limited hours worked by the shops and offices (A. Volgin [chairman of the People's Control Committee of Moscow oblast] in *Pravda*, December 20, 1982, p. 3). Other available data come from a large-scale, random sample of Soviet émigrés to the United States; for most of them, their last normal work period in the Soviet Union was during 1978 or 1979. Of these respondents, 41 per cent answered positively to the question: "While you were working at that job, did you sometimes use work time for personal business (like shopping or running errands)?" (Gregory [1985], p. 27). However, it is unclear (at least to this writer) whether either the 41 or the 73 per cent figures should be considered high or low by international standards.

[23] For the Soviet Union, see Lantsev (1976), especially pp. 68–70. For the other countries, see Salowsky (1983). It is true that the Soviet economy is somewhat less generous than are these countries in its continuation of wage payments for sickness. (One hundred per cent payment is made only after individuals have been in the labor force for eight years or longer.)

[24] See, for example, Schrettl (1982), p. 64, and W. D. Connor in Kahan and Ruble (1979), p. 318.

pretend to pay us and we pretend to work," as Hedrick Smith put it) with the presence of a normal rate of absenteeism. In such an analysis, $u_1 \cdot f_1$ would be taken as being less than the opportunity cost at any relevant level of effort, thus causing workers to reduce their effort to the minimum consistent with retaining their jobs. But since absenteeism is a particularly convenient way of reducing effort, analysis of this type should predict high Soviet absenteeism.

Labor hoarding in a stochastic, steady-state economy

"Labor hoarding," as a component in "hidden reserves," is a phenomenon commented on in the Soviet press as well as in Western writing about the Soviet Union. The broad category of hidden reserves can be divided into three categories, only the third being of interest here.

The first category deals with labor productivity, and Soviet discussion considers various obstacles to its improvement. Concentration is particularly upon incentive problems and upon the obstacles both to dismissal and to reassignment of workers.[25]

The second category constitutes successful efforts by enterprises to have excess labor force needs incorporated into their manpower plans and thus into their wage fund plans as well. One author, basing herself on 1975–77 data for enterprises of a West Siberian city, concluded that unavailability of 1 to 5 per cent of the planned labor force is a normal occurrence that is covered by hidden reserves.[26] Since the requesting of excess manpower, with accompanying wage funds, is virtually costless to the enterprise, it is not surprising that such requests are common. But aggregate data comparing available manpower to planned manpower during the middle 1970s suggest that the effect of such over-requests was greater on the wage fund that on the manpower available in enterprises.[27]

[25] See Manevich (1980), pp. 87–88 and *Ref.*, 1981, 11, E57.

[26] N. V. Chernina in *Izv. sib. otd.*, 1981, 11 (September 1981), p. 127. Data studied consist of output-plan fulfillment in relation to the percentage of planned labor that the enterprise had available to it.

    During these years, labor force plans were made by the enterprises themselves and were uncontrolled by higher authorities. Thus manpower plans during this period may well have been ignored by higher authorities in setting wage fund plans for enterprises. Nevertheless, what presumably mattered to enterprise management was that the existence of padding in such plans was virtually certain to have either a zero or positive (but not negative) effect on wage fund availability, and the reverse for the magnitude of planned labor productivity.

[27] These data refer to the regular excess during the 1970s of the planned number of all industrial employees, as expressed in the sum of approved annual plans of enterprises, compared with actual labor availability; such excess was in the order of six to ten per cent.

It is the third category alone that can properly be viewed as constituting labor hoarding. "Excess" employees are desired by management because of both stochastic and seasonal factors: late deliveries of materials, and the resulting need for excess labor when the supplies do arrive if production targets are to be met on time; changes of production plans during the course of the planning year; the requirement to unload freight cars whenever they may arrive; the obligation to send employees for temporary work both in agriculture and in various unskilled municipal maintenance and warehousing services.[28]

Whether hoarding for such purposes (that we shall, only partly correctly, call stochastic) should be viewed by the Center as being anti-social depends upon the Center's weighting of different objectives. From the point of view of maximizing labor productivity and minimizing costs per unit of output, it would be appropriate to frown upon such hoarding by management. But it seems reasonable to assume that, to the Center as well as to enterprise managements, plan fulfillment of production targets is more important.[29] From this standpoint, the relevant issue is that of whether alternative sources of labor flexibility exist.

Given overfull employment, no supply of temporary labor can normally be found. Part-time work is rarely used in the Soviet Union and, in any case, would be of no help in meeting the above needs. The use of extensive overtime appears to be the only significant alternative method possible under Soviet conditions.

Overtime in the Soviet economy is legally restricted. Not only can it be used solely under specified conditions, but any individual is limited to not more than four hours within a two-day period and not over one hundred twenty hours within a year.[30] However, trade union control over the

(See Chapter 2 and, especially, A. Dadashev in *V.E.*, 1979, 8, pp. 41–42.)

On the other hand, both Soviet industry and the Soviet state sector as a whole were able to engage considerably more manpower through at least 1975 than had been projected in the relevant five year plans. (See Anna-Jutta Pietsch in Lane [1986], p. 181.) One might argue that it was the annual enterprise requests for more labor, resulting directly in higher annual wage fund plans, that consistently brought more workers than had been forecast into the state sector. This latter is a reversal of the argument made in the text. However, I reject such comparisons with five year plan projections because of the unreliability of the latter when judged as forecasts of virtually any aspect of the Soviet economy.

28 See Knishnik and Levikov (1983), p. 48ff.; S. M. Zverev in *E.K.O.*, 1984, 5, p. 46; and, especially, *Ref.*, 1981, 11, E57.

29 Western literature sometimes implicitly denies this. See H.-H Höhmann in *B.B.O.I.S.*, 1984, 28, pp. 16–17, who holds that temporary relief of labor shortages could be achieved by what he believes to be the current reduction of labor hoarding. Although he explicitly recognizes that such hoarding is directed to fulfillment of output plans, he apparently views the reduction of hoarding as being helpful in achieving the goals of the Center.

30 M. E. Pankin in *S.T.*, 1982, 6, pp. 108–11, and Moskoff (1984), pp. 73–74.

reasons permitted for overtime was observed to be extremely slack in the one Soviet study that I have seen dealing with the records of enterprises over a number of years,[31] and some overtime is said to go unrecorded along with similarly unrecorded leaves that are given in compensation.[32]

On a national, aggregative basis, officially recorded overtime in industry was practically nil during 1974–75. Average weekly hours worked in industry by blue-collar workers, including overtime but excluding paid non-working time of nursing mothers, of youth under eighteen years, and all other such legally reduced working hours (especially prevalent in individual trades and branches) was 0.1 hour less than the June 1977 standard workweek that excluded overtime but did include these privileged non-working times.[33] It is difficult to believe that average recorded overtime of blue-collar workers during these years could have reached one hour a week.

A Soviet study conducted some time between 1963 and 1966 is the only one that I know purporting to report actual overtime worked on people's principal job. This study covered 2,700 people in a stratified sample representing the adult population of the Soviet Union as a whole. Of blue-collar workers, 22.5 per cent had a working day of eight hours, and 6.5 per cent worked nine hours or more.[34] Since the change-over from the seven hour, six day week had not yet occurred by 1966, overtime among blue-collar workers that was not compensated by time off must have averaged a minimum of 0.4 hours weekly in this sample. Such overtime for "intelligentsia not engaged in production" was a minimum of one hour weekly.

Data as to actual overtime work are also available for 1973 with regard to a sample of Jewish emigrants to Israel; the sample, however, is non-random, is two-thirds white-collar, covers all urban sectors but only for those organizations located in the European part of the Soviet Union, and is heavily over-weighted by emigrants from Western territories added to the Soviet Union since 1939. In this sample, average overtime worked by men on their normal jobs was 1.6 hours weekly, and by women was 0.9 hours weekly. The figure was substantially higher (twelve to thirteen hours) for those working any overtime, but only 13 per cent of men and 7 per cent of women fell into this category.[35] If these data exclude overtime

---

[31] A. Akhumov and Iu. Shvetsov in *S.T.*, 1984, 7, pp. 102–03.
[32] E. Manevich in *V.E.*, 1981, 9, p. 59.
[33] Compare *V.E.*, 1976, 8, p. 92, and *V.E.*, 1983, 4, p. 65.
[34] Grushin (1967), especially p. 43.
[35] Ofer *et al.* (1979), pp. 3, 7, 18, and 25. Of the respondents, 62 per cent came from an area with only 8 per cent of the country's urban population.

compensated with free time, they seem reasonably consistent with the national sample of the 1960s.

The above data suggest that an estimate of actual total overtime in the Soviet Union as averaging not more than one to two hours weekly for manual workers may not be far off. This is clearly insufficient to provide the flexibility needed under Soviet conditions for the fulfillment of output targets in industry. Thus the third category of "hoarding" seems to represent a *faute de mieux desideratum*, not only for enterprise managers but also for the Center.

Critical for our analysis is the importance to the Center of such "hoarding." The hypothetical desirability is contrary to what is suggested by one reason sometimes given in the West for the hoarding of labor by Soviet managers: namely, that managers are risk avoiders. It is argued that this causes them to prefer, given their enterprise wage funds, a level of employment in their enterprises that is higher than would maximize the expected value of the objective function of a risk-neutral manager (utility from maximizing output, profits, or what have you). Since the Center is concerned with risk only on a more aggregative level than that of the enterprise, its preferred level of employment in enterprise (k) should be lower. The implication of this argument is that the Center would not wish to create conditions that allow managers to hoard as much labor as they desire, given the wage funds of the enterprises.

This argument holds only if we concentrate exclusively on the high variances of the timing of receipts of complementary inputs of raw materials, of pressures to lend workers to agriculture and to local municipal construction, etc. and ignore the effect of high variance of other variables which operate in the opposite direction. The most important such variable is $R_{k,t}$, defined as the number of quits during period (t) by those workers in enterprise (k) who had worked there during ($t-1$). As discussed in Chapter 2, enterprise management faces a trade-off between the number of workers it can employ with a given wage fund and its proportion of old to new workers, since the quit rate will vary inversely with the wage paid. Assuming that skills are often enterprise specific, management in determining its wage policy must choose between the quantity and quality of its workers. $R_{k,t}$ is an inverse function of $w_{1,k,t}/E_{k,t}$ (the wage per unit of effort).

The moment that we consider the existence of variance of R_k around the expected value of R_k, given both ($w_{1,k,t}/E_{k,t}$) and the wages provided in (t) by other enterprises of the locality, there is a collapse of the argument that risk aversion necessarily has a positive effect on labor hoarding. *Ceteris paribus*, the existence of variance in R_k will lead the risk averse enterprise manager to prefer a higher wage level, and thereby a lower employment level, than would maximize his objective function. The case is quite symmetrical to that arising from variances that cause him to prefer a higher employment level. The result is that, under Soviet conditions, risk aversion by management has no obvious direction of bias in its net effect on managerial choice.

If labor hoarding as I have defined it is desirable both for management and for the Center, it appears at first blush to be disadvantageous to blue-collar workers of the enterprise. For it restricts the average of labor productivity over the year, and thus reduces the wage fund available per employee with a standard level of skill. Since industrial workers have relatively little at stake in plan fulfillment by their enterprise – receiving only something like 10 per cent of their earnings above wage rates out of the material-stimulation fund, compared with 90 per cent from the wage fund[36] – it is not too important to them that such labor hoarding is needed for plan fulfillment. One might thus expect resistance by blue-collar workers to any replacement-hiring by enterprises that occurs so as to maintain in the face of quits the existing level of "surplus labor." Particularly in the light of national campaigns to increase labor productivity, such financially motivated resistance by manual workers might be hard for enterprise managements to ignore.

From the point of view of the Center, it is therefore important to eliminate organized group pressure by blue-collar workers against new hirings that are intended to create and maintain the labor "surpluses" needed for plan fulfillment in the face of stochastic disturbances. Our model provides a means for such elimination of pressure, since $u(h_1)$, in (8.7) is less than $-u_2$ (their opportunity cost of effort), and thus workers – when acting as a group – are glad to reduce their work effort.

An alternative means for the Center to resist such blue-collar pressure would be to attach blue-collar incentives primarily to plan fulfillment by

---

[36] The figure is for the 1970s and is only very approximate. It is based upon the statement by D. Dymentman in *P.Kh.*, 1980, 8, p. 112 that blue-collar workers of industry were then receiving only 3 to 4 per cent of their bonus plus piece-rate earnings from the material-stimulation fund, and upon the application of these percentages to the breakdown during 1969–72 of total receipts by blue-collar workers of light industry from this fund (Nazarov [1975], pp. 271–72).

Even if the true figure were double the calculated one, the discrepancy would have only limited significance for the argument in the text.

A study conducted during 1980–81 in three large enterprises of the pulp and paper industry is said to have shown that earnings of manual workers there were essentially unaffected by any results other than output (L. Bliakhman in *S.T.*, 1984, 1, p. 84).

the enterprise. But such attachment would violate the Soviet incentive principle embodied in constraint (4.11) of Model A. The negative side effects, through strengthening dysfunctional enterprise behavior arising out of constraint (4.16) concerning the inevitability of important externalities to the enterprise, would probably be much larger than the potential gains.

ALTERNATIVE EXPLANATIONS OF OVERFULL EMPLOYMENT IN THE FACE OF SHOCKS

The existence of employers of last resort

Two types of employers of last resort exist in the Soviet economy: one urban, and the second rural.

Such urban employers are the variety of organizations whose allocated wage fund is insufficient to permit them to offer competitive wages for the number of personnel that they require, and who thus normally have unfilled positions. As seen in Chapter 2, these organizations are usually financed from the budget rather than from the sale of products or services, and their otherwise unsatisfied manpower needs have been met by temporary assignment of workers that are on the payrolls of non-budgetary enterprises. Since such organizations presumably do not have the same scope as do self-financing (*khozraschet*) enterprises to increase employee earnings above fixed wage rates, one would imagine that they often have unused wage funds – or, at least, can obtain them from their budgetary supervisors if they are able to find additional workers at their low wages. Although no figures are available as to the scope of such urban labor shortages that are met by temporary assignment, it seems clear that these shortages have grown along with those on farms.

Collective and state farms are the rural counterpart. Children brought up on collective farms have the right to remain there as members once they reach sixteen years of age. When attractive employment opportunities are scarce in neighboring urban areas, one might expect farm youth to delay migration to the cities. Since the collective farms have always been substantial net suppliers of labor to the cities, pulsation of gross out-migration in time with local urban labor conditions could do much to equilibrate supply and demand on local urban labor markets in the presence of shocks.

With regard to gross in-migration to farms, such pulsation is probably much more muted in the Soviet Union than it would be in Western agriculture. This is because of the traditional administrative and even legal difficulty encountered in leaving a collective farm once one is a member. But this environment is also likely to mute sharply the pulsation of out-migration. Would-be migrants are prone to seize the opportunity offered by particular temporal situations (e.g. discharge from military duty), rather than to take the risk of delay. Similar muting of the pulsation of migration in both directions also presumably occurs on the state farms, although to a lesser degree.

Pulsation is doubtless much more to be observed in the acceptance of temporary, seasonal work off the farm; but quantitatively, such seasonal work must have been relatively unimportant by the mid-1960s. For, although production by seasonal branches of the economy did not lose its seasonality over time, their labor force did. The difficulty of recruiting seasonal labor caused the relevant enterprises to concentrate upon employing permanent workers. We see this in construction,[37] as well as in sugar beet processing, food canning, and fishing.[38]

The functioning of the collective-farm sector was historically important in containing what would otherwise have constituted structural urban employment – created by a disproportion between available labor and its necessary complement of urban productive capital. This, however, was a transitional problem finally resolved by capital accumulation in the urban areas; it seems no longer to exist on a national level. The importance of Soviet farms for absorbing shocks to the urban labor force is enhanced by the comparative size of the labor force of this sector relative to that in agriculture in contemporary developed Western countries, but it has been sharply reduced by the barriers to exit-on-demand.

The explanation of the absorption of shocks to employment in terms of the existence of urban and rural employees of last resort would seem to have some power. This type of disequilibrium in Soviet labor markets clearly does exist. But no data are available, to my knowledge, that would permit econometric analysis of the situation. In the face of such absence of information, I can only offer the judgment that the proposed explanation is unlikely to be able to account for more than a portion of the observed shock absorption. Furthermore, it cannot be used to explain either the observed

---

[37] In 1965, third quarter employment in construction in the Russian Republic was only 4 per cent higher than that of the first quarter. A similar figure applied even to East Siberia (Antosenkov and Kupriianova [1970], pp. 5–6).

[38] E. I. Bonn *et al.* and L. M. Danilov *et al.* in *Problemy ispol'zovaniia* (1973), pp. 82–87 and 186. In the sugar beet industry, which is the most seasonal of all, off-season employment is 71 per cent of the peak-season labor force.

data of industrial absenteeism or the situation with regard to "labor hoarding."

The "rival hypothesis" of Chapter 3

This hypothesis, it will be remembered, extends the concept of disequilibrium in some limited Soviet labor markets to cover all labor markets. We will examine this hypothesis in the form presented in (3.4), where the border condition of the maximum achievable net inflow of number of new workers is assumed to prevent the enterprise from ever reaching the desired equilibrium in the use of its assigned wage fund.

As was pointed out at the beginning of this chapter, this hypothesis has no difficulty in explaining overfull employment in the face of random shocks; the permanent excess of enterprise demand for labor over supply is a sufficient condition. On the other hand, since this hypothesis makes no use of the distinction between w_1 and w_2, it offers no help in understanding why Soviet absenteeism is not considerably higher than is in fact the case, nor why one does not see labor-force resistance to net hirings in the enterprise. It is in these latter respects that this rival hypothesis does more poorly than does the JROE model in explaining adjustment to shocks.

Where it performs particularly well is in explaining the major growth during the 1950s and 1970s in the detachment of workers from State enterprises for temporary assignment to agriculture and to unskilled urban work (see Chapter 2). This has become more than a response to seasonal labor needs, and has become a means of allowing some organizations to pay well below the market rate all year round for the kinds of unskilled labor that they require.

The "rival hypothesis" provides a powerful drive for ever-increasing egalitarianism in income distribution among workers and employees within the State sector. Since it posits (in 3.4d) that managements are always willing to reduce earnings in their enterprises so as to obtain additional personnel, and furthermore since skills are irrelevant to managers to the degree that personnel in any case will be used for loans of labor to other organizations or for carrying out such jobs as emergency loading and unloading of freight cars, enterprises are implicitly viewed as bidding for skilled labor only to the extent that the gross inflow of relatively cheap, unskilled labor is limited.

This sort of egalitarian trend has indeed occurred.[39] But, on the basis of the hypothesis, one might have expected it to have moved much further

[39] A. Bergson in *J.E.L.*, XXII, 3 (September 1984), pp. 1052–1099 and especially p. 1063.

and faster than has been the case. It would not be unreasonable, if one accepts this hypothesis, to think that the Soviet Center has acted to ameliorate the levelling trend by removing an ever-growing portion of the demand for such labor from that portion of the market which must be equilibrated through wages.

The JROE sub-model concerning shocks provides no help in explaining the rapid growth in temporary assignments. It must depend upon the broader Model B treatment, as developed in Chapters 6 and 7, that explains over-investment in education accompanied by retention of unskilled jobs. It is this that it must use to account for the ever-increasing difficulty of recruiting unskilled labor for hard physical work.

THE SHCHEKINO MOVEMENT: EXPLANATIONS

Explanations in terms of models

It is clear that the JROE Model B has no difficulty in explaining the failure of the Shchekino movement to expand more rapidly and substantially. For the movement directly threatens the assumed Central objective of overfull employment on a locality level and, even more sharply, the goal of avoiding both dismissal and obligatory job change within the existing enterprise. These reasons have long been cited both in Soviet and Western literature as being important in explaining its failure.[40]

In contrast, the "rival hypothesis" provides no explanation. If the low level of dismissals and overfull employment at the level of the individual locality are solely results of permanent overheating of the economy, then there is no reason for resistance either by the Center or by enterprise managers to developments that will bring the local labor markets somewhat closer to equilibrium.

The third model that we have used, Model A with no JROE objectives, is similar to Model B in that it has no difficulty in accounting for the observed phenomenon. Constraint (4.4b), that restricts to a brief timespan Schumpeterian rents provided to employees of a given enterprise, is sufficient to explain the failure of the movement to develop. For it is precisely the enjoyment of such rents for a period of at least three to five years that has

---

[40] Examples of such references in Soviet literature include L. Dorokhova and T. Doroshenko in *S.T.*, 1980, 4, p. 99, and G. Popov in *Pravda*, December 27, 1980, p. 3. For Western references, see D. A. Dyker in Schapiro and Godson (1981), p. 60; those cited by P. Rutland in *Soviet Studies*, XXXVI, 3 (July 1984), p. 360; and especially the Soviet emigrant Kushnirsky (1982), pp. 36 and 42.

generally been viewed as a necessary component in any long-term success of the movement.

We may, however, wonder why there should have been the stubborn refusal in practice – although not at all in Soviet theory[41] – to provide stability of the wage fund (or wage fund per unit of output) over a period of several years. True, one can readily understand the difficulty for the Center of determining stable production programs for individual enterprises several years in advance; this holds particularly with regard to product mix, and the latter is crucial since the labor content of different products produced by the same enterprise is often very different. If the wage fund per unit of output were kept at a predetermined level (or at several such levels, changing periodically) over a number of years, there would be major winners and losers among enterprises simply because of annual changes in planned product mix.[42] Equity considerations argue strongly against such setting of the wage fund.[43] But, of course, one can interpret the permitting of the existence of Schumpeterian rents anywhere in the world as implying a trade-off of equity for efficiency. The question is why such a trade-off is rejected in the Soviet Union, although the near counterpart of quasi-rents on private investment in concrete forms of human capital has always been accepted without question.

[41] See P. Rutland in *Soviet Studies*, XXXVI, 3 (July 1984), p. 359 for the Government's approval in principle in 1971 of longrun wage norms per unit of output, and see G. E. Schroeder in *J.E.C.* (1983), pp. 69–70 for the 1979 decree scheduling their general introduction in industry by 1983.

[42] For products produced *within the same enterprise*, the range of variation of planned labor productivity as measured in gross value is 14.6 to 1, and as measured in net value it is 10.7 to 1. (These data come from a study of the 1982 plans for over 320 enterprises in fifteen ministries, as reported by N. Rozhkova and I. Gorelik in *P.Kh.*, 1984, 6, p. 86). Changes in product mix (presumably between years and at the reasonably high level of aggregation of enterprise product mix plans) increased labor requirements by an average of 3.6 per cent of the original number of employees in the 53 per cent of enterprises whose product mix had become more labor intensive, and reduced it by an average of 2.6 per cent in 44 per cent of the enterprises. Only 3 per cent of the enterprises studied were unaffected in their labor productivity by changes in product mix. (Data relate to 161 enterprises in eleven ministries. It is unclear whether these data, like the previous set, come from a study of 1982 plans. See *ibid.*, pp. 86–87.)

[43] On the other hand, it is not at all clear to what degree annual plans for enterprises actually take account of changes in planned product mix. Two authors from the Research Institute of Labor claim that, although plans are supposed to take account of these changes, in fact they generally do not (*ibid.*). Difficulties in actually doing so are shown by the great differences between plants in the production conditions for identical products, and thus in the wide differences in planned labor productivity (*ibid.*, p. 89, and P. G. Bunich in *E.K.O.*, 1980, 7, pp. 9–11).
    Despite such difficulties and Soviet comments, it does not seem plausible that gross changes in an enterprise's planned product mix are ignored both in the setting of its plan and in subsequent revisions during the year.

The labor market and JROE

261

One could, for example, imagine a procedure in which the wage fund per unit of output (or of value-added) was determined by the Center in each year (t) for year ($t+5$). Enterprises whose product mix, or production conditions, had changed favorably by ($t+5$) would be allowed to keep the assigned planned wage funds. Those whose product mix had changed unfavorably, at least to a significant degree, would be compensated by the Center through an arbitrary increase of wage fund. Such asymmetrical treatment would be inflationary, but this inflationary influence could be countered by basing the original ($t+5$) wage fund on a lower calculation of annual nominal wage increase than is currently used.

An objection to the proposed rolling-plan that is just as serious as that based on equity considerations is that it would imply a significant degree of abdication of control over the rate of national inflation. Wage fund determination, the level set for various social security payments made in cash, and the prices paid by the government for products delivered by the collective farms are the three principal instruments available to the Center for controlling the demand for consumer goods by the public as a whole. Currently, changes in rates of growth of per capita consumption supplies can be balanced with a one year lag by similar changes in these components of demand; thus the annual increase in nominal earnings per industrial blue-collar worker fell from 4.4 per cent during 1969–76 to 2.6 per cent during 1976–83.[44] Such rapid changes on the demand side would have to be renounced if multi-year planning of wage funds were widely adopted.

In my mind, it is an open question as to whether one can properly explain the retention by the Soviet leadership of constraint (4.4b) of Model A by the equity and inflationary costs that would have been involved in their renunciation. After all, the further increase in the inflation rate in recent issues – years of unusually drastic reduction in the growth of real per capita consumption levels – would at most have been only of the order of 2 per cent per annum if the lead time for wage fund decisions had been extended from one year to five. An alternative explanation for the maintaining of these constraints is that the productivity advantages of multi-year planning of wage funds could not in any case be attained without jeopardizing the hypothesized JROE objectives.

Ad hoc explanations

A first possible explanation is that the Shchekino method is only appropriate for a very limited sector of industry. The movement originated in the

[44] *Narkhoz SSSR*, various issues.

chemical and petrochemical sector, and its development has been strongest in such continuous process industries.[45] It has been argued by some Soviet authors that it is most appropriate for these industries where change in product mix and output has little effect on manning requirements, and where the latter are essentially a function of the equipment in place. Here wage funds can, in theory, be set for long periods, particularly when such funds apply only to existing shops within an enterprise and not to physical extensions of the enterprise.[46]

Other Soviet authors[47] and administrative bodies[48] have opposed this view, holding that the method can be applied in every branch of the national economy. Rutland maintains, correctly in my opinion, that the "recent adoption of the scheme by many thousands of varied enterprises would seem to lend support to the universalist argument."[49]

A second possible explanation is that branch ministries have been reluctant to see the Shchekino movement cover too many enterprises within their branch because of the operational headaches that this would cause to the ministry. Ministerial problems with Shchekino have been described as ranging from the difficulty of maintaining a stable multi-year wage fund for more than a handful of enterprises under the ministry's supervision to the need for developing branchwide norms of labor expenditure per unit of output.[50]

CONCLUSION AS TO THE TESTING OF THE JROE MODEL B

This chapter began by confronting Model B with the need for explaining overfull employment at a locality level in the presence of random shocks. A sub-model was developed to reconcile Model B with the observed stylized fact.

The "rival hypothesis" performs better than the JROE sub-model in one respect: it gives a more convincing explanation of the major growth of temporary assignments as a means of filling unskilled and lowpaid jobs.

---

[45] Out of a total of 410 Shchekino enterprises in Soviet industry in November 1975, 220 were in the chemical, petrochemical and oil refining industries, and another 100 were in the pulp and paper industry (A. V. Bachurin in *C.D.S.P.*, XXX, 39 [October 25, 1978], p. 4). As of 1979, only the first three industries above were said to have introduced the Shchekino methods satisfactorily (A. Dadashev in *V.E.*, 1979, 8, p. 40).

[46] For such limited stability of wage funds in some Shchekino enterprises, see Baranenkova (1974), pp. 127–28.

[47] Kheifets (1974), pp. 24–25 and 57–65.   [48] I. Iunak in *S.T.*, 1984, 4, p. 9.

[49] P. Rutland in *Soviet Studies*, XXXVI, 3 (July 1984), p. 351.

[50] A. Mirgaleev in *V.E.*, 1977, 10, pp. 108–09; I. Denisenko in *ABSEES*, 56 (September 1978); T. A. Baranenkova in *Problemy povysheniia effektivnosti* (1983), p. 68.

In all other respects, the JROE sub-model performs better. It explains both the observed fact of the degree of Soviet industrial absenteeism, as well as the absence of worker resistance to labor hoarding by enterprises within a given year and given wage fund. The first is explained by the setting of absenteeism $= \alpha(f_1)$ where $\alpha \leqslant 0$, while the second is explained by modelling such resistance $= \beta\,(h_1)$ where $\beta \geqslant 0$. The "rival hypothesis" offers no explanation for these twin phenomena; it could posit that workers are always ready to accept a reduction in monthly pay in exchange for less work effort, but then it would also predict high absenteeism. Second, the JROE main model – from which the sub-model derives – accounts for the failure of development of the Shchekino movement, while the "rival hypothesis" has nothing to say about this. The "rival hypothesis" could be combined with Model A, and together they would yield a reasonably satisfactory explanation as to Shchekino; but it is then Model A that would be providing the explanation.

Our result in this chapter is particularly strong. We began by confronting the JROE Model B with a puzzle that presented no difficulty to the "rival hypothesis." We ended not only with showing the greater domain of Model B than of the "rival hypothesis," but we also have been able to explain by means of Model B the twin facts of non-excessive absenteeism and non-resistance by workers to hoarding of labor by managements. No alternative hypothesis, even an *ad hoc* one, has been proposed to explain the simultaneous existence of these two apparent facts.

Part 3

9

Some applications

This chapter is a bit of a hodge-podge. It is not intended to be a treatment that further tests the JROE hypothesis, rather, it constitutes an application of the hypothesis to two disparate topics, and the examination of a third topic in Soviet labor markets from the perspective of theory that was developed by other writers in order to deal with markets in developed capitalist economies.

THE SUPPLY SIDE OF THE SECOND ECONOMY

I here define the Soviet second economy as consisting of the production of all goods and services outside of the socialist sector.[1] Much of such production is quite legal (particularly that of farmers on private plots), and a good deal of the rest would be legal if the producers chose to declare their income and pay taxes on it.

A portion of such work is done under conditions where there is no diseconomy compared to socialist production with regard to the obtaining of materials and capital equipment in the proper proportions relative to labor: private tutoring is an example.[2] A second portion does suffer from such diseconomies (particularly an unfavorable land/labor ratio), but compensates by being permitted higher average sales prices: agricultural goods produced on private plots and sold on the collective-farm markets.

A third major portion of such work represents a combination of work outside of the socialist sector and of theft of materials from the socialist

---

[1] This is narrower than the definition given by Gregory Grossman, which includes not only this category but also all production and exchange that is, in some significant respect, in knowing contravention of existing law (in *Problems of Communism*, 26, 5 [September–October 1977], p. 25).

[2] Expenditures on such tutoring are estimated to equal one-fifth of the budget for general secondary education in the Soviet Union as a whole (V. Z. Rogovin in *C.D.S.P.*, XXIV, 10 [April 7, 1982], p. 6).

sector: e.g. repair of privately owned cars.[3] Since the two activities are necessary complements if the final service is to be produced in the private sector, it is difficult to attempt to calculate what is the hourly earning for the factor of work alone.

Aside from agricultural products, the work of seasonal construction gangs in rural areas (the *shabashniki*) probably represents the product of manual labor in which the component of theft of state materials or time plays the smallest role. These private contractors are estimated to have executed about eight per cent of all construction and installation work in the Soviet Union during 1976–80, and 43 per cent of that of Kazakhstan during 1978.[4] Such seasonal workers could expect in 1982 to earn one thousand rubles monthly,[5] four times the average earnings (three times the daily rate) of all state-employed construction workers in the Soviet Union, although for seven days a week of intense work and with travel expenses (and perhaps bribes) coming out of the pay.

High earnings for intense construction work are also found in other countries such as Italy, and are often similarly accompanied there by legal violations and by non-coverage under the obligatory social security system.[6] In these countries as in the Soviet Union, such work is conducted by other than large and stable employer organizations, is not regulated by trade unions, and is normally outside of the law in one or another fashion. One has the impression that such practices go further in the Soviet Union than in developed capitalist countries, but this impression may be mistaken. What is certain is that it is only in socialist countries such as the Soviet Union that such work is conducted exclusively outside of the generally accepted property relationship governing production.

In commenting on the same phenomenon in Hungary, where it seems to be still more prevalent than in the Soviet Union, Kornai writes that "There is a widespread, very industrious and self-driven stratum of the Hungarian population that opts for hard work, almost up to the biological limit of capacity or even beyond it in order to get consumption goods. Certainly this is one of the secrets of the frequently mentioned 'Hungarian wonder'. One of the features of the 1979–1982 measures is

[3] P. Volin in *C.D.S.P.*, XXX, 40 (November 1, 1978), pp. 1–4, and *C.D.S.P.*, XXXIII, 52 (January 27, 1982), p. 15.
[4] A. Brovin in *S.T.*, 1983, 10, p. 80.
[5] N. Kvizhinadze and Iu. Mikhailov, *ABSEES*, 70 (May 1983), 158 F09-F11 8.04 07997.
[6] For such work in Italy by skilled workers who are between twenty-five and thirty-five years old and at their physical peak, interviews show that earnings are twice or more regular wages (Paola Villa in Wilkinson [1981], pp. 143–49).

that it . . . tries to remove at least the administrative obstacles for those who are voluntarily lengthening the worktime with the aim of personal gain."[7]

What are the options facing the Soviet worker who wishes to provide more effort in order to raise his standard of living? As we saw in Chapter 8, overtime is a possibility: in the mid-1960s, 29 per cent of a national sample of blue-collar workers worked an average of at least six hours of overtime weekly.[8] Second regular jobs are also possible; some 1.5 per cent of all workers in the socialist sector hold them. But 75 per cent of all such second jobs in 1977 were in the service sector,[9] in contrast to only 26 per cent of all first jobs, and these service jobs were primarily either for professionals (as in education and in health) or were in badly paid sectors such as retail trade and public catering. The third possibility consists of occasional outside work for pay: if we assume that the 1977 data as to second regular jobs also applied to the 1960s, an additional 3.5 per cent of the workers in the socialist sector – and some 1.5 per cent of manual workers – then did such work for at least an average of an hour a day.[10]

Data for 1973 for Estonia show that 39 per cent of the "occasional work" was being done for private individuals rather than for the socialist sector. For those who did such work, the average time spent on it weekly was 6.2 hours in jobs for private individuals, and 8.9 hours for the socialist sector. Hourly earnings for the socialist sector were some 80 per cent of hourly earnings of full-time employees in the Soviet national economy as a whole, in contrast to work for private parties where it was 140 per cent of the national average.[11]

The first feature that is striking about the Estonian data is that, out of the total sample of working age labor force in the socialist sector of the republic, 18 per cent engaged in one or another form of moonlighting. An average of about thirteen hours weekly was spent on all forms of moon-

[7] J. Kornai in *J.C.E.*, 7, 3 (September 1983), pp. 240–41.
[8] Grushin (1967), especially p. 43.
[9] Study of January 1, 1977 covering the entire labor force of the Soviet Union (A. Novitskii in *E.N.*, 1979, 9, p. 50).
[10] Grushin (1967), pp. 45–46.
[11] Second jobs in the socialist sector paid an hourly rate only half of the national full-time average (Kh. Khanson in *Sotsial'naia struktura. trud* [1975], pp. 117 and 122–23). I am obliged to Michael Swafford for allowing me to read this and other small edition Soviet volumes.

Hourly earnings of full-time employees in the entire Soviet national economy are calculated by dividing annual money earnings by the number of days (multiplied by eight hours) actually worked.

A sample of forty-nine production workers among urban emigrants to Israel had in the same year an hourly earnings rate when privately employed that was 171 per cent of that given for the total Lithuanian sample (Ofer and Vinokur [1980], p. 24).

lighting together (not including overtime). Of the total number of moon-lighters, two-thirds worked on "occasional jobs" and one third on per-manent second jobs.[12]

Given this substantial degree of moonlighting for a fifth of the total Estonian sample, the second striking feature is one that the Soviet author himself found surprising; namely, that moonlighting does not appear to have any significant effect on the amount of free time[13] enjoyed by the worker. The Soviet author suggests that this must be because the work is frequently done within so-called "official worktime." I might add that the relatively low role of second jobs in total moonlighting is fully consistent with this conclusion: such jobs are probably more difficult to perform during regular working hours than are "occasional jobs."

Discussion in terms of the JROE sub-model of Chapter 8

In treating overfull employment in the face of shocks, I posited in (8.6) that group social pressure within socialist enterprises constrains the effort level of the individual on his principal job to be less than the individual's opportunity cost per unit of effort. Given the ratchet effect in planning, lower management – as we saw in Chapter 2 – has an interest in preserving such constraint. Higher authorities cannot seriously combat this social pressure without jeopardizing their own lexicographic goal of overfull employment at the level of individual localities.

The individual can increase his effort level, and be paid for it, by leaving the socialist sector entirely at least for seasonal periods (e.g. when on vacation from his principal job). Rural construction gangs (*shabashniki*) are the arch-type of those making this decision. The group has no need to constrain the effort of the individual in such gangs because the work is not done repetitively for the same customer, according to plan, and through

---

[12] Regular second jobs in the Soviet Union in 1977 were most prevalent in the Baltic republics (A. Novitskii in *E.N.*, 1979, 9, p. 50), and the same may also be true of "occasional work." Thus we should be cautious about extending to the Soviet Union as a whole the figure for the extent of Estonian moonlighting.

See H. Khansen, p. 115 and 122 for the data, and T. Iarve, pp. 145–51 for a description of the sample, in *Sotsial'naia struktura. trud* (1975). The sample is a stratified, clustered random sample of all members of the permanent labor force in Estonia who were between eighteen and fifty-five (sixty for men) years of age. Sample size was 2,300 and there were almost no refusals to answer. The sample description is the fullest I have seen for a Soviet study.

[13] "Free time" is defined as time remaining for leisure after deducting work time, travel time, time for eating, sleeping, etc., time for shopping, housekeeping, and taking care of children. (See, for example, V. D. Patrushev in *S.I.*, 1974, 1, p. 90.)

state-controlled arrangements, but rather on private contract with a specific collective farm or state farm and is paid according to work done.

A second means of increasing the effort level is to increase the hours worked, e.g. through overtime or through taking a second job in the socialist sector. This, however, has the disadvantage to the worker of increasing effort only through an elongation of worktime, leaving unaffected the intensity of the effort per hour worked.

A third means is combination of the two: performing "occasional work" after hours spent on the principal job. Where such work is done for private parties, the worker is unconstrained in the effort he exerts per hour. Where it is for the socialist sector on a piece-work basis, he is probably also relatively unconstrained; in this case, it is both because no one knows how many hours he has really worked and because no tight work group exists which could set constraints. However, such piece-work that is performed at home for the socialist sector is available mainly only to a very limited portion of the labor force (e.g. translators and designers).

A fourth means, however, would seem in general to be the most attractive to all parties under conditions where it is feasible. This is the means that we seem to see in the Estonian sample: carrying out of "occasional work" during the main duty hours. In general, the monthly effort level $E_{i,t}$ on the main job can be kept equal to or less than normal effort $(\tilde{E})$ either through the customary means of restraining the intensity of work per hour, or by allowing high intensity accompanied by a reduction in the hours actually worked monthly on the principal job. The hours saved by the latter method can be used for "occasional work" – either on the premises of the principal job or perhaps elsewhere – and possibly even for holding a second regular job.

This fourth means is attractive to the individual worker, since he can increase his earnings without expanding the number of hours spent in the workplace. It is acceptable to the work group, as there is no ratchet effort downward on future payments per unit of effort; this is because planners above the enterprise level do not, in setting the wage funds of future years, take account of the higher intensity of work since it has not been registered in the output of the planned enterprise. Finally, it is attractive to local management since it increases the ability of the enterprise to compete for labor and to dissuade those workers with enterprise-specific skills from quitting, while at the same time being costless in terms both of effect on meeting production targets and of staying within the allotted wage fund. It is true that problems arise for management if the "outside jobs" are done with the materials of the enterprise; the risk of discovery of such theft is combined with the difficulty of meeting enterprise output targets with less than the allotted amounts of material inputs. But theft need not always be an accompaniment of "occasional work" during duty hours, although there is little question that it must frequently be so.

From the point of view of the Center as well, all four of the above means have their attractive side. All four provide additional labor resources to the economy that would otherwise not be available. Moreover, while such labor is in part used directly to supply private customers, much and probably most of such work is for the socialist sector. True, one would expect that methods two and three would be preferred by the Center, but the first and fourth seem to have a greater potential for eliciting additional labor effort.

This is not to deny the unattractive aspect for the Center of the above means of expanding labor inputs. The private sector grows, including making contracts to supply the socialist sector with processed material goods and services (both the *shabashniki* working as groups, and individuals supplying "occasional work"). Much of this work is, of necessity, illegal; at a minimum, this is so for "stealing time from the state" which is the basis for the fourth method. Transaction costs are high and differential availability of complementary factors of production seem likely to make the marginal product per unit of work effort less than it is in the normal socialist sector. Nevertheless, here is a means of continuing a variant of what has been the traditional means of Soviet expansion: "extensive growth" based on increase in the volume of factors of production.

Given the posited lexicographic overfull employment objective, as well as the need to absorb stochastic shocks at the level of individual localities, it would seem that the Soviet economy has no better means available for eliciting intensity of effort from those individuals who are glad to supply it at the proper price.

INVENTORIES AS AN EMPLOYMENT BUFFER

In general, in the Soviet economy, there is no problem of insufficient demand for goods produced. But this problem does sometimes arise in the sphere of consumer items, particularly for consumer durables. Starting with bicycles and cameras, the problem of insufficient demand has hit at various times watches, sewing machines, radio receivers, television sets, refrigerators, and washing machines, as well as a few other durables such as electric irons. To some degree, it is a question of the product mix that is produced being different from what is demanded; but that is a general phenomenon in the Soviet economy, and one that usually does not result in unsold surpluses. The principal difficulty is, rather, that plant capacity is geared to an unsaturated consumer market, and that its products cannot find an outlet when household stocks become sufficient and demand is restricted primarily to replacement.

We are not discussing here a major sector of the Soviet economy, although it is one whose relative importance has been steadily increasing. Between 1960 and 1974, consumer durable production increased from 5.2 to 8.6 per cent of Soviet national income used.[14] (These percentages are sharply inflated relative to direct employment both because production of durables is expressed in gross value while national income is a value-added concept, and because both numerator and denominator are calculated in prices that include indirect taxes which are probably on average exceptionally high on consumer durables.) Thus occasional sharp reductions in output for specific products, accompanied either by dismissals or obligatory job changes, could well fall within ε_3 of (3.3) that protects workers against such actions. Furthermore, a substantial portion of consumer durables is produced by enterprises with other specialties;[15] the defense industry plays a large role in this regard. Presumably, product conversion should create less of a problem for the employees of such enterprises than of specialized plants.

Nevertheless, as one would expect from our JROE hypothesis, anecdotal evidence suggests that considerable pains are taken to avoid such output declines. The often recounted, but never to my knowledge authenticated, story of suppression of a better light bulb patent in the United States has its authenticated Soviet version. Since the common Soviet phenomenon of frequent increases and decreases of voltage wears out bulbs much faster than would a steady current, Soviet bulb life can be increased substantially by providing higher voltage bulbs. During the 1970s, the producing

---

[14] Both numerator and denominator are expressed in current prices. Consumer durables refer to the Russian expression "naibolee vazhnye tovary kul'turno-bytovogo naznache-niia i khoziaistvennogo obikhoda, prednaznachenykh dlia prodazhi naseleniiu". Passenger cars have been added in by me for 1974. Percentages are calculated from Lokshin (1975), pp. 186 and 192, and from *V.S.*, 1984, 2, p. 80. Comparison with *Narkhoz* 1983, p. 122 suggests that the figure had reached over 11.7 per cent by 1982.

[15] As of early 1971, there were 31 enterprises producing refrigerators, of which only 14 specialized in such production. For other products, the comparable figures were: washing machines – 35 and 11; electric irons – 23 and 2; electric shavers – 13 and 2; vacuum cleaners – 11 and 0; electric stoves – 24 and 0. (Lokshin [1975], p. 190.)

In 1975, the Ministry of Machinery for Light and Food Industry and of Household Appliances produced only 41 per cent of all refrigerators, 32 per cent of all washing machines, and 4 per cent of all vacuum cleaners (*C.D.S.P.*, XXXI, 2 [February 7, 1979], p. 13).

ministry, the Ministry of Trade, and the State Planning Commission of the Soviet Union agreed to forbid such provision "in order to expand trade sales and to secure full loading of the capacity of electric bulb plants."[16] A more common case is one cited in 1983 when a certain type of refrigerator was scheduled to be taken out of production as obsolete, but 50,000 units of the obsolete product were nevertheless planned for 1984 production in one plant alone. The minister of the industry, in explaining this decision in *Izvestiia*, asked what there would be for the collective to work on otherwise? The same minister justified the accepting of bad quality polystyrene by this plant on the ground that rejection would have meant closing the refrigerator plant. Can you imagine what that would be like? he asked the reader.[17]

Given the problem of sudden declines in demand for consumer durables, and our expectation from the JROE hypothesis that efforts would be made to shield production from these changes, it is interesting to look at the evolution of the inventories of these finished consumer durables. To what extent have they been used as a buffer for fluctuations in demand, and has such usage been successful in the longrun?

Production and inventory changes for selected consumer durables

In this section, the production data refer to industry, the sales data to the retail trade network (including cooperatives), and inventories of finished goods to retail trade unless otherwise specified. The sources consist of various issues of *Narkhoz SSSR* and of *Vneshniaia* (1982) except where indicated. All data are in terms of physical units of the particular class of products; since it is generally the higher priced products within a family of consumer durables that enjoy a larger ratio of demand to supply, physical inventory/sales ratios are higher than would be those expressed in value terms.

Finished goods in general are held to only a minor degree by Soviet producers. For knitted clothing on January 1, 1974, for example, only 9 per cent of the value of finished stocks were held in industry and the wholesale network together.[18] Thus our use of the change in retail trade inventories as

---

[16] V. D. Belkin in *E.K.O.*, 1982, 2, pp. 78–79; the quotation marks are given by the Soviet author. Another source blames the action entirely on the Ministry of Trade and the State Planning Commission. The order forbidding such production was rescinded, but the Soviet commentator wondered if the rescinding would last only so long as there was a shortage of light bulbs on the market-place (P. Volin in *ABSEES*, 61 [May 1980], 7).

[17] I. I. Pudnov, minister of the producing industry, in *C.D.S.P.*, XXXV, 41 (November 9, 1983), pp. 6–7.

[18] Lokshin (1975), p. 61.

a proxy for that of total inventories of finished goods is probably not too serious a problem; but no data are known to me as to the proportions in which changes in inventories are typically distributed among producers, wholesalers, and retailers.

Production data, at the level of aggregation we are using (e.g. refrigerators of all models), can be considered to reflect decisions by the State Planning Commission as to production plans and materials allocations. Sales reflect decisions by consumers. Inventories held by retail trade are essentially the residual, since retail trade stores have little choice as to what to purchase. Thus production plans also constitute decisions by the Center as to expected inventory holdings. Although it should not be anticipated that Center-expected inventories will equal realized inventories, my analysis will proceed on the basis that they are equal and thus that the Center planned the realized inventory holdings. I shall also assume in the treatment of individual products that employment and output move together.

Turning to those durables for which we have data (which exclude only cameras among major durables), passenger cars and vacuum cleaners present no difficulties of saturated demand.[19] They shall thus be ignored.

Bicycles. Bicycle production had one indicated period of decline: by 30 per cent between 1958 and 1960, after having increased by four and one-half fold between 1950 and 1958. Production in 1965 was still 6 per cent below that of 1958.

But retail sales showed no such sharp decline. They fell by little more than 3 per cent between 1958 and 1960, although growth did not begin again until 1964. Retail sales had been essentially stagnant between 1956 and 1958, in which year production was some 118 per cent of retail sales. Retail stocks had been allowed to rise to a number of units equivalent to 256 working days of retail sales. The reaction to stagnation and then slight decline of sales was to bring the accumulating inventories back into line by a major cut in production; in 1960, output was only 87 per cent of domestic retail sales plus exports.[20] By the end of 1960, stocks (measured in days of sales) had been reduced to 46 per cent of the end-1958 level. They were

---

[19] For vacuum cleaners, production and stock data are in Potapovskii (1973), pp. 41 and 44. Retail sales data are from *Narkhoz*.

[20] See Lokshin (1975), pp. 208–11. Production and export data are exclusively for bicycles while retail sales and stocks are broader, but the additional items included in retail sales constituted only 8 per cent of bicycle production in 1960 and 13 per cent in 1965. In the comparison of production with sales, the identical product definition is used.

then allowed by 1964 and 1965 to mount again to 64 per cent of the 1958 figure, and even reached 73 per cent in 1970.

The next instance of a significant drop in retail sales was in 1976, with the one year percentage decline in sales being the same as the two year downswing between 1958 and 1960. But this time, stock levels had been brought down earlier to their lowest level since 1962. Production on this occasion was held constant.

The 1958–60 incident was probably the first case of market saturation and undesired inventory accumulation in the Soviet Union in thirty years. After having allowed inventories to pile up through continued production growth as demand levelled, Soviet authorities acted abruptly to eliminate the unaccustomed inventory holdings. Not only did they act aggressively in sales policy (cutting prices and introducing the use of consumer credit), but they were even more aggressive in production policy. There is no indication here of any attention being paid to employment considerations.

Clocks and watches. This industry was the next one hit by a decline in sales. After retail sales had increased at an annual rate of 14 per cent between 1950 and 1958, it levelled off in 1959, and then declined at an annual rate of 5 per cent during the following four years. Retail stocks had mounted sharply during the latter part of the period of growth: at an annual rate of 34 per cent between 1955 and 1958 as measured in days of sales. The tale so far is similar to that of bicycles.

However, this time the reaction to sales decline was to hold production constant and instead to accumulate stocks. Production never fell by even as much as 1 per cent in any year, and it rose slightly between 1959 and 1963 as sales fell by 21 per cent. Stocks increased by two-thirds as measured in days of sale, reaching 306 days in 1963.

The use of retail inventories as a buffer was sufficient fully to protect employment. Output was never forced into decline, and grew steadily. This was not only because of exports – which grew from 15 to 28 per cent of retail sales plus exports between 1960 and 1970 – but also because retail sales showed no further declines.

One might describe this experience as the result of learning by the Center that inventories can be allowed to work themselves off slowly. (During 1969–75, the last period for which we have inventory data, stocks in terms of days of sales were back to the 1955 level.) But what is interesting is that it was the Ministry of *Trade* that argued against cutting back production and closing plants. Trade viewed the problem as consisting of prices, quality and product mix; apparently it did not wish permanently to lose sales as would have occurred if the industry had been reduced in size.[21] Thus it is not at all clear that employment considerations played any major role in the inventory-buffer decision.

Minor products. During at least the years of the 1950s and 1960s, production of minor durables was allowed to bounce around from year to year. Electric-iron production, for example, moved up to 309 in 1955 (1953 production = 100), down to 97 in 1957, up to 505 in 1963, down to 213 in 1965, and had reached 790 by 1974. Meat grinder production moved similarly. So, it is said, did razor blades. Blame was placed primarily upon faulty predictions of consumer demand.[22]

It is perhaps indicative that such major bounces are observed only in the case of such minor products. This may be because the effect on total output and employment of individual plants was relatively negligible. It is true, of course, that equipment usage must have declined sharply when output fell (certainly for razor blades); but this could be considered as a minor cost.

Sewing machines. This was the third of our products to reach maturity as an industry. (Camera production seems to have reached its first peak earlier, about the same time as bicycles.) Production was reduced much more brutally than in either of the previous two industries; however, the longer term marketing perspectives were also by far the worst.

Production and retail sales moved together in close harmony during the period of growth. Substantial decline occurred in both during the same years in the following period, but this decline was much sharper in the case of production than it was in sales. On the other hand, the sales decline continued some four years longer; at the end of the period, both had declined roughly equally.

	Annual rate of change (percentage)	
	Retail sales	*Production*
1951–58	+23.9	+23.3
1959–62	+ 5.7	+ 5.6
1963–65	−15.1	−20.7
1965–69	− 7.4	+13.4
1969–83	+ 1.4	+ 2.1 (1970–83)

[21] *Organizatsiia i metody* (1971), pp. 7–8.
[22] See Hanson (1968), p. 191; *Organizatsiia i metody* (1971), p. 8; Levin (1973), p. 36; and Lokshin (1975), p. 14.

Some easing of the situation occurred through foreign trade; net imports in 1960 of 8.8 per cent of retail sales changed to net exports in 1970 of 4.1 per cent of retail sales plus net exports. But this could help only to a limited degree.

Retail inventories moved up very sharply in terms of days of sales when measured against 1958; but that year's inventory ratio seems to have been exceptionally low for Soviet conditions. More reasonable is to take the end of 1975 as a base; this is the last year given, and the lowest figure after 1960. End-year 1962 = 184 (end-year 1975 = 100) and end-year 1964 = 356. Inventories had been accumulating in relation to 1975 levels for only one year before production was slashed.

Not only was production cut far more sharply than in any other case for which I have information, but it was also done in a unique fashion. Production of sewing machines was stopped in all factories in the country (including those specializing in such production) except for one. Twenty years later, this enterprise was still the only producer of sewing machines in the Soviet Union.[23]

For this product, it is perfectly clear that nothing was done to ease employment problems. On the other hand, it may well be that there were none of much significance. Sewing-machine production is usually carried out with rather general purpose light machining equipment and skills, and there may have been no difficulty for workers to have switched to the production of other products in the same plants and without retraining of consequence.

Radio and television receivers. Both of these went from a stage of rapid growth to stationary output with limited production pains, and even these pains occurred because of earlier excess accumulation of inventories as sales had mounted rapidly.

Annual rate of change
(percentage)

Television sets			Radios		
Period	Retail sales	Production	Period	Retail sales	Production
1966–70	+10.8	+12.8	1951–55	+28.5	+27.0
1971–72	+10.4	− 5.1	1956–62	+ 2.3	+ 2.6
1973–82	+ 0.3	+ 1.7	1963–71	+ 4.1	+ 3.5
			1972–83	+ 0.5	+ 0.5

[23] See *Organizatsiia i metody* (1971), pp. 6–7; Potapovskii (1973), pp. 5–6; and V. Egorov in *C.D.S.P.*, XXXVI, 15 (May 9, 1984), p. 23.

Televison production declined in only one year (1971), but then by the substantial figure of 13 per cent. Since color television remained negligible for some time thereafter, this decline could not have been because of factory conversion to color. Retail stocks had been built up to 127 days of sales by the end of 1971 – no huge figure by the standards of Soviet durables – and then were reduced to 51 days within two years. Partly the reduction occurred through an aggressive internal sales policy, including a large-scale trading-in of sets at the rather substantial average figure of 314 rubles per set.[24] Expanding exports were also partly responsible. But certainly, for a reason that remains unclear, the large single-year production reduction was the main factor in the inventory reduction.

Similarly, radio stocks were allowed to accumulate sharply, although a few years later than those of television. Retail stocks of radios went from 115 days of sales at the end of 1970 to 194 days at the end of 1973, despite the fact that production had been cut back in 1973.

On the face of it, these inventory policies seem to have functioned in complete neglect of employment considerations. However, if one considers radio and televison as a single industry, every production decline in one was counter-balanced by a production increase in the other.[25] It seems likely (although there is no evidence which is available to me on the subject) that in this period there was sufficient overlap between radio and television production in the same factories that they may be combined when viewed from an employment standpoint.

Refrigerators. This product was the last of our group of consumer durables to have a break in its growth rate. Refrigerators showed rapid and continuous expansion through 1973, with domestic sales and production increasing at an annual rate of 11.2 and 11.4 per cent respectively during the last five years. Thereafter, through at least 1983, domestic sales stabilized. During this period, there were five dispersed years of declines; but of these, only 1982 saw a reduction greater than 3.4 per cent. Production similarly had

[24] Lokshin (1975), pp. 198–200.
[25] The full listing of the relevant years is as follows:

| Years of decline | Percentage change in production | |
	Television	Radio
1971	−12.9	+12.5
1973	+ 4.9	− 2.6
1975	+ 6.0	− 4.3
1979	+ 1.5	− 3.2

Moreover, in 1979, color television – described as three times as labor-intensive as black and white (Lokshin [1975], pp. 198–200) – increased by 27 per cent.

five years of decline, although such decline was slightly smaller than the declines in domestic sales. Nevertheless, production increased between 1973 and 1983 by 5.1 per cent in contrast to a decline in domestic sales of 3.8 per cent.

During the first half of the 1970s, the difference between production growth and retail sales was to a considerable degree compensated by an increase in net exports. The same was true to a much lesser degree during the second half of this decade. Yet inventories doubled during the first half, and increased by 160 per cent during the second half.[26] During the first half of the 1970s, retail inventories probably grew little if any more than would have been desired by planners for reasons unrelated to the maintenance of production.[27] The continued expansion during the second half of the 1970s is unexplained.

There is no reason to believe that expansion of inventories was used as a means of maintaining employment either in refrigerator assembly or in compressor plants. While it is true that the industry was very slow in converting to the size of refrigerators demanded by consumers,[28] there is also no reason to believe that such conversion would have been required to maintain employment. Thus neither the growth in inventories, nor the failure to convert promptly to consumer demand, had any obvious effect on the ability of the Center to meet its JROE objective.

Washing machines. Domestic sales and production increased rapidly through 1969, expanding during the last five of these years at annual rates of 11.8 and 12.5 per cent for sales and production respectively. During the next two years, however, sales and production each declined by a total of about 20 per cent – although with the reduction in production lagging sales by one year. Between 1971 and 1973, sales fell by an additional 17 per cent, while production dropped even more rapidly and stocks were reduced during 1972–75. Thereafter, domestic sales came back somewhat and by 1983 constituted 125 per cent of the 1973 level, although still only 85 per cent of the 1969 peak. Production in 1983 was 81 per cent of the 1970 peak. Meanwhile, gross exports had risen from a negligible figure in 1970 to 6 per cent of retail sales plus exports during both 1975 and 1980.

Retail trade stocks increased from 29 to 171 working days of retail sales

---

[26] M. Darbinian in *P.Kh.*, 1985, 1, p. 24.
[27] From 17 to 49 days of sales in January, a period when stocks must have been much higher than in the summer (Lokshin [1975], p. 202).
[28] See, for example, A. G. Lovko and N. I. Bugain in *E.K.O.*, 1979, 6, pp. 25–31, and M. Darbinian in *P.Kh.*, 1985, 1, pp. 24–25.

between January 1 of 1968 and of 1971,[29] with half of the increase occurring during 1970. The increase during 1968 and 1969 had nothing to do with the preservation of employment, but the 1970 increase can be explained in terms of this objective. What is striking, however, is that expansion of inventories was a mechanism employed to maintain job rights for only one year at most; thereafter, production was cut back severely. Of course, with the benefit of hindsight we can say that it would have been impossible to protect production levels indefinitely by inventory accumulation, since retail sales never recovered to the 1969 level. Nevertheless, it is notable that the effort lasted for such a short time.

One of the methods by which production was reduced appears to have been through the elimination of enterprises which had produced washing machines but had never specialized in such production. Thus between the beginning of 1971 and 1980, the number of enterprises producing washing machines was reduced from thirty five to twenty four; but the latter figure was still double the number of specializing enterprises as of early 1971.[30] The eleven enterprises eliminated from such output presumably faced much less of a conversion problem than would specialized enterprises.

As for specialist enterprises, data exist for the third largest producer in the Soviet Union, whose output peaked in 1970 with 5 per cent of total Soviet production. Output in 1971 in this enterprise was only 55 per cent of 1970 output, in contrast to 77 per cent for the industry as a whole.[31] Although demand for semi-automatic rather than hand-wringer washers was greater than supply, the enterprise did not respond by conversion.[32]

This enterprise, however, was also the producer of two other products: gas stoves and electric bulbs. Despite the fact that in 1971 it sharply expanded its production of these two products, and was apparently producing more than its planned output of washing machines, it nevertheless had great difficulty in meeting its total 1971 output-value plan and probably did not meet that for 1972. The reason for such difficulty seems to have been primarily labor shortage, perhaps caused by the fact that the quit rate of its labor force was 50 per cent during 1971 and was still running at an annual rate of 40 per cent during the first ten months of 1972. In view of the enterprise's shortage of labor compared to its production program,

[29] Lokshin (1975), pp. 203–04.
[30] Lokshin (1975), p. 190, and V. Romaniuk in *C.D.S.P.*, XXXII, 32 (September 10, 1980), p. 18.
[31] This was the Frunzenskii EVM plant in the Central Asian Kirgizskaia Republic (Potapovskii [1973], pp. 47–48).
[32] *Ibid.* The absence of such conversion is shown by the failure of per unit costs to increase in either 1970 or 1971.

even after the plan for its principal single product had been reduced to a major degree, there is no reason to believe that for this plant the reduction in the output target for washing machines created any significant difficulties in the preserving of job rights.[33]

Conclusion

The above excursion into inventory policy has proved a failure with regard to casting light on the usefulness of our JROE hypothesis. Of the six major consumer durables examined, it is only in the cases of clocks and watches and of washing machines that one may reasonably interpret Soviet inventory policy as having been significantly affected by considerations of maintenance of employment; even for these two product groups, it is problematic whether such consideration was important. On the other hand, production declines were significant only in the cases of bicycles, sewing machines, and washing machines; for the latter two, we can say with the benefit of hindsight that inventory accumulation could not have served as a buffer to prevent a cutback in production. Bicycles and watches and clocks appear to be the only important consumer durables for which inventory accumulation could have performed this function, and in the second case they did indeed act as such a buffer. Thus the only missed opportunity was in bicycles in 1958–60, and this was probably the first time since the 1920s in which retail sales of any product were disappointingly low. Planners' reaction to such a first instance should probably not be taken as reflecting a well thought out policy, but rather should be viewed as a knee-jerk reaction.

It is for this reason that I do not regard this section as discrediting the JROE hypothesis. Nevertheless, it must be admitted that this hypothesis has not proven applicable to an area where the first expectation would have been that of relevance.

PRIMARY AND SECONDARY LABOR MARKETS

Dual labor markets

The objective of this section is to see what can be said about Soviet labor markets in terms of the concept of dual labor materials. To what degree do Soviet labor markets exhibit the characteristics suggested in this theory

---

[33] *Sovetskaia Kirgiziia*, November 22, 1970, April 29, 1971, and December 2, 1972.

that was developed originally in order to explain work behavior of minority groups in the United States?

The first difficulty lies in selecting the characteristics indicated by the "theory." The problem lies not only in the very limited agreement by the espousers of the theory, but also in the fact that contradictory viewpoints have been expressed at different times by the leading exponent (M. J. Piore). A listing of principal features, as expressed by exponents or sympathizers, is as follows:

(1) Primary market jobs combine several of the following traits: high wages, good working conditions, chances for advancement, employment stability and job security, and equity and due process in the administration of work rules. Jobs in the secondary labor market have the reverse characteristics.[34]

(2) The most important characteristic distinguishing between jobs in the primary and secondary markets consists of the behavioral characteristics, particularly that of employment stability, imposed on the labor force in the primary market.[35]

(3) Participants in the secondary labor market typically do not wish to enter the primary market. They are "target workers," aiming only to earn a set sum of money. They reject entering the primary labor market because there they would have lower-paid jobs, since they would themselves have to bear the costs of training. But they expect never to profit from such training, as they do not wish to remain in the labor market.[36]

(4) The cause of rigidification of markets is unlikely to be found either in investment in human capital, or in differential worker attitudes toward risk combined with the development of implicit contracts in the primary sector.[37]

(5) The central hypothesis is that there is very little mobility between the two markets in the course of individual work careers, with the exception of white male teenagers who often begin in the secondary market.[38]

(6) Mobility between the markets is not the central issue. What matters is that the behavioral characteristics of the actors, and the nature of their human experience, differ as between the markets.[39]

[34] M. J. Piore in Gordon (1971), p. 91.
[35] *Ibid.*, and Piore as described by Gordon in *ibid.*, pp. 210–12.
[36] M. J. Piore in Piore (1979), pp. 174, 198, 12–13.
[37] M. J. Piore in Berger and Piore (1980), pp. 26, 49.
[38] D. M. Gordon in Coxon and Jones (1975), pp. 213–14.
[39] M. J. Piore in Berger and Piore (1980), pp. 16–17.

(7)   Piore is described as being unique among theorists of the dual labor market in having consistently denied the assumption that economic sectors defined by firms are congruent with those defined by labor markets. Piore views primary employers as having some secondary jobs, and secondary employers as having some primary jobs.[40]

(8)   Job ladders, that may but need not be accompanied by increasing job skills, are a characteristic of a relatively closed market internal to the individual company. Such ladders are found in the primary rather than in the secondary labor market.[41]

(9)   There is disagreement among dual market theorists as to whether the distinction between sectors arises primarily out of different characteristics of the individuals or of the jobs. However, the moulding of individuals by the jobs they hold is described as an important part of the theory.[42]

Clearly we can use the dual market theory as a standard against which to analyze Soviet labor markets only by stereotyping the theory. This is, indeed, the approach that will be followed.

The second difficulty with the use of the "theory" is that there is no particular reason to expect it to apply to the Soviet Union. It originated out of research on minority groups in the United States,[43] but the only clearly relevant minorities in the Soviet labor market are women and youth. The theory is closely linked to uncertainty in product markets, and to differential treatment of worker groups with regard to their bearing this uncertainty (through dismissals) rather than having it fall entirely on employers.[44] In the Soviet Union, however, this type of "secondary labor market" would have to be restricted to workers operating under fixed-term contracts, and such workers are overwhelmingly seasonal. Finally, Marxists and radical economists have linked the segregation of labor markets to efforts by employers to divide what would otherwise be a united working class; the historical development of the secondary labor market in the U.S., France and Italy is treated by Piore as constituting a response to sudden upsurges of labor militancy.[45] While this could be viewed as relevant to the labor market in Poland by the time of the emergence of the Solidarity movement, labor militancy in the Soviet Union since at least the middle 1920s has been insufficient to make such a linkage seem applicable there.

[40] R. B. Althauser and A. L. Kalleberg in Berg (1981), p. 139.
[41] Piore of 1975, and P. B. Doeringer and Piore (1971), as treated in Berg (1981), pp. 123–27. D. M. Gordon in Coxon and Jones (1975), pp. 214–15.
[42] Gordon in Coxon and Jones (1975), pp. 215–17, and P. Ryan in Wilkinson (1981), pp. 14–15.   [43] D. M. Gordon in Coxon and Jones (1975), p. 208.
[44] M. J. Piore in Berger and Piore (1980), pp. 6–11.   [45] *Ibid.*, pp. 24–26, 49.

For our purposes, we require operational predictions from the dual-market theory. Such predictions (9.1) and (9.2), and one necessary assumption (9.3), all drawn from a very stereotyped model, constitute the following set:

Primary market jobs are characterized by high wages, good working conditions, the existence of job ladders, and low labor turnover. Jobs in the secondary market are characterized by the reverse. $\qquad$ (9.1)

There is little mobility by individuals, with the exception of youth, between the two labor markets. $\qquad$ (9.2)

Labor markets and products produced by the employing enterprise can be treated as being in general congruent; however, particular trades or groups may – as exceptions – have to be treated separately. $\qquad$ (9.3)

Soviet sectoral labor markets

Relative earnings of sectors and occupations. Data for 1979 and 1983 as to average monthly earnings on their principal jobs of all workers and employees (but not collective farmers) show the following:[46]

	(average for the entire economy = 100)
Coal industry	180
Water transport	139
Construction (excluding design work)	124
Lumbering	123
All industry	110
Engineering and metalfabricating	110
Agriculture	93
Food industry (excluding fishing, which is highly paid)	90
Light industry (essentially, textiles, garments, and footwear)	89
Trade and public catering	79
Housing, communal services, and everyday household services	78
Education	76
Health and social insurance	72

[46] *Narkhoz 1983*, pp. 393–94 and Kunel'skii (1981), p. 158. The data for major sectors of the economy are for 1983, and those for sub-sectors of industry for 1979. Ia. Gomberg and L. Sushkina in *E.N.*, 1982, 1, p. 61 give data for manual workers alone by sub-sectors of industry; these figures are reasonably consistent with those in the text.

Within major sectors, ordinary white-collar employees (excluding professional and managerial) received earnings that in 1983 in industry were 76 per cent of those of manual workers in that sector, and in construction were 68 per cent of those of manual workers there.[47]

Distinguishing between these labor markets purely on the basis of average earnings in the principal job has the disadvantage of ignoring earnings both from second jobs and from the second economy. Taking account of these factors perhaps eliminates the state sector of agriculture and the health sector from those of low earnings; but it does not seem to eliminate the trade sector.[48]

Modifying the official earnings data by the above considerations, we can categorize low earning sectors and occupations as consisting of

non-professional, non-managerial white-collar employees regardless of
   sector
education
housing, communal services, and everyday household services
trade and public catering
light industry
food industry, excluding fishing   (9.4)

These constitute our candidates for the secondary labor market in the Soviet Union on the basis of an earnings criterion.

Quit rates by sector. Dual-market theory applied to the Soviet Union would predict a high quit rate in the secondary labor market relative to the primary one. In contrast, Okun's unified search model predicts only *slightly* higher quit rates in low-paying jobs since workers in these positions, given their short time horizon, have low acceptance wages as is demonstrated by the fact that they accepted these jobs in the first place. (Acceptance implies that the worker found the pay at or above his acceptance wage.)[49]

In making inter-sectoral comparisons of quit rates,[50] the two most important characteristics to hold constant are sex and age. As in all countries, quits are much higher among youth than among more settled

[47] *Narkhoz 1983*, pp. 393–94.
[48] See Ofer and Vinokur (1980), pp. 17, 35, and 38. Their data relate to the estimated sum of earnings in the second economy about 1973 by a sample of Soviet emigrants to Israel. While those working in trade who indicated such earnings did have high private sector earnings relative to those in other sectors, the proportion of people in trade who indicated such earnings was low.
[49] Okun (1981), pp. 47–48. The emphasis in the text is Okun's.
[50] The available data are quits plus disciplinary dismissals (*tekuchest'*). But since quits constitute over 90 per cent of the total, little confusion is created by calling them "quits."

Table 9.1 *Age and sex of labor force engaged in primarily physical work* (percentage)

Sector and Sub-branch	Age (1970)[d]			Female sex					
	< 20 years	20–29 years	≥ 55 years	U.S.S.R.					Russian Republic
				1965[e]	1970[d]	1974[e]	1975[e]	circa 1980	1969[h]
All in the national labor force, engaged primarily in physical work	9	23	8		46				
Of these:									
Within industry					46	48			
Engineering and metalfabricating	14	32	4	39	16[b]	42			43
Textiles	18	27	3	73	85	72			72
Garments	16	28	3	84	93	86			87
Tanning and furs	10	20	8	64	68	69			
Footwear	16	23	7	66	54				
Food (presumably including fishing)	10	22	6	55	27	58			59
Trade and public catering	10	28	4	72	91[c]		76	84[f]	
Communal and everyday household services	10	22	6	53[a]	79		53[a]	high[g]	

Notes:

[a] Housing and communal services and everyday household services.

[b] This figure is clearly far too low for this branch; application of this percentage to the absolute figure of women workers that is given in the same source would show this sector as constituting well over half of total industrial employment.

[c] Twenty per cent of all females working in trade and public catering were described as engaged in primarily mental work. This group is not included in the above figures.

Sources:

[d] TsSU, *Itogi perepisi 1970*, VI, pp. 448–58 and 165–66. These population census data relate to particular manual occupations, that are then apparently aggregated by branch of the economy.

[e] Tatarinova (1979), pp. 20–21 and 42, and TsSU, *Zhenshchiny* (1975), p. 38, for manual workers in industry and its branches.

[f] TsSU, *Zhenshchiny* (1982), p. 7 for 1981.

[g] G. Sergeeva, L. Chizhova in *S.T.*, 1981, 4, p. 119.

[h] A. E. Kotliar *et al.* in *Problemy ratsional'nogo* (1973), p. 384. Presumably, these data provide full coverage of manual workers in the respective branches.

workers. As to sex, females are described as having a quit rate 11 to 51 per cent lower than that of males within the same sub-branch of industry.[51] In six of ten sub-branches studied during the second half of the 1960s, the actual figure was 10 to 22 per cent lower, in three it was 28 to 39 per cent, and in only one was it higher than male (19 per cent higher).[52] In the total labor force in 1976 of a city taken as representative of cities of the Russian Republic, females had a lower quit rate in each age group above that of nineteen years.[53]

Fortunately, data exist in the 1970 census as to these two characteristics by occupation, and occupations have been grouped by branch in the population-census data. These as well as other statistics are presented in Table 9.1. Since data in the table for the food branch presumably includes fishing (a high-earnings and high quit-rate sub-branch), figures for this sub-branch should be ignored in the analysis.

These 1970 data from the population census are not very satisfactory, as they apparently relate only to occupations that could be reasonably allocated to different branches. The figure for engineering and metalfabricating, in particular, is patently absurd. Statistics for the Russian Republic some five months earlier are presumably more reliable; but they cover only a few of the branches of interest. It is believed, however, that the population census data can be used with reasonable reliability to show the feminine nature of the low wage branches. Census data as to age are naturally also suspect, but they are all that are available.

The data for all manual workers in the economy are heavily affected by agriculture, with its high percentage of females and low percentage of youth. They are also highly affected by the inclusion of branches like coal mining that require such physical strength that one would not expect to find many women employed there. Engineering and metalfabricating seems to constitute the best large branch to use as a standard of comparison for low-wage sectors, it is both urban and is available to women from the point of view of required strength.

Judged either by the standard of engineering and metalfabricating or of the economy as a whole, all our low-wage sectors (including education, which is not treated in Table 9.1) are heavily female industries. The possible exception is that of communal and everyday household services. Non-professional, non-managerial white-collar employees are overwhelm-

[51] D. N. Karpukhin and A. V. Shteiner in *E.K.O.*, 1978, 3, pp. 43–44.
[52] Studies by the Research Institute of Labor of the Soviet Union during 1966–70 (A. V. Shteiner, E. I. Bonn and I. T. Deriabina in *Dvizhenie rabochikh kadrov* [1973], p. 183).
[53] Data are from a 1976 sample of enterprises in Orel, a city of 300,000 population (A. Kotliar and I. Kirpa in *Naselenie i trudovye resursy RSFSR* [1982], p. 13).

Table 9.2 *Quits by manual workers according to branch*
(Engineering and metalfabricating of the same area and year = 100)

Area and year	All	Light industry			Household services	Housing and communal services	Trade and public catering	All industry
		Textiles	Garments	Footwear				
U.S.S.R.								
1960	114							
1965	111							140
1967	115							119
1970	119							122
1974	118							116
late 1970s						> average		106
Russian Republic								
1965	114	122						125
1967	115							126
1970					103^b			
1974					112^b			
1976					137^b			
Russian Republic large cities [a]								
1979						> average (total turnover)[c]	lowest category (total turnover)[c]	
Georgian Republic								
1965	90	86	86	110				103
1970	100	96	96	122				107
1973	100	91	91	113				104

Notes:

[a] From a sample study of nineteen cities, each having a population between 100,000 and 500,000.

[b] Calculated on the basis of comparison with the quit rate during 1967 in engineering and metalfabricating.

[c] Although total turnover includes departures of the young caused by military conscription and by being enrolled in full-time education, and departures of the elderly through retirement and death, the age distribution of these sectors suggests that relative total turnover between branches can be used as a proxy for the relative quit rate.

Sources: *Problemy eckonomicheskoi* (1968), p. 114; Rusanov (1971), p. 111; Khurtsidze (1975), pp. 251–52; Nazarov (1975), p. 210; Maslova (1976), p. 141; A. Novitskii in *P.Kh.*, 1978, 8, p. 132; *Trudovye resursy SSSR* (1979), p. 237; *Zaniatost' naseleniia* (1983), pp. 140–42.

ingly clerical and are also primarily female.[54] This fact probably biases our low-wage sectors toward a low quit rate, although such bias is not certain. One might argue that those women who find themselves in higher paid and

[54] In industrial enterprises in 1974, women constituted 84 per cent of this labor force (TsSU, *Zhenshchiny* [1975], p. 39).

non-feminine sectors and occupations have a stronger tendency to remain there than do men in these sectors, but that the justification for such reluctance to quit is not present in lower paid sectors.

As to the age of the labor force, light industry is approximately the same as engineering and metalfabricating. The two low-paid non-industrial sectors have a labor force that is somewhat older and that thus should exhibit a lower quit rate; but the differences are not enormous.

Table 9.2 presents the best data available as to quit rates. Some additional figures are available for comparisons of sub-branches of industry within individual regions,[55] and these are confirmatory. The quit rate in light industry is consistently a bit higher than that in engineering and metalfabricating, although it varies around the rate for industry as a whole. The one set of data available shows the quit rate as being the same in the textile as in the garment industry (these, together, constitute 88 per cent of light industry employment),[56] although earnings in the former sector were some 13 to 18 per cent higher than in the latter.[57] The quit rate in housing and communal services is qualitatively described as above average,[58] and that in household services is higher than the engineering and metalfabricating rate, particularly in 1976. On the other hand, trade and public catering seems to be below that of engineering. The educational sector in large cities is described elsewhere as having the lowest turnover of all branches.[59]

All in all, the quit rate is indeed higher in low-wage sectors than in others, but the degree of difference seems to be more consistent with the prediction of Okun's unified search model than with that of the dual-labor-markets hypothesis. Although neither the sharpness of the two theories nor the quality of the data are such as to allow us to discriminate accurately as to the consistency of Soviet labor market conditions with one or the other of the hypotheses, there is nothing in the data that shows a major distinction with regard to quit rates as between the primary and secondary Soviet labor markets.

[55] *Problemy ekonomicheskoi* (1968), pp. 114–15, and Rusanov (1971), p. 111.
[56] Employment of manual workers according to the industrial census of August 2, 1965 (Krevnevich [1971], pp. 104, 251, and 258).
[57] Data for manual workers in 1965 and 1980 (Ia. Gomberg and L. Sushkina in *E.N.*, 1982, 1, p. 61), and for professional and managerial personnel in 1969 (Komarov [1972], p. 190).
[58] This is confirmed by a sample for 1976 from the city of Orel; Orel was chosen as a typical city of the Russian Republic in the 250–500,000 population size category (A. E. Kotliar *et al.* in *Dvizhenie rabochei sily* [1982], p. 35). In this major study, total turnover in this sector together with household services was roughly 150 per cent of that in industry.
[59] *Ibid.*, p. 35. Turnover in education was about 60 per cent of that in industry.

Mobility between sectors. A single set of Soviet data is available for analyzing inter-sectoral mobility.[60] These figures come from a study executed in 1979 in nineteen cities of the Russian Republic, the cities ranging in size from 100,000 to 500,000 population. The data are presented in the source in the form of a matrix of inflows and outflows during 1979 between enterprises of seven sectors of the urban economy, with each sector being weighted both as a source of outflows and as a target of inflows.[61] The seven sectors consist of the following:

1. Industry
2. Construction
3. Agriculture and forestry
4. Trade and public catering
5. Housing, communal services and everyday household services
6. Transport and communications
7. Other branches

It is sectors 4 and 5 that are of interest, as being the low-wage sectors.

When one considers the probability (P_{ii}) that a person leaving an enterprise in sector (i) finds his next job also in sector (i), with this probability taken as a percentage of the weighted average for all seven sectors of the probability of re-entering the same sector that had just been left, and taking account of the relative number of total entrants into each sector from all such quits, we find that the resulting X_{ii} is:

$$X_{11} = 0.80 \quad X_{22} = 1.51 \quad X_{33} = 1.51 \quad X_{44} = 2.55 \quad X_{55} = 1.73$$

[60] Two other similar data sets have been developed, one for the region (*krai*) of Krasnodar in 1969, and the second for the city of Orel in 1979. But the materials have not been published in a form usable for this analysis. (See Breev [1977] and A. E. Kotliar *et al.* in *Dvizhenie rabochei sily* [1982].)

[61] A. E. Kotliar and V. V. Trubin in *Zaniatost' naselenie* (1983), p. 145. The objectives of the authors are methodological, and presumably for this reason they refer to the matrix as an "example" (pp. 145 and 148). But there is nothing to suggest that the figures are anything but the result of the empirical study.

Unfortunately, I know nothing more about the study.

The inflow and outflow data are calculated from the figures of the local labor offices. In the Russian Republic about 1980, some 29 per cent of all hirings by enterprises (excluding people sent to the enterprise after having finished specialized education, those coming through transfers, etc.) in those cities that had labor offices was done through them. But the figure may be smaller on average for the cities of the size studied here. (I. Maslova in *S.T.*, 1981, 7, p. 67; I. Maslova in *Problemy povysheniia effektivnosti* [1983], pp. 238–39; A. Kotliar in *E.N.*, 1984, 3, p. 57.)

Dependence on the data of the local labor offices in all probability skews the sample of job changers somewhat toward the lower educated and lower skilled strata of job seekers. (Data are available only for 1974, and the situation might have changed somewhat in the following five years. See Kotliar and Trubin [1978], pp. 55–58.) However, it is unclear what if any effect such sample bias should have on the results cited below.

$X_{66} = 1.69 \quad X_{77} = 1.21$

where $X_{ii} = [P_{ii}/(\sum\limits_{j=1}^{7} P_{ji}) (\sum\limits_{i=1}^{7} P_{ij})]/\sum\limits_{i=1}^{7} N_{ii}[\text{numerator}]/\sum\limits_{i=1}^{7} N_{ii}$

and N_{ii} = the number quitting an enterprise in sector
$\quad\quad (i)$ and entering another in the same sector   (9.4)

An individual quitting one of our two low-wage sectors can thus be seen to be considerably more likely that the average member of the labor force to take his next job within the same sector.

We now inquire into the probability that an individual leaving sector (i) finds his next job in sector (j) where $i \neq j$, with this probability taken as a percentage of the weighted average for all sectors of those entering the (jth) sector from some other sector. Reporting the results only for our two low-paid sectors, we obtain:

$Z_{41} = 1.06 \quad Z_{42} = 0.66 \quad Z_{43} = 0.69 \quad Z_{45} = 1.11 \quad Z_{46} = 0.72 \quad Z_{47} = 1.12$
$Z_{51} = 0.94 \quad Z_{52} = 0.88 \quad Z_{53} = 1.03 \quad Z_{54} = 1.24 \quad Z_{56} = 0.92 \quad Z_{57} = 1.37$

where $Z_{ij} = P_{ij}/\sum\limits_{\substack{j=1 \\ j \neq i}}^{7} P_{ij}$ (9.5)

We see that people leaving either of our two low-paid sectors are most likely to enter either the other low-paid sector or the sector of "other branches." Unfortunately, we know nothing about whether sector seven is similarly low paid.

These results do indeed show limited mobility of employment between the low-paid sector and the remainder of the urban economy. But whether this limitation is enough to fit the model of the dual labor market is doubtful. After all, one would be surprised if there were not in general something about the characteristics of an individual working in a low-paid branch that would cause his next job to be in the same or a similar branch. Such characteristics might include health, educational, and personality characteristics, preference for fringe benefits (e.g. closeness of the job to residence) as compared with wages, and the length of the individual's time horizon in a job-search process. The above percentages for intra-sectoral mobility strike me as no higher than can be accounted for by the above features.

Job ladders. The theory of dual labor markets characterize primary labor markets, in contrast to secondary labor markets, as being the ones in which job ladders exist. Our Soviet data on this subject relate to the textile branch and to the branch of engineering and metalfabricating. In contradiction to the theory, it is in the low-paid textile branch that job ladders appear to be more common; this holds particularly for females.

The first indication of this is the degree of formal on-the-job training of manual workers in light industry (essentially textiles and garments). Some 27–28 per cent of these manual workers take courses annually to raise their skills; this figure excludes the courses for workers newly hired into the enterprise. This percentage is described as being twice as high as that for the national economy as a whole.[62] It is particularly striking in view of the fact that light industry is so feminine in character, and that usually females in the Soviet Union engage less in after-hours training than do men because of their respective home and family responsibilities.

The second indication is that the average skill classification of manual workers as a whole is higher in light industry than it is in engineering and metalfabricating, despite the fact that Soviet writers agree that the skill requirements of work are, on average, greater in the latter industrial branch.[63]

More impressive are the differences as to skill classification for females alone. In a study carried out in the Russian Republic during 1969–72 in enterprises selected from branches with a high concentration of female manual workers, the proportion of women to all workers in the various skill grades was found to be the following:[64]

Skill classification	Textile branch	Ball bearings and instruments
	(percentage of female to total manual workers)	
1st (lowest)	30	90
2nd	66	80
3rd	80	66
4th	58	23
5th	77	8
6th (highest)	32	4

Similarly, only 2.2 per cent of all women over age forty who were working in the above engineering industry enterprises were in either of the top two grades, while 33 per cent of those in textiles, and 22 per cent of

[62] V. Denisov in *S.T.*, 1980, 10, pp. 93–94.

[63] Average skill grade in 1972 was 3.5 versus 3.1, and in 1975 was 3.2 versus 3.1 (V. Moskovich in *V.E.*, 1979, 6, p. 58). For Soviet evaluations, see Bliakhman (1978), pp. 102–03 for textiles, and Iu. Anan'eva in *S.T.*, 1979, 10, pp. 83–85 for garments and footwear.

[64] Kotliar and Turchaninova (1975), pp. 63–74. Similar data from other studies are presented in L. Mamonova and O. Gruzdeva in *S.T.*, 1983, 3, pp. 109–13, and in *Ref.*, 1984, 2, 2 E52.

those in garments, were in these grades.[65] In the engineering industry, women remain an average of 4.6 years in the lowest skill grade, compared to 1.5 years for men. They remain twice as long as men in the second grade, and one and a half times as long in the third grade.[66] Such a sex difference does not appear to hold in light industry.

Light industry has a higher proportion of total employees who are under twenty-five years of age than does either engineering and metalfabricating or industry as a whole.[67] This is because the branch serves for many young girls as a way-station to other sectors, particularly for rural youth beginning an urban work career. At the same time, a part of the group of young women remain in the individual textile and garment enterprise for a long time.[68] It is this latter sub-group of women that gets on to the job ladder and moves upward with seniority.

In textiles, some 40 per cent of enterprises studied provide lower work norms (an average of 30 per cent lower), with compensatingly higher piece-rates, to women over the age of forty-five who are spinners, twisters of yarn, or weavers.[69] (These are the trades which entitle women to early retirement at the age of fifty.) But this practice is general neither in the industry as a whole nor, apparently, in any given region or sub-branch, and it is carried out at the discretion of the enterprise. One may assume that such special conditions would not be given to a new recruit to an enterprise even if she were of the appropriate age. Here, then, is a major additional *de facto* rung to the textile job ladder which rewards seniority. I have not read of anything like this existing either in engineering and metalfabricating nor in other average- to high-paid branches.

From the standpoint of Soviet enterprise recruitment policy, although not from that of the dual labor market theory, the existence of firmer job ladders in textiles than in engineering makes perfect sense. It is the low-paid branches that are constrained by their planned wage funds to provide earnings below what are available elsewhere, and thus it is enterprises of such branches that must supply compensating advantages to their workers if they are to retain them. Part of such compensation is to provide a higher proportion of jobs in the middle and higher skill

[65] *Ibid.*   [66] D. N. Karpukhin and A. V. Shteiner in *E.K.O.*, 1978, 3, p. 42.

[67] In June 1973, 37 per cent of the employees in the garment industry, and 31 per cent of those in the textile industry, were under age twenty-five. This compares with 24 per cent for industry as a whole and 26 per cent for engineering and metalfabricating. (*V.S.*, 1974, 5, pp. 94–95.)

[68] E. V. Klopov *et al.* in *Sotsial'noe razvitie* (1977), p. 53.

[69] Study of 49 enterprises with over 100,000 total employees, probably carried out during the second half of the 1970s (L. Shokhina in *Pered vykhodom* [1982], pp. 69–70).

classifications; not only does this practice offer non-pecuniary incentives, but it is also a means of inflating the planned wage fund of the enterprise in the next period. More significant, presumably, is the creation of a job ladder linked to seniority in the individual enterprise, with a kink upward at an age where manual piece-workers would normally see their incomes decline. Such a job ladder is easiest to create in a sector where there are relatively few jobs that require worker skills which cannot readily be learned through plant seniority combined with taking some factory courses.

The situation is different in non-industrial low-paid sectors, where the compensation offered is the slower pace of work than elsewhere. But it is also different in the engineering industry, where the creation of an intra-enterprise job ladder would imply relinquishing recruitment of skilled and well-paid manual workers from outside. Such self-abnegation is less necessary for management in engineering than in textiles because of the relative average earnings in the two branches; but it would also have a much higher opportunity cost there, since it would often imply foregoing genuine required skills that are not available on the internal job market.

Special groups of individuals

Four minority groups are worth distinguishing as potential candidates to be the objects of discrimination at work. These are the same groups with which we would be concerned in other industrialized countries: women, youth, ethnic minorities, and older employees. It is only the fourth that will be considered in any depth whatsoever.

By the term "discrimination" I here mean either of two different actions on the part of the employer. The first is that of providing an individual who is a member of this group with lower earnings for the work done, with poorer opportunities for promotion, or with higher probability of dismissal or obligatory job change, than he would receive if not a member. The second is that of using the group as a classificatory device for determining the probable work characteristics of an individual falling into the group, and thus determining promotion opportunities for the individual on the basis of the average work characteristics of the group rather than the specific characteristics of the individual. Our concern here is only with the employer and not, for example, with the educational system.

For the first three minority groups, it is clear that average earnings of women, youth, and native Central Asians are lower than those of the "majority" group. This, however, does not necessarily show discrimination as defined above.

For women, one may indeed suspect discrimination from the substantial differences between young males and females as to the period spent in lower manual skill grades in industry generally. But Alastair McAuley, whose book is probably the best on this subject, suggests that one cannot expect women's equality without a women's protest movement that is aimed at the general male population rather than at the authorities alone. Soviet women currently hold two jobs, one being that of taking care of household and children, and the quality of their paid work naturally suffers from this fact.[70]

As to the other two groups, youths seem the most likely candidates for discrimination. Many must move into low-paid sectors in their first job because of inability to find work in better-paid sectors.[71] In general, as newcomers to enterprises, they must work their way up between skill categories regardless of their actual capacities, and they are most likely to be short-changed with regard both to bonuses and to the distribution of work that affects the level of piece-work earnings.[72]

As to Central Asian Muslims, both discrimination and reverse discrimination must be at work. I know of no basis on which to hazard a guess as to their relative strengths.

Pension-age employees. Employees above pension age constitute a group of considerable interest; but only contradictory and fragmentary data are available concerning them. Population census data indicate that of this entire group (over fifty-four or fifty-five years of age, depending on whether the individuals are female or male), 23 per cent worked in 1959, 13 per cent in 1970 (following changes of pension laws), and only 11 per cent in 1979.[73]

---

[70] McAuley (1981). The above is my reading of his conclusion; it is more implied than explicit.

[71] In one county (*raion*) in the Sverdlovsk region, only 4 per cent of a sample of that year's group of graduates of general secondary education expressed a desire (when filling out a questionnaire the day before final exams) to go to work in the sector of everyday household services, another 15 per cent wished to go to work elsewhere, and the rest to continue their education. In fact, of all such graduates in the county that year, 54 per cent went to work in everyday household services, and none went to work elsewhere. The purpose of the article was to show disappointment of pupils' hopes for further education, rather than their inability to work in the sector they preferred. (S. M. Gusev in *Trudovye resursy i sovershenstovanie* [1975], pp. 67–70.)

[72] See Iu. N. Udovichenko (a factory director) in *E.K.O.*, 1980, 10, p. 34. He views the second aspect of discrimination as dictated by the kernel of the labor force made up of old timers, and he deplores it because of its effect of leading to a high quit rate of youth.

[73] L. Chizhova in *S.T.*, 1984, 8, p. 90.

Similarly, 1970 census data showed that 24 per cent of fifty-five to fifty-nine years of age worked, but only 7 per cent of women and 26 per cent of men between the ages of sixty to sixty-nine.[74] Comparable American data for 1967 for full-time workers working at least fifty weeks a year are 30, 16, and 47 per cent respectively.[75] Soviet census data presumably count as working only those holding "permanent" jobs who can be considered as full-time, full-year workers.[76] Such census data indicate no increase in the labor-force participation of this group during the 1970s, and show considerably lower participation rates than those of the same age cohorts in the United States during roughly the same period.

Statistics as to the proportion of all old-age pensioners who were working are sharply different. Here the figures rise during the 1970s to reach 34 per cent in 1983.[77] Since the absolute figure given implies that the total number of such old-age pensioners was then 81 per cent of what the total age cohort had been in 1970 (they constituted 94 per cent in 1978),[78] this figure – and others like it – seems totally inconsistent with the census data. Even considering that these statistics are not restricted to full-time and full-year workers, inconsistency is indicated by the fact that we are dealing with a difference in participation rates of something like three to one. Using these figures, the proportion of pension age people working in the Soviet Union in 1983 was virtually the same as the proportion of the same age cohort in the United States in 1967 that worked either full-time or part-time, full-year or part-year (34 vs. 38 per cent).[79] This is despite the fact that part-time work in the Soviet Union is virtually restricted to agriculture.

The above materials show that data limitations in this field are so severe that we cannot even tell whether or not there exists an interesting problem in Soviet labor participation. Namely, the problem of explaining why the Soviet participation rate is considerably lower than the American for the older age groups, while it is considerably higher for females under fifty-five years of age. Given these data limitations, which pervade all investigated aspects of the work behavior of post-pension-age Soviet citizens, very little can be done in investigating the special group of older workers.

The most important *possible* type of discrimination against older workers is that they are not subject to the protection of (3.3) against both dismissal and obligatory job change. Retirement age may serve as an end to the individual enterprise's otherwise open-ended commitment to retain

[74] Lantsev (1976), p. 119.   [75] *Demographic* (1975), p. 89.
[76] Rapawy (1976), p. 14.
[77] M. Kravchenko (vice-chairman of the State Committee on Labor of the Soviet Union), in *S.T.*, 1983, 12, pp. 8–9.
[78] *V.S.*, 1979, 2, p. 79.   [79] Compare with *Demographic* (1975), p. 89.

workers in the same jobs regardless either of the enterprise's need for them or of their ability to continue to perform satisfactorily.

Some flimsy evidence exists to support the existence of this type of discrimination. At two different times, the leading relevant Soviet journal found it necessary to print legal opinion to the effect that pension age workers may be dismissed only on grounds that are applicable to all workers;[80] evidently, this was not clear to all managers. A leading labor economist wrote that, after the passing of the 1956 pension law which was said to have doubled the average value of pensions, the situation had changed from the previous one in which enterprises could not dismiss personnel incapable of working at full capacity.[81] During the mid-1970s, out of all former personnel who were no longer working in a sample of Academy of Science institutes, one-third of those questioned indicated that they had stopped working and gone on pension because of reduction of staff.[82] In a sample of primarily white-collar Jewish emigrants to the United States, 11 per cent of those who stopped work immediately on reaching pension age did so because their superiors wanted them to quit.[83] In 1965 in the Leningrad engineering industry, it was said that the only blue-collar workers kept on after reaching retirement age were those who were specialists most valuable to the enterprise.[84] Of non-working female old-age pensioners in the mid-1970s, a substantially higher proportion of those with education above fourth grade wished to return to work than was the case for those with less education;[85] this difference might well be due to the former group having earlier worked in positions that were easier to fill on the labor market. Some 60 to 80 per cent of managers interviewed at this time viewed the employment of pension age people as required only by the situation of labor deficit in the economy.[86] A major study in the Russian Republic showed that one-third of those old-age pensioners currently working were no longer in the same job they had held when reaching pension age;[87] this figure is sufficiently high to suggest the existence of dismissals.

[80] *S.T.*, 1970, 5, pp. 139–40, and *S.T.*, 1974, 6, p. 156.
[81] E. G. Antosenkov in *Opyt* (1969), p. 15.
[82] Sample of nine institutes in Moscow and Kiev of the Academies of Science of the Soviet Union and of the Ukraine; the study was carried out during 1975–76 (M. Ia. Sonin and K. A. Lainer in *S.I.*, 1979, 1, p. 131).
[83] Madison (1981), p. 35. Ten individuals stopped work for this reason.
[84] Bliakhman, Sochilin, and Shkaratan (1968), pp. 60–62.
[85] Study of over 10,000 non-working old-age pensioners in the Russian Republic in 1973/74 and 1976/77 (Novitskii and Mil' [1981], pp. 73–75).
[86] *Ibid.*, pp. 80 and 211. It is unclear, however, whether this opinion may be limited only to the hiring of such people who had earlier left their pre-pension job.
[87] *Ibid.*, p. 209.

Certainly this evidence is insufficient to prove anything, particularly since other references exist that point in the opposite direction. But it is sufficient to raise the issue of whether discrimination against the older worker exists in the Soviet economy, and of whether his *de facto* protection against dismissal or obligatory job change is less than that of younger employees.

Conclusion

Our stereotyped form of the dual labor market hypothesis contained three predictions: high negative correlation between the sectoral wage level and both the quit rate and the existence of job ladders in that sector, and low mobility of individuals between the primary and secondary labor markets. Qualitatively, the two predictions dealing with labor mobility are corroborated by the data, while the prediction as to where job ladders are to be found is not. However, the quantitative differences in quit rate between sectors, and between intra-secondary-market sector mobility and inter-sectoral mobility, do not seem sufficient to permit one to conclude that the dual labor market theory has particular empirical relevance to the Soviet economy. In this respect, of course, the Soviet labor market may be no different than that of developed capitalist economies.[88]

In general, I believe that the data presented as to labor force behavior are quite well explained by standard neoclassical theory applied within the Soviet institutional setting.

[88] See Glen G. Cain in *J.E.L.*, XIV, 4 (December 1976), p. 1231.

I O

Conclusion

This study has focused on the examination of labor markets in the Soviet Union. Critical to the analysis is the conception that labor is distributed among potential employers through an equating of supply and demand by means of the price mechanism. True, there are exceptions, principal of which has been the rapidly growing assignment of employees to short-term temporary duty as unskilled labor in agriculture or in other low-paying sectors of the economy. Nevertheless, the labor market is viewed as functioning much more effectively on the whole than is the market for commodities (other than those agricultural products sold on the urban collective-farm markets).

For this reason, the approach taken has consisted not of utilizing disequilibrium models, as is a current fad in the study of centrally planned economies, but instead of assuming an equilibrating market. A consequence of this assumption is to downplay the importance both of labor shortages and of labor surpluses in the Soviet economy, two supposed phenomena that have been given great prominence both in Soviet and in Western descriptions of the economy of the 1970s and 1980s.

Denigration of the significance of either shortages or surpluses is, of course, a viewpoint adopted only in the light of the constraints facing the enterprises that together represent the principal demand side of the labor market. Subject to the fungible wage fund made available to them for the current year, and to reasonable expectations as to their own abilities to influence a change in such planned wage funds in future periods, and also subject to highly competitive labor markets due to the existence of overfull employment and to a substantial rate of labor turnover, enterprises are viewed as spending their funds so as to avoid both surpluses and shortages.

This view is not at all in conflict with the notion that Soviet enterprise managers may wish to accumulate more labor than would be appropriate solely in order to maximize labor productivity given the other available inputs, or even more than would be desired by managers in other societies where they are not subject to evaluation according to the criterion of plan fulfillment under conditions of considerable uncertainty as to the timing of delivery of intermediate inputs. Neither of these accumulations constitutes surpluses in the usual sense of representing disequilibrium.

Similarly, the equilibrium treatment is not in conflict with the fact that enterprise managers would generally be happy to hire more workers if they were granted increased planned wage funds, and that they may justify their claims for such funds on the basis of shortage. Such managerial behavior is explained by the fact that it is the wage fund rather than cost or profitability targets that represents the significant constraint on their accumulation of labor, which latter is desired so as to make easier the fulfillment of value-added and sales targets. This so-called "shortage" phenomenon is a variant on the commonplace that no one is surprised to find users citing shortage in the case of goods for which they pay a zero price.

The only quantitative data of which I am aware that relate to perceptions of "surplus labor" come from the large-scale interview project studying Soviet émigrés to the United States who had last worked under normal conditions in the Soviet Union during the late 1970s. Asked as to whether their organization's plan could have been fulfilled with fewer workers, 47 per cent felt that this would not have been possible and only 35 per cent felt that the number of workers could have been reduced by ten per cent or more.[1] The author of the paper, correctly in my opinion, assesses this evaluation as reflecting a perception by those on the job of relatively little redundant labor.

As to the existence of labor shortages in the Soviet economy, one indication of this might be taken to be the growing use of temporary short-term assignments of personnel normally employed in other enterprises and sectors. But here it is striking that such assignments are made *only* to enterprises in sectors with very limited available wage funds per employee; they do not occur even in the lowest paid sectors of industry. Thus what we seem to see here is the working of a deliberate national policy of supplying part of the labor needs of the economy through allocation rather than through a market system, and of increasing the scope of allocation as changes in labor-market conditions raise equilibrium wages for unskilled workers in certain sectors at a rate unacceptable to a Center

[1] Gregory (1985), p. 11. Respondents are from all sectors of the economy.

which must allocate wage funds or otherwise provide such funds in other ways (for collective farms). It is not surprising that the supply schedules for different types of labor, in different parts of the country, should change over time; no more than this (with the shift being to the left for the supply schedules of unskilled labor), plus the hypothesized response of the Center to such change, is indicated by the growth in these short-term assignments. Nor is it surprising that recipients of labor allocations, for which they pay less than market-equilibrium wages, should believe that they face shortages.

The second and more significant indication of shortage is the secular decline in the proportion of industrial equipment that is utilized for more than a single shift, despite the fact that this decline is deplored by spokesmen of the Center. To a large degree, this decline is a result of the fact that the burden of adjustment of labor demand to changing relative wages is thrown upon shortrun modifications that take as given the stock of capital equipment, and that investments are largely shielded from the adjustment process. With the investment process protected from the impact of the relative availabilities of factors of production, it is not surprising that the process should culminate in a poor match between the stocks of capital and labor. Such a mismatch may alternatively be described as an excess of capital equipment or as a shortage of labor.

Here we do indeed have true shortage. This is not in the sense that an individual enterprise management, given its wage fund, is unable to allocate it in such a way as to equalize the marginal value of product (measuring product in terms of the utility weights of management, rather than necessarily in prices) per ruble spent on different types of labor. Rather, it is in the sense that the Center is unable to allocate wage funds among all the organizations of the economy so as to obtain full utilization of all existing capital stock.

Such shortage at the national level seems at first glance to fit in well with the view of János Kornai that socialist societies constitute disequilibrium, shortage economies. Kornai views such societies as inevitably evolving over time into a state of labor shortage, and then remaining in this state. The reason for such an evolution is their almost insatiable demand for investment.

My position, however, is different in two respects from that of Kornai. The first is that the labor shortage exists only at the national rather than at the enterprise level. Kornai's "soft budget constraint," which in his treatment operates at the micro level, does not appear in my analysis and does not seem needed to explain labor market behavior. It is this which has allowed me to use an equilibrium approach to labor markets since it is the enterprises, rather than the Center, that are taken as constituting the actors on the demand side in such markets.

The second difference is that in my view it is not excess investment *per se* that has resulted in labor shortages; rather it is the intra-sectoral composition of fixed investment – and specifically the failure to adopt labor-saving investments – that has led to the labor/capital disproportions. The reason for such "inappropriate" composition of investment is viewed as totally unrelated to Kornai's insatiable demand for investment as a whole; instead, it is considered to be necessitated by the requirements of the JROE lexicographic preferences of the Center.

THE COSTS OF THE JROE POLICY

This book has been written in terms of testing the Job Rights-Overfull Employment (JROE) hypotheses, in contrast to a rival hypothesis whose simplest form is that of "over-heating," largely in terms of the relative domain of these two alternatives. However, it could have been written in terms of assuming the JROE explanations of the agreed-upon stylized facts, and then inquiring into the costs to the economy that must be borne because the Center has lexicographic JROE preferences. It is the second approach that will be taken here in the Conclusion, doing little more than rewriting the results of Chapters 5 through 8.

The particular cost, associated with the stylized labor market facts, that has been concentrated upon by both Soviet and foreign analysts has not yet been mentioned in this book. Such lack of attention has not been because of my belief that this factor is unimportant, but rather is due to its irrelevance to the testing of the JROE hypotheses. This cost is the absence of the effect of the "discipline of the market-place" on the individual worker, preventing behavior which would lead to quick dismissal in capitalist economies, particularly when these economies are not similarly characterized by overfull employment.

The resultant behavior found in the Soviet economy – drunkenness on the job and a low level of effort at the workplace – does not seem to be a product of the job-rights preference of the Center; such behavior seems to be treated as constituting a voluntary renunciation of such a right, and is viewed as comparable in this respect to the quitting of a job. Nevertheless, this behavior is widely observed both because of Soviet overfull employment conditions and because the dismissal of malfeasants by enterprises is commonly viewed as at least partly antisocial since it amounts to throwing the burden of dealing with these people on to the shoulders of others (their next employers). As was indicated in Chapter 3, dismissals for disciplinary reasons seem to average 1 to 2 per cent annually of the total industrial labor force. It is the overfull employment conditions which both directly and indirectly prevent it from being higher.

A second cost of the JROE preference function, this time associated specifically with the job-rights component, has been hypothesized in Chapter 5 to be the inability of the Center to control detailed product mix produced within a given assortment category which is itself laid down in the production plans set for enterprises. Similarly, such detailed product mix is unresponsive to user desires, and is determined anarchistically when judged either from the viewpoint of the Center or from that of the user. This result is associated with pricing behavior. For similar reasons, the Center is highly constrained in pursuing its own objectives with regard to the mix of consumer goods produced; this latter result may be viewed as a benefit from the viewpoint of consumers, but it can scarcely be so considered by the Center.

The inability to control detailed product mix appears to bear much of the responsibility for the incapacity of the combined planning/market system to provide, with any acceptable degree of certainty, an efficient mix of inputs either of intermediate goods or of capital goods to producing enterprises. Chapter 5 has argued that this incapacity is not entirely or even primarily a result of the utilization of administrative-planning methods; instead, it results from price-setting institutions which constitute necessary conditions for the attainment of job rights.

Once more, as in the case of the issue of labor shortage at the micro level, a different causation pattern is seen than that posited by Kornai. Instead of the "soft budget constraint" being held responsible for the uncertainty and inappropriateness of mix that is observed in enterprise supply, I find the lexicographic job-rights preference to be the key causal factor.

The third major cost of the JROE preference function stems, like the second, from the job-rights aspect. This cost, elaborated in Chapter 6, is the failure to adopt labor-saving fixed investments despite the fact that labor shortages lead to an inability to utilize fully the fixed productive capital stock that has been and is currently being built. Labor-saving fixed investments, whether it be unskilled or skilled manual labor that would be economized, have been avoided in a fashion that seems hard to explain on other grounds.

The fourth major cost, this time stemming from the overfull employment rather than from the job-rights element of the JROE function, consists of what must be considered as over-expansion of formal education at various levels if such expansion is viewed as being an investment in human capital. This argument was developed in Chapter 7.

A final major cost lies in the realm of incentives at the workshop level. In the interview project of Soviet émigrés to the United States whose last year of normal work activity in the Soviet economy was in the late 1970s, 58 per cent of the respondents listed "lack of incentives" as *the* principal reason for poor labor productivity.[2] The economic system, bad management, and apathetic or drunk workers came far behind as perceived causes.

Paul Gregory interprets this result as representing the absence of what is regarded as a "fair" return for effort.[3] But an alternative explanation, consistent with the treatment in Chapter 8, is that it represents the organized group pressure on the rate buster who increases his work effort beyond the "normal," with this pressure resulting from the ratchet effect in the formation of each production unit's planned wage fund. As was discussed in Chapter 8, such group pressure is instrumental in serving the Center's overfull employment objective; it obviates what would otherwise be pressure by such blue-collar workers against their own enterprises in the carrying out of hirings designed to create and maintain overfull employment within the narrow geographic district at the expense of average labor productivity in the individual enterprises. In the light of stochastic reductions in labor demand and in allocated wage funds in other enterprises, that reduce the gross hirings by such units in the face of a constant quit rate and thus cut back their stock of workers, such compensatory net hiring is required to avoid local unemployment.

The hypothesized incentive effect to restrain group labor effort, despite the incentive provided to the individual to work harder (as shown by the presence of Soviet absenteeism rates which are not abnormally high by international standards), could quite reasonably have been described by the Soviet émigrés as constituting the lack of incentives for higher productivity. Yet without such an incentive effect, the Center's lexicographically preferred overfull employment objective might well be unattainable.

The above costs of the JROE policy are substantial. They exercise a major influence in preventing the attainment of higher national production levels and richer standards of living. The trade-off involved in the implicit decision by Soviet leaders to grant lexicographic preference to the attainment of JROE objectives is of major significance for the Soviet economic system.

An important consequence of this attribution of the above dysfunctions

[2] Gregory (1985), pp. 13, 19, and Table 1.   [3] *Ibid.*, p. 20.

to the JROE policy is that such costs are treated as being exogenous to the central physical planning methods by which the Soviet economy is directed. They are dysfunctions arising from policy decisions, rather than from the nature of the economic system itself. As such, it *may* be easier for Soviet leaders to make changes which substantially ameliorate these negative features of their economy.

THE JROE POLICY: ITS REASONS AND FUTURE

It was stressed in the Introduction that the JROE policy should be considered as lexicographically preferred by Soviet leaders only within a certain domain of level of achievement of other arguments in the social welfare function. (See (1.1).) If the performance of the economy along conventional dimensions, e.g. the rate of growth of gross national product, were to fall below some unspecified level for a similarly unspecified period of time, one might expect that the economy would have moved out of the relevant domain and that the JROE hypotheses would no longer apply. What has been significant for this book is that, during the period of the 1960s through the mid-1980s, the Soviet economy remained within this domain.

The first question to be raised here is that of why the JROE policy has been given lexicographic preference in the Soviet Union despite its high costs. The two contending hypotheses are that Soviet leaders as a group have personal utility functions which contain as arguments the JROE objectives with the assumed lexicographic strength, and on the other hand that they feel politically obliged to give preference to these objectives as part of an "implicit contract" with labor.

Personally, I would stress that only a monocausal view of history would compel us to choose between these two hypotheses, as opposed to treating the two as complementary. To the degree that overfull employment and job rights are considered as fundamental and popular achievements of the socialist regime in the Soviet Union, renunciation of such achievements could be as unattractive to the Soviet leaders themselves as it would be politically dangerous to them. Nevertheless, it would be useful for us to have some perspective as to the relative force of these two motivations; this would serve as a first possible step in inquiring into the likelihood of the Soviet economy moving during this century out of the relevant domain of the JROE hypothesis.

When the issue arose prominently in a discussion of my study in the context of an industrial relations seminar, the group showed a strong preference for the "implicit contract" explanation. One knowledgeable participant went so far as to suggest that the term "political fear" should be used rather than "job rights." But this group preference had, so far as I could see, no factual underpinning.

It may be relevant to point out here, as was done earlier in Chapter 3, that job rights in the Soviet Union rest more on an informal than on a legal basis. In particular, redundancy dismissals have always been permitted under Soviet law, and without the necessity for any "golden handshake" or unemployment insurance whatsoever. The legal provision that an enterprise is responsible for finding another job for a dismissed worker dates from 1928; the only post-war legal action in this regard consisted of decisions by the Council of Ministers of the Soviet Union in 1957, and once again in 1962, cancelling such responsibility – but such decisions never were put into effect. In 1984, the Soviet Union's Supreme Court implicitly interpreted the current legal position as entailing no such enterprise responsibility. Similarly, the protection from dismissal of individual non-managerial and non-professional personnel whose work is unsatisfactory is by custom rather than by law.

Our problem is that such disparity between the legal and actual situation is subject to two conflicting interpretations. The first is that the legal situation represents the preferences of Soviet leaders, and that the actual situation represents these leaders' decisions in the light of "implicit contract" and "political fear" which bind them. The second is that the actual situation represents the leaders' preferences, and that the legal status deviates from this as a precaution in case the leaders should in the future feel that the economy has moved outside the relevant domain of their JROE preferences. This second interpretation could (but need not) be taken as implying that "implicit contract" considerations do not play a major role, since otherwise they would be imbedded in the legal provisions rather than risking by their exclusion needless antagonism of the labor force of the country.

The second question to be raised is that of the future prospects with regard to maintenance of the JROE preferences. The message here is the common one that we should be cautious in reading too much into straws in the wind.

The 1957 and 1962 decrees of the Council of Ministers of the Soviet Union cancelling enterprise responsibility for finding another job for redundant workers should be taken as representing the weakening of job security. But nothing resulted from these decisions.

Peter Hauslohner has offered an interpretation (based partly upon interviews in the Soviet Union) of the 1965 Soviet economic reforms as envisioning a trade-off between job security and higher consumer income.[4] Hauslohner agrees that job security emerged unscathed from these reforms, but he takes the position that it was not absolutely clear ahead of time that this would happen.

Hungary at the end of the 1970s experimented with redundancy dismissals. I have been told that Hungarian officials in the following months viewed this as having been a laudable and courageous experiment, never to be repeated.

In 1980, a Soviet managerial expert suggested in an article in *Pravda* a system of guaranteed employment in a public works program with minimum wages for those dismissed because of redundancy. To my knowledge, there has been no follow-up on this proposal.

In January 1986, there was a report that over three thousand officials who had been dismissed in a recent reorganization of agricultural ministries and state committees had been promised full pay for up to three months if they were unable to find jobs during that period.[5] At the same time, a Soviet author was quoted as referring to the possibility of massive short-term future unemployment as the result of redundancy dismissals.[6]

Sixteen years earlier, similar officials had been guaranteed preservation of their average earnings for three months provided that they used this period to learn a production trade.[7] This special privilege was presumably provided in compensation for the fact that it was intended that the relevant group was to be struck by substantial dismissals, and that the customary organizational responsibility for finding comparable jobs would not apply. There is no reason to think that the late-1985 measure goes much further than its 1970 precedent. As to the comment on the possibility of future unemployment, occasional predictions of large-scale redundancy dismissals are nothing new in the Soviet press.

It is always possible that Soviet leaders will at some time consider that the economy has moved outside the domain in which JROE policy should apply. If the economy should indeed be threatened with crisis, as is periodically predicted by various Western commentators, it seems to me

---

[4] Hauslohner (1984), p. 236 and Chapter 3, *infra*.

[5] *New York Times*, January 9, 1986, pp. 1 and 6. Part of this was confirmed by V. Kostakov in *Sovetskaia Kul'tura*, January 4, 1986, p. 3, referring to a government decree.

[6] *Ibid*.

[7] Decree of the SSSR Council of Ministers of February 27, 1970 (Baranenkova [1974], pp. 120–21). Reference was to all administrative personnel dismissed as a result of modernization of the administrative apparatus.

most probable that such a conclusion would be drawn and that major improvement in traditional economic indicators would result. But the psychological and political costs of such a decision would be high. One should be extremely cautious in predicting any such development.

Appendix

Easy-reference verbal treatment of algebraic formulae

This appendix is intended particularly for the non-economist, who may wish for simpler but sufficient verbal expressions of the concepts treated in the formulae used throughout the book. The entire book will be treated consecutively in this appendix, except that the formulae of Chapter 5 will be omitted on the ground that the detailed arguments of that chapter will in any case be inaccessible to most non-economists.

CHAPTER 2, P. 65, THE OBJECTIVE FUNCTION TO BE MAXIMIZED

The management of the enterprise tries to achieve its goals (whatever these may be) to the greatest extent possible, subject to its performance plan, to the various non-human physical inputs assigned to it, and to the money available for the payment of wages. Whatever connection may exist between achieved performance within a given year and the plan assigned for the following year is ignored.

Faced with this problem, the management must choose between having a large number of employees and a smaller number who must be paid more but who are individually more effective producers. In particular, we concentrate upon enterprise-specific skills, and use "old" workers (i.e. those employed there in previous years) as a proxy for those having such skills. Given both the relative productivity of these different types of workers and the earnings that must be paid them, the management determines the mix appropriate for that enterprise at that time.

CHAPTER 3

(3.1):

This hypothesis is stated in (3.1) in the text:
Within each small locality of the country – defined in terms of the practicality of commuting to work from an individual's current residence – the probability is

minimal that an unemployed individual will remain unemployed for longer than a month, provided that he is willing to take any job which he is capable of performing. This job may well require a skill level below that of the job seeker.

(3.2):

The degree of on-the-job idleness that is unwanted by the individual worker is restricted, with a very high probability, to a moderate number of days in the year. In saying this, work at a reduced pace for a multiple of days is taken as the equivalent of complete idleness for a single day.

The implications of this hypothesis are that unwanted idleness which is technologically or organizationally unavoidable must be spread by management reasonably equally among the current members of the workforce of the enterprise, and that the composition of the enterprise's labor force must at all times be kept in harmony with the production program and with the technology used to produce it.

(3.3):

Any given individual has a very low probability either of being dismissed from his current enterprise or of being forced to change jobs within that enterprise.

(3.4):

Managers of enterprises attempt to combine a maximum likelihood of plan fulfillment and maximum expected earnings per standardized member of their labor force. Both of these goals apply both to the present and to all future years. In order to retain manual workers with enterprise-specific skills, the enterprise must pay them higher earnings than would be needed to recruit workers from outside. Thus, as stated above for Chapter 2, p. 65, management faces a trade-off between the total size of the workforce and the average productivity of the individual worker. This trade-off is forced by the fact that the funds available within a given year to pay labor are relatively fixed.

In contrast to the situation in the maximization of the objective function of Chapter 2, p. 65, managers here take account of the ratchet effect of achieved performance within a given year on the plan assigned for the following year. Faced with the trade-off situation described, but taking account of the ratchet effect of achieved labor productivity in the current year, it is hypothesized that enterprise managers would always prefer to engage more workers currently than they are in fact able to hire and keep. They would be willing to accept lower average worker productivity and more labor turnover as an acceptable price to be paid for a larger labor force. But the supply of labor available to them on the market-place (at the low earnings level that would be necessary if the individual enterprise were to stretch its wage fund to cover more workers) is insufficient to meet these managerial desires.

CHAPTER 4

(4.14):

Enterprise actions represent a response to two different phenomena. The first of these is motivational: the effect on their own lifetime earnings – both from short-term bonuses and from career development with its concomitant effect on base salary – that managers expect would result from the alternative decisions that they themselves are empowered to make. The second phenomenon is the past history of promotional decisions that has determined which individuals currently hold the enterprise management spots, and thus who are making the enterprise decisions that determine enterprise actions.

The above analysis concentrates entirely upon the effect of the decisions of the enterprise managers on the enterprise's actions. It treats these decisions as being taken within the framework of plans set by higher bodies, of labor and materials supply constraints, of attitudes of non-managerial groups both within the enterprise and outside, etc. Thus all of these other factors are held constant, and so ignored, in the equation.

CHAPTER 6, P. 179

The explanation offered by Model A treats the rate of change in the occupational structure of the economy as being determined by two causal factors: the speed of diffusion of technical innovation on the one hand, and the rate of growth of the capital/labor ratio on the other. It concentrates the analysis upon the first of these causal factors, and deals directly with why the speed of diffusion is low in the Soviet economy.

In contrast, the explanation provided by Model B treats the speed of diffusion of technical innovation as being itself determined by the two other factors mentioned above. The analysis concentrates upon explaining the rate of change in the occupational structure of the economy, and uses this rate as the means for indirect explanation of the low speed of diffusion of technical innovation.

(6.2):

This statement of the problem faced by the Center provides the analytic core for the Model B explanation as to the speed of diffusion of technical innovation that has been described immediately above. The Center attempts to maximize the rate of growth of per capita final product that is consistent with its own hypothesized JROE lexicographic preferences. This constrained maximization is achieved by a joint decision as to the rate of growth of investment and as to the rate of change in the occupational structure of the economy. (It is the second that incorporates the JROE elements of the decision.)

Once the Center has made this joint decision, the speed of diffusion of technical innovations that is desired by the Center falls out automatically.

A critical assumption of the analysis is that the resulting speed of diffusion satisfactory to the Center is sufficiently low so that it can be achieved at the factory floor. Thus the bottleneck to a higher speed of diffusion is a combination of the Center's own JROE preferences and of its preference as to the share of the national product to be devoted to investment.

CHAPTER 8

(8.1):

The work effort of a single individual has no appreciable effect on the payments made in future periods for a given amount of effort. In other words, assuming that a ratchet effect exists in the determination of an enterprise's planned wage fund, the performance of any single worker does not exert any ratchet effect. This result is due to the assumption that there are a large number of workers in the enterprise, and thus that each individual's share of the total effort put forth by the workforce is small enough so that for this purpose it can be ignored.

(8.2):

The monthly pay earned and received by a given individual in a single period is labelled $[w_{1,t}]$. This increases with the work effort of that individual during that period. However, the increase in pay need not necessarily be proportional.

(8.3):

The change in career earnings of the individual, so long as he remains a manual worker in the same enterprise, which result both from his personal effort and from that of the workgroup as a whole during the current period, is labelled $[w_{2,t}]$. Such career earnings increase with the effort of the individual himself in the current period, but decline with the average effort exerted by the group as a whole during the same period. The decline occurs as a result of the ratchet effect in the determination of the enterprise's planned wage fund for future periods.

Appendix

(8.4):

The utility of the individual worker in the current period increases with the growth in his expected career earnings, but declines with the amount of effort that he himself exerts during the current period. In other words, the individual gains satisfaction from increases in money income and feels a psychic loss as he works harder on the job. (The latter may be due to the fact that he cannot use this increased effort for earning additional income in moonlighting elsewhere. Thus the psychic loss applies even to workaholics.) But the money income of concern here consists of the earnings that he expects over his entire career, rather than solely that which he receives in the current period.

(8.5):

Group social pressure can constrain the individual to exert no more than the amount of effort that is normal in the society, but it cannot compel him to exert less than this.

(8.6):

The monthly pay earned and received in a single period by an individual always increases the utility of that individual at least sufficiently so as to compensate for the reduction in his utility from the effort he exerted to earn that pay. Put in another fashion, individuals do not put forth more effort on the job than they wish to, taking account of the effect of such effort upon their personal income.

(8.7):

The change in career earnings of the individual, if all individuals alike would increase their current effort, would be less than the average individual's reduction in utility from the increased current effort itself. In short, if the individual assumes that all other members of the workgroup will act as he does, he prefers not to increase his work effort.

(8.8):

In determining the group response to the income-effort nexus, and thus in determining the maximum amount of effort that it wishes to permit its individual members to exert, the group reacts to the effect of increased effort on career earnings rather than to its effect on pay earned and received in a single period.

(8.9):

Assume the ineffectiveness of possible group resistance to the increase of average work effort between two periods, when this average in the first period had been depressed to below normal through the presence of excess workers. Then each individual worker will be motivated to exert at least the socially normal effort, which by assumption is in turn equal to what he had exerted in previous periods.

(8.10):

As a result of a slight extension of the earlier assumption that group social pressure cannot compel the individual worker to exert less than the normal amount of effort, the group is unable to keep average effort per man in the second period below the normal effort.

(8.12):

For a given absolute change in work effort from its normal amount, and including the income effect of this change, the increase in group welfare from a reduction in average effort is considerably more substantial than is the decline in group welfare from an increase in effort.

(8.13):

The individual worker makes his decision to quit a particular enterprise, or to hire-on there from another one, in terms of his expectation of the monthly pay to be earned and received in the next period. Since he is here making a decision as to whether or not to change enterprises, he does not take account of the ratchet effect of the group effort exerted during that period within either of these enterprises. The ratchet effect here referred to is on the earnings per unit of effort to be received in the future within that same enterprise.

Bibliography

Adam, Jan (ed.), *Employment Policies in the Soviet Union and Eastern Europe*, London and Basingstoke: Macmillan, 1982.

Afanas'evskii, E. A., *Legkaia promyshlennost: ekonomicheskie problemy razmeshcheniia*, Moscow: Mysl', 1976.

Aitov, N. A., *Tekhnicheskii progress i dvizhenie rabochikh kadrov*, Moscow: Ekonomika, 1972.

Amann, Ronald, Julian M. Cooper, R. W. Davies (eds.), *The Technological Level of Soviet Industry*, New Haven and London: Yale University Press, 1977.

Amtliche Nachrichten der Bundesanstalt für Arbeitsvermittlung und Arbeitslosenversicherung (A.N.B.A.).

Antosenkov, E., Z. Kupriianova, *Tekuchest' rabochikh kadrov v stroitel'stvo*, Novosibirsk: Nauka, 1970.

Antosenkov, E., Z. V. Kupriianova, *Tendentsii v tekuchesti rabochikh kadrov*, Novosibirsk: Nauka, 1977.

Arutiunian, Iu. V., *Sotsial'naia struktura sel'skogo naseleniia SSSR*, Moscow: Mysl', 1971.

Baranenkova, T. A., *Vysvobozhdenie rabochei sily i ulushchenie ee ispol'zovaniia pri sotsializme*, Moscow: Nauka, 1974.

Belwe, Katharina, *Die Fluktuation Werktätiger als Ausdruck sozialer Konflikte in der DDR*, Bonn: Gesamtdeutsches Institut Bundesanstalt für gesamtdeutsche Aufgaben, 1982.

Berg, Ivar (ed.), *Sociological Perspectives on Labor Markets*, New York: Academic Press, 1981.

Berger, Suzanne, Michael J. Piore, *Dualism and Discontinuity in Industrial Societies*, Cambridge: Cambridge University Press, 1980.

Bergson, Abram, *Essays in Normative Economics*, Cambridge, Mass.: Belknap, 1966.

Bergson, Abram, Herbert S. Levine (eds.), *The Soviet Economy: Toward the Year 2000*, London, Boston, Sydney: George Allen & Unwin, 1983.

Berliner, Joseph S., *The Innovation Decision in Soviet Industry*, Cambridge, Mass. and London: The M.I.T. Press, 1976.

Bliakhman, L. S., *Proizvodstvennyi kollektiv: v pomoshch' rukoviditeliu*, Moscow: Politizdat, 1978.

Bliakhman, L. S., B. C. Sochilin, O. I. Shkaratan, *Podbor i rasstanovka kadrov na predpriiatii*, Moscow: Ekonomika, 1968.

Bliakhman, L. S., A. G. Zdravomyslov, O. I. Shkaratan, *Dvizhenie rabochei sily na promyshlennykh predpriiatiiakh*, Moscow: Ekonomika, 1965.

Boderskova, N. I., *Trudovoi stazh rabochikh i sluzhashchikh*, Moscow: Iuridicheskaia literatura, 1975.

Bornstein, Morris, Zvi Gitelman, William Zimmerman (eds.), *East-West Relations and the Future of Eastern Europe: Politics and Economics*, London, Boston, Sydney: George Allen & Unwin, 1981.

Breev, B. D., *Podvizhnost' naseleniia i trudovykh resursov*, Moscow: Statistika, 1977.

Bunz, Axel R., Rolf Jansen, Konrad Schacht, *Qualität des Arbeitslebens: Soziale Kennziffern zur Arbeitszufriedenheit und Berufschancen*. Der Bundesminister für Arbeit und Sozialordnung, Dec. 1973.

Butler, W. E., *Soviet Law*, London: Butterworths, 1983.

Byrnes, Robert F. (ed.), *After Brezhnev: Sources of Soviet Conduct in the 1980s*, Bloomington: Indiana University Press, 1983.

Cambridge Encyclopedia of Russia and the Soviet Union, Cambridge: Cambridge University Press, 1982.

Campbell, Angus, *The Sense of Well-Being in America*, New York: McGraw-Hill, 1981.

Chandler, Clark John, "The effects of the private sector on the labor behavior of Soviet collective farmers" (University of Michigan dissertation, 1978), Ann Arbor: University Microfilms International 1707, 1978.

Chernova, E. P., *Trudovye resursy promyshlennosti Kirgizii*, Frunze: Ilim, 1970.

Coxon, A. P. M., C. L. Jones (eds.), *Social Mobility: Selected Readings*, Harmondsworth, Middlesex: Penguin Education, 1975.

Creedy, John (ed.), *The Economics of Unemployment in Britain*, London: Butterworths, 1981.

Demographic and Economic Characteristics of the Aged: 1968 Social Security Survey. Social Security Administration, Office of Research and Statistics, Research Report Nr. 45. DHEW Publication Nr. (SSA) 75-11802. Washington, D.C.: G.P.O., 1975.

Demograficheskie aspekty zaniatosti, Moscow: Statistika, 1975.

Denison, E. F., W. K. Chung, *How Japan's Economy Grew So Fast*, Washington, D.C.: Brookings Institution, 1976.

De Witt, N., *Education and Professional Employment in the USSR*, Washington, D.C.: National Science Foundation, 1961.

Doeringer, Peter B., Michael J. Piore, *Internal Labor Markets and Manpower Analysis*, Lexington, Mass: Heath Lexington Books, 1971.

Dokhody trudiashchikhsia i sotsial'nye problemy urovniia zhizni naseleniia SSSR. Editor: G. S. Sakisian. Moscow: Goskomtrud SSSR, 1973.

Dolishnii, M. I., *Formirovanie i ispol'zovanie trudovykh resursov*, Kiev: Naukova dumka, 1978.

Dubovoi, P. F., E. N. Zhil'stov, *Sovmeshchenie professii i ego material'noe stimulirovanie*, Moscow: Ekonomika, 1971.

Dvizhenie rabochikh kadrov na promyshlennykh predpriiatiiakh (teoreticheski i metodicheskie voprosy analiza tekuchesti). Editor: E. G. Antosenkov. Moscow: Ekonomika, 1974.

Dvizhenie rabochikh kadrov v promyshlennosti. Editor: L. M. Danilov. Moscow: Statistika, 1973.

Dvizhenie rabochei sily v krupnom gorode. Editor: A. E. Kotliar. Moscow: Finansy i statistika, 1982.

Economic Commission for Europe, Secretariat, *Economic Survey of Europe in 1984–1985*, New York: United Nations, 1985.

Feshbach, Murray, "Employment trends and policies in the U.S.S.R.," prepared for the 14th International CESES Seminar, August 1978.

Formirovanie i stabilizatsiia kvalifitsirovannykh kadrov promyshlennosti i stroitel'stva, Novosibirk: Nauka, 1982.

Freeman, Richard B. and David A. Wise (eds.), *The Youth Labor Market Problem: Its Nature, Causes, and Consequences*, Chicago and London: University of Chicago Press, 1982.

Geliuta, A. M., V. I. Staroverov, *Sotsial'nyi oblik rabochego-intelligenta*, Moscow: Mysl', 1977.

Gershanov, E. M., V. I. Nikitinskii, *Priem na rabotu, perevod, i uvol'nenie rabochikh i sluzhashchikh*, Moscow: Iuridicheskai literatura, 1975.

Gomulka, Stanislaw, *Growth, Innovation and Reform in Eastern Europe*, Madison: University of Wisconsin Press, forthcoming.

Gordon, David M. (ed.), *Problems in Political Economy: An Urban Perspective*, Lexington: D. C. Heath, 1971

Granick, David, *Management of the Industrial Firm in the USSR*, New York: Columbia University Press, 1954.

Granick, David, *The Red Manager*, New York: Doubleday, 1960.

Granick, David, *Soviet Metal-Fabricating and Economic Development*, Madison, Milwaukee and London: University of Wisconsin Press, 1967.

Gregory, Paul, "Productivity, slack, and time theft in the Soviet economy: evidence from the Soviet interview project," unpublished report, December 1985.

Grushin, B., *Svobodnoe vremia*, Moscow: Mysl', 1967.

Gur'ianov, S. Kh., L. A. Kostin, *Trud i zarabotnaia plata na predpriiatii*, second revised and enlarged edition, Moscow: Ekonomika, 1973.

Guroff, Gregory, Fred V. Carstensen (eds.), *Entrepreneurship in Russia and the Soviet Union*, Princeton: Princeton University Press, 1983.

Hanson, Philip, *The Consumer in the Soviet Economy*, London, Melbourne, Toronto: Macmillan, 1968.

Hauslohner, Peter Austin, "Managing the Soviet labor market: politics and policymaking under Brezhnev" (University of Michigan dissertation, 1984), Ann Arbor: University Microfilms International, 1984.

Hazard, John N., *Managing Change in the USSR* (The Goodhart Lectures 1982), Cambridge: Cambridge University Press, 1983.

Hilker, Tons Henrich, *Ungarns Wirtschaftsmechanismus im Wandel zwischen Plan und Markt*, Frankfurt am Main: Peter Lang, 1983.

Hough, Jerry F., *The Soviet Prefects*, Cambridge, Mass.: Harvard University Press, 1969.

Hough, Jerry F., *The Soviet Union and Social Science Theory*, Cambridge, Mass. and London: Harvard University Press, 1977.

Ioffe, Olympiad S., Peter B. Maggs, *Soviet Law in Theory and Practice*, London, Rome, New York: Oceana Publications, 1983.

Joint Economic Committee of the Congress of the United States, 89th Congress, 1st Session, *New Directions in the Soviet Economy*, Vol. 2A, Washington, D.C.: G.P.O., 1966.

Joint Economic Committee of the Congress of the United States, 96th Congress, 1st Session, *Soviet Economy in a Time of Change*, Vol. 1, Washington, D.C.: G.P.O., 1979.

Joint Economic Committee of the Congress of the United States, 97th Congress, 2nd Session, *Soviet Economy in the 1980's*, Washington, D.C.: G.P.O., 1983.

Kahan, Arcadius, Blair A. Ruble (eds.), *Industrial Labor in the U.S.S.R.*, New York: Pergamon Press, 1979.

Kamerman, Sheila B., Alfred J. Kahn, *Child Care, Family Benefits, and Working Benefits*, New York: Columbia University Press, 1981.

Kaminskii, I. N., *Zarabotnaia plata i material'noe stimulirovanie na ugol'nykh shakhtakh*, Moscow: Nedra, 1967.

Katsenelinboigen, Aron, *Studies in Soviet Economic Planning*, White Plains, New York: M. E. Sharpe, Inc., 1978.

Kharchenko, A. K., A. S. Minevich, Z. S. Chaika, *Trudoemkost' dobychi i pererabotki ugli*, Moscow: Nedra, 1970.

Kheifets, L. S., *Uvelichenie vypuska produktsii s men'shei chislennost'iu rabotnikov (ispol'zovanie opyta shchekinskogo khimicheskogo kombinata)*, Moscow: Ekonomika, 1974.

Kheinman, S. A., *Organizatsiia proizvodstva i proizvoditel'nost' truda v promyshlennosti SSSR*, Moscow: Institut ekonomiki AN SSSR, 1961.

Khurtsidze, N. K., *Problemy proizvoditel'nosti truda*, Tbilis': Metsnireva, 1975.

Knabe, Bernd, "Zur Volkszählung 1979 in der UdSSR," in *Berichte des Bundesinstituts für ostwissenschaftliche und internationale Studien*, 12–1979.

Knishnik, S., A. Levikov, *Gibt es in der Sowjetunion einen Arbeitskräftemangel?* Moscow: APN-Verlag, 1983.

Komarov, V. E., *Ekonomicheskie problemy podgotovki i ispol'zovaniia kadrov spetsialistov*, Moscow: Ekonomika, 1972.

Kornai, János, *Economics of Shortage*, Amsterdam, New York, Oxford: North-Holland Publishing Company, 1980.

Kostin, L. A., *Proizvoditel'nost' truda i tekhnicheskii progress*, Moscow: Ekonomika, 1974.

Kostin, L. A., *Trudovye resursy v odinnatsatoi piatiletke*, Moscow: Ekonomika, 1981.

Kotliar, A. E., V. V. Trubin, *Problemy regulirovaniia pereraspredeleniia rabochei sily*, Moscow: Ekonomika, 1978.

Kotliar, A. E., S. Ia. Turchaninova, *Zaniatost' zhenshchin v proizvodstve*, Moscow: Statistika, 1975.

Krevnevich, V. V., *Vliianie nauchno-tekhnicheskogo progressa na izmenenie struktury rabochego klassa SSSR*, Moscow: Nauka, 1971.

Kunel'skii, L. E., *Zarabotnaia plata i stimulirovanie truda: sotsial'no-ekonomicheskii aspekt*, Moscow: Ekonomika, 1981.

Kurman, M. V., *Dvizhenie rabochikh kadrov promyshlennogo predpriiatiia*, Moscow: Statistika, 1971.

Kurotchenko, V. S., *Material'no tekhnicheskoe snabzhenie v novykh usloviiakh khoziaistvovaniia*, Moscow: Ekonomika, 1975.

Kushnirsky, Fyodor I., *Soviet Economic Planning, 1965–1980*, Boulder: Westview Press, 1982.

Lampert, Nicholas, *Whistleblowing in the Soviet Union*, London and Basingstoke: Macmillan, 1985.

Lane, David (ed.), *Labour and Employment in the USSR*, Brighton and New York: Wheatsheaf Books Ltd. and New York University Press, 1986.

Lantsev, M. S., *Sotsial'noe obespechenie v SSSR*, Moscow: Ekonomika, 1976.

Lebedeva, L. I., *Trud rabochei molodezhi v narodnom khoziaistve Kirgizii*, Frunze: Ilim, 1977.

Levin, A. I., *Izuchenie i prognozirovanie sprosa naseleniia*, Moscow: Znanie, 1973.

Linz, Susan J. "Managerial autonomy in Soviet firms," Irvine Economics Paper No. 86-35 (January 6, 1986).

Lokshin, R. A., *Spros proizvodstvo torgovlia*, Moscow: Ekonomika, 1975.

Madison, Bernice, "The Soviet social welfare system as experienced and evaluated by consumers and personnel," unpublished report of September 1981.

Malinvaud, E., M. O. L. Bacharach (eds.), *Activity Analysis in the Theory of Growth and Planning*, London: I.E A./Macmillan, 1967.

Manevich, E. L., *Voprosy truda v SSSR*, Moscow: Nauka, 1980.

Mangutov, I. S., *Inzhener. sotsiologo-ekonomicheskii ocherk*, 2nd edition, Moscow: Sovetskaia Rossiia, 1980.

Markov, V. I., *Oplata truda v sisteme upravleniia ekonomikoi razvitogo sotsializma*, Moscow: Ekonomika, 1980.

Mashenkov, V. F., *Proizvoditel'nost' truda v sel'skom khoziaistve*, Moscow: Kolos, 1974.

Maslova, I. S., *Ekonomicheskie voprosy pereraspredeleniia rabochei sily pri sotsializme*, Moscow: Nauka, 1976.

Materialy vesoiuznoi nauchnoi konferentsii po problemam narodonaseleniia zakvakaz'ia, Erevan: NII ekonomiki i planirovaniia Gosplana Armianskoi SSR, 1968.

Matthews, Mervyn, *Education in the Soviet Union: Policies and Institutions since Stalin*, London: George Allen & Unwin, 1982.

Maurice, M., F. Sellier, J.-J. Silvestre, *Politique d'éducation et organisation industrielle en France et en Allemagne*, Paris: Presses universitaires de France, 1982.

McAuley, Alastair, *Economic Welfare in the Soviet Union*, Madison, Wis.: Univ. of Wisconsin Press, 1979.

McAuley, Alastair, *Women's Work and Wages in the Soviet Union*, London: George Allen & Unwin, 1981.

McAuley, Alastair, Ann Helgeson, "Soviet labour supply and manpower utilisation 1960–2000," unpublished manuscript, 1978.

McAuley, Mary, *Labour Disputes in Soviet Russia 1957–1965*, Oxford: Clarendon Press, 1969.

Migratsiia naseleniia RSFSR, Moscow: Statistika, 1973.

Migratsiia sel'skogo naseleniia. Editor: T. I. Zaslavskaia. Moscow: Mysl', 1970.

Migratsionnaia podvizhnost' naseleniia v SSSR. Editors: B. S. Khorev and V. M. Moseenko. Moscow: Statistika, 1974.

Moskoff, William, *Labour and Leisure in the Soviet Union*, London and Basingstoke: Macmillan Press, 1984.

Naselenie i trudovye resursy RSFSR. Narodnonaselenie, Vypusk 40, Moscow: Finansy i statistika, 1982.

Naselenie SSSR. Spravochnik, Moscow: Politizdat, 1974.

Naselenie, trudovye resursy SSSR (problemy razmeschcheniia i puti ikh resheniia), Moscow: Mysl', 1971.

NATO Directorate of Economic Affairs, *The USSR in the 1980s*, Brussels: 1978.

Nazarov, M. G., *Mnogofaktornyi analiz proizvoditel'nosti truda v tekstil'noi promyshlennosti*, Moscow: Legkaia industriia, 1975.

Nikitinskii, V. I., V. E. Paniugin, *Dela ob uvol'nenii rabochikh i sluzhashchikh*, Moscow: Iuridicheskaia literatura, 1973.

Nogee, J. L. (ed.), *Soviet Politics: Russia after Brezhnev*, New York: Praeger Special Studies, 1985.

Normativnye akty po ispol'zovaniiu trudovykh resursov. Editor: K. A. Novikov. Moscow: Iuridicheskaia literatura, 1972.

North, Douglas C., R. P. Thomas, *The Rise of the Western World: A New Economic History*, Cambridge: Cambridge University Press, 1973.

Novgorodskii, Iu. F., N. N. Ottenberg, N. M. Khaikin, *Tekhnicheskii progress i sovershenstvovanie podgotovki kadrov*, Moscow: Ekonomika, 1973.

Novitskii, A. G., G. V. Mil', *Zaniatost' pensionerov, sotsial'no-demograficheskii aspekt*, Moscow: Finansy i statistiki, 1981.

Obrazovatel'naia i sotsial'no-professional'naia struktura naseleniia SSSR, Moscow: Statistika, 1975.

Ofer, Gur, Aaron Vinokur, Yechiel Bar-Chaim, "Family budget survey of Soviet emigrants in the Soviet Union," RAND P-6015, Santa Monica: July 1979.

Ofer, Gur, Aaron Vinokur, "Private sources of income of the Soviet urban household," RAND R-2359-NA, Santa Monica: August 1980.

Okun, Arthur M., *Prices and Quantities: A Macroeconomic Analysis*, Washington, D.C.: Brookings Institution, 1981.

Omel'ianenko, B. L. *Tekhnicheskii progress i sovremennye trebovaniia k urovniu kvalifikatsii i podgotovke rabochikh kadrov*, Moscow: Vysshaia shkola, 1973.

Opyt issledovaniia peremeny truda v promyshlennosti, Novosibirsk: Nauka, 1969.

Organizatsiia i metody izucheniia sprosa, Moscow: Ministerstvo torgovli SSSR, VNIIKS, 1971.

Osnovnye problemy ratsional'nogo ispol'zovaniia trudovykh resursov v SSSR, Moscow: Nauka, 1971.

Otnoshenie k trudu i tekuchest' kadrov. Editors: E. G. Antosenkov and V. A. Kalmyk. Novosibirsk: Sibirskoe otdelenie AN SSSR i Novosibirskii gosudarstvennyi universitet, 1970.

Pashkov, A. S., *Pravovoe regulirovanie podgotovki i raspredeleniia kadrov*, Leningrad: Leningradskii universitet, 1966.

Pavlenkov, V. A., *Dvizhenie rabochei sily v usloviiakh razvitogo sotsializma*, Moscow: MGU, 1976.

Pered vykhodom na pensiiu, Moscow: Ministerstvo vysshego i srednego spetsial'nogo obrazovaniia SSSR, 1982.

Piore, Michael J. (ed.), *Unemployment and Inflation: Institutionalist and Structuralist Views*, White Plains, New York: M. E. Sharpe, Inc., 1979.

Potapovskii, V. *Tekhnicheskii progress i pokupatel'skii spros*, Frunze: Kyrgyzstan, 1973.

Problemy ekonomicheskoi effektivnosti razmeshcheniia sotsialisticheskogo proizvodstzva v SSSR, Moscow: Nauka, 1968.

Problemy ispol'zovaniia rabochei sily v usloviiakh nauchno-tekhnicheskoi revoliutsii, Moscow: Ekonomika, 1973.

Problemy povysheniia effektivnosti ispol'zovaniia rabochei sily v SSSR, Moscow: Nauka, 1983.

Problemy ratsional'nogo ispol'zovaniia trudovykh resursov, Moscow: Ekonomika, 1973.

Problemy razmeshcheniia trudovykh resursov, Moscow: Ekonomika, 1973.

Problemy vosproizvodstva i migratsiia naseleniia, Moscow: Institut sotsiologicheskikh issledovanii, AN SSSR, 1981.

Professional'naia podgotovka rabochikh kadrov. Editor: V. B. Belkin. Moscow: TsNILTR, 1980.

Proizvoditel'nost' truda – vazhneishii faktor povysheniia effektivnosti proizvodstva Editor: P. A. Khromov. Moscow: Nauka, 1982.

Protsessy izmeneniia sotsial'noi struktury v sovetskom obshchestve, Vypusk 2, Sverdlovsk: 1967.

Prudinskii, A. M., *Trudovoe zakonodatel'stvo ob uvol'nenii s predpriiatii gornoi promyshlennosti*, Moscow: Iuridicheskaia literatura, 1966.

Puti razvitiia malykh i srednykh gorodov tsentral'nykh ekonomicheskikh raionov SSSR, Moscow: Gosplan SSSR, 1967.

Rapawy, Stephen, "Estimates and projections of the labor force and civilian employment in the U.S.S.R. 1950 to 1990." U.S. Dept of Commerce, Bureau of Economic Analysis, *Foreign Economic Report* No. 10 (September 1976).

Rees, Albert, George P. Shultz, *Workers and Wages in an Urban Labor Market*, Chicago & London: University of Chicago Press, 1970.

Regional'nye problemy naseleniia i trudovye resursy SSSR. Editors: V. G. Kostakov and E. L. Manevich. Moscow: Statistika, 1978.

Resheniia partii i pravitel'stva po knoziaistvennam voprosam. 13 (April 1979–March 1981). Moscow: Politizdat, 1981.

Rusanov, E. S., *Raspredelenie i ispol'zovanie trudovykh resursov SSSR*, Moscow: Ekonomika, 1971.

Ruzavina, E. I., *Zaniatost' v usloviiakh intensifikatsii proizvodstva*, Moscow: Statistika, 1975.

Rzheshevskii, V. A., *Ekonomicheskie eksperimenty v promyshlennosti*, Moscow: Ekonomika, 1975.

Salowsky, Heinz, *Fehlzeiten – ein internationaler Vergleich*, Cologne: Deutscher Instituts-Verlag, 1983.

Sbytova, L. S., *Struktura zaniatosti i effektivnost' proizvodstva*, Moscow: Nauka, 1982.

Schaefer, Reinhard, Carola Schmidt, Jürgen Wahse, *Disponibilität – Mobilität – Fluktuation*, Berlin: Akademie-Verlag, 1982.

Schapiro, Leonard, Joseph Godson (eds), *The Soviet Worker: Illusions and Realities*, London and Basingstoke: Macmillan, 1981.

Schrettl, Wolfram, "Consumption, effort, and growth in Soviet-type economies," (Boston University dissertation, 1982), Ann Arbor and London: University Microfilms International.

Sevost'ianov, G. M., *Trudovoe zakonodatel'stvo na predpriiatiiakh lesnoi promyshlennosti i lesnogo khoziaistva*, Moscow: Lesnaia promyshlennost', 1975.

Shafranova, O. I., *Professional'nyi sostav rabochikh promyshlennosti SSSR*, Moscow: Statistika, 1972.

Shkaratan, O. I., *Promyshlennoe predpriiatie*, Moscow: Mysl', 1978.

Shapiro, V. D., *Sotsial'naia aktivnost' pozhilykh liudei v SSSR*, Moscow: Nauka, 1983.

Shkurko, S. I., *Po primeru Shchekinskogo khimkombinata: stimulirovanie rosta proizvoditel'nosti truda*, Moscow: Ekonomika, 1971.

Shkurko, S. I., *Stimulirovanie kachestva i effektivnosti proizvodstva*, Moscow: Mysl', 1977.

Sidorova, M. I., *Vozmeshchenie neobkhodimykh zatrat i formirovanie fonda vosproizvodstva rabochei sily v kolkhozakh*, Moscow: Nauka, 1972.

Smirnov, D. D., *Priem na rabotu, perevod i uvol'nenie rabochikh i sluzhashchikh v SSSR*, Moscow: Znanie, 1969.

Smirnov, V. N., *Distsiplina truda v SSSR (sotsial'nye i pravovye problemy)*, Leningrad: Leningradskii universitet, 1972.

Sonin, M.Ia., *Razvitie narodonaseleniia, ekonomicheskii aspekt*, Moscow: Statistika, 1980.

Soskiev, A. B., *Vosproizvodstvo i ispol'zovanie trudovykh resursov sel'skogo khoziaistva*, Moscow: Kolos, 1978.

Sotsial'naia struktura. trud. svobodnoe vremia, Tallin: Institut istoriia, An Estonskoi SSR, 1975.

Sotsial'no-ekonomicheskie voprosy organizatsii truda. Editor: V. S. Nemchenko. Moscow: MGU, 1974.

Sotsial'noe razvitie rabochego klassa SSSR. Editors: E. V. Klopov, V. N. Shubkin, L. A. Gordon. Moscow: Nauka, 1977.

Sotsial'nye problemy truda i obrazovaniia, Vypusk I, Riga: 1969.

Sotsial'nye problemy truda na promyshlennykh predpriiatiiakh. Ufimskii aviatsionnyi institut im. Ordzhonikidze, *Trudy*, vypusk 42. Ufa: 1971.

Staroverov, V. I., *Sotsial'no-demograficheskie problemy derevni*, Moscow: Nauka, 1975.

Statistisches Jahrbuch 1984 für die Bundesrepublik Deutschland, Stuttgart and Mainz: W. Kolhammer, 1984.

Steklova, A. N., *Kontrol' za raskhodovaniem fondov zarabotnoi platy*, Moscow: Finansy, 1976.

Sukhov, A. A., *Trudovaia mobil'nost' pri sotsializme*, Moscow: Ekonomika, 1981.

Tarasov, A. M., *Podgotovka kadrov dlia kapital'nogo stroitel'stva*, Moscow: Stroizdat, 1979.

Tatarinova, N. I., *Primenenie truda zhenshchin v narodnom khoziaistve SSSR*, Moscow: Nauka, 1979.

Tomiak, J. J. (ed.), *Soviet Education in the 1980s*, London, Canberra and New York: Croom Helm and St Martin's Press, 1983.

Topilin, A. V., *Territorial'noe pereraspredelenie trudovykh resursov v SSSR*, Moscow: Ekonomika, 1975.

Trudovoe pravo i povyshenie effektivnosti obshchestvennogo proizvodstva, Moscow: Nauka, 1972.

Trudovye resursy: formirovanie i ispol'zovanie. Editor: E. V. Kasimovskii. Moscow: Ekonomika, 1975.

Trudovye resursy i sovershenstvovanie ikh ispol'zovanie v sovremennykh usloviiakh. Sverdlovskii gosudarstvennyi pedagogicheskii institut, Ministerstvo prosveshcheniia RSFSR, *Nauchnye trudy*, sbornik 227, Sverdlovsk: 1975.

Trudovye resursy: sotsial'no-ekonomicheskii analiz. Editor: V. G. Kostakov. Moscow: Ekonomika, 1976.

Trudovye resursy SSSR. Editor: L. A. Kostin. Moscow: Ekonomika, 1979.

Trufanov, I. P., *Problemy byta gorodskogo naseleniia SSSR*, Leningrad: Leningradskii universitet: 1973.

Tsepin, A. I., *Priem, perevod i uvol'nenie s raboty*, Moscow: Moskovskii rabochii, 1973.

TsSU pri Sovete Ministrov SSSR, *Chislennost' i sostav naseleniia SSSR: po dannym vsesoiuznoi perepisi naseleniia 1979 goda*, Moscow: Finansy i statistika, 1984.

TsSU SSSR, *Itogi vsesoiuznoi perepisi naseleniia 1959 goda RSFSR*, Moscow: Gosstatizdat, 1963.

TsSU SSSR, *Itogi vsesoiuznoi perepisi naseleniia 1959 goda SSSR (svodnyi tom)*, Moscow: Gosstatizdat, 1962.

TsSU SSSR, *Itogi vsesoiuznoi perepisi naseleniia 1970 goda*, Moscow: Statistika, 1972–74.

TsSU SSSR, *Narodnoe obrazovanie, nauka i kul'tura v SSSR*, Moscow: Statistika, 1977.

TsSU SSSR, *Naselenie SSSR 1973. Statisticheskii sbornik*, Moscow: Statistika, 1975.

TsSU SSSR, *Sel'skoe khoziaistvo SSSR: Statisticheskii sbornik*, Moscow: Statistika, 1971.

TsSU SSSR, *Trud v SSSR*, Moscow: Statistika, 1968.

TsSU SSSR, *Zhenshchiny v SSSR*, Moscow: Statistika, 1975 and 1982.

U.S. Bureau of the Census, *Statistical Abstract of the United States*, Washington, D.C.: G.P.O.

U.S. Department of Labor, Bureau of Labor Statistics, *Employment and Earnings, 1909–75*, Bulletin 1312–8, Washington, D.C.: G.P.O., 1976.

U.S., *Economic Report of the President*, Washington, D.C.: G.P.O.

Vasil'ev, E. K., L. M. Chistiakova, *Effektivnost' oplaty upravlencheskogo truda promyshlennosti*, Moscow: Ekonomika, 1972.

Vasil'eva, E. K., *Obraz zhizni gorodskoi sem'i*, Moscow: Finansy i statistika, 1981.

Vasil'eva, E. K., *Sotsial'no ekonomicheskaia struktura naseleniia SSSR (statistiko-demograficheskii analiz)*, Moscow: Statistika, 1978.

Vasil'eva, E. K., *Sotsial'no-professional'nyi uroven' gorodskoi molodezhi*, Leningrad: 1973.

Verein für Sozialpolitik, Gesellschaft für Wirschafts- und Sozialwissenschaften. Neue Folge Band 142. *Wachstumverlangsamung und Konjunkturzyklen in unterschiedlichen Wirtschaftssystemen*, 1984.

Vneshniaia torgovlia SSSR 1922–1981. Ministerstvo vneshnei torgovli. Moscow: Finansy i statistika, 1982.

Vodomerov, N., *Ispol'zovanie rabochego vremeni i effektivnost' proizvodstva*, Riga: Liesma, 1975.

Voprosy teorii i praktiki upravleniia trudovymi resursami. Editor: A. E. Kotliar. Moscow: TsNILTR, 1983.

Vosproizvodstvo i ratsional'noi ispol'zovanie rabochei sily v narodnom khoziaistve respubliki, I and II, Tallin: Goskomtrud ESSR, Tallinskii politekhnicheskii institut, i Institut ekonomiki, AN ESSR, 1975.

Wädekin, Karl-Eugen, *Privatproduzenten in der sowjetischen Landwirtschaft*, Köln: Verlag Wissenschaft und Politik, 1967.

Wages and Labour Mobility, Paris: O.E.C.D., July 1965.

Wilkinson, Frank (ed.), *The Dynamics of Labour Market Segmentation*, London: Academic Press, 1981.

Zaniatost' naseleniia: izuchenie i regulirovanie, Moscow: Finansy i Statistika, 1983.

Zaniatost' v nebol'shikh gorodakh (ekonomiko-demograficheskii aspekt). Editor: A. E. Kotliar. Moscow: Statistika, 1978.

Zimbalist, A. (ed.), *Comparative Economic Systems: an Assessment of Knowledge, Theory and Method*, Boston: Kluwer-Nijhoff, 1984.

Index

absenteeism: dismissal for, 90–1; in forestry areas, 88; and work effort compared with other countries, 112, 248–51, 263, 305

Academy of Science institutes in Moscow and Kiev: (1975–6) study on pensions, 96, 298

accounting, financial, 39–40

Acharkan, V., 35n104

administrative district (*raion*), 36

administrative staff: redundancy, 96–7, 308n7

advertising, 140

Afanas'evskii, E. A., 75n10

age: beginning of labor, 222n67; labor force participation by, 25, 80 (Table 3.1), 287 (Table 9.1); quit rate by, 13, 100–1, 286, 289–90; *see also* pensionable age, people of

agent-principal model, 130–2

agriculture: average monthly earnings, 285; intersectoral mobility, 291; organized recruitment of urban workers, 20, 38–40, 256–7, 258; quits and dismissals, 14; retirement rates for equipment, 195; second economy, 267; use of 1973 constant prices still in 1983, 139n9; vocational training and education for, 212, 214, 216; *see also* farms, collective; farms, state

Albertini, Edward, 176 note

Altai region, west Siberia, 192

Althauser, R. B., 49n156

Amann, Ronald, 174n10

Anan'ev, V., 44n138

Anikeeva, F. B., 26n59

Aninova, O., 16nf

Antosenkov, E. G., 35n104, 74n9, 76n12, 298n81

apprenticeship system, German, 215

arbitration: pre- and post-contract in producer-purchaser agreements, 147–8

arrests, 13n4

artists, research and creative, 92

Arutiunian, Iu. V., 28n65

Asia, Central: discrimination against natives of, 295–6; favourable discrimination for Muslim nationalities, 227, 296; lack of adaptability of rural youth, 75n10, 221

assets, fixed: retirement rates, 194–7 (Table 6.5)

Australia: quit rates and separation rates, 15 (Table 2.1), 16, 17, 112

Automotive Service Association, Russian Republic, 28n61

auto-repair, 28n61; private, 268

Avis, George, 230

Azerbaidzhan Republic: employment quotas, 50n157; materials handling, 185

Bachurin, A. V., 59n196, 107n90, 139n11, 262n45

Baku: population growth, 31n81

Baranenkova, T. A., 98n63, 65, 99n67, 308n7

Barinov, V., 38n118

barter, 134, 144, 147

Batkaev, R., 41n

Bauer, T., 106n89, 199

Bauman University, 233

Bayesian priors, 117, 123–5, 126, 127, 129, 132n19, 163

Belkin, V. D., 274n16

Belorussian Republic: collective farms, 14n13; no transfer of unused wage fund, 56

Belwe, Katharina, 15–16nf

benefits: fringe, 66; sickness, 34

Berezina, 37n116

Bergson, Abram, 137, 143, 171n1

Berliner, Joseph S.: on dismissals for redundancy, 93, 95–6; on number of industrial items produced, 128n14; on pricing of new products, 141n13

bicycles, 272, 275–6, 282

birth: rate too low, 80; time between jobs for, 77n12; *see also* maternity leave

Bliakhman, L. S., 45n144, 255n36

blue-collar occupations: absenteeism compared with Western countries, 248–9, 250; capital/labor substitution in, 199–201; declining (1959–70), 177 (Table 6.3); and education, 203n6, 210–11, 219; educational discrimination in favour of, 227–32; potential resistance to extra hirings, 240, 244–5, 255–6, 305; Soviet compared with US, 175–9 (Table 6.2); *see also* manual workers

Boderskova, N. I., 34n99

Bohnet, Armin, 174n10

Bonn, E. I., 93n46

bonuses: allowable, 53; incentives, 130, 132n19; managerial, 58, 63, 148n22; for manual workers in industry, 43n135, 48; no regulations on proportion of wage fund for, 54; and ratchet effect, 60n199; supplementary funds, 52n167; use of wage fund for, 55–7

Boretsky, Michael, 174n10

Brezhnev, Leonid Ilich, 118n2

bribes, 90, 147, 203

Britain, Great, *see* United Kingdom

buildings: industry, *see* construction industry; for new equipment, 195n65

Burakovskii, M., 227n81

Bureau of Labor Statistics, US: layoffs and separations data, 15nb, 101n73, 111

bureaucracy, Weberian model of, 123

bus-drivers: earnings in Moscow and Leningrad, 48

C.D.S.P. *see Current Digest of the Soviet Press*

cameras, 272, 275, 277

Campbell, Angus, 73

Campbell, Robert, 188

Canada, 194

capacity utilization, 273; slack in 164–5, 200

capital: accumulation in urban areas, 257; heavy investment in fixed and low

returns, 120, 171–201; utilization inadequate, 187–8, 302

capital/labor ratios, 171–9; annual rates of increase in, 172–3 (Table 6.1); correlation with occupational change, 174, 176 (Table 6.2); substitution, 171, 173, 181, 187–8, 199–201; *see also* equipment, industrial

capital/labor substitution, 184–90, 199–201; *see also* equipment, industrial

capitalist countries: and compulsory job change, 221; elites compared with Soviet, 119; labor policies compared with Soviet, 12; job rights, 84–5; and job security, 105; market discipline, 303; rate of gross hires for unemployment, 237; reputation for price stability, 148; trade union monopolies in, 48

career advancement, 130–2

carpenters, 178

cars, passenger, 273n14, 275; *see also* auto-repair

Carstensen, Fred V., 133

catering, public, 285, 286, 289–90, 291

censuses, 79: one-day, 73n4, 164–5n35

Center: attitude to extra work, 272; constraints on, 123–33; determines wage fund for each enterprise, 42; and education as investment, 113, 202–5, 233–4; and JROE hypotheses, 70–9; maximization behavior, 1–3, 117–35; motivational system, 129–35; ownership and control by, 125–9; possibility of control over relative earnings, 45–6; possible liberation from consumer demand in price-setting, 141n14; and requests for additional personnel, 68–9, 106; social and organized recruitment by 20; *see also* leadership, Soviet; planning, central

Central Statistical Office: educational aspirations of rural secondary school children, 228; graduations data, 204; maintenance workers, 197; number of people in various trades, 185; one-day censuses, 73n4, 164–5n35; reductions of grade during wage reforms, 44; (1976–80) redundancy study, 94, 96; (1978) study of earning levels of manual workers, 45n144, 47–8

centralism", "democratic, 102–3

Chung, W. K., 173n8

Cheban, I., 91n39

Cheliabinsk sovnarkhoz: redundancies, 96n52
chemical industry: and petrochemical sector, 262; wage supplements in, 48
Chernina, N. V., 51n161, 251n26
Chernova, E. P., 84n29, 89
Chicago school of sociology, 203
childcare, *see* nursery facilities
China: job rights, 109–10
Chistiakova, L. M., 52n167
Chubuk, I. F., 26n59
Chupeev, V., 30n75
Churbanov, V., 234n100
cities: migration between, 31–4; population growth rates, 31
class mobility: education and promotion of, 226–32
clerical personnel (*sluzhashchie*), 50
clocks, 276–7, 282
coal mining: average earnings, 43, 48, 285; pit closures (late 1960s), 97; towns and housewives, 82, 83
Cobb–Douglas functions, 171, 173
Cohn, Stanley H., 172note, 176nb, 194–5
collective farms, *see* farms, collective
Committee on Labor of the Ukraine, 22
communal services, 285, 286, 289–90, 291
Communist party: Central Committee decree (1979) on obligatory secondment of personnel, 40n130; local authorities' pressure for overfull employment, 84, 246–7; members directed to work, 17; power-preservation for functionnaries, 121, 170; vested interests, 118n2
commuting and labor market in cities, 33–4
competition: price-setting in conditions analogous to, 150–4
Comsomol organization: social recruitment, 19
constitution, Soviet: on the right to choose occupation "taking account of social need", 97–8
constraints on maximization of objective function, 118, 123–33, 300: hard and soft (Kornai), 5, 52, 57; ideological, 123–4, 125; JROE as one among a number of, 2, 3, 70–113; psychological and social 123; re economic coordination, 125–9; re incentives, 129–33; wage fund as a "hard", 57–9, 68–9, 106
construction industry: average monthly earnings, 285, 286; intersectoral mobility,

291; non-allocated producer goods for, 169; organized and social recruitment in, 18, 19, 37–8, 257; private seasonal gangs in rural areas (*shabashniki*), 268, 270–1, 272; quits and dismissals, 14; retirement rates for equipment, 195
consumer goods: annual price setting, 158, 168; control of demand for, 261; orders for durables, 169; price-setting problems, 138, 140–3 – solution, 157–8; problem of insufficient demand for some durables, 272–82; *see also* producer goods
consumers: choice, 126–7, 128, 139–43; sovereignty distrusted, 126, 128, 143; tastes and advertising, 140; welfare of final, 122
contracts: employment 36; fixed-term labor, 13, 19; "implicit" of leadership with labor, 3, 306–7; producer-purchaser, 147–8
Cooper, Julian, 223
Council of Ministers of the Soviet Union: (1977) approved product aggregates for bonus calculations, 137n5; decrees (1957, 1962) on responsibility of administration to find another position for a redundant employee, 98n63, 307; (1970) redundancy pay for administrative personnel dismissed because of modernization, 308n7
Courts, the: appeals against dismissal, 92, 103–5
criminality and dismissal, 91
Current Digest of the Soviet Press (C.D.S.P.), 28n61, 35n101

Dadashev, A., 50n160, 262n45
Danilov, L. M., 13n4, 21n37, 89na, 93n47, 184note
David, Paul, 193n61
Davidovich, Ia. A., 32n86
Davydova, G. V., 165n35
defense industry, 273
Denison, E. F., 173n8
designers, 271: industrial, 222–3
discipline, dismissals for violation of labor, 12–13, 15na, 87, 88–91, 110; and job rights, 88; as proportion of labour force, 88–9 (Table 3.2), 304; reluctance to sanction, 91
discrimination, social: in education, 226–32
dismissals: bindingness of constraint, 99–102, 161, 223; compensation for illegal, 104; due to reorganization of state

committees, 308; groups unprotected from, 92, 295–9; legal grounds for, 90; legal restrictions on, 102–5, 307; low probability of, 86–7; potential objects of, 87–99; in quit rate, 12–13, 110–11; reasons for, 36–7; reluctance of enterprise to make, 5–6, 91, 98–9, 105–13, 303; *see also* discipline; incompetence; quit rate; redundancy

Divilov, S., 50n157

Doane, D. P., 151n23

Dobrusin, A. M., 99n67

Doeringer, Peter B., 45n141

Donbass region, 83

Dorokhova, L. S., 217n57

drunkenness, 90, 303

dual labor markets, *see* labor markets, primary and secondary

Dunstan, J., 207n11

Dymentman, D. 255n36

earnings, labor: individual's marginal, 62–3; lost during study, 203–5; non-monetary, 66; planning of per employee, 106–7, 126; relative to basic wage rates, 11, 41, 44, 45–9; relative per sector, 285–6; should be directly proportional to quantity and quality of work, 39, 45, 129; structure of industrial manual workers', 41–2 (Table 2.4); *see also* wage rates

economies of scale: failure to realize in production, 145–6; and optimum combination of different types of labor, 163

economy, Soviet: constraints affecting coordination, 125–9; efficiency question, 2n2, 4–5, 40, 120, 129–33; fundamental concern with job provision, 76; inability to absorb educational surplus, 219–20, 233–4; malfunctions in, 4–5, 133–5, 145–6, 303–6; reforms (1965), 307–8; *see also* growth, economic; second economy

education: as a consumer good, 232–3; earnings in, 44, 285, 286; as economic investment in human capital, 113, 202–5, 233–4; for its own sake, 233; and JROE, 202–34; and need for occupation change, 220–6; over-investment in, 112, 205–19, 259, 305; and promotion of class mobility, 226–32; quit rate, 290; standards, 208; supply and demand conditions for different levels of, 205–19

education, full-time: or part-time, 215, 223–6, 231–2; transfers for, not quits, 13, 16n18, 29

education, higher (*vuzy*): expansion (1950s and 60s), 206–8; graduations, 204; job direction for graduates of, 18, 22; private return, 205n7; supply and demand for, 212–14; foreign, 207; *see also* university education

education, part-time 223–6, 231–2; drop-out rate, 224

education, primary, 202, 206

education, secondary: completion of, 207–8; electives, 207n11; examinations, 207, 208, 209n21; extension debate, 203n4, 205; grades, 8th and 10th, 204, 205, 207n11; length of compared with West European, 206–7; universal as pre-vocational, 203, 206; *see also* junior college; tutoring, private

education, vocational, 203: social functions of, 215–17; supply and demand conditions, 214–19; *see also* vocational schools

effort, work, 303; adjustment of average per worker when shocks in overfull employment, 240–56, 313–15; of individual constrained by group pressure, 62–3, 243, 270, 305, 314; options for Soviet worker to raise his standard of living, 269–72; ratchet effect on wage fund and, 62–4, 305

electoral pressures, freedom from, 119

electrical equipment industry: relative earnings of piece-work manual workers, 46–7 (Table 2.5)

élite, Soviet, 119

emigration: applying for and job rights, 86

émigrés: to Israel, 253, 269n11, 286n48; to US, 250n22, 301

employees: demand for additional, 68–9; human dignity of, 73, 166; only short-term advantages from success of an enterprise, 125–6; proportion of old to new, 67; restrictions on job change, 28–37; temporary and seasonal, lack of job rights, 85; *see also* workers

employers: contributions for building of houses, 35n101; of last resort, urban and rural, 256–8; rejection of job applicants, 110; restriction in changing set tasks for individual employee, 36–7; *see also* managers, enterprise employment: contract, 36; guaranteed in public works program (Popov's suggestion), 97–8, 308; interruption of, *see* work service, continuous; inventories as buffer, 272–82; length within same enterprise, 101–2; planned growth, 57n187; *see also* full employment; overfull employment

employment offices, municipal, 20–2

employment quota: actual against planned, 49–52, 56; enforcement 51–2; linked to managerial pay, 105, 129–30, 191; maximum average (1965–70), and (1980), 50; and nominal earnings per employee, 106–7; *see also* hiring

engineering industry: average monthly earnings, 49, 285; job ladders in, 293, 295; materials handling in, 184–5, 190–1; proportion of investment in, 189; quit rate, 288–9; "skill category", 46note; 1976 study of hourly paid time-workers by skill grade, 47; temporary residence permits for workers in Moscow, 32n86; (1967–8) workers performing at a higher grade than wage level, 53

engineers: in applied research and design, 222–3; education, 211, 213–14, 224–6

enterprises: comparison of earnings in a given trade among, 49; self-financing (*khozraschet*), 256; size of Soviet industrial compared with Western, 164; *see also* mangers, enterprise

equality: for different nationalities, 226; for women, 73, 296

equipment, industrial, 164–5: decline in intershift and intra-shift usage, 173n7, 188, 193, 302; (1973) decree for expansion in plant capacity for building of, 186; extent of retirements of, 194–7 (Table 6.5); mainline production in engineering, 164–5n35; mechanized in materials handling, 185–7; new, and redundancy, 93; obsolescence, 196, 198; replacement and maintenance workers, 194–9; scrapping rate compared with West, 196, 197n68, 199; service life, 196–7, 198

Estonia: auxiliary and mainline production workers, 186; "occasional work", 269–70; university preparatory divisions, 230

eviction, 35

extractive industries, 13; *see also* coal mining

families: and educational discrimination, 227–32; organized resettlement of farm, 20; with pre-school age children and "helping" members, 74n8; (1974–5) study of employment in Leningrad, 80

Far East: organized resettlement of farm families to, 20; projected net labor force movement to, 236

farmers, collective: full employment and seasonal slack period, 75; pension law, 175, 177na, 178; resettlement of, 20, 22

farms, collective: absence of right to leave locality, 28, 29, 257; conditions of occupancy, 23–4; incentives, 27–8; markets, 140, 159, 169, 267; ownership, 125; resignation from and migration to urban areas, 14; secondment of urban workers to, 38–40, 256–7; separation rates, 30; special legal status and power to evict quitting workers, 35

farms, state: absorption of shocks to urban labor force, 256–7; organized resettlement, 20, 22; ownership, 125; separation rates, 30

Fedorenko, N. P., 137–8n5

Feshbach, Murray, 204nf, 222n67

Fil'ev, V., 94n49

Filippov, F., 211n32, 213n36, 219n65, 232n95

finished goods, 274–5

fishing, 13, 19, 257, 285, 288

food industry: average monthly earnings, 285, 286; employees in, 287, 288; processing, 84n29, 257; in Russian Republic, 101

foodstuffs: retail prices, 159n27

foreign trade: and decline in consumer demand, 276, 278, 279, 280; inefficiency re choice of product aggregates, 133

foreman category in engineering, 223n69, 225

forestry: female white collar absenteeism rare in areas of, 88, intersectoral mobility, 291; temporary transfers, 37n117; *see also* lumbering industry

formulae, algebraic: easy reference verbal treatment of, 310–15

France: length and coverage of secondary education, 206, 208; nursery facilities, 74n8; retirement rate for equipment, 194; secondary labor market, 284; separation rates, 16note

Frunzenskii EVM plant, 281n31

full employment: hypothesis, 70–105; Kornai on, 73

Fundamentals of Labor Law (1970), 37n114, 98n63

Gailgalas, B. P., 49n154, 89nc

garment industry, 83n27, 84n29: knitted stocks, 274; quits in, 289–90

geographic restrictions on job changes, 28–34

Georgian Republic: quits by manual workers, 289

German Democratic Republic: quit rates and separation rates, 15 (Table 2.1), 17

German Federal Republic: absenteeism, 249, 250; apprenticeship system, 215; length and coverage of secondary education, 206–8; nursery facilities, 74n8; quit rates and separation rates, 15 (Table 2.1), 16, 112; (1972) redundancy study, 96; retirement rate of equipment, 194

Gershanov, E. M., 36n110

Gilitskii, F., 14n13

glavki (subdivision of ministry), 146

GNP, *see* gross national product

Gomberg, Ia., 285n46

Gomulka, Stanislaw, 172–3n5

goods, *see* consumer goods; producer goods

Gor'kii: excess of supply over demand for skilled workers, 219n65; junior college graduates as blue-collar workers, 211; redundancy dismissals in, 99; shortage of unskilled labor, 189n48

Gorlin, A. C., 151n23

Gosplan SSSR, 60n199

graduates: annual figures, 204 (Table 7.1), 206; certificates, 208; of full-time schools directed to work, 17, 20, 218–19; full-time students as percentage of all, 205 (Table 7.2), 223–6

Granick, David, 7n6, 59n195, 117n1, 129n15, 133, 145n20, 151n23, 200n76, 202n1, 227n81

Great Britain, *see* United Kingdom

Gregory, Paul, 250n22, 301n1, 305

Grigorev, A., 225n76

gross national product (GNP): objective function in terms of growth of, 160, 306

Grossman, Greogry, 267n1

Grossman, P., 23n45

Grotseskul, G. N., 238n5

group: management as upholder of values of, 62–3; pressure constraining individual effort, 62–3, 243, 270, 305, 314

growth, economic: objective function of Center, 122, 160; trade-off between "extensive" and "intensive", 119–20, 159, 272

Guroff, Gregory, 133

Guser, S. M., 84n28, 296n71

Hajenko, F., 96n51

Hanson, Philip, 28n61

Hauslohner, Peter Austin, 7: on consensus of élite, 119n3; on 1965 economic reforms, 307–8; on eviction of workers who quit, 35n106; on interests of Communist Party functionaries, 121n6; on job assignment, 17n19, 18n20, 22n44; moral obligation of enterprise to find jobs for redundant employees, 98n63, 99n71; reduction in length of work week leads to more female labor force participation, 27; on social contract, 3n4; Ufa-Kaluga experiment, 123n8

health: earnings, 44, 285; problems and job transfer, 92; *see also* sickness benefit

Helgeson, Ann, 28n64

Hicks-neutral technological change, 171, 172n5, 173

Hilker, T. H., 2n2

hiring: absence of resistance to extra, 240, 244–7, 255, 305; by the enterprises themselves, 20–2; channels used in Russian Republic, 21–2 (Table 2.2); make-work, 84; mix of, 110; obligations toward youth, 236–7; planned, 17–23; quantity of, 112–13

Höhmann, H.-H., 252n29

Hough, Jerry F., 118n2

household economy, private: quits into, 14n17; women in, 82, 83

household services, 285, 286, 289–90, 291

housing: average monthly earnings in, 285, 286; and intersectoral mobility, 291; national legislation (1981), 35n106; non-allocated producer goods for, 169; quit rate, 289–90; restrictions on job change, 34–6; shortages, 36; *see also* residence permits

human capital: education as investment in, 113, 202–5, 233–4, 260; excess supply of, 205–19 – explanations, 219–34

Hungary: "Hungarian wonder" (Kornai),

Hungary *cont.*
268; job rights hypothesis as explanation of economic behavior of, 7; Kornai's view as to experience of, 57; power of Communist Party functionaries, 121; redundancy dismissals experiment (1970s), 308; (1968) reforms in economy, 126

Iagodkin, V., 93n46, 96n52
Iankovskaia, E. A., 83n27
ideology: commitment to keep relative prices stable, 168–9; constraint on maximization, 123–4, 125; traditional socialist, 125–6
idleness: constraint of unwanted, 78–9, 160–7, 182, 246, 311; humiliation of (Kornai), 73, 75
incentives: to change occupation, 220–6; constraints on system, 6, 129–33, 163; to misinform Center about quasi-rents, 129; negative effects of price-setting, 142; and obligation to work in the socialist sector, 27–8; payments, 41note, 42; and poor labor productivity, 305; in Shchekino experiment, 238; system as rules of behavior for managers, 137; *see also* Model A
income: creation or distribution in job rights, 71, 72, 308; egalitarianism in distribution, 1, 258–9; maintenance and guarantee of minimum, 78–9, 86; and no-idleness constraint, 162; *see also* national income
incompetence and dismissal, 87, 91–3
industry: intersectoral mobility, 291; lack of demand for graduates of junior colleges, 209–10; (1965) reform in, 58n192; *see also* manual workers in industry
inflation: capital rate of, 172note; and rolling plan for wage fund, 261; and wage fund constraints, 59, 106
information-processing: limits to Center's, 123, 128, 129, 133, 137
innovations, technological: diffusion rate slow, 174, 190; disincentive for managers re employment quota, 191; effect on mix of materials allocation, 180; regarded as externality to utility function by managers, 179; shift towards labor-augmenting type, 172–3n5; subsidizing cost of implementation, 179; *see also* equipment, industrial

input-output relations, 129, 137; inconsistency in, 133
institutions: creation by Center of economic, 117–18; decision-making by, 106; regulations and incentives coordinating, 120; vested interests of, 118n2
inventories: as employment buffer, 272–82
investment: allocation of, 134, 199–201; cycles of Bauer, 199; cycles of Kornai, 69, 105–6; fixed, 106n89; fixed and JROE, 171–201, 303–4, 313; and labor/capital imbalance, 120, 302–3; and objective function of Center, 122
investment in human capital, 112, 113, 202–5: problem of excess, 209–12
irons, electric, 272, 273n15, 277
Israel, Jewish emigrants to: on overtime, 253; on private earnings, 269n11, 286n48
Italy: absenteeism, 249, 250; high earnings for construction work, 268; retirement rates of fixed assets, 194; secondary labor market, 284
Iun', O. M., 128n14, 137n5
Ivanov, I. I., 210n27
Ivanov, S., 96n52
Ivanovo, 82
Izvestiia, 274

Japan: absenteeism, 249n19; comparison of secondary education system with Soviet, 207n11; equal opportunity of education between social classes, 228; job rights, 85; technological change and capital/labor ratio, 173
Jews: discrimination against, 227; emigrants to Israel, 253; white-collar emigrants to US, 298
job changes: adaptability and, 220–6; geographic restrictions on, 28–34; low probability of being obligatory, 86–7; obligation to make specific, 37–40, 96; restrictions on specific, 34–7; *see also* transfers, job
job directions, *see* hiring, planned; organized recruitment; social recruitment; transfers, job
job evaluation: influence on US relative earnings, 45n141
job ladders, 284, 285, 292–5
job performance: ability and willingness for, 76–7; inability for and dismissal, 87, 91–3, 110

job refusal: rights of, 21
job rights, 71, 84–105; hypothesis, 78–9, 85; and inability of Center to control product mix or adopt labor-saving fixed investments, 304; informal basis, 307; or "political fear", 307; *see also* JROE hypotheses
job search, 71–2: period of, 76–7, 79, 81, 82, 226, 311; as voluntary unemployment, 71–2, 79
job security, 2n2, 105; legal protection, 92–3; and overfull employment, 105; trade-off between higher consumer income and, 308; weakening, 307; *see also* dismissals
job vacancies: planned hiring in filling of, 17–23
jobs, second: regular, 269, 271; *see also* moonlighters
JROE hypotheses (Job Rights-Overfull Employment), 1–8, 70–113; applications, 267–99; costs of policy, 303–6; domain, 3–4, 6, 136, 306, 308; fixed investment and, 171–201; fixed prices and, 136–70; job rights in, 85–7; labor market and, 235–63; policy – its reasons and future, 306–9; set of, 70–9; *see also* maximization problem
junior college ("specialized secondary education"): compared with German *Fachhochschule*, 206; job direction for graduates of, 18, 22, 211; stipendia, 209; supply and demand conditions, 208–12, 219

Kahn, Alfred J., 74n8
Kalinin, I., 128n14
Kalleberg, A. L., 49n156
Kaluga: disciplinary dismissals, 89; -Ufa experiment with employment bureaus, 20, 21n37, 123n8
Kamerman, Sheila B., 74n8
Kaminskii, I. N., 43n134
Kartashova, L., 89–90n34
Katsenelinboigen, Aron: on eviction, 35; on fungilibility of wage fund at ministerial level, 53n168; on redundancy dismissals in Gor'kii, 99
Kaufman, Roger T., 112n95
Kazakhstan: mechanizers' training, 216n53; private contractors in construction work, 268; rural youth, 221

Kazan: occupational mobility and education, 227n84, 228n85
Khabarin, E., 214n41
Khanson, Kh., 269n11
Khar'kov: commuters in, 33
Kheifets, L., 48n153, 60n197, 93n46, 190n50, 238n5, 239n6
Khorev, B., 32n88
Khotin, Leonid, 27
Kiev: Academy of Science retirements study, 96, 298; housing for employees, 35; population growth, 31n80
Kinsburskii, A. V., 204note, 209n21, 224n72
Kiperman, G., 59n196
Kirgizian Republic: disciplinary dismissals, 89; Frunzenskii EVM plant, 281n31; (1958–67) hirings beyond enterprise plan limits, 84; quit rate (1963), 101–2
Kirichenko, V., 234n100
Kirpa, I., 288n53
Klimonov, V. P., 223n69
Knishnik, S., 183n18
Komarov, V. E., 222n68
Konovalova, N., 165n35
Kornai, János: hard and soft constraints, 5, 52, 57, 106; on "Hungarian wonder", 268; on investment cycles, 68–9, 105–6; on socialist societies, 302; on unemployment, 73, 166; "vegetative mechanisms", 180n16
Kostakov, V., 107n90, 308n5
Kostin, L. A., 39n125, 75n10, 107n90
Kotliar, A. E., 21n39, 22, 51n164, 287nh, 288n53, 290n58, 291n61
Kovalev, A. I., 184nf, 185n20
Krasnodar region (*krai*), 291n60
Krasovskii, V., 165n35, 188n40, 200
Kremliakov, V. A., 83n27
Krevnevich, V. V., 184note
Kriukov, I. Ia., 165n35
Krueger, Gary, 147
Krylov, P., 139n9
Kuhn-Tucker conditions, 151, 161
Kulagin, E., 214n41
Kulikov, V., 104n87
Kunel'skii, L. E., 189n50, 285n46
Kuprianova, Z. R., 76n12, 89nf
Kurbatova, G. Ia., 198n73
Kuz'min, V. A., 217n54
Kvasha, Ia., 164n30

labor allocation, 17–20: Center's belief in

labor allocation *cont.*
  inefficiency of, 127–8; policy of by
  temporary assignments, 301–2
labor camps, forced, 12
Labor Code (1970), 36n111, 37n114,
  98n63, 66
labor disputes, 102–3
labor force: age and sex in physical work,
  287 (Table 9.1); change in educational
  level, 180, 183, 189; female participation,
  see women; observed degree of
  participation in socialist sector, 79–82
  (Table 3.1); reductions (1960s)
  compared with US, 176 (Table 6.2);
  reductions in declining occupations
  (1959–70), 177 (Table 6.3) *see also*
  seniority
labor hoarding, 78, 105, 251–6, 263
labor market, Soviet, 11–69: attempts to
  control effective demand, 49–52, 68;
  equilibrium assumption, 11, 300–3;
  existence of, 12–23; and JROE
  hypotheses, 70–84, 235–63; limits on
  working of, 11, 23–40; literature on, 7;
  nature of, 12–40, 105; setting of prices in,
  40–65, 300
labor market disequilibrium hypothesis,
  5–6, 105–13: confronted with
  observations, 109–13; modifications,
  107–9; and overall employment with
  shocks, 235, 236n2, 257–9
labor markets, primary and secondary,
  67n209, 282–99: hypotheses, 285; Piore's
  theory, 283–4; sectoral Soviet, 285–95
labor militancy, 284–5
Labor Research Institute of the Soviet
  Union, 14, 39n125: study of older
  manual workers in non-mechanized jobs
  in industry, 192
labor shortage; hypothesis, 67–9, 188,
  199–201; *see also* labor market
  disequilibrium hypothesis; indications of,
  300–3; and labor hoarding, 252n29; at
  national level, 302
labor surplus, 300: and educational
  overinvestment, 112–13, 180–1, 205–19,
  305; at enterprise level, 251–6, 301
labor turnover, *see* job changes; quit rates
Lagrangian maximization problem, 150,
  152, 161
Lainer, K. A., 298n82
Laki, Mihaly, 174n10
Lampert, Nicholas, 104n82, 86, 87

Lange, O., 137
Lapidus, Gail W., 26n59
Laskavy, A., 76n12
layoffs, 100, 110
Le Monde, 28n62
leadership, Soviet: concern with job
  provision, 76; minor ideological
  prejudices, 124; personal utility function,
  306; rational and traditional Marxist,
  120; trade-off in implicit JROE objective,
  305
legislation: on dismissals, 102–5, 307;
  sentencing of unemployed people to
  compulsory work (1961), 24
Leighton, Linda 101n73
leisure: and money income preferences,
  123; moonlighting and, 270; or "poor"
  job, 82–3
Leningrad: bus drivers' earnings, 48;
  commuters, 33; employment office, 21;
  families study (1974–5), 80; foremen with
  higher education, 223n69, 225;
  in-migrants, 32; machinebuilding
  enterprises, 31–2; parental occupation
  and probability of pupil continuing
  education beyond secondary level, 231–2
  (Table 7.3); pensionable age people in
  engineering, 298; population, 31; trade
  union factory committees and dismissals
  (1962–3), 103; vocational education in,
  217
Levikov, A., 183n18
Levine, Herbert S., 141n14
Lewis, Tracy, R., 130n16
light bulb manufacture, 273–4
light industry: average monthly earnings,
  285, 286; job ladders in, 293–5;
  on-the-job training, 293; quits by manual
  workers, 289–90
limitchiki, 32n85
Linz, Susan J., 59n194
Lithuania: approved manpower plans, 51;
  private earnings, 269n11
Livshits, R., 34n99
Lobanov, V., 212n36
local authorities: enterprise manpower
  planning, 51, 84, 246–7; temporary
  assignments for unskilled work, 180
local commissions for job placement of
  youth, 22–3
locality: and JROE hypothesis of frictional
  unemployment, 76–8, 82–4, 87, 235–7,
  259, 310–11; restrictions on job changes,

locality *cont.*
28–34; of work in multi-plant enterprise
    as "population point", 36
logging, *see* lumbering industry
Lokshin, P., 138n7, 158n25
Lokshin, R. A., 273n14, 275n20,
    279n25
looms, shuttleless: replacement of electric
    motors in, 54–5
Lubcke, K., 15–16nf
lumbering industry, 13, 19, 178, 285
L'vov: commuters, 33

McAuley, Alastair: appeals to Courts about
    dismissals, 104n82; and earnings in
    education and health, 44n140; on legal
    role of higher trade unions, 102n78; and
    "official" poverty line, 75n11; structure
    of all industry earnings, 41na (Table
    2.4), 42; wage drift, 42; on women's
    position, 25n55, 296
machinebuilding, 31–2, 145n20: wage rates,
    44
machinists: redundancy study, 94–5 (Table
    3.3); and vocational education, 218
maintenance work on equipment, 186n32,
    196, 197–9
Malakhin, V., 98n62
Malinvaud, E., 137
Malova, V. A., 213n36
managerial personnel, 50, 52: earnings, 54,
    214n41; education, 209, 210; in line
    management, 224–5; responsible posts,
    no job rights, 85, 86, 92
managers, enterprise: active role in
    absorption of employment shocks, 236,
    244–7; appointed and removed by
    Center, 126, 129; evaluation re plan
    fulfilment, 246, 301; failure to internalize
    Center's objective function, 132–3,
    134–5, 163, 179; incentives to avoid
    overexpenditure of wage fund, 58, 63–4;
    incentives to misinform about production
    capacities, 134; motivation and
    incentives for, 130–3, 312; reputation
    with higher authorities, 55; requirement
    to adjust to labor supply situation,
    180–1, 301; responsibility to relocate
    redundant employees, 98–9; risk
    avoiders, 254–5; rules of behavior for,
    136–7; salaries linked to number of
    personnel, 105, 129–30, 191; trade-off
    available to, 11, 65–9, 107–9, 254, 298,

310, 311–12; *see also* maximization
    problem
Manevich, E. L., 74n8, 77n12, 81n19,
    144n18: on redundancy, 97, 98n65
manpower plans, *see* employment quota
manual workers in industry, 13, 50, 288:
    auxiliary and mainline production,
    186–7; graduates of vocational schools,
    17; job ladders for, 293–5; organized and
    social recruitment of, 18–20, 22;
    separation rate, 13–16, 288–9 (Table
    9.2); structure of earnings, 41 (Table
    2.4); *see also* workers, unskilled;
    piece-workers
markets: collective farm, 140, 159, 169, 267;
    expansion of role in Yugoslavia and
    Hungary, 121; grey, 144; role in Soviet
    economy, 121; *see also* labor market,
    Soviet
Markov, V. I., 13n10, 41n
Markov chain, 131
Marrese, Michael, 106n89
Marxism, 120, 284
Mashenkov, V. F., 39n125
Maslova, I. S.: on dismissals, 89, 90n35; on
    employment bureaus, 20n36, 21n37, 39,
    40, 291n61; on redundancy, 93n46,
    96n52
material-stimulation fund, 52, 64–5, 139:
    allocation of, 48; incentives from, 41note;
    labour productivity and, 50
materials-allocation plans, 136–48: effect of
    technological innovations on, 180; and
    producer goods, 143, 147, 149, 152–5,
    158, 169; and product mix, 164–6; setting
    of and above-plan production, 156–7; *see
    also* supply difficulties
materials-handling: introduction of
    technology into, 185–7, 190, 192–3, 199;
    unskilled workers in, 183–5 (Table 6.4)
maternity leave, 25n55
Matrozova, I. I., 77n12, 93n46, 47
Matthews, Mervyn, 207n11, 217n57
maximization problem: of objective
    function for Center, 1–3, 117–35, 310; of
    enterprise management, 6, 65–7, 145–57,
    160–7, 310; model for testing JROE
    hypotheses, 6, 117–35; *see also* JROE;
    labor market disequilibrium hypothesis;
    Model A; Model B
meat-grinders, 277
mechanics, auto, 28n61, 90
"mechanizers", *see* tractor-machinists

medical schools, 203n5
Melentev, N. R., 239n8
Merson, A., 213n38
metalfabricating industry, 285, 288–9; equipment, 165n35, 198; job ladders in, 293
migration: from collective farms, 28–9, 30; rural-urban, 29–31, 82, 256–7; self-betterment explanation (Zaslavskaia), 82–3; urban in-, 31–4; and vocational training of rural youth, 215–16
military: compulsory service and labor market, 12, 13, 29, 229; decline in utilization of equipment, 165n35; personnel in occupation change data, 175n12; and return on vocational education of service, 218
Mincer, Jacob, 101n73
ministries: and fungibility of wage fund, 52–3, 55–6; industrial, 51, 146, 151n23; national, 31; problems with Shchekino experiment in branch, 262; reorganization of agricultural and dismissals, 308; and revision of planned wage funds, 59
Ministry of Machinery for Light and Food Industry and of Household Appliances, Soviet Union, 273n15
Ministry of Trade, Soviet Union: on consumer goods production and demand, 140n12, 169, 276–7; forbids higher voltage light bulb production, 274
minorities, national: discrimination for and against, 203n6, 227, 295–6; work behavior in US, 283–4
mobility, labor, 5: intersectoral, 291–2; and regional unemployment, 82–4; restrictions on, 28–34, 111n94; *see also* job changes; migration
Model A, 117, 121–35: explanation of Shchekino movement, 259–61; objective function and constraints re economic coordination, 125–9 – re incentives, 129–33; and proposed solutions to prices of producer and consumer goods, 159–60; and Soviet occupational change data, 179–83, 312
Model B. 117, 135: explanation of excess supply of human capital, 220–6, 259; explanation of Shchekino movement, 259; and occupational change data, 181–3; and overfull employment at local

level in face of frequent shocks, 235–8, 262–3; and proposed solutions to prices of producer and consumer goods 160–7; and reluctance to implement technological innovations, 183–201, 312
Moldavian Republic, 91, 104n83
monopolies, natural: treatment in Europe and US, 124
moonlighters, 73, 269–70
Moscow: bus drivers' earnings, 48; commuters, 33; employment office, 21; hiring of out-of-town workers, 32; organized recruitment, 32; population plan, 31; quits and dismissals in industry, 14; vocational education, 217, 218
Moscow *oblast*: dismissals' appeals of small enterprises, 104n85; part-day absences, 250n22
Moskalenko, V. K., 239n8
Moskovich, V., 44n138
mothers of young children, 72, 74, 92
motivational principles, 129–33; *see also* incentives

Narkhoz SSSR, 17n19, 38n124, 125, 159n27, 274, 275n19, 285n46
national income, 72, 273
natural units of production evaluation, 139n11, 144, 146
neoclassical theory, 4, 299: extensions, 118–21
Netherlands, the, 249, 250
Nikitinskii, L. V., 98n63
Nikitinskii, V. I., 37n114, 102n78, 103n80, 104n85
North, Douglas C., 4n5
Northwest region: rural migration in, 29–30
notice requirement, 34, 226
Novitskii, A., 269n9, 270n12, 298n85
Novosibirsk oblast', W. Siberia: collective and state farm separation rates, 30; (1964–81) studies of engineering workers, 92, 102, 211; time between jobs, 76n12, 81
nursery facilities, 72, 74
Nuti, D. M., 59n196, 143

O'Dell, F., 218n61
ob' 'edineniia, all Union, 146
obligation to work in socialist sector, 23–8, 243–4; and labor market, 247–8
obshchestvennyi, see social recruitment

"occasional work", 269–72
occupation: ability to change, 220–6;
    change of (1959–70), 174, 175–9 –
    explanation, 179–83; parental and
    probability of pupil continuing education
    beyond secondary level, 231 (Table 7.3);
    right of individual to choose his, 97–8; by
    sector, 285–6; *see also* job changes; skills
Ofer, Gur, 253n35, 269n11, 286n48
oil refining industries, 262n45
Okun, Arthur M.: unified search model,
    286, 290
Okun'kov, L., 36n107
Omel'ianenko, B. L., 184nc
Opyt, 34n98
Orel': hiring through local commissions,
    23n45; (1979) intersectoral mobility,
    291n60; (1976) quit rates, 288n53,
    290n58
organized recruitment (*orgnabor*) 18–19, 20,
    22: departure before end of period,
    90n35; in Moscow, 32
Ostrovskaia, R. T., 217n54
overfull employment, 70–84: definition, 1;
    in each locality and skill flexibility, 222;
    in face of frequent shocks, 235–8 –
    explanations, 256–9, JROE model,
    240–56; and job security, 105; JROE set
    of hypotheses, 70–9, 85; and
    overexpansion of education, 220–6, 305;
    why does Center allow? 106–7
overheating, economic, 5, 85, 110, 259, 303
overtime, 269, 271: legal restrictions on,
    252–3; extent, 253–4

packers, 184 (Table 6.4)
Palterovich, D., 165n35, 179n15, 195n64,
    196n67
Paniugin, V. E., 37n114, 102n78, 103n80,
    104n85
Pankin, M., 76n12
Panteleev, N., 21n40, 188n41, 44
paper industry, 255n36, 262n45
parasitism, 24, 28, 247–8: laws against, 24
Parfenov, V., 76n12
part-time education, *see* education,
    part-time
part-time work, 16, 72, 73–4, 252, 297
Pashkov, A. S., 18n20
passports, internal, 28: and rural workers
    on state farms (1932, 1940) decrees,
    28n64, 30
Pavlenkov, V. A., 14n17, 35n104

peat industry, 19
Pechorskii coal basin, 42–3
pension law: (1956), 27, 74n9, 298, (1970),
    74n9, 296; collective farm, 175, 177na,
    178; continuous work service and, 34
pensionable age, people of: as child-rearing
    help, 74n8; discrimination against, 295,
    296–9; labor force participation rate,
    80–1; liable to dismissal or obligatory job
    change, 96, 297; right to work and
    employment of, 74, 74–5n9, 86
People's Commissariat of Labor of Russian
    Republic: 1928 decree on responsibility
    of enterprise to find another position for
    redundant employee, 98n63
Petrunina, N. A., 192n59
physicians: earnings, 44n140, 214
piece-workers, 42: payments, 43–4, 48, 53,
    79, 130, 161; relative earnings in
    electrical equipment industry, 46–7
    (Table 2.5); relatively unconstrained,
    271; skill difference in earnings, 162
Pietrzynski, G., 15nf
Piore, M. J.: dual labor market theory,
    283–4; on job evaluation, 45n141
Pirogov, V., 76n12
plan enforcement: and efficiency, 120, 126,
    129, 133, 159–60
planning, central: for labor or market
    relationship, 11, 17–23, 23–40; mistakes
    as shocks, 236; in non-taut production,
    149, 151–4 (Fig. 5.1), 167–8; objectives
    of, 1–5, 6, 117–35; organized on sectoral
    basis, 237; relationship with
    performance, 126, 129; sovereignty, 127,
    141n14, 142–3; in taut production,
    148–9, 150–1, 168; welfare, 1–4; *see also*
    State Planning Commission
plans, five year, 57n187, 61–2, 139n11, 202,
    252
Plotnitskii, G., 64n202
pluralism, 118
Plyshevskii, B., 139n9
Poland: secondary labor market, 284;
    technological chance and overcoming of
    supply difficulties, 174n11
Poliakov, V. T., 138n7, 141n13
policy choices of Center, 1–5, 117–18: and
    dysfunctions, 305–6
Politbureau, 99, 118n2
political constraints, 120, 170
political opposition: exclusion from job
    rights, 85, 86

Poltorak, I. S., 17n19, 20
polytechnical education, 207n11
Popov, G.: proposed redundancy scheme
    payments in public works program, 97–8
population: growth in suburbs, 33–4;
    planned, 31; urban growth rates, 31
Population Censuses: labor force
    participation data, 79
Portes, Richard, 59n196
Potapovskii, V., 275n19
poverty, 75, 174n11
power preservation, 120, 121, 170
Pravda, 34n98, 91, 97, 99n71, 238n5, 239n6,
    308
prices in the labor market: and control over
    labor usage, 127–8; setting of, 11, 40–65
prices of product: annual changes by
    aggregate (1949–54), 138, 141, 142, 168;
    current, 138, 139; fixed and JROE,
    136–67, 304 – alternative explanations,
    167–70; indices attempted (1948–9), 139;
    revision (1982) and subsidization of
    innovation, 179n15; set by individual
    product, 137–8; if set by producers,
    154–6; shadow different for identical
    input aggregates, 134, 139; system of
    constant, 138–9; *see also* retail prices;
    wholesale prices
private plots of agricultural employees,
    23–4, 27, 125, 267
private sector: growth of, 272; household,
    14n17; work, 27
probationary period: no protection from
    dismissal during, 92
producer goods: non-allocated, 169;
    price-setting problem, 143–8; solution,
    148–57, 159, 168; *see also* products
product, final: growth of per capita, 122
product aggregates: chosen for import as
    opposed to export, 133; and individual
    product, 146–7, 157; planning in terms
    of, 127, 128, 136–7, 142; substitutability
    in production and in use, 163–4; total
    number, 158; transformation within,
    144–5, 148
product mix: accords with no-idleness
    constraints, 161–7; anarchy in
    determination, 133–4, 145, 146–8, 304;
    Central determination of final and
    intermediate, 126–9, 154; changes in
    annual planned and wage fund, 260–1; in
    consumer goods, 128, 140–3; and
    efficiency, 148–57; planning via prices,

139n11; and problem of insufficient
    demand for some consumer durables,
    272–82; in producer goods, 143, 144–8
production: above-plan, 144, 155–7;
    changes in functions, 162–3; of consumer
    goods and demand, 140n12; evaluation
    in terms of constant, current prices or
    natural units, 139n11, 144, 146; and
    inventory changes for some consumer
    durables, 274–82; ownership of means of,
    125; plans, 143, 148–54, 157; process –
    adaptation to capital/labor ratio,
    172–201; technological change in, 93, 99,
    163
productivity, factor-: rate of, 119–20n5,
    171–3
productivity, labor: current and planned re
    wage fund, 60–4; improvements in and
    short-term increase in earnings, 240–7;
    and labor hoarding, 251; and labor
    surpluses, 112–13; lack of incentives and
    poor, 305; materials stock and extra,
    244n14; and size of material-stimulation
    fund, 50; and wage rates, 44; *see also*
    effort, work; Shchekino experiment
products: intermediate, 27, 127, 128; new,
    134–5, 139, 141, 222
professional personnel, 50, 52: earnings of,
    54, 214n41; education, 209, 210
promotion, *see* career advancement
Prudinskii, A. M., 17n19, 91n38
psychological aspects of unemployment, 73
PTU, *see* vocational schools
public service: job rights, 85, 97–8, 308
Pudnov, I. I., 274n17
pulp and paper industry, 255n36, 262n45

quasi-rents: Schumpeterian, 61, 238,
    259–60; short-term enjoyment by
    employees, 125–6, 129, 259–60
queuing system of labor distribution, 40
quit rates, 12–17, 81: definition, 16n18;
    disciplinary dismissals in, 88–90; and
    dismissal constraint, 99–102;
    manipulation of, 67; and natural wastage
    of labor, 220, 226; relative US and
    Soviet, 101n73, 111–12; by sector,
    286–90; Soviet annual in international
    perspective, 15 (Table 2.1), 100–1, 113;
    structure of, 100–1

rabochie, 183n19; *see also* blue-collar
    occupations; manual workers

radio receivers, 272, 278–9
raion (administrative district), 36
Raiu, O. M., 205n7
ratchet effect, *see* wage fund
razor blades, 277
recruitment: by enterprises themselves,
  20–2; policy and textile industry, 294–5;
  see also organized recruitment; social
  recruitment
redundancy of personnel: definition, 93–4;
  and dismissal, 87, 93–102, 110, 307–8;
  legal criteria, 37; payments, 97–8;
  predictions of large scale, 307–8;
  responsibility of enterprise to find
  another job, 98–9
Rees, Albert, 49n156
refrigerators, 272, 273n15, 274, 279–80
regional aspects of unemployment, *see*
  locality
Renner, T. M., 216n53
rents, Schumpeterian, *see* quasi-rents
repair, *see* maintenance work
research personnel: applied, size of staff,
  222–3; re-certification, 92
resettlement, agricultural: organized, 20,
  22
residence permits: temporary and
  in-migration to cities, 32–4
retail trade, 55, 138, 139, 274–5
retirements, 101n74, 192–3: job rights, 13,
  296–9
retraining: payment during, 97
Reynolds, R. T., 207n9
Reznik, I. G., 224n71
Riabushkin, T. V., 189n48
Rogovin, V. Z., 267n2
Rogovskii, N., 50n157, 60n199, 139n11
Romanov, Grigorii, 99
Romanov, N. N., 104n82
Romma, F., 14n13
Rosefielde, Steven, 12n2
Rozenova, L. I., 180n15
Ruble, Blair, 37n114, 103n80
Rukavishnikov, V. O., 228n85
Rumer, Boris, 195n63
rural: female workforce participation, 26;
  -urban educational inequality, 288; *see
  also* migration
Rusanov, E. S., 13n8, 89nf
Russian Republic: disciplinary dismissals,
  89; employment in construction, 257n37;
  engineering industry materials handling,
  185; food industry, 101; job directions in,

17n19, 18–19, 22–3; mechanizers'
  education, 216; mobility between sectors,
  291; new industrial plant with unfilled
  work places (1971–5), 188; number of
  approved working places, 50, 51; orders
  for consumer durables, 169; quit rates,
  288, 289; skill classifications, 293; slack
  in capacity utilization, 164; spread of
  Shchekino experiment, 239; study of
  pensionable age in jobs, 298; university
  preparation divisions, 230; use of manual
  workers outside main shift, 188
Rutkevich, M. N., 204nd, 208n14, 213n40,
  232n95
Rutland, Peter: on Shchekino experiment,
  238n5, 260n41, 262
Ruzavina, E. I., 96n52

Safronov, N., 186n28, 197n68
salaries, 44: (1965) decree setting
  white-collar, 55–6; linked to number of
  personnel, 105, 191; supplements to,
  53
sales tax, 127, 138
Salowsky, Heinz, 249n19
Sarkisiants, G., 74n8
Sazonov, S., 30n75
Sbytova, L. S., 203n2
Schaefer, Reinhard, 15nf
Schrettl, Wolfram, 123n8
Schroeder, G. E., 260n41
Schultz, George P., 49n156
Schumpeter, J., 239: quasi-rents, 61, 238,
  259–60
"scientific revolution", 234
scientists, physical, 222–3
second economy: definition, 267; earnings
  from, 286; opportunities for work in,
  243–4; supply side of, 267–72; urbanites,
  27–8
seconding, obligatory, *see* temporary jobs;
  transfers, job
sectoral labor markets, 285–95: job ladders,
  292–5; mobility between, 291–2; quit rate
  by sector, 286–90; relative earnings and
  occupations, 285–6, 288–9; for unskilled,
  191–3
Semenchenko, A., 38n118
seniority of labor force, 43, 294
separation rate, *see* quit rate
Sergeeva, G. P., 24n54, 74n8
services sector: quits and dismissals, 14;
  second jobs in, 269

Sevost'ianov, G. M., 37n117, 102n78, 104n87

sewing machines, 272, 277–8, 282

sex: exclusion from vocational schools on basis of, 218; labor force participation by, 80 (Table 3.1), 83, 287 (Table 9.1); quit rates by, 286, 288–90

shabashniki (seasonal construction gangs in rural areas), 268, 270–1, 272

Shagalov, Ia., 186n28, 197n68

Shaikin, V. P., 157n24

Shaozhi, Su, 124n9

Shapiro, V. D., 74n8

Sharlet, R., 24n53

shavers, electric, 273n15

Shchekino experiment, 45, 55–6, 94: enterprises studied, 96n52; its failure to develop, 238–40, 263 – explanations, 259–62

Shchekinskii chemical combinat, 60, 99, 182–3, 238–9

Shinakova, G. I., 217n57

Shirov, A., 186n28, 197n68

Shiskina, L. A., 90n35

Shkaratan, O. I.: on foremen, 225n75; on occupational mobility, 227n84, 228n85; on vocational training for blue-collar workers, 217n56, 57, 233n99

Shkurko, S. I.: on five year plan, 61n200; on relative earnings and wage rates, 45–6, 48; on Shchekino experiment, 238n5

shocks to economy: absorption and offsetting of, 236–8; overfull employment and, 235–8 – JROE model, 240–56, other explanations, 256–9; role of farms, 256–7

shoe orders, 169

Shokin, A. I., 39n128

Shokhina, L., 294n69

Shukhgapter, M. L., 185n20

Shul'ga, Iu. E., 17n19, 20

Siberia: departure before end of organized recruitment period, 90n35; employment in construction in East 257n37; housewives, 83; projected net labor force movement to, 236; resettlement of farm families in, 20

sickness benefits, 34

Sidorova, Zh., 52n166

skill-grade: classifications in light industry, 293–5; downgrading threat, 44, 85–6, 92; and earnings correlation, 47–9, 162, 163; in engineering industry, 46 note; of

fathers in educational discrimination, 227–32; inability to find job at one's own, 72, 74, 77; workers performing at higher than wage level, 53; *see also* job ladders

skills: change of and redundancy, 94–5 (Table 3.3); change in required by technological change, 174; comparison of earnings among enterprises, 48–9; defined narrowly, 36, 49, 225; education and adaptability of, 220–6; enterprise-specific ignored in Central wage fund planning, 67, 108–9, 310; learning of new plus old, 48; reclassification, 41na, 44n140, 53, 96–7; supplementary payments for combining where labor shortage exists, 53

Slepykh, V. I., 60n198

sluzhashchie (clerical personnel), 50

Smirnov, D. D., 36n107

Smith, Hedrick, 251

Sobranie postanovlenii pravitel'stva SSSR (SP SSSR), 13n10

social insurance, 285

social pressure, 38, 63, 90; *see also* group

social recruitment, 18, 19–20, 22, 37–8

social security payments, 261

socialist countries, other: comparison with labor market observations, 109–10

socialist sector: obligation to work in, 23–8, 247–8; work outside and within, 267–71, 272

Solidarity movement, 284–5

Solov'ev, A., 50n160, 74n9

Sonin, M. Ia., 25, 298n82

Sozinov, V., 98n65

Sozykin, A. G., 89nf

SP SSSR (Sobranie postanovlenii pravitel'stva), 13n10

specialist workers: no job protection, 92; and permanent residence permits, 33; proportions of senior to rank-and-file, 48

spetsial'nost, 36, 182, 213; *see also* skills

Staroverov, V. I., 29–30n 70, 72, 73

State, Intelligence and Research Bureau, US: on labor camps, 12n2

State Bank: and employment quotas, 52n165; refusal to release funds for wage payments beyond the allotted amount, 58

State Committee of Labor of the Russian Republic: Central Laboratory of Labor Resources, 22; wage rates, 41

State Committee of Labor of the Soviet Union: on labor shortage, 188; Research

State Committee *cont.*
Institute redundancy studies, 93n47, 94, 96
State Committee on science and Technology of the Soviet Union: scrapping rate of equipment, 197n68
State Planning Commission of the Soviet Union: (1977) approved product aggregates for bonus calculations, 137n5; on bonuses, 54; employment plans (1972–79), 50; improvements in light bulb production rejected, 274; national wage fund based on manpower estimates lower than sum of enterprise plans, 107n90; non-allocated materials, 169; production plans and materials allocation, 275
stazhirovka (on-the-job training period), 18
steel towns, 82, 83
Steklova, A. N. 58n192
Stolzel, J., 15nf
Stolzenberg, R. M., 49n156
stoves, electric, 273n15, 281
Strumilin, S. G., 202, 203
students, full-time: as percentage of all graduates, 205 (Table 7.2), 223–6; receiving scholarships, 80;/teacher ratio, 224n71; as "unemployed", 72
Subotskii, Iu. V., 128n14
suburbanites, 33–4
sugar beet industry, 257
Sukhov, A. A., 14n14
suppliers for production 145–6, 147–8: temporary credits to meet bills of, 58n188
supply difficulties: in change of mix required by innovation, 180; delivery conditions, 166; technological change in overcoming, 174n11
Supreme Court of Russian Republic: (1979) decision on obligatory transfer within an enterprise, 36n107; (1975) decision on right of collective farms to evict hired employees who quit, 35; dismissal decision, 103n80
Supreme Court of the Soviet Union: (1967) decision on dismissal for absenteeism, 90; (1984) ruling on redundancy, 98n63, 307; (1975) survey of dismissal appeals, 104n82
Sushkina, L., 285n46
Sverdlovsk region: desire of collective farmers and blue-collar workers for higher education for their children, 228;

university entrants, 229; youth in household services, 296n71
Swafford, Michael, 269n11
Sweden: absenteeism, 249; pre-school child care, 74n8

Tallin(n): permission required to become permanent resident, 31
Tartu, Estonia, 205n7
Tashkent: population growth, 31n80
Taylor, Frederick W., 130
teachers: education of, 212–13n36; low earnings, 44n140, 214; no job protection, 92;/student ratios, 224
technicians: education of, 208–12
technological change: "innovation of poverty", 174n11; and labor/capital ratio, 171–201; in production, slow rate, 163; and redundancy, 93, 99; *see also* innovations, technological
tekhnikumy, see junior college
tekuchest' (quits plus dismissals for labor discipline), 88, 286n50
television sets, 272, 278–9
temporary jobs: assignments and shocks to labor force, 256–7, 258, 262; included in quit rates, 15nb; and in-migration to cities, 31–4; as labor allocation, 301; loans for non-industrial sector, 191–3, 252; obligatory transfers, 37–40, 47, 86, 111; seasonal, 257; in unskilled work, 180, 213, 300
textile industry: Central Asian, 75n10; education of spinners and carders, 218; in Ivanovo, 82; job ladders in, 292–5; quits from 289–90; replacement of electric motors of shuttleless looms, 54–5
theft of materials for "occasional work" during duty hours, 271–2
Thomas, R. P., 4n5
time: Center's rate of preference, 122; managers' rate of preference, 130–2; "stealing from the state", 28n61, 272
Tomiak, J., 224n71
totalitarianism, 118
tractorist-machinists (mechanizers): agricultural secondment, 38; data on job changes, 30; vocational training for, 216
trade employees, 285, 286, 289–90, 291
trade unions: and allocation of wage fund among personnel within enterprise, 65; and cases of dismissal, 90–1, 92, 102–3; control over reasons for overtime, 252–3;

trade unions *cont.*
  factory committees, 102–3; monopolies in
    capitalist countries, 48; (1965) ruling of
    central council on dismissal for
    absenteeism as last resort, 91n38
trades, *see* skills
training, on-the-job: compared with
    vocational education, 217–19; of manual
    workers in light industry, 293; payments
    during re-, 97; period (*stazhirovka*) 18
transfers, job: decision (1979) of the
    Supreme Court 36n107; for disciplinary
    reasons, 37; health problems and, 92; of
    industrial manual workers, 18, 20, 22; for
    military service and full-time study, 13;
    obligatory permanent, 111; obligatory
    temporary, 37–40, 86, 111; protection
    against obligatory, 92; for redundancy
    reasons, 94–7; refusal of permanent, 36;
    of specific job, 37–40; within an
    enterprise, 36–40, 94–6
translators, 271
transport and communications sector:
    intersectoral mobility, 291; water, 285
transportation crosshauls, extensive, 146
Trubin, V. V., 21n39, 291n61
truck drivers: agricultural secondment, 38
Trufanov, I. P., 225n75
Tsvetkov, B., 186n28
"turnpike" approach, 122
tutoring, private, 267
Tyson, L., 2n2

Udovichenko, Iu. N., 90n35, 296n72
Ufa: Aviation Institute, 213; -Kaluga
    experiment of employment bureaus, 20,
    21n37, 123n8
Ukraine: Committee on Labor, 22; job
    directions in 17n19; labor bureaus in, 22;
    quits and dismissals in industrial manual
    labor force, 14; slack in capacity
    utilization, 164; use of manual workers
    outside main shift, 188
Ukrainskii, D., 128n14, 139n11
"under-employment", 72: spread of, 78–9
unemployment: avoidance of, 236;
    categories excluded from, 73–5; concern
    with social aspects and *per se*, 73–6;
    definition problem, 72–3, 77;
    involuntary, 71, 76n12, 77, 85, *see also*
    redundancy; regional aspects of, 82–4;
    voluntary, *see* job search
unemployment, frictional: acceptable, 75–7;

and disequilibrium hypothesis, 109, 235;
    long-term among migrants, 82; observed
    degree of, 71–2, 79–82; voluntary, 76n12,
    81
United Kingdom: gross hires and
    unemployment 237; length of secondary
    education, 206; quit rates and separation
    rates, 15 (Table 2.1), 16, 112; retirement
    rates of equipment, 194, 195
Unites States of America: absenteeism, 249;
    affirmative action doctrine, 226;
    comparison with Soviet occupational
    change (1960–70), 175–9 (Table 6.2);
    downgrading and dismissal, 92, 110–11;
    earnings relative to a trade between
    enterprises, 49n156; émigrés on
    absenteeism, 250n22 – on surplus labor,
    301; and equal educational opportunity
    between social classes, 228; female labor
    force participation, 24–6 (Table 2.3);
    length of secondary education, 206–7;
    materials handling technology, 190;
    metalcutting machine tools, 198; nursery
    facilities, 74n8; pattern of change of
    personnel in research, 223; pensionable
    age people in jobs, 297, 298; problem of
    defining unemployment, 72, 73; quit
    rates and total separation, 15 (Table
    2.1), 16, 100–1, 111; retirement rates of
    equipment, 194, 195; suppression of
    better light bulb patent, 273; unskilled
    materials handlers, 185; work behavior of
    minority groups, 283–4
university education: dairy, 212n36;
    discrimination in admissions, 227–32;
    length of, 206; one-year preparatory
    sections, 229–30; (1950s) two-year
    obligatory work experience prior to, 229
Urals: earnings per skill-grade of heavy
    industrial manual workers (1960s), 47;
    housewives, 83; students wishing to go to
    junior college, 209; unemployed (1967),
    84
urban: female workforce participation, 26;
    transfer of workers to farming, 38–40; *see
    also* cities; migration
Usminskaia, S. A., 84n28
utility function: individual's, 122–3;
    manager's, 130–2; personal of leadership,
    306
Utokov, A. A., 213n36
Uvarov, V., 38n118, 72n1
Uzbekistan: parasites in, 24

vacations, 34, 76n12, 81
vacuum cleaners, 273, 275
Vasil'ev, E. K., 52n167
Vasil'eva, E. K., 203n5, 227n84
"vegetative mechanisms" (Kornai), 180n16
vertical integration: within ministries, 145–6
Vestnik statistiki (V.S.) 17n19
Villa, Paola, 268n6
Vilna, Lithuania: disciplinary dismissals, 89
Vincentz, Volkhart, 212n33
Vinokur, Aaron, 269n11, 286n48
Vneshniaia torgovlia SSSR, 274
vocational schools (PTU), 207–8, 216–17: graduates of, 17, 17–18n20, 22, 90n35, 204, 206; few girls in, 218
Volgin, A., 250n22
Volin, P., 274n16
Voronin, E., 21n37, 107n90
VS. (*Vestnik statistiki*), 17n19
Vukolova, A. N., 93n46
vuzy, see education, higher
vysvobozhdenie (a version of redundancy), 93n46

Wädekin, Karl-Eugen, 23n47, 125n10
wage drift (McAuley), 42–3
wage fund, 42, 46, 52–65, 139: fungibility of, 52–7, 300; as a "hard" constraint, 57–9, 106, 301; "ratchet" effect on, 60–4, 238, 240, 305; redistribution of, 161–2; repayments of overexpenditure, 57–9; rolling-plan, 261; savings, 53; stability predetermined in Shchekino experiment, 238–40, 260; unused, 56–7, 60; use by enterprise, 52–65; wage rates and, 40–9
wage rates: fixed, 11, 41; and relative earnings, 44–5; revisions (1956–60, 1973–5) in industry, 43–4; against wage fund, 40–9; see also earnings, labor
wage supplements: officially recognized (1970s), 45; regional percentage, 48; use of wage fund in, 55–7; see also bonuses
warehousing workforce, unskilled, 183–4 (Table 6.4)
washing machines, 272, 273n15, 280–1, 282
watches, 272, 276–7, 282
water transport, 285
weather: shocks to economy, 236
weaving industry, 54, 165n35
Weber, Max, 120, 123

Weitzman, M. L., 137, 171n1,2, 173n6, 188n37
welfare function: planners', 1–4, 122, 233, 306
whistle-blowers, 86
white-collar personnel: absenteeism compared with West, 249; (1965) decree setting salaries, 55–6; educational discrimination against children of, 227n81; job direction of, 18; reclassification of, 96–7; relative earnings, 286; rewarded from material-stimulation fund, 241n10
White Russia: excess of supply over demand for skilled workers, 219n65; state university entrants, 230, 232n96
wholesale prices, 139–40: setting of, 138, 148–57
Wiles, Peter: on mobility restrictions on collective farmers, 28–9; Soviet labor policy compared with capitalist, 12
women: absence of work for, 84; discrimination against at work, 295–8; full employment as foundation of equal rights for, 73, 296; job ladders in light industry, 293–5; in labor force (1959–70), 24–7 (Table 2.3), 80 (Table 3.1), 83–4, 181, 183, 192, 286–90; non-working, 26, 82, 83; over 45, special privileges to keep them working, 53, 294; pregnant, 92; see also housewives; mothers
work: compulsory, 23–8; experience prior to university, 229; hours of, 27, 253, 271; "official time", moonlighting within, 270; service, 34, 226; see also part-time work
workers: control over enterprises, 125–6, 129; "discouraged", 73–4; new, 67, 244n13; "target", 283
workers, unskilled: buying out of, 192n57; evolution in industry, 183–7 (Table 6.4) – explanation, 187–94; reductions in occupations, 177–8; segmented markets for, 191–3

Xiaoping, Deng, 124

youth, discrimination against, 295–6; immigration to cities, 32–3; job placement of, 22–3; period between full-time education and first job, 81; protection against dismissal or obligatiory transfer, 92–3; quit rates, 286; time between jobs to study, 77n12; unemployed, 77n12,

youth *cont.*
81n19; vocational education for rural,
215–16
Yugoslavia: job rights, 109–10; possible for
same-skill employees to earn different
incomes, 125; powers of Communist
Party functionaries, 121

Zabulis, G., 209n21

Zaitsev, G., 38n118, 72n1
Zalavskii, I. E., 217n54
Zaslavskaia, T. I., 83
Zaslavskii, I., 44n140
Zelenskii, A. G., 186n32
Zhemanova, M. P., 84n28
Zimbalist, Andrew, 133
Ziuzin, D. I., 75n10
Zlotnitskaia, T., 45n144